ANIMALS & MEN

ISSUES 16-20

THE JOURNAL OF THE CENTRE FOR FORTEAN ZOOLOGY

NEW HORIZONS

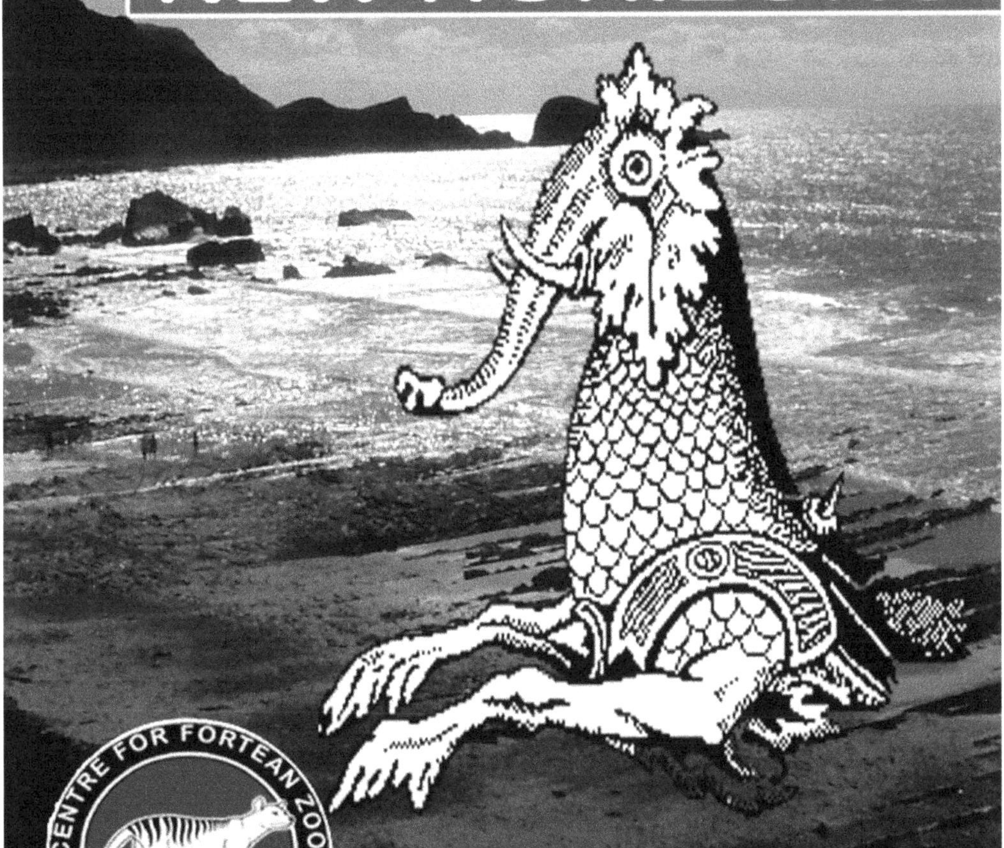

THE CENTRE FOR FORTEAN ZOOLOGY
www.cfz.org.uk

Edited by Jon Downes

Typeset by Jonathan Downes,
Cover and Layout by PussyOringgg for CFZ Communications
Using Microsoft Word 2000, Microsoft , Publisher 2000, Adobe Photoshop CS.

First published in Great Britain by CFZ Press

**CFZ Press
Myrtle Cottage
Woolsery
Bideford
North Devon
EX39 5QR**

© CFZ MMX

All rights reserved. Without limiting the rights under copyright reserved above, no part of this publication may be reproduced, stored in or introduced into a retrieval system, or transmitted, in any form of by any means (electronic, mechanical, photocopying, recording or otherwise), without the prior written permission of both the copyright owners and the publishers of this book.

ISBN: 978-1-905723-56-0

Contents

5.	*My Back Pages* by Jonathan Downes
11.	*Answering the Call of Monsters* by Richard Freeman
17.	*Animals & Men* Issue 16 Spring 1998
67.	*Giant Lizards in the English Countryside* by Darren Naish
69.	*Animals & Men* Issue 17 Christmas 1998
119.	*Animals & Men* Issue 18 Christmas 1998
169.	*Animals & Men* Issue 19 Spring 1999
219.	*Animals & Men* Issue 20 Spring 1998
269.	About the CFZ

My Back Pages

Putting together this fourth volume of collected editions of *Animals & Men* has not been an entirely enjoyable experience, although it has been an eye-opening one. It is an open secret that during the late 1990s my life was not as ordered, nor indeed as respectable as it is now. I was divorced from my first wife in 1997 and for some years I drank, smoked, and ingested more chemicals than – with the benefit of hindsight – was altogether sensible. My romantic life was complicated to say the least and, although by the standards of today's youth my behaviour was not particularly outrageous, it did gain me an unfortunate reputation in some quarters. I strongly suspect that it was the rigours of my somewhat dissolute lifestyle, which some pundits have blamed for the apparently shoddy appearance of some of the magazines that we released in the years 1998/9. This is actually not true.

The real reason why the production values of some these issues leaves something to be desired, is because – as we always have, and indeed still do at the CFZ – we were pushing ourselves far beyond our ability. I had been publishing fanzines since the early 1980s. In fact, at various times between 1969 and 1977 I was involved in producing diverse unofficial school newspapers, so I suppose my involvement in the alternative publishing scene goes back as far as that. It had been a major part of my life, indeed one of my major sources of income ever since 1987 when my first wife and I started (and I blush to admit this) a fanzine called *Spanish Train* dedicated to Alison's favourite pop singer, a short geezer with stupid eyebrows, but an unimpeachable aristocratic pedigree. However, I learnt the fanzine editor's art using a manual typewriter, Letraset (for those not in the know this was a commercially available range of alphabeticised rub on transfers which were available in a range of fonts and sizes), glue, scissors and sheer determination. As I had also learnt my art during the fag end of the punk rock movement and the neo-hippy movement of the late 1980s where squiggly lines, jumbled lettering and a bizarre mixture of fonts and typography designed to show how alternative we all were was des rigeur, the transition from anarchic music magazines designed to be sold at rock festivals to a cryptozoological journal designed to be taken seriously was quite a difficult one to engineer. However, we managed it.

From the late 1980s onwards, we were aware that the magazines that people took seriously were put together on computers called PCs, and in late 1997 we finally acquired one. Before that we had produced the first 15 issues of *Animals & Men* and indeed the first two yearbooks on an Amiga 1200 games machine (I remember with a grin how when we finally upgraded to the aforementioned Amiga 1200 from an Amiga 500+ that I had bought back in 1994 Graham and I were so impressed to have a whole megabyte of memory). Whilst we had learnt the basics of producing a magazine that was not aimed to be read by pilled up crusties some years before, and had already dispensed with the gratuitous wavy lines and unnecessary font changes which, with hindsight, so marred much of our musical output, the real problem was that neither Graham nor I had more than the vaguest of ideas how to use a PC. I think that during one of his stints on the dole Graham had been taught the rudiments, but I had never even touched one before and had never heard of such things as PDFs. We also didn't have a scanner, and as ridiculous as it sounds we had to pay a funny little bloke, whose name I can't remember, a fiver a time to scan pictures in for us.

Re-mastering the magazines for a new format threw up a load of technical challenges and I thank the Lord for Adobe Photoshop, without which the whole project would never have seen fruition. I am not going to bore you with long, boastful look how clever I am descriptions because there is actually nothing particularly clever about what I've had to do; it is merely being tedious, painstaking and often irritating.

No, it is not the technical side of this which I have found either upsetting or uplifting; it is the personal side of it. At the time of writing, in the spring of 2010 the CFZ is – as always – in a state of flux, but has basically achieved the position that I always wanted it to. It is a full-time organisation with offices in America, Australia and New Zealand and at any one time we are carrying out research projects at various locations across the world. Indeed my dear wife Corinna and I have only just returned from a two and a half week sojourn in southern Texas studying the mysterious blue dogs which have been reported across the Lone Star State for the last five or six years, but it was not always so. Back in 1998 and 1999 when the magazines, which can be found in this current collection, were originally published Graham, Richard and I were living on tiny incomes in Exeter. Then, as now, we were dependant on the generosity and kindness of members of what I had always thought of as the CFZ family. Over the years the

CFZ family has become a very close and tight knit entity and it is heart warming to note how many people who were involved back in 1998/1999 are still involved today. Names like Nick Redfern, Neil Arnold, Nick Molloy, and Richard Muirhead are as familiar to the people who read our daily online magazine in 2010 as they were to the people who read *Animals & Men* when the magazines included in this collection were first published.

However, there are some faces who were integral parts of the CFZ family back in the day who are no longer with us. Some like Clin Keeling are dead. Others, like Tom Anderson have drifted away and would be welcome back at any time. Others have left in a more acrimonious fashion and one was even expelled. There is a peculiar irony to this. It has been suggested in certain quarters that the people who are no longer with the CFZ left because they were somehow offended by the eccentricities of me, Graham and Richard who have been running the CFZ more or less amicably since 1997. This is just not true. Nor, have they left because of their own eccentricities; most of the more extreme members of the CFZ from the halcyon days of the end of the 20th Century. No, the reason that most of our quondam associates have buggered off into the sunset is purely for financial reasons. Although I am not a renunciate and I am quite prepared to accept that money is a necessary evil, it is not a subject that I find of any great interest.

In 2006 after years of penury I inherited a small but significant amount of money and a medium sized house from my late father. And almost overnight once I had money people, including some that I had known for years, saw it as their purpose in life to have me share it with them. Others, once I finally found myself in the position of being able to fulfil my stated ambitions for the last decade and a half of establishing the CFZ on a sound, philosophical footing showed themselves up and revealed their true colours. When we were not in the position to be able to run the CFZ in the way that we wished these philosophical differences either didn't matter or remained hidden. Once I put my money (and my life and that of my newly acquired wife and family) where my mouth was, it made all the difference in the world.

I have always been reasonably open about my influences, and about the men whose work has massively influenced my own. Strangely (and this had been both a curse and a blessing) I have met, and worked, with several of my heroes. Others (thankfully) I have not. Some of my heroes, like Gerald Durrell and Tony 'Doc' Shiels, are probably self-evident to anyone who has ever read any of my books, or had more than the vaguest perusal of the CFZ website. Others may surprise even some people who know me quite well. One man without whom the CFZ, CFZ Press and the volume that you a reading at the moment could not possibly exist is a bloke called Jeremy John Ratter, better known to people of a certain age as Penny Rimbaud who is best known as the drummer for a spectacularly inept punk rock band called Crass. In 1967 he assumed the tenancy of a dilapidated house in the Essex countryside where he started an artistic and cultural community based around his own singular anarchist philosophy which has continued ever since and is as of 2010 still going strong. Now, Crass' music was often bloody awful. It was needlessly abrasive and lyrically often went far beyond what one would expect from a group of foul-mouthed hod-carriers with Tourette's syndrome and certainly not what one would expect from people of Ratter's social background. But the thing that is really extraordinary is that an ever-shifting band of brothers and sisters based around the same nucleus of people produced a diverse range of books, records, and films as well as work in other media such as art exhibitions and performance pieces and did so whilst all the time maintaining complete control over the methods of production and dissemination. I met them on a couple of occasions in 1982 and what I learnt from them both politically and commercially has stayed with me ever since and shaped my life in the intervening years.

Now, whereas we don't agree about a lot of things, Richard Freeman, Graham Inglis and I have shared the basic political, social and cultural precepts which define the CFZ and how it is run, and I think that it is worth noting that whilst we have had some pretty major disagreements over the years (especially Graham and I) we are all still here a decade and a half after we first started working together. I am also particularly lucky in that my wife understands what I am trying to achieve and how I try to achieve it, and since we first got together in the late winter of 2005 she has been by my side.

We all have the same basic philosophy in common, for example we believe that zoos and museums should be places of education, temples where one worships at the altar of Mother Nature if you will rather than somewhere where the great unwashed go to gawp at animals, have their faces painted and learn circus skills. We believe that the only point of having an event like our annual Weird Weekend is so that we can draw the general public into what we do and that conferences that perpetuate a culture of elitism and secrecy are counter-productive. Sadly some people over the last few years have not only disagreed with us but have done their best to stop us carrying out our chosen path.

It is this that has led to the most uncomfortable parts of my re-formatting the 1998 and 1999 issues of *Animals & Men* for this current volume. It saddens me to see the work of people who I once considered friends and who are now, I feel, at the very best misguided fools and at the very worst actual enemies. However, like my mentor in things anarchocyndicatively I do not believe in trying to rewrite history.

Recently all has not been well in the Crass camp. Although the band split up in 1984, and stopped living together in 1989, there are a plethora of artistic and business reasons why they have had to remain in contact. Recently, sadly, they have split into two armed camps; one led by Rimbaud also including two of the singers and the graphic artist, and the others, led by bass player Pete Wright who threatens to spill the beans about the schisms within the band even back in the glory days of the punk rock revolution in the early 1980s if he doesn't get his own way regarding such thorny problems as re-issues and re-mastering of the band's legacy. This drama, which means very little on the world stage, but a surprising amount to some of us of a certain age for whom Crass was a shining example of how things *should* be done has been playing out as I have been carrying out my own re-mastering and re-issue programme.

In the past five years, there have been more arguments, disagreements and general schisms within the CFZ than ever were before. However, unlike Crass we have always been fairly open about such things and I don't think anyone has ever expected me in particular to be a cuddly, fluffy bunny who never loses his temper.

Carrying out this particular bout of re-formatting has been a real trip down memory lane. It covers the immediate aftermath of our first ever foreign trip and a time when the nascent CFZ, and the three-man team who run it were really beginning to find their feet. Not all the memories that have come flooding back into my head over the past few weeks have been sad ones. 1998 and 1999 were strange years, but exciting ones; they were the years in which we first tried to utilise the power of the internet, during which we first tried to make films, during which on a budget of absolutely nothing we still managed to keep a punishing publishing programme more or less on schedule, and they were times during which the Centre for Fortean Zoology we know today, now the largest organisation of its kind in the world was really forged. They were strange days, they were exciting days, and despite the heartache I wouldn't have missed them for the world.

Jon Downes,
Woolsery, North Devon
April 2010

Publisher's note: Please be aware that these are broadly facsimile reprints of magazines published considerably over a decade ago and any and all adverts are included for the sake of verisimilitude and are no longer applicable in any shape or form. Likewise the Exeter address quoted liberally within is now a private household and any and all correspondence should be directed to our current abode in North Devon (see title page).

Answering the Call of Monsters

I have always loved monsters. The large, the spectacular, and the weird; monsters in all their glorious forms. I suppose it dates back to the early 1970s and an episode of a *Doctor Who* adventure called *Terror of the Autons*. It involved a grotesque plastic doll that was possessed by an alien intelligence called the Nestene. It killed by spitting a fast drying mist of liquid plastic over the mouth and nose of the victim, thus suffocating them. In the scene that sticks in my mind it was lying in the back seat of a car. Triggered by the body heat of its victim it twitched into life like a homicidal, grossly deformed version of Morph from *Take Hart*. From that day till this I was hooked on both monsters and *Dr Who*.

I heard the story of St George and the Dragon as a child and found it laughably stupid. A knight on his mouse of a horse with a puny lance and sword had about as much chance of slaying the dragon as a cockroach riding a hamster and armed with a cocktail stick would have of slaying a bulldog in plate armour. I was always on the side of the dragon.

Likewise, in monster movies (on which I was weaned) I was always rooting for monster over the stupid humans. I still prefer films where the monster wins.

Wildlife films were another great influence

in my formative years. I recall sitting enraptured each week with my granddad watching *Life on Earth* with the great David Attenborough who, soon after, presented a series on monsters called *Fabulous Animals*. Sadly this excellent series still remains unreleased on DVD and my enquiries to the BBC have been answered with 'there are no plans to release it'. Another forgotten show was *The World About Us* that had amazing titles featuring a swirling golden globe that was composed of metallic strips and evocative music that hinted at adventures in far off lands. Each episode transported the viewer to some exotic locale and looked at some amazing creature.

Whilst other kids were collecting football cards or playing football like mindless zombies, I was turning over stones and searching through the long grass for mini-beasts and collecting the monsters from the backs of packets of *Monster Munch*.

I never did and never will share the un-ambitious, dull, soul destroying interests of the average man. Too many people waste their lives in boring 9 to 5 jobs. Too many people have ambition eradicated from them at an early age. When I was getting ready to leave school I said I wanted to be a zookeeper. Everyone said it was a pipe dream and I would never achieve it, but I'm a great believer in making your own destiny. I left school, got a job at Twycross Zoo in the West Midlands and became head or reptiles.

I worked in the zoo for several years breeding a number of rare reptiles. However, I hated the management and their petty, spiteful, counterproductive ways. I saw over thirty fellow keepers leave for exactly the same reason. Then one morning after years of abuse I snapped, and told the zoo director (who knew nothing about animals whatsoever) where she could stick her job.

The next few years were spent in a wilderness, working mainly on building sites. I hated this as it bored me beyond reason and the conversation revolved around sport and soap operas, two things I despise.

Finally I decided to go to university and study zoology. I ended up in Leeds, which, socially, was the best place I have ever lived. My three years there were among the happiest in my life.

The course however, did not match up. Lecturers used textbooks thirty years out of date and made errors that would shame a schoolboy. One lecturer in palaeontology could not tell the difference between a triceratops and a protoceratops or a mammoth or a mastodon. The same man gave a lecture about how sauropod dinosaurs live their whole lives in water having their great weight buoyed up. This was a theory disproved before I was born! Elsewhere lecturers did not know the scientific names of animals or how many species were in a particular family. It was quite disillusioning.

However whilst in Leeds I met many great forteans such as Steve Jones (the UK's first Pagan magistrate and noted folklorist), Phil Thorley, John Tinsley and Andrew McPherson (all students of the occult) and Paul Bennett (expert in the history and legends of Ilkley Moor, a renowned window area).

One summer's holiday I was in Cornwall with two friends. We had spent the morning putting out bait for the beast of Bodmin and had planned to return that night to check it. We decided to have dinner at the famous *Jamaica Inn*. At the time the inn played host to Potter's Museum of Curiosities. This was an amazing collection of Fortean items including incredible dioramas of stuffed animals. These included kittens getting married, guinea pigs playing cricket, squirrels duelling, rats drinking, frogs on swings, rabbits in school and the Death of Cock Robin with all the animals from the rhyme included. They were made in the 19th Century by Victorian taxidermist Walter Potter (1835-1918). He also collected a number of heterogeneous objects of interest such as the head of a man-eating crocodile, a model church made out of feathers and two headed lambs.

This, to me, is the essence of what a museum should be. Old, dusty, fascinating. Each object telling its own queer tale in echoing rooms and corridors. I hate the sanitised, clean, computer graphic orientated, interactive museums of today. We can till see a glimmer of what Potters was like in places like Ilfracombe Museum and other small collections.

Tragically, when its current owners became too infirm to run the museum, it closed and this remarkable and unique collection was broken up and sold off. Artist Damien Hurst tried to buy the collection for £1,000,000 but alas his noble effort was too late.

But I digress.

It was in the foyer of Potter's Museum that I came across a little magazine called *Animals & Men*. It wasn't as rude as it sounded and it had a picture of 'the surgeon's photograph' on the front. I decided to buy a copy. This is one of those little, seemingly insignificant events that actually turn your life on to a whole new path. I enjoyed the little cryptozoological mag and decided to subscribe. A few issues down the line I had become the Yorkshire rep for something call *The Centre for Fortean Zoology*, a group dedicated to the study of anomalous creatures, animal folklore and the weirder aspects of zoology. I had no idea this group existed but I wanted in.

I began writing letters and then articles including one on dragon legends in Yorkshire that made it to the front cover with an illustration by Lisa Allegri that looked more like Ermintrude the cow from *The Magic Roundabout* than it did a dragon.

I met *Animals & Men* editor Jon at one of the *Fortean Times* Unconventions where I had been booked to do a talk on dragons. He wasn't quite what I had expected, looking somewhat like a cross between 1970s wrestler Giant Haystacks and a grizzled gold prospector from the old west. We got on very well as two eccentrics and spent a boozy weekend together along with Jon's best mate and sidekick Graham who had the look of a Mexican bandit / desperado. He mentioned living in a place called 'Holne Court'. I let my imagination run away with me a little bit at the time as I imagined Holne Court to be some grand mansion and Jon to be some eccentric millionaire. I envisioned the CFZ as a globe trotting organisation ready to launch expeditions in search of cryptids at the drop of a hat. In my mind's eye it was all high, leather back chairs, huge libraries, globes of the world that opened up into drinks cabinets and rolling acres of parkland.

As it turned out Holne Court wasn't like that at all. I visited Jon for the first time just after he had split up with his first wife. I discovered that the mansion of my imagination was a freezing cold, dilapidated, two up, two down house on an unpleasant estate. I recall the first time I visited the only food and drink he had in the house was coke (which I hate) and quiche.

Despite having my dreams of living in Jane Austen style splendour dashed I visited Jon, Graham, and Toby the dog on a number of occasions and took part in several TV programmes with them including Jon Ronson's *For the Love Of*, which was my first foray into television.

Jon decided to give me a permanent role in the CFZ and took me on as Zoological Director. The following few years were like some kind of cross between *The X Files* and *The Young Ones*. Imagine if you will that Mulder and Scully had been three middle-aged men with no cash. Together we investigated big cats, animal mutilation and lake and sea monsters.

The early days of my involvement with the CFZ seem like a different world now. The dingy little house seemed to be a magnet for every loony in Exeter. A brain damaged paranoiac cripple, a transvestite jester and a woman who looked like *Biffa Bacon*'s Mum from *Viz*. As well as monster sightings we got dragged into cases involving a man who thought he had been kidnapped by his own time travelling descendents who cured him of cancer, and an alcoholic poltergeist witness. There was also a retired couple who claimed to have been visited by Martians and Venusians who landed their invisible spaceships next to the equally invisible pyramids in the field behind their house on the outskirts of Exeter. Of course, all of these folk were prime candidates for an indefinite stay in the squirrel farm but one odd story given from those days made me pause for thought.

One night we were 'phoned by a man claiming to be from a secret cabal of international arms dealers who were also fanatical cryptozoologists. He claimed that they ran several secret, private zoos in which they were breeding thylacines, Queensland tigers and moas. They also had a 45 foot reticulated python. I would have been inclined to dismiss his wild story as the ravings of a fantasist but there were a couple of points that bothered me. In one of our many 'phone conversations he mentioned a new weapon, a kind of gun that could fire a million bullets in ten minutes. It sounded impossible but a few weeks later I saw the very device the fellow had been describing featured on an episode of *Tomorrow's World*. He was also remarkably well informed about the zoo world and in particular about the behind the scenes part, the who's who of zoo owners, directors and so on. On balance I think he was probably just a well-informed fantasist, probably. We made *Animals & Men* in the old-fashioned cut and paste way, until Jon got the first proper CFZ computer. It all felt very DIY back in those days, photocopying and stapling the magazine. I well recall the first CFZ website and how primitive it looked by today's standards.

Yes the old CFZ has come along way since then. We thought trekking up to a pet cemetery in Haldon Hills a few miles outside of Exeter to investigate some creature that had been digging up animal corpses and eating them was an adventure. A trip to Cornwall in search of Morgawr or Owlman was a major adventure. Loch Ness was just too far away for us to think of attempting. Now we travel the world in search of monsters and mysterious beasts. Thanks to my involvement with the CFZ I have seen places most people only dream about and have had adventures that seem right out of a 1930s pulp fiction magazine.

I have yet to see a true cryptid but I know they are out there. Too many good, well trusted people have seen them, including close friends. Yes, monsters do exist and maybe one day I will be lucky enough to see one face to face. I'm not a rich man, nor do I ever expect to be. But I have heard the monsters calling and I'm spending my life answering that call.

Richard Freeman,
Exeter
April 2010

Issue 16

Spring 1998

This was the first issue that I had ever tried to put together on a PC. We bought our first PC at the end of 1997 with the advance that I got from Domra for the second edition of *The Owlman and Others*. My whole relationship with Domra was an unfortunate one, and I was far from satisfied with the production values, especially of the first volume, which didn't even have my name on the cover for some obscure reason of the publisher. But it paid for our first PC - a P1 with 1.25 gb of memory. It cost nearly £1,000, and I boughgt it from my former dope dealer.

Unfortunately, I had no more than the sketchiest idea of how to use it, which is why so much of the first few issues is so apparently shoddy. This issue, by the way, was the only one in this volume in which the master copy on the CFZ archive computer was so dodgy that we were unable to reconstitute anything from it. The version you see here was taken from a scan...

Animals & Men **Collected Editions Volume 4**   **New Horizons**

ANIMALS & MEN

The journal of The Centre for Fortean Zoology

The Search for The Chupacabra; Snakes with Legs; Giant Lizards in Hampshire?; The Eastern Cougar and much more........

Issue 16   £2.00

ANIMALS & MEN # 16

THE CURRENT CREW OF THE CFZ MOTHERSHIP
(SOMETIMES KNOWN AS THE BOYS, GIRLS AND DOG OF
THE OLD BRIGADE) ARE:

Director: Jonathan Downes
Assistant Director: Graham Inglis
Gothic invoker of spiders / Assistant Editor: Richard Freeman
Toby the CFZ dog

Magazine cartoonist and Newsfile artwork: Mark North
Newsagent from Nowhere: Richard Muirhead
Associate founding editor: Jan Williams
Additional artwork: Lisa Allegri

CONSULTANTS

Consulting Editor and Cryptozoological Consultant:
Dr Bernard Heuvelmans
Zoological Consultant: Clinton Keeling
Cryptozoological Consultant: Dr Karl Shuker
Cetological and Plaentological Consultant: Darren Naish
Zoological Consultant: Chris Moiser
Surrealchemist in Residence: Tony 'Doc' Shiels
Computer Consultant: David Simons

REGIONAL REPRESENTATIVES - UK

Scotland: Tom Anderson
Surrey: Nick Smith
Yorkshire: Richard Freeman
Somerset: Dave McNally
West Midlands: Dr Karl Shuker
Kent: Neil Arnold
Sussex: Sally Parsons
Hampshire: Darren Naish
Leicestershire: Alistair Curzon
Cumbria: Brian Goodwin
S Wales & Salop: Jon Mattias
Tyneside: Simon Elsdon

REGIONAL REPRESENTATIVES - OUTSIDE UK

Switzerland: Sunila Sen-Gupta
Spain: Alberto Lopez Acha and Angel Morant Fores
Germany: Hermann Reichenbach and Wolfgang Schmidt
France: Francois de Sarre
Denmark: Lars Thomas and Erik Sorensen
Eire: The Wizard of the Western World
Mexico: Dr R A Lara Palmeros
Canada: Ben Roesch

"In her abnormalities, nature reveals her secrets." (Goethe)

WHO'S WHO & WHAT'S WHAT

CONTENTS

3 Editorial
4 Newsfile
14 Newsfile Extra: Eastern Cougars
17 At Last: Snakes With Legs! by Darren Naish

20 Only Fools And Goatsuckers:
Expedition Report: the hunt for the Chupacabra, by
Jonathan Downes
24 The Quagga Project Update, by Chris Moiser
24 Bestiary: The Manticore, by Ade Dimmick
25 Conversation Pieces, by Richard Freeman

26 North of the Border, by Tom Anderson
27 Clinton's Cogitations, by Clinton Keeling
30 A Collection of Cat Curiosities,
by Richard Muirhead

32 Cryptoherps in Indiana, by Brad La Grange
35 Werewolves of London Again,
by Gypsy Sherred
37 What's Afoot? By Richard Freeman

38 The Tristate Bigfoot Conference,
by Chad Arment
39 Giant Lizards in the English Countryside?
by Darren Naish

40 Letters
43 Reviews: websites, magazines, books
46 CFZ Publications
47 Back issues; Methods of Payment.

ANIMALS & MEN

CFZ, 15 Holne Court, Exwick, Exeter,
Devon, EX4 2NA, England

SUBSCRIPTIONS:

For a 4-issue subscription:
£8 UK   £9 EEC
£14 US/Canada/Oz/NZ (airmail)
£15 Rest of World.
Please see "Methods of Payment" on p47.

ANIMALS & MEN # 16

THE GREAT DAYS OF ZOOLOGY...
...ARE NOT DONE!

EDITORIAL

Dear Friends,

Welcome to a somewhat belated issue sixteen of Animals & Men. The delay is simple. When we started The Centre for Fortean Zoology four or five years ago it was purely an organisation aimed at amassing information, most usually by research in museums, libraries and second-hand book shops.

Now we have made the quantum leap into hands-on research. This does mean, however, as we are still a non profit making organisation, that our publication schedule has suffered somewhat. Many apologies have to go out to everyone who ordered the 1998 yearbook at Christmas and didn't get it until April. Unfortunately (or fortunately - depending which viewpoint you take) we disappeared off to Mexico, Florida and Puerto Rico in January and we have been in the field (literally) hunting for the elusive 'Beast of Haldon' since almost a week after we arrived back in the UK.

Apologies also have to go out to everyone who was expecting this issue of Animals & Men to be the first printed in colour.

It would have been if it wasn't for the fact that a certain UFO magazine who was propping up our income to a ridiculous degree went bust soon after Christmas then we would now be the proud owners of a colour printer. All things being equal, we will be in colour as of issue seventeen (which SHOULD be out on time in July).

Two other big changes have taken place within the infrastructure of the CFZ within the last six months. Firstly wee have now acquired a Pentium 166 computer, which is responsible for the far better type quality that you will notice with this issue and which has also helped us with our first forays into cyberspace.

As regular readers will notice this is the beginning of a new phase in Animals & Men - the ethos of the "Global Village" which made so much sense when we were addled young hippies (well, at least Graham and I were), has now become a reality through the Internet. We are rapidly becoming part of that virtual community and if the CFZ is going to move successfully into the 21st Century then we have to embrace the new technology as fervently as possible.

(Thanx once again, by the way to Darren Naish for another libellous piccy of me in a Cryptozoological iconographical pose)

The other change within the CFZ is the advent of Richard Freeman as a permanent member of the CFZ faculty. He has been a mate of ours for years and we share similar tastes in music, pseudo science, and lifestyle. He is actually moving down to CFZ Mansions in June and we're gonna have FUN FUN FUN until "Tony" takes the "funding" away.....

Slainte

JonD

jon@eclipse.co.uk

NEWSFILE

Compiled and collated by **Graham Inglis, Richard Freeman** and **The Editor**

LAKE AND SEA MONSTERS

Lend us a couple of Squid 'till payday...

Steve O'Shea's quest for *Archituethis dux* continues apace. The latest specimen that he has secured is ten metres long and weighs an incredible three hundred kilos.

"*This is a whopper - just massive,*" Mr. O'Shea said of the female squid recently caught by the Ministry of Fisheries Scientific Observer programme, near Mernoo Bank, about 200km off the East Coast of Christchurch.

He has four giant squid in his collection at Niwa's great point lab and hopes to prove that the creatures lives for only two years and are coming to New Zealand water to breed and die. "*There is little known about them because they live so deep. They are one of the last mysteries of the water,*" He said. "*We don't even know how many species there are.*" If his theory is correct, he would expect more giant squid

ANIMALS & MEN # 16

NEWSFILE

to be spotted or caught in the next few months and then not be seen again for two years. O'Shea is dissecting and preserving the squid with the help of Professor Chung-Cheng Lu, a visiting expert from the Zoology Department in the National Chung Hsing University in Taiwan. *"The Bay of Plenty Times"*, New Zealand 13/2/98.

EDITOR'S NOTE: Information posted on the Internet a few days later suggested that O'Shea had secured yet another specimen of this elusive cephalopod. Another earnest seeker after cephalopodical (if that is the word) truth is Dr Clyde Roper who was featured in the January issue of National Geographic magazine (page 91) in a photo of him examining a beached sperm whale carcass in New Zealand. The caption for that photo stated:

"A sperm whale carcass in New Zealand shows signs of a struggle - sucker marks - leading marine biologists Clyde Roper and Malcolm Clarke to suspect a giant squid. Up to 60 feet long, it is a mystery mollusc, having never been seen alive in its deep sea lair. Roper hopes to change all that by lowering a robotic camera into a 3,000-foot canyon just off shore of this New Zealand beach."

Another fine Ness.......

EDITOR'S NOTE: Those jolly nice chaps at the Copyright Liberation Front have been unable to locate a copy of this latest Nessie pic in a format that they are able to half-inch so we therefore have restricted ourselves to quoting the Reuters report in full...

INVERNESS, Scotland (Reuters) - An amateur photographer who snapped mysterious happenings in Scotland's Loch Ness has puzzled experts and led to renewed speculation about the existence of the monster said to live in the lake. Scottish pet food salesman Richard White noticed something strange in the loch as he drove along its eastern bank and realized it could be the elusive "Nessie."

"I always carry a camera in my van in case of a road accident," the former soldier told a Scottish news agency on Monday. *"I was on my way to Foyers, a small village above the loch, as part of a regular sales run, when I noticed an unusual disturbance halfway across the loch toward Urquhart Castle on the opposite bank. I stopped to take a look and remembered I had the camera, so I got it out and just started reeling off the photos,"* he said.

White, 53, has been awarded 500 pounds ($825) by a firm of British bookmakers which offers a prize for the best "Nessie" image of the year. Sightings of the mysterious monster, often described as having a long neck and a large body like a brontosaurus, have been reported since the 15th century.

Around two million tourists flock to the murky loch each year hoping to get a glimpse of the beast.

"This is a remarkable sequence, some of the best 'Nessie' photos that I have ever seen," said Gary Campbell, president of the Official Loch Ness Monster Fan Club. White and Campbell did not want to go public until the pictures had been analyzed by scientists using computer enhancement techniques. Campbell said the fact that experts had been unable to decide exactly what the pictures showed only added to the mystery of the Loch Ness monster.

"With so many of the photos taken of 'something' in Loch turning out to be a boat's wake or some other

ANIMALS & MEN # 16

NEWSFILE

everyday object, it is great to have a real mystery on our hands," he said. In February last year, a Scottish auxiliary coast guard officer said he had found the monster's secret lair on the bottom of the 23-mile (37-km) long loch.

Song of Norway

"An international team of experts plans to search a Norwegian lake with the latest technology in August in the hopes of putting an end to a 250-year-old legend about a sea serpent, the expedition head said on Wednesday. Jan-Ove Sundberg, a Swedish freelance journalist who has been fascinated by the legend for more than 25 years and who participated in a previous unsuccessful search in

1977, does not believe the legend -- he believes the "beast" could be a new large eel species. A team of zoologists from Norway, Canada, the United States, Great Britain, Italy and Russia will take part in the 17-day search, financed by the Seljord municipality in the Telemark region of southern Norway. The participants are all specialists in searching for unknown species, and have studied similar phenomena in their respective countries, including the famed Loch Ness Monster in Scotland, the Champ in the U.S., Ogopogo in Canada and Vorota in Russia.

Sundberg believes previous expeditions may have been unsuccessful because of improper equipment.

"The animal in the Seljord Lake may have been affected (by the equipment) and taken off," he said. But zoologist Torfinn Oermen at Oslo's Zoological Museum is sceptical about the search, and believes the chances of finding an undiscovered species in the cold lakes of the Nordic region are very small. Oermen noted that there are eels measuring up to 10 feet in oceans, "but there are no eels that big in the cold lakes up here in the north," he said.

And, he added, "the Seljord Lake is too far from the ocean for a sea animal to have remained there since the ice age." Oermen believes the explanation behind the sea serpent legend could be similar to a case cleared up at the Suldal Lake in the neighbouring Rogaland region back in 1893, where witnesses claimed to have seen a large, black, smelly monster rise from the water, and then descend never to be seen again. According to Oermen, a sawmill was located next to the lake." (UPI)

Editor's Note: I have to admit that I fail to see what a sawmill has to do with anything, but that is the way of things There is a possibility that three of the CFZ posse will be accompanying this expedition but this has yet to be confirmed.

MYSTERY CATS

CUMBRIA

Mary Kavanagh wrote to The Whitehaven News to share her amazement at what she believes may have been a leopard or puma. A passenger on a train travelling through Silecroft, near Millom, was shocked to see what she describes as *"a large cat-like animal"* prowling through a field.

Animals & Men Collected Editions Volume 4 **New Horizons**

ANIMALS & MEN # 16

Radio 4 ran a news item on the "Today" programme on Friday morning where some other wildlife 'expert' [whose name I forget] advised that there were various big cats roaming about the UK, but humans had nothing to fear from these animals.

His theory was that after the passing of the Dangerous Wild Animals act in 1976, some owners set their large cats free rather than register them. These animals have since bred and retreated to rural areas of the UK. They survive by preying on livestock, hence disembowelled sheep etc. But they are far more likely to run away than attack any of us. According to the Fortean Times one was even frightened off by a domestic cat whose territory it had wandered into...

Given that big cats can easily survive in far more inhospitable areas such as the cold regions of the former Soviet union, I find no reason to disbelieve this explanation. They are rarely seen, though, as such cats are elusive. Try finding a pet cat when it does not want to be found.

Some sceptics say that some 'alien big cats' are only large domestic cats - maybe [some breeds can indeed get to 3-4 feet long], but a domestic cat is only a domesticated Asian/African jungle cat, and can interbreed with many of the smaller wild cat species such as the above..

In the words of an old lady interviewed by journals after a sighting: "If it is a domestic cat, I wouldn't care to have it sat in front of my fireplace".

Not surprising - perhaps on her pension she would never have been able to afford that much Whiskas ....

Alex"

BALMORAL, SCOTLAND

A gamekeeper gunning for the Beast of Balmoral killed the local church minister's tortoiseshell cat, police believe. A spokesman for the Invercauld Estate said that the gamekeeper had been reprimanded, and told to study the difference between domestic and feral cats. Daily Mail 15/12/97

NEWSFILE

MEXICO

Ironically, at the same time as the CFZ posse and a Channel 4 film crew were in Mexico investigating chupacabra reports there was also an incident involving an out of place lion cub which was found hiding under a car in one of Mexico City's roughest neighborhoods. It was captured with lassos and taken to a zoo by firemen who said. "We took it to a circus but they said they didn't have any lions, so we took it to the Chapultepec Zoo instead."

The 6-month-old female lion was found by traffic reporters working for a Mexico City radio station in the asphalt jungle of Doctores, one of the capital's most crime-ridden areas early on Tuesday February 3, 1998. "I hope it eats some of the criminals," said a caller to the radio station, Radio Rojo, when the escapee was reported. *New York Daily News* February 4, 1998

The Frogman Cometh

Martin Pickersgill, the intrepid frog hunter who abandoned his girlfriend in order to walk across Africa in search of reed frogs (see A&M 14 and 15) has come up with the best scam we have heard of yet. He is auctioning off the right to name the eight previously unknown species of frog discovered by him to fund an expedition to Africa in search of the tokoloshe, a species of hominid he glimpsed as a 15 year old in Africa. The tokoloshe is said to be 3 - 4 ft tall &

ANIMALS & MEN # 16

possessed of the strength of 10 men. It is said to be a creature of Bantu folklore. *The Observer 1.3.98*

Lakeland BHM..

Brian Goodwin has really come into his own this issue as our intrepid Cumbrian correspondent. He sent us this reader's letter to 'The Whitehaven News':

Sir - Following your story that you ran in The News on February 19th, 1998, I would like to recount the tale of a sighting made by myself some weeks ago.

While walking my dog on the evening of Sunday, January 25th on the road out of Beckermet towards the A595, I passed Nursery Woods. The time was approximately 16.45. It was starting to get dark so my visibility was not that good, but as I walked past the woods I heard the snapping of branches.

Thinking it was a deer or another animal, I stopped to try and see what it was. Looking through the trees I noticed a large creature covered in a sort of ginger brown hair that seemed to be drinking from a pond about 150 metres into the woods. As the lighting was getting bad I was straining to make out what the animal was but as I stopped and stared it appeared to see me, at which point it reared up onto its hind legs and made off slowly further into the woods. I would estimate its height when upright to be approximately six feet and six inches and its weight to be about 14 stone.

This was not a man as it was naked except for its covering of hair. Also it was not a deer as it made off on its hind legs.

After the sighting I rushed to my home in Beckermet and told my wife what I had witnessed. Let me assure you, this is not a hoax. I was going to report the incident to the police but my wife persuaded me not to for fear of ridicule. I have lived in Beckermet for seven years and walk past these woods almost every day and have never witnessed anything like it before or since.

Name and address withheld by agreement. Source - *'The Whitehaven News'* 5th March

NEWSFILE

EDITOR'S NOTE: This sighting only goes to underline my suggestion above that the sighting reported in the same newspaper on the 19th February and included in this Newsfile under 'Mystery Cats', should possibly be redefined as a putative BHM zooform phenomenon.

Nepalese Monkey Business

Dr. Mukesh Kumar Chalise, a Primatologist and Associate Professor of Biology at Kathmandu University claims that he has "traced a new monkey group, little known to the scientific literature, in the Makalu-Barun area in the eastern hills of the Kingdom of Nepal". He claims that they are very different to

ANIMALS & MEN # 16

NEWSFILE

other animals known from the region. *(EnviroLink Network)*

Beetle Revival

A "Maid of Kent" 2.5 cm staphylinidae beetle (*Emus hirtus*), presumed extinct for decades, has reappeared: a specimen was found in 1997 in a public lavatory. *(Sunday Telegraph 9/11/97 via Exotic Zoology)*

Wainscott Moth

A moth, *Sedina buettneri*, known as Blair's Wainscott, has reappeared in Dorset, probably having crossed from the continent. It was declared extinct in Britain in 1950. - *Daily Telegraph 27/12/97*.

Much play was made in the papers of this revival as its extinction followed the defeat of Atlee's Labour administration and its return is a few months after Tony Blair's "New Labour" party won power. A spokesman welcomed the news but conceded that there'd be political repercussions if a road gets built through its habitat.

Siberian Tiger

BEIJING (AP) — United Nations researchers recently found traces of as many as six Siberian tigers — a species on the verge of extinction — in northeast China's Changbai Mountains.

They also found signs of wild leopards, another endangered species, the state-run Xinhua News Agency reported Saturday.

The experts from China, Russia and the United States have been to Russia and plan to travel to North Korea to find out how many Siberian tigers remain in the wild and how to protect them, Xinhua said.

It said the group did not actually see the tigers, but found footprints, droppings and discarded bones of their prey.

Threatened by destruction of their habitat and poaching, only 300 Siberian tigers are believed to survive in the wild, most of them in Russia.

Three other subspecies of tiger -- Bengal, Indochinese, Sumatran and Siberian -- are also endangered and the South China tiger is close to extinction.

OTHER STORIES

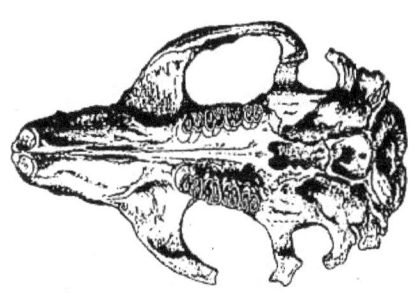

BUT IS IT ART?

BUFFALO, N.Y., Jan. 6 (UPI) -- The slogan for a 9,000-pound Asian elephant at the Buffalo Zoo could be "Will Paint for Food." Fourteen-year-old Surapa (SUHR-rah-pah) has caused a sensation in the zoo's gift shop, where the pachyderm has sold more than 60 paintings for $25 each. Elephant keeper (and art instructor) Daryl Hoffman told United Press International that he stumbled on to painting looking for something for the zoo's three elephants to do on winter afternoons. The lumbering mammals apparently get bored during the long Buffalo winters just like people do, so Hoffman taught them how to paint. He said one of his beasts, Jyothi (JOH-dee), took no interest, and Sheba, a former circus elephant, dabbles. But Surapa has become a star, producing works that some have compared to abstracts hanging in Buffalo's Albright-Knox Art Gallery.

ANIMALS & MEN # 16

NEWSFILE

Hoffman says after a few missteps, his charges caught on quickly. He said: *"Since the elephants were used to eating anything handed to them, they ate the first brushes, but they soon caught on that if they applied the paint to canvas, they would get fruit."* Hoffman says the paintings are so successful that zoo officials want to paint t-shirts as well.

Just don't expect any still-lifes.

WHO IS RESPONSIBLE FOR NESSIE?

Government papers just released reveal confusion in high places over the legal status of the Loch Ness monster. In the 1930s the police, unsure of their powers if they ever had to protect Nessie from hunters, wanted to know where they stood legally. It seems a hunting party planned (in some unspecified manner) to tranquilise the monster. There were also concerns over public disorder and traffic disruption if a confirmed sighting were to occur.

More than one government department has a say in matters relating to fish, but they declined to act, on the not unreasonable grounds that there was no evidence that Nessie is a fish.

In response to one inquiry about Nessie, a government official said, "I think this letter has been in every other department than Monty Python's Ministry of Funny Walks - which might be the best place for it..."

The Guardian ; The Daily Mail 1/1/98

FALLING FROGS (LITERALLY)

Editor's Note: OK I admit it - It ain't my pun - It comes, like this story, from the pen of the irrepressible Daev Walsh:

Concern at low frog numbers in Irish midlands

Laois, Offaly and Westmeath have recorded low numbers in the first Irish Frog Survey which was carried out because of growing concern about the future of the creature in Ireland. The survey, organised by the Irish Peatland Conservation Council (IPCC), involved more than 900 schoolchildren from every county in Ireland, and was intended as the first comprehensive overview of the spread of the amphibian over the country.

The survey found that frogs reproduce in every county in the Republic but low returns from Laois, Offaly and Westmeath have posed questions for the organisers. Twelve counties returned fewer than 10 records and according to Dr Peter Foss, chairman of the IPCC, this may indicate a low density of frogs in the counties involved. *"Alternatively, it may indicate a low density of human population, low school cover, unsuitable habitats or counties with extensive areas under intensive agriculture,"* he said.

"This certainly calls for more research because we would have expected more reports, especially from bog pools in the Midlands."

He said 50 per cent of reports located frogs in man-made ponds and this was a helpful indication at a time when it
appeared the frog is under threat.

"Modern farming practices destroy frog habitats and the use of pesticides and chemicals kills them. They are a wonderful indicator of a clean environment," said Dr Foss.

The survey had most returns from counties Cork, Donegal, Dublin, Galway, Waterford and Limerick. Dr Foss said it was estimated that 7 per cent of frog spawn located during the survey survived to become juvenile frogs.

He said the IPCC received telephone calls from distressed house owners claiming that large numbers of frogs were trying to invade their homes.

He said this was because the common frog goes to the same pond to breed every year and always follows the same path to that pond. *"If a house is built in the middle of their path they will try to go through rather than go around it,"* he said.

Animals & Men Collected Editions Volume 4 — New Horizons

ANIMALS & MEN # 16

NEWSFILE

Who's afraid of the big bad.....

EDITOR'S NOTE: The following notice was posted on an Animals IRC Newsgroup on the Internet on December 17th 1997...

The U.S. Fish and Wildlife Service (FWS) is offering a reward of up to $2,500 for information leading to the arrest and conviction of those responsible for injuring a gray wolf on December 13 on Birch Lake near Babbitt, Minnesota in eastern St. Louis County. Because of the extent of its injuries, the wolf was later destroyed.

After receiving a call from a local resident, a Minnesota Department of Natural Resources Conservation Officer found the critically injured wolf on Birch Lake. Snowmobile tracks on the lake surface indicated the animal had been struck twice by snowmobiles. Although still able to run after the initial strike, upon being struck a second time the animal suffered two broken legs and apparent internal injuries. After discovering the condition of the animal, the Conservation Officer was forced to destroy it. No arrests have been made in the case.

Because of their listing on the federal threatened species list, gray wolves are protected under the Endangered Species Act. The fine for "taking" (killing, harming or harassing) a threatened species such as the gray wolf within the United States is $25,000 and/or six months in federal prison. Protecting endangered and threatened species and restoring them to a secure status in the wild is the primary objective of the FWS endangered species program.

This illegal killing follows a related incident in Marshall County during the firearms deer season, when a radio-collared wolf was shot. The Marshall County wolf had been part of a research program conducted by biologists at the Agassiz National Wildlife Refuge near Middle River, Minnesota.

Anyone having information pertaining to these incidents should contact a FWS Special Agent at (218) 720-5357 or Turn In Poachers (TIP) at (800) 652-9093. Callers may remain anonymous.

Who's grooming the badgers ready for the Badger parade?

Badgers enjoy protection as they raise the dead. Badgers who have taken up residence in one of Ireland's oldest graveyards are exhuming the bones of the dead and causing extreme distress to relatives. But it emerged yesterday that the relatives of those buried at the Yew Tree graveyard near Monasterevan, Co Kildare, cannot legally interfere with the sett, which is protected by law. The cemetery, which is on the site of the old monastery founded by St Evan in 570 AD, is off the main Monasterevan/Bracknagh road and local people still bury their dead there. The last funeral to the cemetery was over a year ago but many local people own graves there which are being systematically dug up by the badgers.

Each night a fresh haul of human bone is taken to the surface. This, according to Richard O'Rourke, who lives in Monasterevan, has been going on for several years. He became aware of the problem when he brought a friend to visit a grave there and they found human bones littering the graveyard.

"It was a horrible sight. I was very shocked and my friend was very disturbed at what we had seen," he said. Mr O'Rourke said he subsequently learned that a state of "war" has existed between local people and the badgers for several years. "There is an annual Mass held there and the locals have been trying to block up the holes to drive the badgers away but they have not succeeded," he said. It was extremely distressing to local people to see the bones of their ancestors being brought to the surface of the graveyard by wild animals, he added. Yesterday, Ms Angela Tinney of Badgerwatch, an organisation dedicated to the preservation of the badger, appealed to the people of the locality not to disturb the sett until May next. She said the badgers are currently breeding and if they were allowed stay until May she would get a licence from Dúchas, the Heritage Department, and move the badgers on. "People should know that badgers are a protected species and they or their habitat cannot be touched without a licence. This has happened before, in Co Mayo, and it was dealt with," she said.

ANIMALS & MEN # 16   NEWSFILE

A spokesman for Dúchas said that this was a highly unusual case; the badgers are protected under the 1976 Wildlife Act but could be moved under Section 34 of the Act under licence. *The Irish Times* Thursday, February 12, 1998

Eel meat again

"Dead" giant eel attacks British fishmonger

LONDON (March 24, 1998 Reuters News Service) - Fishmonger John Hogg will never feel quite the same about dead fish after facing by a gigantic, enraged conger eel that apparently rose from the grave. Hogg had been quietly sorting through the boxes of catch early last Friday when the enormous, shark-like creature reared up, snapping its razor-like teeth inches from the terrified fishmonger's face. "For a moment I thought I was a goner. It was so big and powerful," said Hogg, who first tried to battle the monster with a broom. But he soon realized he had no hope of overpowering the 6-foot eel, which weighed about 150 pounds and abandoned his shop for 11 hours until he was quite sure it was dead. "By the end of the day it will all be cut up and sold. It's like a bony cod steak but it's an acquired taste, and I'll be trying some of this one," said Hogg.

Whoa...a real boa?

EDITOR'S NOTE: OK It's another steal from Daev Walsh but his puns are eminently stealable...

In A&M15 we printed a story of an incredible monster in Peru. In his `Cogitations` elsewhere during this issue Clin Keeling heaps scorn upon the story. This, however, appears to be another account of the same event, and this time one which appears to have a little more credibility...

LIMA - Luis Iluma was playing soccer in a village deep in Peru's Amazon jungle on Tuesday when he saw a black boa constrictor the size of two passenger buses slither by. According to Nuevo Tacna inhabitants, a 130-foot long serpent with a diameter of about 15 feet crashed through the jungle undergrowth, felling trees and forging a ditch wide enough to drive a tractor through." (Reuters).

Editor's Note: Another Reuters Report a few days later, courtesy of Daev Walsh reads:

.... a 'black boa constrictor the size of two passenger buses slithered by the Peruvian village of Nuevo Tacna, deep in the Amazonian jungle. This creature was allegedly 40 metres long and about five metres in diameter, felled trees, and left 'a ditch wide enough to drive a tractor through'. There were five witnesses, and three hundred people felt its passing as it made for the river Napo. The reports were treated with scepticism by Peru's national radio stations, and it was suggested that heavy machinery was misidentified. This idea was dropped when the local authorities pointed out that the jungle in the area was far too dense for such mechanical goings on. The mayor of Mainas 170 miles (270 km) from Lima, Jorge Chavez reckons that 'there really is something to the villagers' versions' of the story.

Interjection from Richard Freeman (Herpetologist of this Parish): Boa constrictors seldom exceed ten feet in length and the record is 18.5 feet. The anaconda, the largest new world constrictor, reaches a length of 23 feet but both are far short of the 130 feet of snake cited by Reuters. A snake of this incredible size would be as helpless on land as a beached whale. This account is therefore either a downright hoax, a monstrous (if you will excuse the pun) exaggeration, or something zooform in nature.

THE "GREY" MENACE (....OK we've been writing for UFO mags for too long)

The red squirrel is believed to have become extinct in one of its last remaining strongholds in England. Wildlife trusts say there have been no reliable sightings of the red around Cannock Chase, in the Midlands, since 1994. Simple competition for food between it and the American grey, rather than direct aggression, is thought to be the cause. "Reds only" zones in Northern

ANIMALS & MEN # 16

England have been declared, where land managers are encouraged to trap greys who infiltrate the area. *Daily Telegraph 7/1/98*

A member of the House of Lords, Lord Inglewood, has called on the UK government to save the red squirrel. He suggested roadside warnings as one way of protecting the red. *BBC Ceefax 26/3/98*. *(What's squirrel language for "greys keep out", one wonders.)*

BIRD STORIES

ONE FOR SORROW...

The magpie, long regarded as responsible for the fall in numbers of small songbirds such as the bullfinch and tree sparrow, has been cleared of blame.

Although magpies do feed on other birds' eggs and chicks, researchers now say the decline is probably due to herbicides, which have almost eliminated the seed-bearing weeds that fed small birds. In some areas, small birds were found to be doing well, despite rising magpie numbers. *Daily Telegraph 16/12/97*

WOT A LARK!

The woodlark is making a comeback in east England, helped by mild winters, replanted woodlands and managed heath and scrubland. *Daily Telegraph 14/2/98*

KIWI

The brown kiwi - a symbol of new Zealand - is heading for extinction, perhaps in 15 years: recorded numbers have more than halved, to 30,000, since 1982. Predators and loss of habitat are cited as reasons. *Daily Mail 1/1/98*

NEWSFILE

TO WIT TO WOO....

Editor's confession: None of my puns are original this ish - that one was from Tony Shiels c.1978....

A mysterious white owl was credited with helping save an Arkansas girl's life after she became lost in canyon country. She was prevented from falling asleep (and thus probably dying of exposure) by her pet dog, Scotty, which kept barking at the owl. A police officer said, "I don't know of any white owls in the county. That's some kind of sign." *Daily Telegraph 30/12/97*

PALAEOBIOLOGY

FOOTPRINTS IN THE SANDS OF TIME

What are believed to be the world's oldest animal droppings have been found on Islay, a Scottish island, in 600 million-year-old rock. Scientists thought the most advanced creatures at that time were jellyfish, but the curved chain of droppings indicates an animal with a mouth and gut. *Daily Telegraph 11/12/97*

DINOSAURS "CRACKED TAILS LIKE WHIPS"

Computer recreations suggest that male sauropods may have been able to whisk their 9 metre tails fast enough to create a miniature sonic boom - the same effect as that of cracking a whip. This effect could have been used to attract mates or to intimidate rivals.

Newsfile Correspondents

Daev Walsh, Brian Goodwin, The Cryptic Clipper, CZOneList

Please continue to send your news items, either to the Editorial address or by e-mail to gl@eclipse.co.uk

Animals & Men Collected Editions Volume 4   **New Horizons**

ANIMALS & MEN # 16   NEWSFILE EXTRA

NEWSFILE EXTRA: EASTERN COUGARS
assembled from various sources by The Editor

The Eastern Cougar - a subspecies of *felis concolor* found, naturally enough, in the eastern parts of the United States of America has long been presumed extinct by mainstream zoologists. Reports have proliferated in recent years, however, and it seems certain that pumas do indeed inhabit places where zoological orthodoxy says that they shouldn't. Unlike the case in Britain where any pumas are certainly either introduced specimens or their descendants the situation in the eastern states of the USA is more problematical.

It seems highly likely that, as has undoubtedly been the case in the UK, captive pumas have escaped (or been deliberately intrduced) into the wild. However, as there is still the possibility that remnants of the original population have survived until the present day then these sightings do, indeed, present a tantalising cryptozoological mystery.

The irony, however, is that even if there are still a few Eastern Pumas around, they have probably been pushed into extinction by genetic dilution from introduced specimens belonging to other subspecies.

Here is a round up of recent news items on the subject:

The Washington Post of 23rd February 1998 carried the following article:

"Cougars, Believed Extinct, May Prowl Park

Wildlife biologists in Shenandoah National Park are using road kill to try to verify whether cougars have returned to the park.

The big cats, also known as mountain lions, are officially listed as extinct in the eastern United States. But Jim Atkinson, a wildlife biologist for the park, and several of his colleagues are convinced they have returned, and they hope to prove it with heat-sensitive cameras set up at six sites in the park.

"It's only a matter of time," Atkinson said recently while baiting one of the sights. "If cougars are present on the mountain--and we really have no doubt that they are--then I think we'll eventually capture one on film."

Park officials have set six bait sites, but have gotten mostly pictures of bears, bobcats and smaller critters feasting.

One dark, grainy photo showed a large, catlike animal with a tawny coat and round head. But the animal's tail, which on a cougar would be two-thirds the length of its body, was lost in the shadows, so the photo is inconclusive. The last known native cougar was killed in Virginia in 1882 in Washington County".

Shenandoah National Park is in Iowa, but putative eastern cougars were also turning up in Tennessee according to an undated news item (taken I think from Associated Press) which was recently posted on the Internet:

CHATTANOOGA -- A cougar and a cub are wandering the New Hope community of Marion County.

Sightings began three months ago. Biologists have studied plaster casts of paw prints and estimate the cougar's weight at 100 pounds.

"In all probability, it's a South American or Western cougar that someone's had in captivity," said Mike Bailey of the Tennessee Wildlife Resources Agency.

"She was probably bred before she was released and they didn't know she was pregnant. And the cat either escaped or it was illegally dumped."

There is a slight possibility the cat is an Eastern cougar, one of the rarest animals in North America. Until the Marion County cats are identified, they are under the protection of the Endangered Species Act, Bailey said.

"The possibility of it being an Eastern cougar is very remote, but we do know that we had a small population of Eastern cougars living in the Smoky Mountains about 20 years ago," he said.

"About that period of time, we had one that was killed in Bledsoe County."

Bailey said there was no reason for New Hope residents to panic. "There's no need to go out and lock up the cows," he said.

An internet-friend of mine with whom I correspond about UFO related animal mutilations sent me the following e-mail in mid-March. We had been chatting on-line the night before about of forthcoming hunt for "The Beast of Haldon" (for the full story see next issue), and she thought that I might be interested in this snippet of information:

Hi Jon,

- 14 -

ANIMALS & MEN # 16

NEWSFILE EXTRA

Just thought you might be interested, one of the regulars in the #ufo room is from a small town near Topeka, Kansas. He was telling me tonight there have been reports of "cougars" around the Topeka area also. Strange...may not mean anything but just thought I'd pass that little tid bit of info along. Makes me wonder why cougars? Would their senses be clueing them into impending earth changes coming so they are relocating to "safe zones"? Or could there be a special attribute unique to the large cats that would from an alien/ufo point of view make them the more desirable animal to put implants in and track as opposed to a deer or squirrel that might be native to the area. Worth taking a chance in upsetting the ecological balance in an area to introduce these animals onto unfamiliar ground? Oh well may not mean a thing, but just wanted to pass it along.

Have a wonderful day!
Arleen

Proving that there is indeed no such thing as a coincidence, within days, veteran US fortean Loren Coleman got in on the Eastern Puma act when he posted these three news reports on The Internet:

PEOPLE PONDER COUGAR ORIGINS - MOUNTAIN LIONS ARE IN NEW ENGLAND, BUT EXPERTS DON'T KNOW IF THEY'RE NATIVE, WANDERERS OR MAYBE LOST PETS.

Published on Wednesday, April 24, 1996
Portland (Maine) Press Herald
Byline: Associated Press

When three mountain lions padded single-file across a snow-covered Vermont lake in 1994, they left behind more than paw prints, droppings and the terrified Craftsbury resident who saw them. The cougars, the first definitely seen in Vermont in more than a century, also raised a question that is being repeated among wildlife specialists along the East Coast.

"Where did they come from? We still don't know," state biologist Cedric Alexander said Tuesday. Alexander has reviewed more than 100 cougar sightings in Vermont since 1991, deeming about 15 percent of them credible.

From Maine to Georgia, people are reporting encounters with cougars, despite scientists' belief that the last of the mountain lions native to the region were wiped out between 50 and 100 years ago. The two notions are not incompatible. Wildlife authorities do not deny the cats, also known as pumas or catamounts, are out there. But they say the animals are either escaped pets or have wandered from their habitat west of the Mississippi River.

"I would bank my reputation that we don't have a viable population," Ken Elowe of the Maine Department of Inland Fisheries and Wildlife told The Boston Globe. "If we did, every place where deer congregate you would find a cougar."

A federal lab confirmed that fur collected last year in Cape Elizabeth, Maine, came from a cougar; high school students have compiled 100 credible sightings in Maine over the last 20 years.

Some of the East Coast sightings can be attributed to exaggeration. One reported cougar found dead in Vermont last month was actually a bobcat; another in Delaware turned out to be a dog.

But the reports in the East coincide with cat trouble in the West, where the thousands of mountain lions that roam California are increasingly encroaching on suburban life. In California, two joggers were killed by cougars in 1994, the first such deaths there since the turn of the century.

Some say they believe the cougars have strayed here, although the nearest known habitat is Minnesota. Others say there have always been native mountain lions that survive deep in the woods. The distinction may be important to biologists. But it is moot to Nancy Davis of Stetson, Maine. Davis' chowchow, Grizzly, was clawed to death in January. State officials say a common bobcat was the culprit. Davis, who says she saw 4-inch-wide pawprints in the snow, is sure a much larger cougar is to blame.

The cat struck quickly and fiercely, yanking the 70-pound dog from the wall to which his leash was bolted and dragging him easily more than 100 feet.

"He was still attached to the end of his run. But whatever it was dragged him down to the side of the road," she said. "He didn't last the night."

Davis wants the state to admit that a cougar killed her dog. That way, she said, residents will know that they should take precautions with their children and pets.

"There's no doubt in my mind, they are here," she said.

Loren's second contribution to the great Eastern Puma debate concerned a batch of 1995 sightings..............

ANIMALS & MEN # 16 — NEWSFILE EXTRA

SIGHTINGS KEEP ALIVE TALK THAT COUGAR PROWLS AT CAPE

REPORTS OF A MOUNTAIN LION IN TOWN ARE UNCONFIRMED, BUT SOME RESIDENTS SAY THEY KNOW WHAT THEY SAW.

Published on Wednesday, January 15, 1997
Portland (Maine) Press Herald
Byline: By Grace F. Murphy Staff Writer

Sleepy Hollow has the headless horseman. Loch Ness may have a monster. Does Cape Elizabeth have mountain lions?

The state says no, and residents remain split over whether a 1995 sighting means the big cats reside in Maine's most affluent town. But mountain lions live, at least in spirit, at the lunch counter at Cape Variety, in conversations at Town Hall and in the thoughts of those who walk or live in the southern end of town.

Clint Hat of Eastman Road has no doubt that the town harbors at least one mountain lion. He says he saw it on his lawn this spring. "After it went through the woods I got on the lawnmower to ride back up to the house. The blades were still turning and if you'd seen the path, I was going back and forth like I was drunk, I was so excited," Hat said. In March 1995, Rosemary Townsend saw what she thought was a lion during a walk in an undeveloped area in the southern part of the town. State game wardens investigated her report, and found hairs that were tested and proved to be like those found on a mountain lion.

None of that convinces residents like Norman Bethel, a retiree who pondered the question at Cape Variety. "I'm not saying there can't be some in the state passing through. I think 90 percent of the sightings are just that. But one on Cape Elizabeth? I don't believe it. If it were here, it's only temporary and there'd be tracks," Bethel said. The lions, also known as cougars, pumas and panthers, are common in Montana, Idaho, Colorado and the Pacific Northwest. They were believed to have been eliminated from Maine in the 1930s, but there have been many sightings across the state since then - all unconfirmed. The animals, which are bigger and have longer tails than bobcats and lynxes, feed on game such as rabbit and deer, which are plentiful in Cape Elizabeth.

State biologists doubt there are mountain lions in Maine, because a 1994 survey of northern Maine counties found no evidence of any. They say that if there was a population in the state, there would be evidence such as tracks, droppings, carcasses or skeletons.

Ken Elowe, director of the Wildlife Division for the state Department of Inland Fisheries and Wildlife, said the division hasn't yet been able to verify sightings.

"We're not saying they didn't see what they said they saw. We just can't verify that they did see a mountain lion," he said. Bob Leeman, Cape Elizabeth's animal control officer and Hat's brother-in-law, said Hat's was the last reported sighting in town. "The state, as far as they're concerned, they still don't recognize (the mountain lion) as existing because nobody has really sighted it and gotten proof other than those hairs" from the animal that Townsend saw, Leeman said.

At the time of Townsend's sighting, state officials speculated that the hairs came from someone's pet mountain lion. There are several registered as pets in the state, but Leeman said there is none registered in Cape Elizabeth. John Costa, a hunter for 20 years, was bow hunting in the woods of southern Cape Elizabeth in the fall of 1995 when he saw a deer streak across a distant field, with a smaller animal running close behind. "At first I thought it was a fawn running with the doe . . . Then I thought it was a coyote taking a deer. But a coyote tends to be black and gray. This thing looked more tan and had a large tail." Costa found no tracks, but in the same area found a half-eaten carcass, three to four days old. The deer's bones were broken, a possible result of a mountain lion's powerful attack, he said. Lester Jordan said he believes Cape Elizabeth is home to mountain lions.

Jordan, a farmer, said he found what he considered to be cougar tracks in his yard in the 1980s, but none since then. He said the state should just admit that some live in Cape Elizabeth. "I have no idea why they'd not admit it," Jordan said. Some residents don't need to see evidence of the big cats to believe they live here. Tom Eismeier, principal of Pond Cove Elementary School, said he was a skeptic until a friend from Vermont explained why he thinks the animals live in that state, and how they could survive on the food supply available in Cape Elizabeth.

"He's an outdoorsman and believes it to be true, and I'm taking his word for it," Eismeier said. Whether his students believe, Eismeier isn't sure. Sarah Dow, a student at Cape Elizabeth High School, said she doesn't believe cougars live in her town, or that it's an issue for her classmates. Karen Pride, who is a Brownie leader with Girl Scouts of America, said it hasn't come up among her scouts because they don't usually camp in Cape Elizabeth.

ANIMALS & MEN # 16

But living in the Shore Road area, where three bear sightings have been reported in the past five years, Pride believes. "It's not a stretch of my imagination that there would be a mountain lion or two," she said.

Townsend, who reported the mountain lion sighting in 1995, said she no longer hears questions about it, except for inquiries from the media and students studying mountain lions. "I don't think the mountain lion is running around town," she said. "There's lots of vegetation and forest, which is heavily populated with deer, and it wouldn't surprise me if there was something like that lion back there. But I don't think they're in every park in Cape Elizabeth."

Finally - another report, also via Loren Coleman and CZOneList, also from 1995. This appears to suggest that the elusive creature was even photographed!

MOUNTAIN LION SIGHTINGS SUBJECT TO INTERPRETATION
WITH HARD EVIDENCE OF THE BEAST LACKING, BIOLOGISTS ARE SKEPTICAL ABOUT WHAT PEOPLE THINK THEY SEE.

Published on Sunday, November 26, 1995
Maine Sunday Telegram, Portland, Maine
Byline: By Roberta Scruggs Staff Writer

An experienced photographer announced with great excitement that he'd snapped a roll of film of a mountain lion - an animal extinct east of the Mississippi for more than 50 years. When he brought the pictures to the New Hampshire Inland Fisheries and Wildlife Department, however, it was clear the creature - spotted across a field in morning light - was a tom cat. "People do see things, nobody disputes that," said Charles Bridges, chief of New Hampshire's fish and wildlife department, "but their interpretation of what they see is anybody's guess."

The mountain lion, also called cougar, panther, puma, and catamount, stands at the center of one of the century's most puzzling wildlife mysteries. If the Eastern mountain lion is extinct, why are so many people seeing it?

Mountain lions are sighted regularly across the eastern United States, including about a dozen times in Maine each year. The Eastern Puma Network, based in Baltimore, reports more than 2,300 sightings since 1983....

This batch of stories just go to prove the truism that quasi-fortean events do, indeed occur in 'clusters' and that with the arrival of the Internet, a medium which has totally reinvented most people's concepts of global communication, these concepts are becoming even more self evident.

NEWSFILE EXTRA

NEWSFILE EXTRA
AT LAST - SNAKES WITH LEGS!
Some Recent Discoveries Relating to the Earliest Snakes

by

Darren Naish

In recent years we have learned much about some of the rather more profound changes that have been made in vertebrate evolutionary history, and a veritable multitude of fossils transitory between certain groups - such as lobe-finned fishes and tetrapods for example - are now known. A sequence of events culminating in development of the armour-encased chelonians (turtles) has recently been outlined (*Nature* 379: 812-5; *Biol. Rev.* 70: 459-547), and more convincingly than ever before. In 1993, the most primitive known amphisbaenian, *Sineoamphisbaena*, was described (*Nature* 366: 57-9), It allowed a re-evaluation of the relationship between this group and other squamates. Similarly, *Eocaecilia* - a Jurassic caecilian with little legs (*Nature* 365: 246-8) - was a significant discovery. Now it is the turn of the snakes. Most zoologists today accept that snakes are most closely related to lizards, and specifically to varanids and related groups. Alternative hypotheses are that snakes are closest to acontiines or *Dibamus* (*Zool. J. Linn. Soc. Lond.* 41: 71-88) or to the amphisbaenians (*C. R. Acad. Sci. Paris*, 294: 563-6). New analyses, which have included the most primitive known fossil snakes as part of the data set, reveal that snakes are part of the varanid group of lizards called the Platynota (*Phil. Trans. R. Soc. Lond.* B352: 53-91) but, surprisingly, they are almost certainly most related to mosasauroids - those sea-going, mostly enormous lizards of the Cretaceous.

Animals & Men Collected Editions Volume 4   **New Horizons**

ANIMALS & MEN # 16   NEWSFILE EXTRA

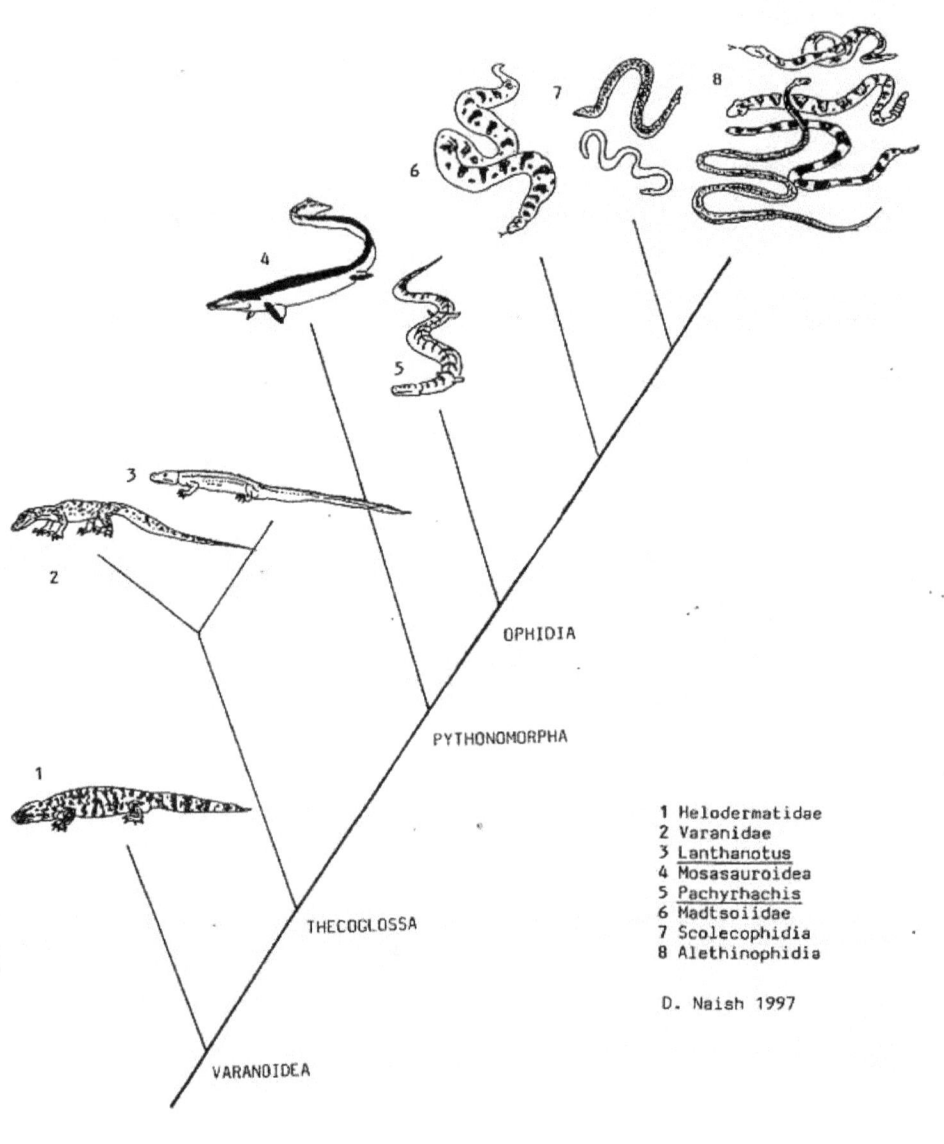

1 Helodermatidae
2 Varanidae
3 Lanthanotus
4 Mosasauroidea
5 Pachyrhachis
6 Madtsoiidae
7 Scolecophidia
8 Alethinophidia

D. Naish 1997

ANIMALS & MEN # 16   NEWSFILE EXTRA

Both groups, sharing 40 specialised characters and therefore a single ancestor, form the Pythonomorpha. This group was actually created by E. D. Cope back in 1869. It fell into disfavour because no subsequent worker ever included both mosasauroids and snakes in the same analysis - until now.

Mosasauroids are marine lizards and the fact that they are close relatives of snakes suggests that snakes may owe their ancestry to an aquatic phase too. This theory would be corroborated if the earliest snakes were found to be marine... and, what do you know, they are (*Nature* 386: 705-9). New work on one of very earliest known snakes, *Pachyrhachis problematicus*, reveals a marine habit for this animal. Interestingly, *Pachyrhachis* has some pachyostotic bones. Pachyostosis - basically, thickening and hypermineralisation of the bone - is a common adaptation in aquatic vertebrates and enables them to use their own bodies (rather than swallowed stones) as ballast. Sirenians and some groups of bottom-feeding marine reptiles have pachyostotic bones.

The primitive status of *Pachyrhachis* is confirmed by the fact that it retains true hindlimbs and a well-developed pelvis (*Jour. Vert. Paleo.* 16: 68A; *Nature* 386: 705-9). It is also more lizard-like than later snakes, and, indeed was initially interpreted as a non-snake platynotan that had convergently evolved the snake body plan. (*Bull. Mus. Natn. Hist. Natl., Paris*, 2: 87-104). But the new work demonstrates that *Pachyrhachis* can properly be regarded as the '*Archaeopteryx*' of the snake world.

Also far more lizard-like than later snakes are another 'wet' group, the madtsoiids. Though first thought to be part of the boa-python group and regarded as a sub-family of them (*Bull. Mus. Natn. Histl.., Paris*, 33: 152-60), madtsoiids are actually very primitive and represent a radiation of primitive, perhaps amphibious snakes that lack the characters seen in advanced snakes - the group that includes all living snakes. Madtsoiids first appear in the Upper Cretaceous and ranged widely in the Southern Hemisphere, being known from African, Madagascan, South American and Indian rocks of this age. A recent and startling discovery is madtsoiid material from Europe (*C.R. Acad. Sci. Paris*, 322: 603-8). Late Cretaceous Europe was a series of archipelagos linking northern Africa with Eurasia and madtsoiids, together with some Southern Hemisphere dinosaur groups (abelisaurs and titanosaurs), were able to island-hop northwards (*Terra Nova* 1: 69-74; *Geol. Mag.* 131: 625-30). Modern boas and pythons are superb mariners - there is one reliable record of a boa travelling nearly 200 miles cross-ocean on a piece of driftwood (*Sea Frontiers* 39: (6): 20-1) - so it should not come as a surprise that these enormous, bulky snakes were able to make crossings from island to island.

And enormous and bulky they were: the biggest madtsoiids achieved lengths of nine metres and were of oil-drum like girth. This is in contrast to giant modern snakes which, even when nine metres in length, are not massive in circumference. According to the Australian palaeoherpetologist Dr. Paul Willis, madtsoiids of these sizes would have weighed in at 800 kg. Or more! Not all madtsoiids were huge though: a small one has recently been reported from the Eocene-Agre Riversleigh deposits in Australia, although exactly how small it is has yet to be announced.

Madtsoiids were not an exclusively Cretaceous group as they survived, in Australia, until very recently - *Wonabi naracoortensis* was hunting wallabies until a few million years ago (e.g., in the Pleistocene). It has been suggested that *Wonabi* was adapted for climbing, perhaps in caves (*Mem. Qd. Mus.* 28: 139-151), but its bulky body has led others to suggest that it was amphibious (*Kadimakara*, Princeton Uni. Press, 156-9). I think, in view of their overall large size, great girth and phylogenetic relationships, that madtsoiids were analogues of certain extant big, bulky snakes - namely anacondas (*Eunectes*) and wart snakes (*Achrochordus*). These modern analogues are amphibious.

ANIMALS & MEN # 16

EXPEDITION REPORT

ONLY FOOLS AND GOATSUCKERS
EXPEDITION REPORT:
Puerto Rico, Mexico and Miami
JANUARY/FEBRUARY 1998

Puerto Rico is an island in the Antilles, and has been a dependent territory (it is no longer politically correct to term them 'colonies') of the United States for a Century now. Previous to the Spanish-American War it had been a colony of Imperial Spain, and even now towns like Old San Juan have a decidedly Mediterranean/Colonial feel to them. When considering the quasi fortean events which have surrounded the island for so many years now, it is, I believe, important to discuss Puerto Rico's unique geographical, political and socio economic position within the Caribbean.

As well as the undoubted influences of Roman Catholic Spain, and the rampant capitalism of the United States (of which the island feels very much a 'poor relation' - whilst we were there the campaign for equal state-hood status was actively and violently going ahead) the socio-cultural influences of the rest of the Caribbean are also very much in evidence. The so called 'Voodoo Republic' of Haiti is only a figurative stonesthrow away, and a belief in the 'old religion' of Santeria - (a bastardised mishmash of West African folk belief practised by generations of slaves and their descendants) and the gorier parts of Judeao-Christian belief) are rampant across the island. It is not surprising that this diverse cultural schizophrenia has led to the formation of a community in which fortean phenomena are so common.

The first reports of what became known as the Moca vampire were in 1973 when on the 21st October, at El Yunque Mountain, in the middle of what remains of Puerto Rico's rain forest nine people saw four "weird" creatures, each of about 5-6 feet (1.5-1.8 m) in height. These creatures were quite active on the mountain slopes and made strenuous efforts to avoid the light of torches shone at them. Branches of trees were found broken and also strange footprints. Over the following months there were a series of attacks on domestic livestock in the area. The attacks were centred in the district of Moca (hence the popular name), and sightings of strange animals, often in conjunction with reports of UFO activity, continued. On the 18th April, 1975. At Ponce, Orlando Franceschi, a farmer, took a shovel out into the backyard of his home, after seeing what he took to be a stray dog. But what the farmer came face to face with was no dog. It had *"long ears, a long nose to the mouth, which was slit* with no lips; two black blobs for eyes and the jawbone of an ape." When this creature walked, it did so swaying from side to side. The reports died down at the end of the 1970s, but about ten years later there were reports of more monsters. Firstly a creature resembling a large porcupine (there are no known porcupines living on the island - indeed there are only a very few indigenous mammals - was reported on the outskirts of the El Yunque rain forest. This animal was reputedly purely vegetarian in diet and lived mostly on plantains (the staple crop of the peasant farmers of Puerto Rico). A few years later other quasi-cryptozoological creatures - Devil Birds were reported from various parts of the island. Researchers at the time claimed that these were an (unnamed species of) native bird which had (for some unknown reason) had the spurs usually attached to the feet of fighting cocks (a sport which is still legal on Puerto Rico), grafted on to their beaks. These reports also petered out after a few months, but in the mid 1990s the animal mutilations started again. This time the culprit was described as El Chupacabra (Spanish for The Goat Sucker - also a derogatory term for prostitutes of the lowest order). This time the reports were much more homogenous in nature and described attacks on a wide range of domestic livestock and there were even disturbing reports of attacks on human beings. Researcher Conrad Goeringer wrote in 1997 that:

"Believers in the chupacabras say that the beast is a hybrid creature, in appearance something which resembles a cross between a giant dog and a lizard. It is said to walk upright on two feet, is capable of flight, and sinks its fangs into victims and kills them by drinking their blood. News reports of chupacabras sightings come from mostly rural areas; and while the mysterious creature seems to prefer farm animals like sheep, goats, and chickens, it has been alleged to attack humans."

A researcher at the Centre for Fortean Zoology, who shall remain nameless described the animal (most famously depicted by Puerto Rican researcher Jorge Martin) as a cross between a kangaroo and Sonic the Hedgehog (a computer game character) on acid! By 1996 the attacks had spread to Mexico, Guatemala and even the mainland United States. The reports continued and in September 1997 we were approached by AVP Films, an independent company to take an expedition to Puerto Rico, Mexico and Miami in the hope of tracking down some witnesses and discovering the truth about the creature. Even as we made preparations to embark on our adventure the attacks continued. his report, for example, was posted on the Internet in December 1997 by researcher Peter Petrisko:

"Utuado, PUERTO RICO - Mysterious attacks on domestic farm animals, in this town 40 miles southwest of San Juan, have triggered rumors of

ANIMALS & MEN # 16 — EXPEDITION REPORT

renewed predation by the Chupacabra ("goat sucker"). Forty-two large white rabbits, some chickens and a duck were found dead on a farm November 20. The dead animals had twin perforations mostly in the stomach region and feet. Most of the perforations were triangular. Researcher Scott Corrales added, "One rabbit had its stomach split, an incision so precise as to only have been made by a surgical instrument or by an expert surgeon. No trace of blood remained in any of the dead animals."

A week before Graham and I embarked to Latin America, the Director - Norman Hull, the Producer - Marcus Sulley, and the Researcher - Tom Tanner, had flown to San Juan (the capital of Puerto Rico) to pave the way for us and a few days before we were due to leave we received an excited e-mail from Tom telling us that there had been a devastating attack on over twenty fighting cocks in a small village near San Juan only the week before. It was obvious that we were going to have an exciting time!

As events transpired - we did!

A day to day day of our expedition can be found on The Internet, and will eventually be available in book form, but for the purposes of this issue of Animals & Men, here are a few excerpts....

THURSDAY 22nd JANUARY 1998 - PUERTO RICO

Our first witness, who by English standards at least, seemed to live in dreadful poverty, was in fact a policewoman and quite well off by the standards of her village. She told us in a mixture of Spanish (translated by Rueben, a New York Policeman who had been `given' to us as an escort and interpreter for the day) and extremely hesitant English, how about eighteen months or so before, she had been hanging out her washing on a line in the back yard - in reality an area of wasteland decorated by pampas grass and the stumps of two moth-eaten banana trees - when she had seen a spinning red light in the sky several miles away between two mountains.

Within days she had experienced a series of attacks on her poultry which were kept in a ramshackle (but extremely secure) coop underneath the house. here, I should perhaps explain, that the house in which she was living had been built on the side of a steep hillock, and the back part of the house was raised from the ground on stilts. The chicken coop was therefore at ground level between them.

She told us how on several occasions she had found members of her flock, outside on the ground although they had previously been locked into the coop for the night. On each occasion, the corpses were totally exsanguinated (presumably through two puncture marks on the neck) but were otherwise unharmed. On one of these occasions she and her brother had seen the animal that they believed was responsible. It was bipedal and looked a little like a kangaroo with spikes sticking out of its back. It had a reptilian face and slit eyes. She drew us a picture which showed a creature remarkably similar to the drawing made so familiar by Puerto Rican UFO researcher Jorge Martin.

She told us how some of the chickens had been covered with a revolting layer of slime which she assumed was saliva. This facet of the chupacabra attacks has been noted elsewhere, and many researchers have hypothesised that this slime is in fact some kind of anti-coagulant which is used - like that in the saliva of a vampire bat - to aid the exsanguination of the chupacabra's victims.

She also drew our attention to an ancient thorn tree just beyond the perimeter wall which surrounded her property. The creature had disappeared into the undergrowth here, she told us, but as it did so it rubbed itself against the tree leaving a revolting stain as if it had been covered with ink. This was too good an opportunity to miss, and so the intrepid team - well, Graham actually, as he is more limber and supple than yours truly - climbed over the wall and negotiated the steep slope to the base of the tree. At the bottom of the slope was what looked suspiciously like an open sewer, and I was very glad that it was Graham, not me who had to avoid falling headfirst into it.

Graham eventually reached the base of the tree, but much to my disappointment he said that there was no sign of any discolouration or stain upon the bark. Mostly for the benefit of the ever-watching cameras (but partly in a vain attempt to secure some sort of specimens) he scraped some bark samples from the base of the tree where our witness and her brother claimed that the stain had once been, and, to preserve some semblance of scientific integrity, took a second bark sample from another part of the tree for use as a control sample. He then negotiated the slippery slope up to join the rest of us, and we went on to visit our next witness.

We didn't have far to go. She lived next door. She, too had seen a mysterious creature but was afraid and refused to talk to us. According to Rueben she was a refugee from Colombia and spoke only her own peculiar dialect of Spanish. She was, he claimed (and I have no reason at all to disbelieve him), both highly superstitious and distrustful of both the police and the media. The political background from whence she had come made this last statement highly believable.

She did, however, provide us with a potentially exciting piece of evidence. Although she did not want to talk to us, she was

- 21 -

ANIMALS & MEN # 16   EXPEDITION REPORT

willing to give us a sample of what she claimed was chupacabra dung.

Highly excited I asked for more information, but was somewhat deflated when, on her instructions (shouted through the barred screen-doors as all the way through our conversations she refused to come outside), Rueben took us to a particularly dry and desiccated piece of ground about fifty feet from the front of her house, and pointed sceptically down to the ground below us. There, coiled malevolently were what I assume were some enormous worm casts. Again, more as a matter of form than for any other reason I took some samples (noting some peculiar indentations on the dry ground next to them) and carried them in a specimen jar to the lady of the house who confirmed (through Rueben) that yes, this was what she meant, and would we please now leave her property.

There was obviously nothing more that we could get out of her. I noted at the time, however, that although what we had collected were almost certainly worm casts, the ground on which we found them was baked solid with the sun and was as hard as concrete. When you add to that the fact that during the rest of our stay on the island, although I examined every piece of waste ground that we passed I never saw any other worm casts even remotely resembling the so-called chupacabra dung of Dorado, it is, perhaps fortunate that I took my specimens back to England with us.

That afternoon we visited a house owned by a man called George who appeared to be a local small-time gangster.

According to the information that we had been given, there had been an attack on over thirty cockerels that had been co-owned by George and his next door neighbour. I will be the first to admit that I have a typically English middle-class stance towards bloodsports and those who practise them, and therefore my sympathies were not altogether with the bereaved farmers. George was the sort of wide-boy who, in he had been English would have lived on the outskirts of somewhere like Harlow New-Town making a living from selling `dodgy motahs` and `bent MOTs`. He was not an immediately likeable person but once we had by-passed his air of bravado we could see that he really was frightened. His business partner Oscar described how he had found the birds found killed and drained of blood and how there had been a trail of three-toed footprints leading across the surface of the yard. We examined one of the chickens and there were indeed two massive puncture wounds on the neck and thorax, and the body appeared bloodless. We took feather samples from around the area of the puncture wounds, hoping that subsequent analysis would show some evidence of the mysterious slime (theorised by some to be an anti-coagulant)

which has been reported on so many of the chupacabra's victims.

Both George and Oscar voiced their fears that the chupacabra would soon stop killing domestic livestock and start to attack human victims. Although there is some evidence that this may have happened in Mexico, the accounts of attacks on humans in Puerto Rico do seem, like Mark Twain's death, to have been somewhat exaggerated.

WEDNESDAY 29th JANUARY 1998 - MEXICO

One of our most promising witnesses was a vet in the town of Puebla, just south of the volcano Popacatapetl. It took several days to track her down but she took us to a smallholding owned by an old Mexican farmer called Dom Pedro. A year before three of his sheep had been attacked by a mysterious creature. According to Soledad, the vet - the first professional on the scene - found that, although the sheep were completely drained of blood, not breathing and their hearts not beating, they were still alive twelve hours after the attack: they reacted to light and touch stimuli, were in great pain and eventually had to be destroyed. As someone with a working knowledge of animal physiology I found this account completely mystifying, and can put forward no scientific rationalisation for it. There were huge crucifixes daubed on the walls of Dom Pedro's farmyard and all over the walls of houses in his village. Again Dom Pedro spoke no English, but even my Spanish is adequate to translate the words "Por protectione de vampiros"...

WEDNESDAY 4th FEBRUARY 1998 - UNITED STATES

Early that morning Graham and I were appearing as special guests on a Radio Programme being broadcast from Fort Lauderdale. The programme rejoiced in the name *"Footy and The Chicks at Six"* and was presented by a New York Irishman called *"Footy"* (who made a series of not particularly funny jokes about Englishmen until I gave him a clenched fist salute and whispered *"Tioefaidh ar Lar"* at him - a technique that has got me out of trouble in Hibernian hostelries on a number of occasions). The *"Chicks at Six"* turned out to be two charming (reasonably) youngish ladies of (obviously) Spanish descent. Much to the chagrin of the Norman who saw his prime directive being compromised, our 'on-air' conversation became sidetracked onto the subject of the skunk ape.

A caller, who identified herself only as 'Denise' described to us her encounter with a chimpanzee type creature that made a strange hooting noise somewhat akin to the electronic feedback from a badly tuned electric guitar. 'Denise' tried to emulate the sound for us, and having done so was slightly libellously compared by 'Footy' to the music made by Rock

ANIMALS & MEN # 16

EXPEDITION REPORT

Group, Aerosmith, who were the special guests on his show immediately after us.

Other callers also described their experiences and it soon became apparent that the 'skunk ape' was as real to the inhabitants of Southern Florida as the big cats which still roam the moorlands of south-western England to the farmers of Bodmin Moor. Unlike the so-called Beast of Bodmin, however, it was also apparent that most of the people who had encountered the 'creature' were of the opinion that it was supernatural in nature rather than a flesh and blood animal. Several callers linked it with the local practise of Santeria - a voodoo-like religion practised all over the Caribbean by descendants of slaves, and other people that we met within the staff of the radio station itself linked it strongly with the UFO reports which had been prevalent in the area over the previous few years.

Thursday 5th February 1998 - HOME AGAIN

The next day we discovered quite how strange the skunk ape phenomenon actually was. Still on the track of El Chupacabra we were filming in Sweetwater, a particularly innocuous suburb of Miami where, allegedly at least, the first Chupacabra killings on the mainland of the United States had taken place. The original witness was not available to see us, and as our schedule was tight we had to be content with interviewing the UFO investigator who had first collated the evidence of the killings.

It soon became evident that the animal that had been seen by the original witness (a worker at a suburban rest home for psycho-geriatrics) had very little to do with the main body of chupacabra attacks which are discussed elsewhere in this book. The animal she had seen was something like a cross between an ape and a shaggy black dog, and moved semi-bipedally leaving a trail of exsanguinated chickens and turkeys behind it.

We were shown plaster casts which were taken at the time and which purport to be taken from tracks found in the area where the beast was seen. The cast resembles that of a very large dog print, but with one incredible difference! It appears to have the finger nails of a human or an ape rather than the claw marks of a canid. I persuaded our freind Vergilio Sanchez from the Miami UFO Centre to let me have a copy as a memento mori, and more by luck than by judgement it arrived safely back in England wrapped in a stolen hotel hand-towel, and as I write is now proudly resting upon the piano in my sitting room. At the time, the connection between UFO reports and a bizarre canine/hominoid hybrid rang a mental bell in the innermost recesses of my mind, reminding me of something I had seen and heard about in Suffolk the previous year, but there was nothing that I could do about it at the time, and as there was more pressing work to do, I mentally filed it in my cerebral in tray, and got on with the job at hand.

When we got back to England, however, the pieces of the puzzle began to fall into place.

As readers of my inky fingered scribblings both here and elsewhere will be aware, I have long taken an interest in the semi-legendary events that took place at the end of December 1980 in Rendlesham Forest in eastern England. Over A period of three nights, what was quite possibly the most significant UFO episode in British history took place and the reverberations from those events have echoed across the world ever since. From my point of view, however, what is particularly interesting is that Rendlesham has been the epicentre for a wide range of episodic high strangeness for many years, and there are several links between the events there and the events that we were investigating half way across the world in southern Florida.

The area between Orford Ness and Rendlesham Forest in Suffolk is a very strange place. As well as being one of the most eastern points in the British Isles it has also been the focus for a wide range of bizarre paranormal activity. Writing in the 13th Century, Ralph of Coggeshall, described a "wild man" caught in fishing nets off Orford Castle. This creature who like so many contemporary sightings of humanoids seen in conjunction with UFOs was seemingly equally at home on land and at sea, lived at the castle for several months. The wild man is not the only item of cryptozoological interest from the Rendlesham area. The lanes of the area are reputedly haunted by giant spectral black dogs (like the one seen by Lady Rendlesham in Leiston Churchyard at the end of the nineteenth century), that pad malevolently but silently along. An even more disturbing spectre called the *shug monkey*, which is described by witnesses as an unholy combination of mastiff and great ape is also seen on occasion, and in recent years the forest has also been the haunt of mysterious black panthers'.

At the end of 1997 I was introduced to a lady called Maxine Pearson who lives in Southend upon Sea. During our long and convoluted telephone conversations about UFOs, crop circles, CIA Mind Control experiments and the like I happened to mention that my real interests lay in cryptozoology and in particular with monster hunting.

Much to my amazement Maxine calmly told me that she was in possession of some video tape which showed the paw print of some huge animal - like that of a cat or a dog, but far bigger and with strange flattened finger nails rather than claws. She thought that it was a print from an alien big cat of some description, but my immediate thought was of the semi-

- 23 -

ANIMALS & MEN # 16   EXPEDITION REPORT/SHORTS

mystical `shug monkey`. When I later found that my friend and colleague Jan Scarff who was brought up in the vicinity of the air bases also knew about the so-called `shug-monkey` I became even more interested, and when, a few weeks later in an unimpressively obscure suburb of Miami I saw a plaster cast and heard a description of a bizarre dog/ape hybrid seen in conjunction with both UFO activity and animal mutilation episodes, another link in the chain was formed. There seems no doubt that there is some connection between the two types of phenomena. What the connection is, however, remains obscure. It would be ridiculously simplistic, to my mind at least, to claim that the hairy humanoids, like Lord Kimbote portrayed in a classic episode of *The X Files*, are the denizens of the mysterious space craft. I think that the truth is far less obvious and far more subtle. Both phenomena are inextricably linked, but are symptoms of something far greater and far less easy to understand.

Tuesday 10th February 1998

After an eight hour flight during which I drank as much whisky as I was allowed (not very much) and then fell asleep, we landed at Heathrow Airport at about eight forty five in the morning. I knew that I could explain the three extra bottles of Tequila in my suitcase, but as I approached the waiting customs officers, and the sign asking us whether we were in possession of any biohazardous material, the hairs on the back of my neck literally began to stand up as I frantically wondered whether the contents of my rucksack counted as "Something to Declare". Feeling like the hapless employee of some Colombian cocaine baron, I smiled sweetly at the forces of law and order and walked unscathed into the cold London air.

When I got home the house was in a reasonable state of chaos and there was a serious amount of tidying up to be done. When, several hours after arriving home Graham had unpacked my computer from where it had been hidden in the loft and I finally managed to access three and a half weeks e-mails, I discovered amongst the assorted rubbish and junk mail this following message from a cryptozoological Newsgroup:

"... my wife found a great battery operated Chupacabras toy at a local shop today. About a foot-high with a devilish face and bloody claws, the chap's automated actions are nothing special, but he sure looks great. Made in China by the "Super S. Heroes" company, this delightful addition to the kids' Easter basket cost $16. Probably available at better toy stores and import-oriented flea markets everywhere."

I looked at my dog, laughed and lit a cigarette. It was obviously going to be one of those days....

The Quagga Project Update
by Chris Moiser

Firstly, 13 of the project zebras at the Elandsberg private reserve are being moved to the Karoo National Park and Addo Elephant Park. This is highly significant for two reasons. The more important of these is that both of these are in the Quagga's original range, and so future breeding of these zebras will hopefully be subject to the same selection pressures that the original quaggas evolved under - the areas, being National Parks, have not changed significantly since the Quagga became extinct. The second factor is that this translocation now means that the National Parks Board are involved in the project, and by inference are giving it their support.

The second major activity, during March, involved the BBC. A film crew from the BBC "*QED*" programme filmed for a programme to be broadcast later in the year, devoted entirely to the Quagga project. It will include interviews with David Barnaby ("*Quaggas and other Zebras*") and Reinhold Rau, the project secretary. Filming for the programme has also taken place at London Zoo and Knowsley Safari Park (there were quaggas in the past at Knowsley Hall). It is hoped to also film in Amsterdam Zoo, where the last quagga died.

BESTIARY: THE MANTICORE
by Ade Dimmick

Ade Dimmick is the Editor of The Dragon Chronicle - essential reading for those with an interest in all things Draconian. Starting with this issue he is giving the readers of "Animals & Men" a guided tour (in his own inimitable style) to the contents of his Draconian Bestiary...

The bestiaries of the middle ages are full of all kinds of weird and wonderful beasts that should more than pique the interests of the average cryptozoologist. The manticore is no exception; a savage predator, with obscure creation mythology links, depicted in medieval heraldry and used as the symbol of jerimiah, the biblical prophet! The manticore or marticoras was a lion/human/scorpion composite, said to have originated in India. Its name comes from the Persian *mardkhora*, which means man-eater. The earliest recorded reference was made by Ctesias, the Greek traveller, physician, priest and historian (c.BC 400).

The manticore can be both male and female. Its head was human, although this was confined to the face and ears. Its azure blue eyes held a hypnotic gaze and its face was said to

ANIMALS & MEN # 16

SHORTS

have been 'deceitfully honest'. Its vermillion red body was that of a lion, sometimes including the tail, but more often the tail was scaled like a serpent's; long and scorpion-like. The tail held poisonous quills which were fired, projectile fashion, at any adversary or prey. Occasionally it was depicted as having bat-like wings, but there is no evidence to suggest that it ever flew. It also had three rows of razor sharp teeth on each jaw, which would tear its victim to pieces. Incidently, its favourite delicacy was human flesh. Its shrill voice resembled the combined sound of the trumpet and flute; it also hissed like a serpent. Other striking physical attributes included extremely powerful legs, which enabled it to jump incredibly high, and run faster than a bird in flight. Because of this, it was virtually impossible to capture or contain. The female of the species, while sharing the same habits and characteristics as the male, differed slightly in appearance. Its whole body was covered in the same serpent-like scales confined to the tail in the male. It also displayed obvious breasts and appeared to have something resembling a phrygian bonnet on its head! The female has also been compared with the Sirens of Greek mythology, and is seen to be representative of the feminine principle connected with the primeval waters and creation mythology. The manticore's natural habitat is said to have been the jungles of Asia. It is documented as the most dangerous and feared of all the jungle creatures, as well as the most dangerous beast *ever* known to Man! It has been suggested that the manticore legend may have been born out of Man's instinctive fear of predators, the living reality of man-eating tigers and folktales of weretigers - a feline version of werewolves.

Conversation pieces

by Richard Freeman

Not all great cryptozoological tales are to be found in mildewed old tomes. You would be amazed at what can turn up in casual conversation. The following two quite astounding accounts emerged TOTALLY unsolicited during conversations where we were talking of totally un-cryptozoological matters.

My girlfriend's late husband, Trevor Butt was an extensively travelled man who had lived and worked in several countries. He spent many years in Australia employed as an animal keeper at a circus. During this time he rescued an aboriginal co-employee from a fire. The two men became bonded in brotherhood from then on. She could not recall the name of her ex husband's aboriginal friend name but he rejoiced in the nickname of "Wombat".

Around 1968 the two friends where visiting Trevor's brother Barry who worked as a national park ranger. All three of them were out walking Barry's dogs near his home in Queensland when they noticed a bizarre animal stealthily approaching them from some undergrowth. At this point in my girlfriend's narrative my ears really pricked up. She described the beast as haveing dark stripes. "Thylacine" was my first thought, but there were more surprises in store. I allowed her to continue without question, and the tale that emerged was amazing. The creature was catlike and had tigerish stripes, however all three knew it was no `tiger`. Trevor and "Wombat" had both worked with true tigers. It had large tufted ears and was rusty coloured with black bands. The animal was as tall as Barry's german shepherd dog but far longer. As soon as the dogs showed an interest in the beast it ran back into the forest and dissapeared. Only one animal fits that description - the so-called "Queensland tiger"!

The second story emerged when Jon, Graham and I were interviewing Mr Rupert Bunts about his puma sighting on Exmoor. Mr Bunts inquired about my zoological interests and when I said that crocodilians were my chief interest he told me a highly interesting tale:

Rupert Bunts had been a soldier in Rhodesia (now Zimbabwe) in the early 70s and one of his jobs was to intercept terrorists from neighbouring Zambia. The easiest way to tell if a man was indeed a terrorist was by his boots, Zambian boots being different from Rhodesian ones. On one occasion a suspect ran into the water in the southern end of Lake Kariba, in an attempt to swim away from the patrols. The ill-fated fellow was siezed and bitten in two by an immense crocodile. Rupert and his companions opened fire on the giant reptile with high-powered SLR rifles. These can send a bullet through a brick wall at one mile range. Not even the armour plate of a giant crocodile could withstand such a barrage. Once the monster lay still they drew alongside in a boat. When dragged ashore and cut open, the luckless suspect's legs were retrieved. His boots were indeed Zambian.

I asked Rupert how big the crocodile was. To my amazement he answered, "Between 25 and 30 feet." The record for the Nile crocodile is 21 ft for one shot by the Duke of Mecklenberg in Tanzania in 1905. Mr Bunts' specimen would be a new record, but sadly the soldiers did not know the importance of their specimen and did not photograph it. Since Mr Bunts actually shot and cut open the animal, I do not think it likely that he could have been mistaken about the size. Both Mr Bunts and my girlfriend Joyce had no idea of the significance of these tales and related them just as incidental conversation. So keep your ears pinned back: you never know what you may hear!

ANIMALS & MEN # 16

COLUMN

North of the Border

A selection of musings from the blurred digits of

Tom "mine's four litres of white lightning" Anderson

Annually there are 40 to 50 cetacean strandings recorded on the UK mainland, of which 70% occur in Scotland.

Until now, only two centres have had the expertise to rescue sea mammals - at Aberdeen and Caithness. However, and beluga or blackfish reading this and contemplating grazing their chin on some intermediate beach will be relieved to learn that squads of re-floaters are currently undergoing training in Caithness. As you can't count on a stranding at any given time, the volunteers use an inflatable 20 ft (6 m) model of a pilot whale and vast quantities of what appears to be soggy tarpaulin.

As most of these dear people are frail creatures of the female persuasion and unable to grasp anything more muscular than a pilchard, never mind the concept of clearing the airways of the aforesaid tarpaulin, it was indeed a painful sight to see.

My final, frustrated and dispareing cry of "Just open the air valve, you stupid bitch, and chuck it out to sea" was not received in the constructive vein in which it had been intended.

My New year's resolution, should I live so long, will be to cease deriding those who believe the year 2000 marks anything at all besides the erection of a rather tasteless and costly marquee at Greenwich.

This is due to recent seismic hints that the day of reckoning is nigh - they have shaken my faith in believing in damn-all.

One interpretation is that it's heaven's judgement on a nation which deifies the Spice Girls and whose idea of social interaction is watching soap operas. Whatever the cause, the punishments have been somewhat bizarre. For example, in July 1997, a mineral bottling plant in Perthshire was rocked by an earthquake (2.7 Richter) thereby negating their labels claiming their water was "still". In August a seven-year-old camel in Merseyside, amusing himself expectorating on tourists, was killed by a bolt of lightning.

And on 7th September a tornado struck a Nottinghamshire farm, hurtling 40 pigs skywards along with their sties. Weathermen blamed a huge drop in air pressure.

Oh yeah?

GRAHAM'S COMMENT: The so-called "millenium" in 2000 is a good excuse for a boozing session, if one needs an excuse (personally, I don't) but otherwise is fairly meaningless. Firstly, the new millenium commences in 2001, not 2000, since the AD calendar commenced from year 1 rather than year zero.

Secondly, the year-count relates to the birth of Jesus, which many historians and theologians now agree occurred in 7 BC and in September, not December - so the millenium should have been celebrated back in 1993. And as regards calendars, the Moslem millenium doesn't occur for another 540 years and the Jewish one is 683 years away. And thirdly, the "round number" aspect of the year 2000 only applies in "base ten" decimal arithmetic: if humans had evolved from a Devonian fish with 8 digits instead of 10, for instance, then the millenium would have happened 320 years ago. So let's keep a sense of perspective as we get pie-eyed on December 31st. And remember to stay away from lifts, aircraft, washing machines, and anything else dependent upon computer chips!

ANIMALS & MEN # 16

CLINTON'S COGITATIONS

Clinton Keeling, veteran zoologist and Zookeeper, and editor of "Mainly About Animals", looks back at the last issue of "Animals & Men".

Another packed issue - and, again, a rich source to draw on from within. Let's look at a few of the more "commentable-upon" points...

I note with a strange blend of irritation and amusement on p.5 that the Institute of Zoology cannot (?) afford the £15,000 allegedly required to examine the Orang Pendek material. I'm sorry, but I just plain, honest-to-God don't believe it -not only that such a sum would be needed but that they haven't got it either. I come upon this sort of thing, backed up by this feeble excuse, so frequently that I'm getting rather tired of firing back my stock rejoinder to such unenthusiastic folk - "If you took only a slight cut in your salaries to release more money to do your work, your incomes would still be above the national average."

Concerning the "Legendary Amazon Forest Monster" wasting valuable space on p.6, just for the record I'll waste a bit more by - well, I was going to say I don't believe a word of it, but on second thoughts I'll replace "word" with "syllable".

I fear I don't agree that the Wallabies dealt with on p.7 have been known to cryptozoologists for years, as they are far outside the realm of cryptozoology, being a well-known and common species - chiefly the Bennett's Wallaby (*Macropus ruficollis bennetti*) artificially introduced here and about whose existence there isn't the slightest doubt. The so-called "wildlife expert" ought to take up plumbing instead [he said that their success indicates how much the British climate has changed in the past few years] as although this species originates on Tasmania it's incredibly hardy, so its survival here isn't a source of wonder at all. We kept the species at the Ashover Zoological Garden, high up in the Peak of Derbyshire (the coldest part of England) but they invariably refused to avail themselves of the straw-filled shelter provided for cold weather, in fact often in the early morning they tucked into their food with small icicles hanging from their fur in an almost chandelier-like manner. It's worth recalling, too, that the first Wallabies released in this country were those belonging to Sir Philip Brocklehurst, who turned them loose on the moorlands above Leek on the Derbyshire/Staffordshire border, where the altitude was even higher than Ashover's - and there wasn't a man-made shelter in sight!

Right, now concerning escaping Iguanas (p.9) I'm going to disagree mildly with our revered Editor - but I'm sure that, as gentlemen, any verbal or written altercation between us will be conducted in a most civilised manner.

He writes, "..*any amateur herpetologist will tell you Iguanas and their relatives are great escape artists and will often disappear from the most securely sealed vivarium...*" but here, surely, the operative word is the one not greatly appreciated by professionals - "amateur".

Yes, this happens all too often in collections operated by amateurs, whereas professionals know exactly what their charges are capable of, so therefore make sure such escapes are impossible. I'm afraid this is quite a problem, especially since, over the last few years, keeping non-domestic species has become such a craze, as the local press loves to batten on such events and so broadcast unfavourable and unwelcome publicity.

Now, don't misunderstand me; some amateur wild animal keepers are good, very good indeed - but unfortunately there are far too many who regard a newly-acquired specimen as something to take down to the pub to show off, or to keep in a compartment totally unsuited for its needs, pending of course its well-publicised escape. These are the ignorant b*****s we can well do without as their antics are currently attracting the attention of the legislators and the law-makers.

ANIMALS & MEN # 16 COLUMN

I thought the article "The Bigfoot Murders" (pp.14-18) was truly excellent, as unlike most of those in cryptozoological publications it didn't frantically and desperately clutch at straws - as, for example, a certain VERY well-known and oft-quoted book does - and in some cases pours scorn on tall tales that some would have grabbed gleefully to their bosoms as proof positive of the "existence" of some non-such. (Just one unfortunate mistake however, on p.15 - "All monkeys and apes ... have fingernails rather than ... claws". No, sorry, Marmosets and Tamarins have claws.

At last, at long last, someone else has the courage to say something I've been saying (to everyone's horror) since the 1950s. Yes, I entirely agree that the famous De Loys photograph (discussed on p.16) is simply that of a perfectly ordinary Spider Monkey (*Ateles sp.*). I mean, damn it, just take another look at it and tell me what the blue-blazes else it can be? When people say words to the effect "no it's not a Spider Monkey but something quite different" I'm reminded of a story by Hans Christian Anderson that I'm sure you know - something about the Emperor's new clothes...

Regarding the tale on the same page about a Yeti killing and eating a number of soldiers, in that case all I can say is that the Ghurkas are not what they used to be, as this is what they'd have been...

Again, at very long last, I've come upon someone else who shares my intense dislike of the Chimpanzee - although to be fair I ought to specify the *adult* Chimpanzee (p.17). I know that in these days when so many people have a sort of "thing" about Anthropoid Apes it's little short of blasphemy to make statements of this sort, so I was beginning to wonder whether I was the only person around who regards the creature as a thoroughly nasty piece of work - in fact perhaps the only species, apart from the domestic dog, I actively dislike.

I might add that I'm a zoologist who specialised in the Primates, but I just cannot like this one. I can speak with a bit of authority too, as I've had quite a lot of experience with it, including having kept a total of six of my own. People often say I'm being unscientific by endowing the species with human attributes that I dislike in Man, but the fact remains no other species affects me in this way. The adult Chimpanzee seems to be mentally unstable (periodically screaming hysterically and throwing itself about both in confinement *and* the wild), unnecessarily aggressive, treacherously violent and with unpleasant personal habits - furthermore it has the unenviable reputation of being the only *wild* animal I've ever known to attack a human child. Less seriously, I'm honest enough *still* to say that a person is/isn't common (vide my remarks in issue 15 of *Animals & Men* on political correctness) and in my view the adult Chimpanzee has the face of a downright pleb., which the Gorilla and Orang Utan certainly hasn't!

In short, thanks Richard Freeman, whoever you are, for a fine and valuable article.

On p.20 mention was made of the so-called Mountain Beaver, also known as the Sewellel (I've never known anyone risk pronouncing this latter verbally; have you?), but rather surprisingly no mention was made of its most remarkable individual characteristic as a species, which I imagine is unique. When it voids faeces it pulls each pellet out from the anus, with the teeth, but why, only the Almighty knows - and he won't split.

Oh dear, I'm about to clash with the editor again... On p.21 it states there are certainly Beavers living wild in this country. O.K., then, being essentially a peace-loving person I'll say so too. The fact remains, however, that if they are "out there" (as a trendy would say) they must have somehow abandoned all their natural instincts, as believe me even a small Beaver lodge and dam can be seen from at least half a mile away and makes itself felt over a very wide area - and I've never heard of any such alterations to our English countryside. How do

ANIMALS & MEN # 16

COLUMN

I know this? Well, folks, I *did* spend three years with the Canadian Wildlife Service...

EDITOR'S NOTE: The beavers on the River Axe which were noted as far back as 1988 by MAFF were brought to my attention by a Mammologist from Exeter University who told me that these animals are indeed building dams on obscuree backwaters of the river. Whether or not they are breeding, however, needs to be discovered by someone with the time to go out and look for them. The farmer who owns the land is reluctant to give out concise information but through the good offices of Exeter University we are hoping that we can mount an expedition to study and film the creatures some time this summer. However, like most of our plans this one is very much open to being rearranged at a moments notice.

Sorry, very sorry, but I just cannot believe that wolverines are rampaging about the British countryside [Terry Hooper's article, pp 22-24 in last issue]. Very occasionally, perhaps, the odd one might have got out, and contrived to remain elusive (contrary to the nature of the species) but I draw the line beyond this.

Just consider a few facts. This is a large species (occasionally it preys on Deer) and is largely diurnal, so by all the laws of averages it shouldn't be long after one has taken up residence in an area that the human population knows all about it, as it certainly doesn't hide from Man. It also has a strange habit (shared by some kinds of Bears but no other animal I can think of offhand) of entering cabins, sheds, outhouses and other structures in search of food *and then wrecking the joint* - and as no such cases seem to have been reported I'm yet again forced to the conclusion that if Wolverines are loose in Wales they seem to have shed their normal behaviour.

Another indication of the value of *Animals & Men* in not blindly accepting each and every "inexplicable" report - in fact its readiness to come up with a logical explanation - appears between pp. 25 and 27 in the article I haven't time to copy out here. [It was by Jan Scarff, telling how he, Jonathan Downes and others located the "Weird Warbling Whatsit of the Westcountry".] I feel strongly that one such paper is worth ten which, as per my earlier comment, clutch forlornly at straws, at least as far as the cause of cryptozoology is concerned.

Again, "Wherefore Art Thou, Nessie" (pp. 28-31) [by Neil Arnold] was first-rate in that it looked at the subject (if in fact there is one) sensibly and objectively - besides being perhaps unique in offering a kind of "guide" to Loch Ness Monster hunters, with its plethora of good tips. Also, although I do not believe in its existence, I share the writer's concern about the trade in souvenirs trivialising the whole concept.

Just one thing, another *bete noir* of mine which I know most other people couldn't care less about, but it absolutely jars on me, as it sounds so discordant, even ugly. The beginning of the last paragraph of the left-hand column on p.29 - "...the castle seemed like it was peering..." Ugh! Yuk! Please, *please*: "..the castle seemed to be..." or "looked as though..." I really do think this Americanism, that has now got so firm a grip on some of us over here, sounds utterly horrible. Believe it or not, but I've even heard schoolteachers using it. It was still a damned good article, though.

As a once-popular catch-phrase used to go, "And that's yer lot" (let me hasten to add I never used it; like most self-educated people I am decidedly pedantic) which, for all I know, might produce sighs of relief, but if, on the other hand, I've contrived to unearth a point or two from the rich bed that is this publication which has proved to be of interest - well, it's something, I suppose.

A COLLECTION OF CAT CURIOSITIES

by

Richard Muirhead

This essay is a result of a search through my files on all sorts of information about cats, mainly but not only the domestic moggie.

There is already an excellently documented account of cat cryptozoology, Karl Shuker's *Mystery Cats of The World*. But to the best of my knowledge the information presented here has not been widely reported before in the canon of cryptozoological or Fortean literature as a whole. I may, of course, be wrong as I have not done an extensive search.

In the second quarter of the Fifteenth Century 'The Master of Game' was published and is now deposited in The Bodleian Library, Oxford. The illustration below is a reproduction of a postcard showing a spotted wildcat from this publication (MS Bodley 546,fol.40 verso). In my opinion, this illustration could be of an earlier European version of the leopard or even an unknown species of felid.

ANIMALS & MEN # 16 — FEATURE

In 1931 Bernard Read published his translation of a late medieval Chinese Materia Medica on Animals which contains some interesting information.

White tigers are referred to as "Han" and black tigers as "Yu". "Piao" was a five toed kind of tiger and when with horns it was termed "Ssu".

EDITOR'S NOTE: The CFZ were, I believe, only the second or third investigation team to arrive on Bodmin Moor after the attacks on livestock at Ninestones Farm in 1993.

Whatever one thinks of the video evidence produced by Mrs Rosemary Rhodes, there is no doubt that she has some spectacularly unusual pussy cats living on her farm.

They are not only particularly large but there is a strain of them that, like the "Piao" mentioned briefly above, had five toes on each of its feet......

The "Ssu" was described in greater length:

"It is shaped like a cat and is the size of a cow. A yellow coat with black spots. Saw-like teeth and hooked claws....It roars like thunder and causes a wind to rise."

Other cat-like or tiger-like animals mentioned here include:

Chiu Erh:

"A huge tiger that lives on a non carnivorous diet but it kills tigers and leopards. It has a white body with black spots and a tail longer than the body".

Po:

"... a piebald horse - a fabulous tiger, body like a horse, white body with a black tail, a single horn, serrated teeth with which it can eat tigers and leopard."

Whilst researching in Northampton library last summer I came across an interesting book called *The Natural History of Northampton-shire with some Account of the Antiquities* by John Morton, published in 1712. It has some interesting things to say about wild-cat colouration:

"I mean in respect of the Colour, which for the main is a dusky Red or Yellow, and that is in all of them; whereas in the Tame ones it is various and uncertain. The She Cats are finshed, and the like Lone-Houses, do sometimes wander into the Neighbouring Woods and are gibb'd by the Wild ones there."

If 'gibb'd' means to mate, and it would seem from the context of the sentencing that it does, this would be interesting confirmation of the view of some cryptozoologists that some of the mystery feral cats of S.W. England may be domestic-wild cat hybrids like the Northamptonshire ones almost three hundred years ago.

The Daily Mail of January 3rd 1995 carried an interesting story of a cat:

... *"who came back from the dead."* The story was that a fourteen year old tabby in Ipswich who was barely able to walk was given a supposedly lethal injection by a vet to put it to sleep.

The vet confirmed that the cat *"had no discernible heartbeat at all "...* but seventeen hours after the injection the cats owner heard a rustling in the box and the cat emerged alive!

EDITOR'S NOTE: this is a common story within the annals of forteana and, indeed within literature as a whole. It was even a scenario mentioned in one of the classic "William" stories by Richmal Crompton, who also, by the way, included lake monsters, ghosts, poltergeist phenomena and aliens amongst other fortean phenomena as inspirations for her stories...

The Northampton Chronicle for September 23rd 1905 carried the following letter:

ANIMALS & MEN # 16

Anomaly in Natural History

Sir, Your readers may be interested in the following anomaly in natural history:-

Mrs.Jackson (wife of Mr Smyth's gamekeeper) put a lame chicken into the basket of her cat with one kitten to nurse.

The cat took kindly to her charge, keeps it warm under her, treats it exactly as she does her kitten, licking it thoroughly clean, etc, and if the chick is taken out of the basket carries it back in her mouth. The chick is doing well, and will soon be independent of its strange foster mother. J.T.Bartlet.

Next we have a cross-over with another well known genre (if that is the right term) of fortean phenomena:

The Daily Telegraph for November 28th 1986 carried a story entitled:

'Cat nap goes with a bang.'

"Firemen were called to a cat which was enveloped in blue flame and blown several feet in the air while sitting in its favourite chair while sitting in its favourite chair in Anmer Lodge old people's home in Stanmore, west London...."

Apart from a psychic phenomenon, the only explanation we can think of is that it was caused by a build-up of static on the cat's fur" said Stanmore fire station officer Harry Bachelor.

Finally, a story appeared in The Oxford Mail of July 9th 1997 about a barking cat!

The cat, Noodles, of Radley near Oxford barked for its breakfast and on investigation it was found that the cat was brought up in a house with dogs in it. " A spokesman for Oxford Animal Sanctuary said:

" This does seem most unusual. "

We at the CFZ would tend to agree !

FEATURE

Cryptoherps in Indiana

by

Brad La Grange

I found these references to cryptozoological herps on a website on Knox County (Indiana) folklore. I have paraphrased them for the benefit of this article.

Alligator in Vincennes?

From the Indianapolis Star, Dec, 1946 p9 c5

According to the story, Ben Melvin and James Auder killed an alligator in Mariah creek. Supposedly the gator came south from Petersburg where one had been released in 1900.

"Big Jim"- Vincennes Commercial, 1908

Giant Rattlesnake in Vincennes area

Starting in 1881, a large rattle snake(12ft long) was reported up and down the Little Wabash. It was reported to have killed a logger, but that is suspect. It returned in 1908(or a descendant?) and was spotted by Sheriff Lee Staley. But Jim did meet his Waterloo when O.H Sullivan shot 'Jim' in Sullivan County whilst 'he' was cavorting in the hog pen. Jim got killed and measured in at 12ft, 5in/ 29 rattles. The skin was mounted but no word as to its location. (Note, a 6ft Timber rattler was mounted in a local bar in Perry County, Indiana until the bar burnt in the 19 60's)

ANIMALS & MEN # 16   FEATURE

EDITOR'S NOTE: writing on The Internet, Richard day and Paul Ingram note:

"A century ago stories of a giant rattlesnake were striking fear in the hearts of the area. Big Jim was reported as the terror of the Wabash, a monster rattler 10 feet long (or longer in some estimates). He made his home at **Rattlesnake Bluff** on the Little Wabash, 12 miles north of Carmi, Ill., although he reportedly ranged up and down the Wabash Valley.

The snake was first noticed in the spring of 1881 when loggers went to log the Skillet Fork bottoms.

According to the story of this confrontation, told with grand detail in 1908 by the Vincennes Commercial, the loggers were driven to shelter in rain to the bluff overhanging the river. A black man in the crew was sent for firewood, but he came back, terrified and empty-handed. The logger, who was named Big Jim, reported seeing a great demon prowling the bluff. Capt. Ed Ballard, in charge of the crew, angrily ordered the man back to his task.

Minutes later a scream was heard from the top of the bluff and Jim hurtled down the bluff and into the flooded river. He was never seen again, though an extensive search was made of the river the next day.

More men ascended the bluff but heard what they said sounded like a thousand rattles. Rain or not, the survivors boated to the Illinois bank of the Wabash in record time.

The Commercial, looking back, said the logging business in the area was set back by stories of the giant snake. Also, other excursions of this of this monster rattler, now called Big Jim in honour of his victim, were reported in succeeding years. Near the bluff one farmer looked into his chicken yard and saw his best Plymouth Rock rooster staring eyeball to eyeball with a giant snake. He emptied a shotgun at the snake, and it disappeared. He said his rooster was never the same again."

Indiana Sea Serpent

This one easily smells of hoax. According to the story, a sixty foot snake with a dogs head lived in Horseshoe pond near Vincennes, as reported in the Vincennes Commercial, April 22, 1892. It was black, and of course, immune to bullets. It showed up again in the south of the state according to the June 17th issue of the Vincennes Commercial, in Big Swan pond, but now with white and black, in addition to red and yellow mottled sides (sounds like the backdrop of a Jefferson Airplane concert). Of course only men of untouchable reproach and great veracity saw this creature.

I'm not convinced of any of the creatures, and I down right don't believe the last one, but, lets not forget the legendary Oscar - the giant snapping turtle of Churbusco, Indiana.

EDITOR'S NOTE: When I lived in Canada during the late 1970's it was strongly believed amongst the local young people that a giant (although I prefer to use the word `outsized` snapping turtle lived in a local swamp.

Together with some intrepid companions and a case of undrinkable local lager (I was only about nineteen at the time) I went in search of this colossal chelonian, but although we saw various turtles of different species (including Common Snappers) we saw nothing even approaching the size of this legendary beast whose name, if I remember correctly was "Big Frank".

- 33 -

Animals & Men Collected Editions Volume 4 — **New Horizons**

ANIMALS & MEN # 16 — FEATURE

Cartoon (Punch 26.5.1909) courtesy Richard Muirhead

Werewolves of London Again
by Gypsy Sherred

In 1947, Victor Brauner invoked a chance encounter between a wolf and a coffee table. Thirty years later, Warren Zevon recorded *Werewolves Of London*. Twenty years later, our gang of surrealchemical detectives continue to encounter lycanthropes in all sorts of provoking magical circumstances.

Brauner's *Wolf Table* (an occasional table in every sense) indicates that lycanthropy is a Genuinely Surreal condition. Surrealism is littered with metamorphoses, entanglements of humans, animals, birds, objects. Lautreamont predicted all this in *Les Chants Du Maldoror*, as his hero warps into a louse, a leech, an octopus, a fly, a rhinoceros, a shark, a spider, a swordfish, a hyena, a mastiff, a black swan and a cricket. Magritte's women turned into fish and weretiger-striped blocks of wood. He was influenced by photographs of carnival freaks in *Variete*, including that of Lionel The Man Dog. Max Ernst conjured up bird headed entities, including rooster-men in *Une Semaine Du Bonte* - and Victor Brauner produced a cock with a wolf's head in *The Philosopher's Stone*.

That cock is a useful clue in this case of werewolves. Howlin' Wolf sang about a Little Red Rooster. August Derleth sent his sleuth Solar Pons into Hotspur territory on the trail of The Tottenham Werewolf. Those Spurs have a rooster as a club symbol. Tod Browning based his film *Freaks* (with its chicken-woman) on a story called *Spurs*, by Tod Robbins. Lionel The Man Dog springs to mind in this connection. Browning also directed *Dracula* - "Ah, the children of the night, what sweet music they make!". The Count can take the form of a wolf, amongst other things.

Cocks, like werewolves, have interesting Freudian connotations. The Freudian might argue that the wolfman, who tries to kill that which he loves the most, is a symbol of unconscious, bestial desires. The early Surrealists were fond of Freud. They would certainly approve of the unconscious erupting into the waking world in a dramatic, lycanthropic fashion.

In 1909, Freud treated a Russian whose case is now referred to as that of 'The Wolf Man.' Freud met Holmes in *The Seven Percent Solution*. Holmes met a devilish canine beastie in *The Hound Of The Baskervilles*. Conan Doyle was influenced by Baring-Gould's books on Dartmoor. The Reverend also wrote *The Book Of Werewolves*, in which The Werewolves Of London can be found.

Warren's song is the key. Like Brauner and Count Dracula, Zevon is of Eastern European extraction. They know all about wolf packs in that part of the world. Another Warren, Warren William, appeared in *The Wolf Man* and *The Lone Wolf* series of movies, incidentally. Anagramatically, Warren gives us Warner, and Warner Oland played Dr. Yogami in the 1935 film *The Werewolf Of London*. He's most famous for playing Charlie Chan. Zevon's Werewolf prowls through Soho with a Chinese menu in his hand.

"He's the hairy handed gent, who ran amok in Kent." Hairy Hands have also manifested, mysteriously, on Dartmoor, startling motorists on the B3212 outside of Postbridge. Kent is

Animals & Men Collected Editions Volume 4 — New Horizons

ANIMALS & MEN # 16   FEATURE

derived from a Celtic word for 'Head'. It was inevitable that those totemic Sea Heads should be involved. *Werewolves Of London* inspires and haunts the Sea Heads Artists Gang. Lycanthropes, like Sea Heads, have "a special loony arrangement with the moon" (Sea Head Lines, Tony Shiels, 1996).

Warren Zevon recorded singles for the White Whale label. "When Moby Dick awoke one morning from unsettling dreams, he found himself changed in his bed of kelp into a monstrous Ahab." This is the opening line of Harlan Ellison's werewolf story *Adrift Just Off The Islets Of Langerhans*. White Whales and White Wolves. The nautical Captain Marryat wrote about *The White Wolf Of The Harz Mountains* in 1839. Henry Hull played the unfortunate lycanthrope in *The Werewolf Of London*. He was also in Alfred Hitchcock's ocean going picture *Lifeboat*. Hull is a word loaded with maritime significance. Hull itself was a whaling port in the bad old days, and is home to a modern day shanty festival.

Sea Wolves of London. Jack London wrote *The Sea Wolf*. The film starred a lupine Ida Lupino, with music by Erich Wolfgang Korngold, famous for his pirate movie scores. Gregory Peck (a roosterish surname) starred in *The Sea Wolves*. He also played Ahab in the Huston version of *Moby Dick*, of course. Patrick MacNee was another one of *The Sea Wolves*. He also turned up in *The Howling*, written by John Sayles (Sails?). Our wolf packs seem determined to run to the sea.

Right at the end of *Werewolves Of London*, just after the line about a werewolf sipping a pina colada, Warren says something off mic. To S.H.A.G.sters at least, this sounds very like "Huh, Strawboys!" "A Sea Head could meet a Strawboy at Oiche Shamna - Hallowe'en" says Tony Shiels. I've probably mentioned this before.

Ah - OOOOO!

Cartoon by Aberdeen's Mr Entertainment

ANIMALS & MEN # 16

What's Afoot?

By
Richard Freeman

About three years ago, Richard Freeman was on holiday in Cornwall when, more by chance than by judgement he drove into the Jamaica Inn complex on Bodmin Moor. At Potter's Museum of Curiosities he purchased a copy of this magazine and after a few months he satarted to wride for us sporadically. Three years later he is a fully fledged member of the Animals & Men posse, and come the summer he will be living with us here at Crypto Mansions. In this, the first of a new series he cuts a swathe through the world of forteana and presents the nearest thing that readers of Animals & Men will ever get to a "What's On" column..............

Some places have a truly awful *genus loci*. Bradford is a case in point. A dire grey leaden pall hangs over the place. I can't imagine it being the slightest bit cheery on a summer's day, let alone a wet weekend in November.

In short, it takes a lot to persuade me to visit Bradford; but visit it I did on November 22nd, the opening day of "The Unexplained", a new display at the National Museum of Photography.

The originally-named exhibition is a collection of Fortean photographs and films. Upon entering, one is met with a slowly-changing series of photographs and films projected onto the wall, intersperced with phrases and quotations from witnesses. Sadly, much as predicted, UFOs get the lion's share.

UFOs are als the first subject tackled as you move on. There are pictures of them, with the date and location, but many are ones that were exposed as hoaxes long ago: there is no mention of this. Several films were also shown on video. To observe some latex dummies being sliced up in someone's converted garage (doubling as Roswell), one is forced to peer through what looks like a fridge door with slits in!

Earth Mysteries fare worse (ETs being more interesting to the sheep-like masses). There is a small collection of crop circle photos and shots of earth lights, but there is no suggestion that earth lights could be an explanation of some UFOs.

A small "show" was run live. This features teenage "actors" recreating several "abduction" scenes. The standard of acting would shame a "teatowels on heads" style infant nativity play. Sadly, we would see more of this troupe.

Home territory next: the cryptozoology display. It had nothing I had not seen before, but was competently done. British big cats (alive and dead), Thylacines, lake and sea monsters, and Bigfoot were all featured. The Dinsdale Nessie film and Patteson's Bigfoot were both shown. Oddly, Bigfoot was given a lot of coverage, while the yeti and other mystery apes were ignored, as were odder entities like Mothman, Owlman and the Chupacabra.

Freak weather was next, with British whirlwinds, waterspouts, ice falls and frog/fish rain. Once again, hoax photos featured, such as the "jerked street lamp" ball lightning.

The Turin Shroud is recreated as a life-size replica, having a small section to itself.

Finally, the main exhibition was rounded off by a recreation of the 1969 moon landings by the talentless group from earlier on. This features an American family watching the event live, whilst a narrator suggests that the moon shots were all hoaxed. The American accents were of a standard which would have made John Keel or Loren Colman dish out a punch or two, had they been present.

In an annexe to the main exhibition is an information room. This is quite good, except for the intelligence-insulting explanations of words like "crypto" in big letters on one of the walls. Here are a collection of folders and books containing information on various Fortean subjects. Crypto-stuff includes Bigfoot, alien

ANIMALS & MEN # 16　　　　　　　　　　　　　　FEATURE

big cats, and lake monsters. The folders are mainly reprints from *F.T.* and *Fate*. *Animals & Men* gets a mention as "an excellent magazine!".

Next to the folders and books is a computer that runs a Fortean program, allowing visitors to choose various subjects. Our own dear editor features in a monologue of his thoughts on mystery animals (with an unfortunate reference to Migo as a pre-zeuglodont whale): apart from that *faux-pas*, this is probably the best thing in the exhibition.

I left feeling that it could have been a lot better. Some life-size models would not have gone amiss, as would some experts to answer questions and do talks.

The exhibition runs until April 19. However, this is a two-part exhibition: the second part runs from April 25 to July 5 1998 at Cartwright Hall - in Bradford (unfortunately!).

The Tristate Bigfoot Conference

by

Chad Arment

(reprinted from CZOneList with the kind permission of the author)

Just got back from this, sponsored by Don Keating in Newcomerstown, Ohio.

My interests in BF are limited to sightings in Ohio and in those areas I've lived (like Harford County, Maryland, where over 100 reports were chronicled by Bob Chance and Mark Opsasnick), but it's basically the only large cryptid in Ohio, so I do maintain some interest in it.

To briefly note: Speakers were Dr. John Bindernagel, Daniel Perez, and Ray Crowe. Bindernagel did an overview of his new book "North American's Great Ape: the Sasquatch" (Beachcomber Books, B.C., Canada: 1998) - it's basic biological data on the animal, taken from some basic assumptions on primate biology and from sighting reports. Chapters include topics: Locomotion and gait, tracks, foraging, elements of ape displays, etc. Not a bad book, somewhat basic, I'd have liked to have seen more ecological data, but can't have everything. My glance through the book has been somewhat cursory for now - I didn't notice many newer reports, but the book isn't really meant to bring new sightings to light, merely to examine older reports from the viewpoint of a wildlife biologist.

Ray Crowe argued that BF is *Homo erectus*, primarily on the grounds that female BF sightings show "human-like" breasts. I disagree, but what the heck. Daniel Perez spoke on two topics - first on his investigation of a Union County, Ohio report 18 years ago (when he first began to recognize that Ohio has quite a bit of "wide open areas") and secondly on his attempt to figure out at what speed the Patterson film was taken.

Perez has acquired a similar camera to the one used for that footage and believes that the film was taken at 16 frames/sec as opposed to the 24 frames/sec that you usually see on television specials (which he contends would provide better evidence for the film's credibility). He also stated that he didn't believe that BF was either man or ape, but rather "it is what it is."

Personally, I think he's cutting hairs a little fine, but again, no big deal.

Also, I spoke briefly with Mark Francis who said that he is working on a website that will include his back issues of the North American Bigfoot Information Network newsletter. (Long title, but easily the most interesting of the BF newsletters I've ever come across.)

As part of this new section we welcome reviews of conferences, exhibitions etc....

ANIMALS & MEN # 16

FEATURE

Giant Lizards in the English Countryside?

by Darren Naish

Like any good cryptozoologist, I have numerous cases on file where people have reported seeing an unusual creature crossing the road, typically at night and typically seen briefly, illuminated in the headlights. The list of such sightings, especially in a global context, is very long and I have given up trying to compile a brief one. Of local interest to me are numerous reports of Hampshire's A.35 of a black A.B.C seen in the small hours.

However, all of this provides me with an incentive to keep my eyes firmly glued to the road whilst driving at night. Thus far I've seen deer, owls, rabbits by the truckload, weasels, cats (not big ones ... yet) and giant lizards.

Oh really?

On Thursday 29th May 1997 I was involved in a car crash: essentially the car I was travelling in met a large wall at high speed. The wall came off OK and fortunately so did everyone else involved. Before you ask, I wasn't driving. But it was on the way back in the R.A.C van, that my sighting occurred. Though the prospect of pushing a severely traumatised mini into a small, inner city garage at 2 a.m. now put a slight downer on an otherwise fun-filled evening, I was nonetheless playing at the 'watch the road' game.

"Well I never - a Giant Lizard!"

Direction of travel

Sightings that have not been reported to the local press include Mr. E.R.Abbott's of early 1982, and the two related to me by Carol Renouf - both made by her husband in October 1991 and on the Christmas Eve of the same year. Like about 98% of A.B.C sightings the world over, these are all spectacularly uninteresting unless you happened to be there at the time: *"I saw a large black cat..."* And? *"Well that's it!"*.

Just in front, about 10m away, a great big lizard jolted out of a hedge on the right and sort of jerked across to the left. Of a uniform dark colour, it was about 1.5m long with a bulky, dragging tail and elongate, heavy neck. The sighting lasted all of three seconds - the only comment being mine: *"What's that???"*

Well, as interesting as giant lizards........

"Hang on a minute - it looks just like a fox pulling a dead rabbit to me..."

ANIMALS & MEN # 16

LETTERS TO THE EDITOR

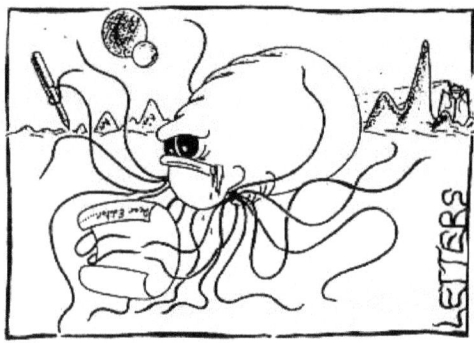

The Editor and his band of merry men welcome an exchange of correspondence on any subject of interest to readers of this magazine. We reserve the right to edit letters and would like to stress that opinions voiced are those of the individual correspondent rather than being necessarily those of the editorial team or the Centre for Fortean Zoology. Every attempt is made not to infringe anyone's moral rights or copyright, and we apologise if we have unwittingly done so.

I thought I saw a Puddy Tat...

Hello Jon,

Just to let you know I saw a strange cat a few weeks ago. It was in Weston Lane, near where I live, at the Weston Road end. At this point, the lane runs between two steep earth banks, covered with vegetation; the cat was going into the bushes, prior to climbing up the slope. It was all black, larger than the usual house cat, and had a long bony body, long legs, a small head and a very long tail. I saw the whole of the cat, but did not get near to it, as by the time I got to the spot, it had disappeared. As far as I know, no one else has seen it, but this area is covered with houses, so it might be somebody's pet. I am keeping a lookout in case I see it again, I frequently pass the spot where I saw it.

Yours, Noela MacKenzie   (Noela@dial.pipex.com)

Editorial Comment: In the last issue we solicited obscene but printable limericks about Tom Anderson. Dr Gail-Nina Anderson (no relation but an expert on vampires) writes:

Dear Jon,

OK, the first problem is that, although it looks reasonable enough on the page, the internal rhythm of the line "There was a young man from Aberdeen" has buggered up any chance of getting your limerick to scan properly even before you've written it. Could Tom not be gently persuaded to move elsewhere, for the sake of poetic harmony?....

Graham's Comment: Perhaps Uppingham (near Leicester)? Anyway, Gail-Nina fuelled herself up on Earl Grey tea and two fried egg sandwiches and penned the following sequence of limericks:

That Tom Anderson can't resist verse
Is a strange Aberdonian curse.
He'll libel his friends
For unspeakable ends
In a manner that's crypto-perverse.

In an area North of the Border
The zoology's all out of order.
There's a curious hominid
Known as the Tominid
Or the Lesser Fanged Ranting Marauder.

Tom's idea of a roaring good time
Involves no lubrication or slime,
Leather, creams, whips or silk,
Or ought of that ilk -

Animals & Men Collected Editions Volume 4   **New Horizons**

ANIMALS & MEN # 16   LETTERS

He'll just stuff you and mount you in rhyme.

Graham's Interjection: Sadly, the next one isn't printable, although we may consider 'posting' it on one of the less salubrious news groups on the Internet...! The one after that isn't obscene but is very good anyway:

With respect for humanity minimal,
Tom's poetry verged on the criminal.
His rhyming was hectic
His puns apoplectic,
And his scansion entirely subliminal.

EDITORIAL COMMENT: Thanks, Gail-Nina - and a free subscription to "Animals & Men" is yours!

ICE ICE BABY

EDITOR'S BLURB: As any regular reader will no doubt have become aware the CFZ Wrecking Crew have become enamoured of The Internet. What used to be the old HELP column in *Animals & Men* has become a regular feature of our e-mail and occasionally it throws up a gem like this one....

Mr. Downes,

I have a question about an exhibit that I have been wondering about since I saw it as a child. The travelling exhibit was called, as I remember, "The Minnesota Ice Man," a supposed prehistoric man frozen in ice. I saw it at the Fashion Square Mall in Saginaw, Michigan in the mid 1970s at a time when there were many reports of Bigfoot sightings in the USA. Was this real? With new technology available today has this frozen "man" been proven to be a fake or genuine? I am sure that the ice block could have been CAT scanned to see if the contents were human or not.

have a great New Year,

Darren Nemeth

EDITOR'S BLURB: as one can no doubt see from the final words of Darren's letter it arrived at what is euphemistically called "The Festive Season" whilst Graham, Richard F and yours truly were drinking a lot and playing interminable games of "Find The Fish" (a completely pointless game akin to "20 Questions" involving fish which was invented by Senor Freeman. In amongst this pointless merriment Richard and I wrote back to Darren:

Dear Darren,

The ice man you saw in the seventies was almost certainly a fake. The supposedly genuine beast was removed from public view in the late sixties when its anonymous owner took it off show. Frank Hanson, the show man who displayed it for the owner, said that in the early days a real specimen was shown. Zoologist Ivan T Sanderson and cryptozoologist Bernard Heuvelmans examined it closely and were convinced it was real. Heuvelmans knocked over a lamp onto the ice block causing it to crack. Both scientists smelt rotting flesh.

The major rumour surrounding the iceman's genesis is that it was shot by a soldier in Vietnam, then smuggled back to the U.S. in a body bag. Later, when the FBI began to show an interest, the owner removed his odd charge. Hanson insists the true beast is still on ice somewhere in California. After this a dummy was substituted for several years. Sanderson and Heuvelmans believed it was a primitive human unlike the yeti that seems to be a colossal ape. There are many tales of such wildmen in Indo-China. If you took any photographs of the creature or have any pix or flyers (handbills) of the sideshow we'd be very interested in seeing them.
Best wishes,

Richard Freeman

A few hours later we received a reply which has historical significance for us at least

ANIMALS & MEN # 16

LETTERS

because it gives us the first account we have ever read from someone who actually saw the exhibit when Hanson et al were still claiming that the corpse was a legitimately cryptozoological exhibit...........

Hi,

Wow, thanks a lot for the information! I wonder the "original" ice man is at now. As far as I remember it was at the Fashion Square Mall in the mid 1970s and was displayed in a casket type refrigerator. Every one paid, I think, 50 cents to $1 to look at it and they could take a long of a look as they pleased for their money. I remember staring at for a long time and distinctly remember seeing a remarkably human leg and hand. Other parts of the body were conveniently concealed, like the face and torso, by ice air bubbles. But like I said, this was extremely life like. One of the promoters told me that it was real and the only way human flesh could be duplicated like that was with a wax dummy but he added that wax would crack if it were kept at such a low temperature. However, I think I remember that the thermometer in the "Casket" did not read such a low temperature as was stated in the literature the ice man had to be kept in. There was a note beside he thermometer saying it was not working, or something like that.

I remember a display at the ice man exhibit that had literature. This included copies of the covers or several books on the subject. Can you tell me what books that were published on the ice man? I would really like to read more about it.

Darren Nemeth

the truth is....

Dear Sir/Madam

My name is Mike Nicholson, I am a psychology undergraduate at Bolton Institute and am currently conducting my final year research project, which constitutes approximately 20% of my overall BSc (Honours) degree.

I am researching the area of paranormal belief and its relationship to both critical thinking and reasoning skills. The basis of my study is that individuals who have high levels of interest and involvement in such phenomena may provide a more accurate picture of the cognitive characteristics of "paranormal believers" than that obtained from participants in previous studies, namely those who were identified as believers via a questionnaire relating to paranormal beliefs. My hypothesis is that individuals who devote a higher proportion of their attention and time to the study of such phenomena will be at least as efficient in their critical thinking and reasoning as non-believers, contrary to what has been suggested by some authors who have previously worked in this area of research.

I was therefore wondering whether it would be possible for your group to help me in my research by allowing me to send you a small selection of brief questionnaires (3 in total). All responses would remain completely confidential, with all participants and groups remaining anonymous. Participants will be able to request information on the progress of the study and will be free to withdraw from the project at any point. The research project will be fully supervised by an academic lecturer at the Institute and upon completion I would be more than happy to forward your group a complete copy of the project for your own perusal. If you would like to help me in my project, or would like further information concerning any aspect of the study, please E-Mail me at the following address:

MEN1CSS@BOLTON.AC.UK

Please leave a postal address if you do wish to take part and I will send you the questionnaire material, along with pre-paid return envelopes. Also, should you know of any other groups/societies that you feel would beinterested in helping me with my research, I would be grateful if you could forward a contact address to me.

Thank you in anticipation for your help.

Your sincerely

Mike Nicholson

ANIMALS & MEN # 16

LETTERS

REVIEWS SECTION

Web Sites

The **CFZ web site** can be found at http://www.eclipse.co.uk/cfz

We update regularly and at the moment have something in the line of forty pages for your online delectation. There are also links to other sites and, as we do with magazines, we welcome exchanges of magazines and the cross-linking of web sites with like-minded (ish) organisations.

The information below is for guidance only: websites may change or close without our knowing!

Out of the Cauldron - witches & pagans festivals and info, including the forthcoming Wisecraft Festival in Yorkshire, is at http://www.pagan.force9.co.uk

Brian Goodwin's excellent site at http://freespace.virgin.net/brian.goodwin/index.htm includes big cats, serpents, dragons, Nessie, and news from Fortean Cumbria.

The English version of **Michel Raynal's** Virtual Institute of Cryptozoology service at http://perso.wanadoo.fr/cryptozoo/welcome.htm is now being developed - with text and pics

The news section on the **Earthly Delights** site at http://www.planet13.co.uk/earthly/EarthlyDelights.htm looks at Bodmin Moor: its terrestrial zodiac, big cats and celtic stones.

Ben Roesch's "Cryptozoology On The Internet" list of crypto sites is at http://www.ncf.carleton.ca/~bz050/HomePage.czlinks.html

And his home page is at http://www.ncf.carleton.ca/~bz050/

Magazines

We welcome an exchange of publications with other magazines who either cover the same broad range of subjects that interest us and our readers or else who make us laugh...

MAINLY ABOUT ANIMALS
A5 32pp Quarterly. Subscrip: £5 per year. C. Keeling, 13 Pound Place, Shalford, Guildford, Surrey. GU4 8HH

Clinton Keeling is editor of this zoological-based magazine, and writes in his own inimitable and sometimes ascerbic style - see pp 24-25 of this issue of *Animals & Men*... Issue 36 (Jan 98) includes part 2 of *"Big Bad Eagles"* by Darren Naish, and pieces on elephant trekking, the Saiga antelope, goldfish fungus, how we can classify Wolverines, and news from various zoological gardens. The magazine is rounded off by Pamela Keeling's beautifully written "Country Corner", with its horticultural and ecological leanings - and its news of their new kitten, Pinkerton!

-43-

Animals & Men Collected Editions Volume 4   New Horizons

ANIMALS & MEN # 16   REVIEWS

MAGONIA
£1.25 John Rimmer, 5 James Tce, Mortlake Churchyard, London SW14 8HB
http://www.magonia.demon.co.uk

Magonia's been running for nearly 30 years now, and is still seeking to "interpret contemporary vision and belief", mainly in the UFO/Fortean areas. Issue 62 examines the UFO/abduction area, looking at the psychology, sociology and trends in testimony behind the phenomenon; and also has the usual no-holds-barred book reviews. For instance, on Nick Redfern's *Covert Agenda*: "If Redfern had thrown out all the rubbish ... the publishers would not have been interested. They know that there a lot of nutters out there."

COVER UP
SUPR (Scottish Unexplained Phenomena Research) A4 12pp
£1.25 David Colman, 49 Limefield Cres., Bathgate, WL, Scotland EH48 1RF

In issue 10 (Mar 98) the internecine wrangling amongst Scottish UFOlogists is still going strong - presumably indicative of a vibrant and thriving 'scene'. Anyway, it's better than the deathly hush of indifference., innit? That aside, there's an interesting editorial on how litigation-obsessed American Interests want legal control over the names McDonald and Nessie; Scottish UFO sightings; and pieces on possible cover-ups in the Vatican and the UK nuclear industry (the former being about some angel or other, whose message is supposedly shut away in a vault! (I think that more likely reasons for general Vatican secrecy are (a) to disguise the extent of their co-operation with Nazi murderers, and (b) to conceal historical evidence that the Pope isn't infallible and that the authority of their church is, like most others, built on an edifice of fear, ignorance and kow-towing to the Establishment...)

ANIMAL NEWS
A5 24pp NAPAK quarterly. (Inquiries to Elaine Storey, 57 Marlboro Ave, Goole, East Yorks, DN14 6JB)

NAPAK was formed in '86 as a voice against increasing legislation facing animal keepers and to promote responsible care of animals. In the Jan-Mar issue, there's letters (help sought and given), an article on Dobermans (a breed of dog that's had a very bad press in the past) and info ranging from snakes to lemmings (non-suicidal ones) to terrapins (turtles). The front cover deserves a mention for its minimalist design - just a circle in a square, and the title and date in small font near the bottom.

MYSTERY MAGAZINE
£2. Bimonthly. A4 38pp MM, 48a Bridge Street, Killamarsh, Derbys, S21 8AJ

The "equivalent of a local *Fortean Times*", issue 2 has UFO reports, loads of weird news snippets, a look at the garbage that goes into pet food, a catalogue of ghosts - 64, including a limping butler at the BBC, and pieces on Chinese dragonlore, and witches. There's less cryptozoological stuff than in issue 1, however.

NETWORK NEWS
A5 24pp. Suggested UK subscription donation is £5. Earthly Delights, PO Box 2, Lostwithiel, Cornwall, PL22 0YY.

Issue 11 is the most recent we have: Diabolical Earth Current. There's a multi-part look at the cult of Princess Diana - before and after her death - with premonitions, conspiracy theories and various after-effects. There's also a look at new-age type graffiti on various ancient structures, including Stonehenge. It seems that the word LIVE daubed on one edifice was not a Liverpool football supporter who ran out of paint!

DEAD OF NIGHT
A4 62pp £2. Lee Walker, 156 Bolton Road East, New Ferry, Merseyside, L62 4RY

Strange news stories, superstitions and conspiracy theories. A consistently brilliant magazine which is highly recommended by all the folk within the Animals & Men shock troops...

EDITOR'S PLUG: My favourite magazine that is currently available within the shambles of weirdness that is broadly known as the fortean marketplace. Here we should like to bid a fond farewell to Uri Geller's Encounters, Enigmas and Sightings magazines which have sadly ceased publication in the last few months. My bank manager will miss you all................

- 44 -

ANIMALS & MEN # 16

BOOK REVIEWS

by Graham Inglis or Jonathan Downes
(where noted)

MIAMI "CHUPACABRAS"
by Virgilio Sanchez-Ocejo.
Pharaoh 1997 US$9.99 PO Box 960771 Miami Fl 33296 USA

Chupacabra, the vampiric "goat sucker", has been affecting the Latin American regions of the world for the past few years (if not longer). This 58 pp book is an orderly collection of witness data, photographs and reactions from those concerned, including the authorities. Jonathan and I met Virgilio during our Miami visit in February and he cooperated with entheusiasm when asked to take part in our documentary on *el Chupacabra*. His investigative entheusiasm shows though in this book, too, while acknowledging that much more information needs to be collected before serious analysis cam be made. The book includes some of his photographs, including one of a pawprint cast that he took near his own home on the outskirts of Miami. A sober resource for the researcher, rather than a popularisation. **GI**

THE DOG WHO RESCUES CATS
The True Story of Ginny

by Philip Gonzalez & Leonore Fleischer.
ISBN 0-684-81924-4 Simon & Schuster 1997. £9.99
160pp.

This is one of the most beautiful stories I have read in a long time. Walt Disney has cashed in on the concept of animals with "loveable human traits" often enough but, when it happens outside Hollywood, this can be rather special.

This is the story of a New York labourer, Philip Gonzales, who, after several bereavements and then suffering serious injury in an industrial accident, adopts - or rather, is adopted by - a small mixed-breed and ill-treated dog, that he calls Ginny. She soon becomes a faithful friend, restimulating his interest in life. Then her liking for cats soon becomes evident, and a pattern starts emerging: her main concern is for animals (and humans) in trouble of some sort. She befriends starving stray cats on wasteground and harasses Philip into going back to them. He soon realises that she wants him to feed them.

Ginny's "radar of the heart", as Philip terms it, leads her to select deaf cats and cats with injuries of various sorts, sometimes in potentially dangerous situations. Philip has had as many as 15 cats in their home at one time, and the dog plays mother to them all.

Compassion in New York can be hard to come by, sometimes. This dog's behaviour and instincts (or efficient use of her senses) make a very remarkable story. **GI**

McX
Amazing True Stories From Scotland's X-Files
Ed: Ron Halliday £6.99 B&W Publishing. ISBN 1-873631-77-4 255pp.

Most of the cases fit in the McYawn "insufficient data" category of unexplained ghosts or UFOs; the most bizarrely cryptozoological item is the mad (allegedly) Earl of Glamis Castle who was supposedly nearly limbless, evil, and the shape of a monsterous hairy egg. Collectors' note: how many points would you get for that? (Glamis and the 'evil egg' were covered in *Goblin Universe #5*). There's also a quick look at the Big Grey Man of Ben MacDui (covered for our *1997 Yearbook* by Dr Karl Shuker and for *Goblin Universe #5* by Phil Johnston - and we had a picture generated from remote viewing, too.) **GI**

- 45 -

Animals & Men Collected Editions Volume 4　　　　　　　　　　　　　　　　　　**New Horizons**

ANIMALS & MEN # 16

OUR OTHER PUBLICATIONS

THE OWLMAN AND OTHERS
by
Jonathan Downes

NEW UPDATED EDITION

240pp with colour cover £12.95

Published by and available from

Domra Publications, 65 Constable Road, Corby, Northants, NN18 0RT, England.

ISBN 0952441764

For the last 20 years girls and young women visiting Mawnan Old Church in southern Cornwall have reported sightings of a 4 to 5 foot tall humanoid creature covered in feathers.

This book examines two decades of evidence of owlman and related matters - including the activities of Tony 'Doc' Shiels - and comes about as close to the truth as anyone ever will.

Can be ordered through bookshops by quoting the ISBN number and Publisher.

MORGAWR: THE MONSTER OF FALMOUTH BAY
by
A. Mawnan-Peller

Now with a new introduction by Tony Shiels, this booklet is available for £1.50 from the CFZ.

THE CFZ YEARBOOK 1998

edited by
Jonathan Downes & Graham Inglis

is finally available...

200pp. £12.50

Published by and available from

CFZ
15 Holne Court, Exwick, Exeter, Devon, EX4 2NA, England.

Contributors:

Tom: Anderson, Neil Arnold, Richard Freeman, Mike Grayson, Martin Jenkins, Roy Kerridge, Chris Moiser, Nick Molloy, Richard Muirhead, Darren Naish, Michael Playfair, and Emmet J. Sweeney.

Subjects:

Giant crocodiles, cryptozoological films, African Stories, Nessie - asking the right questions, Nessie - diary of a hunt, Ichthyosaur evolution, Mammoths and the Comet, Sea Serpents, Amerindian icons, Strange Snake stories, an alphabetical guide to water monsters, the Fortean Fauna of Percy Fawcett, and The Zambesi River God.

How to Order:

Please see METHODS OF PAYMENT on page 47.

Animals & Men Collected Editions Volume 4   **New Horizons**

ANIMALS & MEN # 16

ANIMALS & MEN
BACK ISSUES: £2 each

Back issues are available from the editorial address (p2). Please see "methods of payment" below.

CONTENTS (all issues also contain news pages, reviews and letters) :

1 Relict Pine Martens, Giant Sloths, Sumatran and Javan Rhinos, Golden Frogs, Frog Falls.
2 Mystery bears in Oxford and The Atlas Mountains, Loch Ness reports, Green Lizards, Woodwose, The Tatzelwurm.
3 Giant Worm in Eastbourne, Lake Monsters of New Guinea. Giant Lizards in Papua, Mystery Cats, Black Dogs on Dartmoor, Scorpion Mystery.
4 Manatees of St Helena, Migo: The Lake Monster of New Britain, The search for the Tasmanian Thylacine.
5 Mystery cats, Loch Ness, More on the "Migo Video", Boars and Pumas, The Hairy Hands of Dartmoor.
6 The Owlman Special; also the Humped Elephants of Nepal, Mystery Cats, Sabre-toothed cats, Mysterious hominids of Africa, The British Nandi Bear?, Bibliography of Cryptozoology books part 1 (by Dr Karl Shuker).
7 Mystery Whales, Strangeness in Scotland, On collecting a cryptid, Bodmin Leopard Skull, Shuker's Cryptozoological Bibliography pt 2.
8 Green Cats and Dogs, Mystery Whales, Quagga Project, Bibliography of Cryptozoological books (3rd & concluding part), Malayan Man Beast.
9 Hong Kong Tiger, Horseman of Lincolnshire, Scottish BHM, Congo Peacock, Mystery Whales.
10 Mystery Moth of Madagascar, Bengal Leopard Cats, The Derry, Wild Boars in Kent, a new Irish lake monster, mystery whales and the truth about the Essex Beach Corpses.
11 The "Walruses Special", also: Feathered Dinosaurs, Ground Sloth Survival in North America, Mystery Whales, Initial Bipedalism.
12 Lions: The Barbary Lion, etc. More Feathered Dinosaurs, Chinese Crabs in the Thames, Mystery Animals of Germany, News from New Zealand.
13 Pangolins; also Moby the Sperm Whale, Barking Beast of Bath, Yorkshire ABCs, Molly the Singing Oyster, Leatherback Turtles, Walruses.
14 The Dragons of Yorkshire, Irish mystery animals, In Search Of "Gambo", Charlie Fort and the Vampire Sheep Slayer - and Jackals; and the first of Clinton's Cogitations (Clin Keeling looks back on and comments on the previous issue).
15 Lake Dakataua "Migo" monster update, The Weird Warbling Whatsit of the Westcountry, The Beast of Llangurig, The Waspman, The Bigfoot "Murders", and three articles on Beavers.

OUR OWN PUBLICATIONS

THE GOBLIN UNIVERSE
BACK ISSUES: £2 each

Back issues are available from the editorial address (p2). Please see "methods of payment" below.

CONTENTS (all issues also contain news pages, letters, and record, magazine and book reviews) :

Issues 1-3 were freebies brought out mainly to publicise the activities of a band called The Amphibians from Outer Space. They also contained dodgy poems about postmen. They are no longer available.

4 St Neot: Weirdest Village in the West? Naked witches, hellhounds and Capel's tomb. The Vampire of St Leonards (Exeter). Cattle Mutilation. Psychic Detectives.
5 Crop Circles & Animal Mutilations. Ghosts of Glamis Castle. Communication with UFOs,. The "nooshpere" and text semantics.
6 Jon and Tina are shown the Rendlesham UFO crash site in Suffolk. Mystery Planets (Karl Shuker). Cannibalism in Scotland. D.I.Y. countries and states.

METHODS OF PAYMENT

Postage and packing is extra: please add 25p (£0.30 non-UK) per magazine and 75p (£0.90 non-UK) per book.

Payment can be made in UK cash, by IMO (an international money order), Eurocheque, or by a cheque drawn on a UK bank. Please make all cheques payable to Jonathan Downes.

Send all orders to CFZ, 15 Holne Court, Exwick, Exeter, Devon, EX4 2NA, England.

Britain is one of the few countries of the world where US dollars do **not** circulate. If making payment in US$ then please add $10 to cover the currency exchange fee.

Cartoon by Mark North

ISSN 1354-0637 Typeset by *"The Boys from the Old Brigade"*
"where are the lads who fought with me when history was made"

Animals & Men Collected Editions Volume 4 — New Horizons

Well I'm not sure how it happened, but back in 1998 when I was preparing issue 16 of *Animals & Men* I managed to cut off the end of Darren Naish's article. Here it is in its entirety..

Giant Lizards in the English Countryside

by Darren Naish

Like any good cryptozoologist, I have numerous cases on file where people have reported seeing an unusual creature crossing the road, typically at night and typically seen briefly, illuminated in the headlights. The list of such sightings, especially in a global context, is very long and I have given up trying to compile a brief one. Of local interest to me are numerous reports of Hampshire's A.35 of a black A.B.C seen in the small hours. Sightings that have not been reported to the local press include Mr. E.R.Abbott's of early 1982, and the two related to me by Carol Renouf - both made by her husband in October 1991 and on the Christmas Eve of the same year. Like about 98% of A.B.C sightings the world over, these are all spectacularly uninteresting unless you happened to be there at the time: "I saw a large black cat..." And? "Well that`s it!".

However, all of this provides me with an incentive to keep my eyes firmly glued to the road whilst driving at night. Thus far I've seen deer, owls, rabbits by the truckload, weasels, cats (not big ones ... yet) and giant lizards.

Oh really?

On Thursday 29th May 1997 I was involved in a car crash: essentially the car I was travelling in met a large wall at high speed. The wall came off OK and fortunately so did everyone else involved. Before you ask, I wasn`t driving. But it was on the way back in the R.A.C van, that my sighting occurred. Though the prospect of pushing a severely traumatised mini into a small, inner city garage at 2 a.m. now put a slight downer on an otherwise fun-filled evening, I was nonetheless playing at the `watch the road` game. Just in front, about 10m away, a great big lizard jolted out of a hedge on the right and sort of jerked across to the left. Of a uniform dark colour, it was about 1.5m long with a bulky, dragging tail and elongate, heavy neck. The sighting lasted all of three seconds - the only comment being mine: "What`s that???"

Well, as interesting as giant lizards in the English countryside are, I'm afraid that a giant lizard it was not. How often do you see foxes run backwards, dragging a dead rabbit along? I'd certainly never seen such a thing before. As you may note from the accompanying illustrations, the profile was superficially like that of some giant lizard, and did have me wondering for a few seconds at least. So, sorry, no giant lizards after all.

Interesting, though, that just a few days later, I saw another fox worthy of particular attention (I am guaranteed of a fox sighting every other night) - one that had big black patches, one on the side of the shoulder and another before the thigh. This was on the campus of Southampton University and was, again, at around 2 a.m. I chased the animal to get a better look: problem is, foxes can run faster than people..... even ones who look for big cats and see giant lizards.

Issue 17

Summer 1998

This was the first issue that had a colour cover, at least the first edition did. Like so many things within the history of the Centre for Fortean Zoology the colour cover was discontinued for reprints between 1998 and 2004 when, for the first time, we had affordable colour printing. This issue saw the beginning of a long, torturous and ultimately irritating sparring match between two contributors: Terry Hooper and Chris Moiser – neither of whom at time of printing twelve years later are associated with the CFZ. With the benefit of hindsight if I had realised at the time that both would leave the CFZ family in a relatively acrimonious manner, I don't think I would have sweated so much blood as editor in trying to be diplomatic. This is the earliest issue for which we have a surviving digital master and it is presented pretty much as it was originally sent out expect with some (but probably not all) of the errors fixed.

Re-reading this issue, I am actually mildly embarrassed at the level of studenty silliness that it contains. The jokes about H P Lovecraft, for example would never be included in the *Animals & Men* of 2010. But the CFZ have always grown up in public, and the point of these re-issues is to present them as historical documents as well as research tools, and whilst we have fixed typos and omissions where possible, to take out crass jokes and inappropriate stupidity would be re-writing history to an almost Stalinist extent, and just to save our blushes, this is something which we are not prepared to do.

Animals & Men Collected Editions Volume 4   New Horizons

Animals & Men
The Journal of the Centre for Fortean Zoology

Is THIS the face of the British "Wolverine"?
Killer Bees; A New species of Beaked Whale?
The Bodmin "Wildcat" video

Issue 17   £2.00

ANIMALS & MEN # 17

THE CURRENT CREW OF THE CFZ MOTHERSHIP ARE:
Director: Jonathan Downes
Deputy Director: Graham Inglis
Assistant Editor: Richard Freeman
Toby the CFZ dog
Magazine cartoonist and artwork: Mark North
Newsagent from nowhere: Richard Muirhead
Maxine Pearson, who does her own inimitable thing
Paranormal research: Gill Bennett
Associate founding editor: Jan Williams
Tour Manager: Nigel Wright
Hedge-Witch: Joyce Howarth
The Happy Medium: Alyson Diffey

CONSULTANTS
Consulting Editor: Dr Bernard Heuvelmans
Cryptozoology: Dr Karl Shuker
Zoology: Clinton Keeling, Chris Moiser
Cetology and Palaentology: Darren Naish

REGIONAL REPRESENTATIVES
Scotland: Tom Anderson
Surrey: Nick Smith
Somerset: Dave McNally
West Midlands: Dr Karl Shuker
Kent: Neil Arnold
Sussex: Sally Parsons
Gtr Manchester & Cheshire: A E Munro
Hampshire: Darren Naish
Leicestershire: Alistair Curzon
Cumbria: Brian Goodwin
Tyneside: Simon Elsdon
Republic of Ireland: Daev Walsh
Switzerland: Sunila Sen-Gupta
Spain: Alberto Acha, Angel Morant Fores
Germany: Hermann Reichenbach and Wolfgang Schmidt
France: Francois de Sarre
Denmark: Lars Thomas, Erik Sorensen
Mexico: Dr R A Lara Palmeros
Canada: Ben Roesch

"In her abnormalities, nature reveals her secrets"
(Goethe)

WHO'S WHO & WHAT'S WHAT

CONTENTS

3 Editorial
4 Newsfile
15 Newsfile Xtra: Killer Bees
16 Newsfile Xtra: Big Cat Video

18 Vertebrate Palaentology, by Darren Naish
27 Wolverines or Muddy Badgers? by Chris Moiser
29 Turtle Tales, by Dr Lars Thomas
30 The Ziphiidae - a possible new species, by Darren Naish

33 Clinton's Cogitations, by Clinton Keeling
35 What's Afoot, by Richard Freeman
37 A Virgin Conference-goer Breaks his Duck, by Nigel Wright

38 Letters
42 Reviews: books, websites, periodicals
46 Back issues and CFZ publications

ANIMALS & MEN

CFZ, 15 Holne Court, Exwick, Exeter, Devon, EX4 2NA, England

http://www.eclipse.co.uk/cfz

SUBSCRIPTIONS:

For a 4-issue (one year) subscription:
£8 UK   £9 EC
£14 US/Canada/Oz/NZ (airmail)
£15 Rest of World.

Please see METHODS OF PAYMENT on p47

ANIMALS & MEN # 17

The Great Days Of Zoology are Not done

Dear Friends,

With this issue it is all change at The Centre for Fortean Zoology. As many of you will, no doubt have noticed we have a new layout and we are, at last, in colour. Finally we have been able to afford the equipment necessary to make our work easier. Hopefully, now we are possessed of at least a smidgen of high tech gadgetry we will be able to resume the standards of production and delivery which we will be the first to admit have slipped somewhat in the last couple of years.

Also, with this issue we can proudly announce yet another NEW publication. Now we are linked into the global media through the wonders of The Internet our news gathering capabilities have increased a hundredfold - for example - this issue we produced seventy two pages of news which had to be whittled down into the NEWSFILE section of this magazine. Obviously we cannot do justice to all the information we have been sent, so as from September 1998 we shall be producing a monthly newsletter in addition to *"Animals & Men"*. If you wish to subscribe merely send a quid for each month that you want to receive it to us at the editorial address. There is no set length for a minimum subscription so you can subscribe for one month or one year - it is all the same to us! As long as enough people want to receive the newsletter we shall continue to publish it.

On a sadder note, one of our major influences - the legendary Fortean Tony "Doc" Shiels has parted company with us as of this issue. He was the "Surrealchemist in Residence" for the CFZ for over three years, but after a series of events over recent months he has become dissatisfied with the state of contemporary forteana and has decided to leave the field. He will be sadly missed, and we hope that at some stage he will return to the fray.

EDITORIAL

When he does there will always be a berth for him aboard the Good Ship CFZ and an open bottle of rum will be waiting for him. Until then, however, in his words *"The Wizard of the Western World has other Fish to Fry"* and in ours *"Doc Shiels has left the building"*.

Let's hope that, like Elvis, he will be back.

On a practical note it means that we will not be republishing his books and so all you guys who ordered any Shiels material can either get a refund or can transfer your credit to the new newsletter or to the 1999 Yearbook or whatever!

On more pleasant subjects, Richard Freeman has now joined the full time inhabitants of Crypto Mansions here in Exeter and has brought his own inimitable style (not to mention an unhealthy obsession with things appertaining to the works of H.P.Lovecraft) to our little hovel in Exeter. He is responsible for the libellous pic of me which is printed below and which I am reliably informed depicts your beloved Editor as Great Cthullu - the sleeper in the corpse city. The young blonde struggling in my tentacles is my own business entirely!

Until next ish, in the words of the immortal "Spinal Tap" *"err... we hope you like our new direction"*...

Jon Downes

Animals & Men Collected Editions Volume 4   New Horizons

ANIMALS & MEN # 17
NEWSFILE
COMPILED THIS ISSUE BY
JON DOWNES AND
RICHARD FREEMAN

NEWSFILE

LAKE AND SEA MONSTERS ETC

SLIME DRENCHED TENDRILS
A deep frozen giant squid, was flown from New Zealand to Kennedy International Airport and then trucked to the American Museum of Natural History on Central Park West. Museum scientists watched anxiously as the creature was slowly revealed in its glory, its tentacles and body curled up in a cramped packing case, its huge eyes hidden from sight.

"It's tremendously exciting," said Dr. Neil Landman, curator of invertebrates at the museum. *"To have a look at a actual giant squid is a dream I've always had. It's gorgeous."* The museum's squid, though a baby, is 25 feet long. Caught in December by fishermen in New Zealand, it is in an excellent state of preservation, and is possibly the best giant squid specimen in existence. Museum scientists plan to inject it with preservatives as soon as it is sufficiently thawed. The 25-foot baby joins the museum's 46-foot model of an adult giant squid, which is featured in the new biodiversity hall.

The museum plans to study the squid carefully, and perhaps eventually to put it on public display, which will depend partly on how well it survives the rigors of thawing. Though the animal is immature the scientists say they should be able to determine its sex. Dr. Landman added that the giants were so poorly understood that the age of the 25-foot specimen was a total mystery. *"Is it 2 years old? Five years old? One hundred years old? Nobody knows. And nobody knows the depth that these animals live at. I'm involved in a project trying to answer these questions"*.

The museum's beast almost got away. In Los Angeles, after the flight from New Zealand, the squid and its packing case proved too heavy for the aircraft that was scheduled to take it the rest of the way. So it had to wait. As a result, the squid landed late at Kennedy, in the afternoon rather than the morning. *"We're really pleased that it got onto the next flight,"* said Dr. Landman, the curator. *"There were a lot of pins and needles."* Among the uncertainties was what might happen if the giant squid started to thaw or emit a strong odour while passing through Customs.

As it turned out, the squid had to go through Customs twice, in both Los Angeles and New York, delaying its arrival still further.

Steve O'Shea, a marine scientist at the National Institute of Water and Atmospheric Research in Wellington, New Zealand, (See A&M16) who accompanied the squid on its flight, said the giant had been captured by commercial fishermen and frozen immediately.

The baby, he added, was one of several recent catches. Mr. O'Shea said the squid was a gift from the New Zealand agency to the museum, which paid about $10,000 for its transportation.

Modern scientists have repeatedly tried to catch the beast and observe it in its

ANIMALS & MEN # 17   NEWSFILE

deep lair, using nets on long lines, submersibles equipped with bright lights and lately, robots tied to long tethers—always to no avail. All that began to change in the last decade off New Zealand. Fishermen and scientists there worked to develop a series of deep commercial fisheries, going after exotic fish for the consumer market. As the pace picked up, the fishermen began occasionally hauling up giant squids that were apparently feeding on dense schools of fish at depths of nearly a mile. A system of reporting was initiated so that Government scientists in Wellington learned of the catches and often received body parts or whole carcasses to study. Recently, the run of landings has picked up and thrown the field into a high state of excitement.

Mr. O'Shea, who is in charge of collecting giant squid data throughout New Zealand waters, from both Government and commercial vessels, said yesterday that the new specimens were in beautiful shape, most especially the one acquired by the museum. In the past, he said, dead animals have often been a shambles, hacked into pieces by fishermen or so bruised and abraded that parts were unrecognizable. *"It's the best specimen that we've had,"* Mr. O'Shea said of the museum's acquisition. *"It's not the largest, but it's the best."* NEW YORK TIMES, June 11, 1998

RICHARD'S COMMENT: the stars are right, and the spawn of Great Cthulu are rising heralding his glorious awakening from his aeon long sleep in the drowned corpse city so he can ravish and slay amongst the world of men again.
EDITORIAL COMMENT: shut up Richard!

LAKE ILIAMNA MONSTER

From the January 1988 issue of ALASKA magazine, page 17: "The Lake Iliamna monster once again has reared its legendary head. On July 27, several, reportedly sober, eyewitnesses say they saw a 10-foot, black "fish" leaping and splashing in the lake, about five miles northwest of Pedro Bay village. Verna Kolyaha was fishing from a skiff with her mother and sister when they saw the creature. Kolyaha approached to within 100 feet of the creature, which she said was shaped like a whale, with a white strip along the fin on its back. *"It made an almost complete circle around us,"* Kolyaha told the *Bristol Bay Times.* Back at the village, Rainbow Bay resort owner Jerry Pippen and pilot Jerry Blandford were airborne within 30 minutes of the sighting, but saw nothing but a large ripple on the lake.

The next day, however, Pippen reported seeing "a really huge seal ... squirting water six to eight feet in the air." Pippen said the animal was cream coloured, with lighter markings. Sightings of a huge creature that lives in the depths of Alaska's largest lake are so persistent that the Alaska Department of Fish and Game keeps an open file labelled, "Lake Iliamna Monster." In 1963, a department biologist was flying his small plane over the lake and for 10 minutes watched a creature that appeared to be about 25 to 30 feet long swimming below the surface. It never came up for air.

The biologist estimated the beast's length by comparing it to the aeroplane's shadow on the water. A number of times in recent years, sport fishermen near the villages of Iliamna and Pedro Bay have reported a big, peculiar, snake-like form moving along at the water's surface. Explanations for the creatures that have been observed range from a lost whale that strayed in from the ocean to a huge sturgeon to a species of freshwater seal. The Native people say the creature is a monster that doesn't like people and upsets boats that stray too far from shore, but there's no scientific evidence to prove any theory."

Wednesday 8th June, 1998, marked one year since the sea monster known as Cadborosaurus was last seen in British Columbian coastal waters, but this could just be a cycle when the numbers of the monster are on the decline, said Ed Bousfield. Bousfield is a research associate with the Royal Ontario Museum, and co-author of the controversial paper which first gave a scientific description to the creature. "El Nino affects the food," he said, "but I think the bigger factor is the noise pollution in the straits. There is so much marine traffic there now, it is driving it away." Bousfield

ANIMALS & MEN # 17 NEWSFILE

caused more controversy, when he presented a scientific paper on his link between Caddy and the mysterious monster of the Okanagan to a recent symposium of cryptozoologists in Kelowna. Bousfield has submitted his paper to two scientific journals for peer review and possible publication. Caddy was a regular visitor around Vancouver Island in the past four years, with more than 20 documented sightings but no photographs. *"There have been 300 sightings in the last century alone,"* he said. *"It has also been seen in nine different lakes in B.C. The connection with Ogopogo is that where you find these sightings, you find sea-run salmon. If there are not as many sightings now it could be that it is going into a low-ebb cycle the same as the salmon are."*

In his paper, Bousfield said the areas where Ogopogo has been seen were all linked to the Pacific, but are now cut off by dams. He said 10,000 years ago Caddy probably followed salmon up streams into lakes in the Columbia and Fraser drainage basins and became landlocked. The similarity of the two creatures with a snakelike body, humps or coils, horselike head, flippers and split tail indicates they are related, he said. *"Glacial and post-glacial evidence suggests that Okanagan's Ogopogo is probably a freshwater form or variant of the reptilian species Cadborosaurus willsi."* Victoria (British Columbia) Times-Colonist Tuesday, 7 July 1998.

THE BEASTS OF THE OLD BRIGADE

Monster-spotters are flocking to Lough Eske, three miles from Donegal Town, for a glimpse of a monster nicknamed `Eskie`. Seamus Caldwell of Harvey's Point Hotel is one of those who believes he *"saw something"* in the icy waters. *"It was 2:30pm on Sunday when a load of the guests starting moving down to the pier to the lake,"* he said. *"They said they had seen something and when I looked out, I saw something moving up and down at about 300m out.* The banqueting manager played down suggestions that his eyes might have been affected by a slack holiday season. *"We're in the business of selling food, not monsters,"* he told The Star. Local Ard na Mana B&B boss Annabel Clarke also believes in the monster, despite seeing nothing herself so far. *"The monster was probably up around Harvey's looking for scraps - he's probably quite hungry and lonely."* But her husband Kieran thinks there maybe a real link between the region and Lough Ness. *"Some lakes in Donegal are said to be connected by current to Scotland,"* he said. *"These creatures can't live forever, they have to find ways to perpetuate themselves so there must be more than one - ours could be a cousin of Nessie. "* (*The Star*, Friday July 3rd 1998)

A FISHY FATWA?

TEHRAN (Reuters) - A game fish from distant California, a marlin, has been caught by an Iranian fisherman in the Gulf, Iran's Fisheries Research Centre said. A tag on its fin indicated the 178 cm (70 inches) long, 35 kg (77 pound) big game fish, caught off the Gulf coast port of Bushehr, had swum thousands of miles from California Perhaps this is some bizarre piscine attempt at revenge for the Iranian victory over the US in the world cup?

SWAMP THING

The Asian swamp eel has been found in canals, ditches, streams and ponds near Tampa and Miami, Fla. The species is spreading and has the capability of invading and harming freshwater ecosystems throughout he Southeast, including the already-besieged Everglades system, according o the U.S. Geological Survey scientists who found the species in Florida.

The exotic creature is a highly adaptable predator, able to breathe air and to live easily in even a few inches of water, especially in warm climates. *"This species exhibits unusual behaviour, appearance and adaptations,"* said Dr. Leo Nico, a biologist with the USGS Florida Caribbean Science Center in Gainesville, Fla.

"It has the potential to spread into freshwater ecosystems throughout the Southeast where it could compete with or prey upon native fishes. Imagine a creature with all the attributes necessary to successfully invade and colonise the Everglades and other southeastern wetlands. Well, the swamp eel may be that creature."

Scientists say they suspect the swamp eel may have escaped from a tropical fish farm or have been a pet released from an aquarium. The species, they believe, is already firmly established in Florida. *CZOneList*

ANIMALS & MEN # 17

OH THE SHARK DEAR.........

On the night of February 20, 1998, three fishermen in Macajalar Bay, Cagayan de Oro, caught a fish they couldn't identify. A local radio station reported the find the following morning. The fish was later hacked into pieces and consumed that day. Subsequent reports, quoting government sources, said the strange fish was a whale shark. But research conducted by this writer using the Internet revealed that it was a megamouth, an extremely rare species with previously only 10 sightings worldwide. *(CZ OneList)*

OUT OF PLACE

SNAIL TALE

PHILADELPHIA (AP) — A species of snail that is considered one of the worst agricultural pests in California has been discovered in Pennsylvania, posing a potentially expensive threat to the state's farms and nurseries. *"The last thing Pennsylvania wants is this snail rampaging across the countryside,"* said David Robinson, a snail specialist for the U. S. Department of Agriculture. *"It's a major pest. It's one of the worst snail problems there is. It feeds on practically anything green and growing."* The brown garden snails were discovered last month in the garden of a Philadelphia schoolteacher, who told officials that they had been in her garden for 10 years. Before that, the snail has not been known to survive the winter in Pennsylvania, though state officials fear it may be adapting. California spends about $7 million a year to battle the snail, which was brought to that state in the 1850s from the Mediterranean, as a delicacy for restaurants. One threat to Pennsylvania agriculture is the direct damage to plants, but other states also might refuse to import Pennsylvania products because of a snail infestation in the state. State officials plan a survey of state parks and commercial greenhouse operations to determine whether the snails have spread beyond the Philadelphia neighborhood where they were discovered. State Department of Agriculture scientists said the snails probably arrived in Philadelphia on garden plants imported from California.

NEWSFILE

CHUPA CADAVER?

The following story was posted on the Internet by (I think) Loren Coleman who lifted it from an Arkansas Newspaper report: *"Treasure hunter Dane Chastain just might have located the biggest treasure of his life. The Oklahoma native says he has discovered and retrieved the decomposed body of an alien being in the woods around Fort Chaffee, Arkansas. In a story broken on Little Rock radio station, KARN News Radio, the body is said to be small in stature, mostly bones at this point but still having skin "like a fish" covering it. The remains also have silver hair and a strange fin protruding from its back. Ft. Chaffee has been held under considerable suspicion by a number of UFO researchers for years andwas most recently in the news in the 80's when hundreds of Cuban refugees were sent there for detention and processing. Chastain is said to be* en route *to the International UFO Museum In Roswell with the remains"*

Full story and photograph in next issue.

YIP YIP BABOON

BOSTON (AP) - Boston Garden lore took on another odd chapter - even after the venerable arena's demolition - with the discovery of monkey bones amid the rubble. Said to house gremlins who plagued visiting basketball teams, the former home of the

ANIMALS & MEN # 17 — NEWSFILE

Boston Celtics built in 1928 was dreaded for problems real and imaginary, but there were never reports of a resident monkey. The mysterious remains found in the wreckage last week prompted demolition workers to pause for a moment of silence. *"The Celtics might have to change their mascot,"* former Garden director Larry Moulter said. *"This obviously was a true fan."* Visiting teams over the years complained about dead spots in the Garden's famed parquet floor and perceived slights like the occasional lack of hot water in the showers, but none ever mentioned a rogue monkey swinging off the backboard to swat away jumpshots. Officials have no idea where the monkey might have come from. The remains didn't look old enough to be from the great monkey escape of 1936, when Frank Buck's "Bring 'Em Back Alive" animal show nearly lost a passel of monkeys during the show. And besides, all those feisty critters were supposedly rounded up. A check with Ringling Bros. and Barnum & Bailey didn't turn up any leads either, despite the fact the circus performed at Boston Garden in 1994. And although monkeys were part of an old "Wizard of Oz" show at the Garden, none of the ones dressed up in wings were reported to have flown the coop. *Boston Globe, Boston, Massachusetts Associated Press, 23 May 1998 Saturday*

GOING TO THE DOGS

25 May 1998 SPOKANE, Wash. (AP) _ There may be only about 500 New Guinea singing dogs in the world and one has spent the past month in the Spokane County Animal Shelter. The dog left the pound on Friday for Cat Tales, an exotic animal park north of Spokane. Scirocco had been languishing on death row while shelter workers tried to find him a home, said Nancy Sattin, the county's animal control director. *"It would have been a shame to have to put him down,'"* Sattin said. The 2 1/2-year-old dog might become a daddy, if a suitable female can be found, said Janice Koler-Matznick, a singing dog expert in Central Point, Oregon. *"It's a big deal,"* she said. *"They're definitely going extinct if we don't do something soon."* The breed was discovered in the early 1900s in the remote highlands of New Guinea, isolated from the rest of the world by the rugged terrain and fierce tribes of the area. The dogs, which can weigh about 25 pounds, got their name from their high-pitched, sing-song howl. Sattin believes Scirocco may have been born at an exotic animal farm in Western Washington and lived in Stevens County for a time. She would not identify the woman who gave the dog to the shelter. *"The woman who owned him just couldn't handle him,"* Sattin said. *"She had trouble keeping him home."* While singing dogs like people and are small animals, they generally don't make good pets. Their instinct to run and hunt small mammals and birds is overpowering. *(Fortean List)*

P-P-P-PICK UP A PENGUIN

RIO DE JANEIRO (Reuters) - Penta the penguin came in from the cold to warm the hearts of Brazilian soccer fans. When the stray penguin turned up in the sea off Rio de Janeiro, surprised beachgoers took it as a sign of luck for the national team in the soccer World Cup and adopted it as a mascot for the team. They draped the bird in a green and yellow national flag after rescuing it and nicknamed it Penta, or Fifth, for the fifth World Cup soccer title the reigning champions were hoping to win in France. They had it pose for TV cameras during public parties after Brazil's 3-0 victory over Morocco before stowing the penguin in a beer cooler to await zoo officials.

SHE'LL BE CAIMAN ROUND THE MOUNTAIN

HAMILTON, Ohio (AP) - What he wanted was a catfish. So Matthew Viars, 17, put his line into the Great Miami River on Tuesday evening with some friends and relaxed under a canopy of stars. He didn't get catfish. What he got was a 6-foot-long alligator. *"We saw a big splash,"* Viars said. *"Its head was up and its tail was moving back and forth in the water."* The mysterious gator hasn't been seen since. It's the second time an unexpected reptile has popped up in the strong-moving river. In December, a 4-foot alligator was pulled from the Great Miami just north of the latest reported sighting. The Butler County sheriff has declared an alligator alert. *"Don't make the gator a bad guy. He's an innocent victim here,"* said Johnny Arnett, a Cincinnati Zoo official advising police. *"People are buying a lot of these animals and finding out that there's too much to handle and just turning them loose."* The zoo doesn't have enough employees to spend days searching for the gator but would be willing - possibly along with a club of reptile enthusiasts - to help catch it.

Boston Globe/Associated Press, 5 June 1998

Animals & Men Collected Editions Volume 4 **New Horizons**

ANIMALS & MEN # 17
A BIT CLOSE TO HOME FOR COMFORT
(WHEN YOU OWN A HOUSE ONLY FORTY MILES SOUTH!)

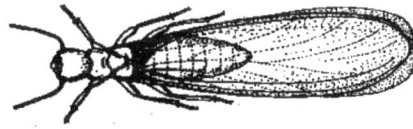

PEST control experts will begin attempts next week to eradicate a colony of more than a million house-eating termites on the north Devon coast (James Landale writes). The voracious bugs from southern Europe, believed to be the most destructive in the world, have eaten their way into two holiday homes. Nick Raynsford, the Construction Minister, said the Environment Department would spend £129,000 on a 12-year programme to wipe out the colony, using a toxin called hexaflumuron.

Termites were first discovered at the two properties overlooking Barnstaple Bay at Saunton four years ago and were thought to have been destroyed by chemical pesticides. But an even greater infestation was discovered two months ago. The 4mm-long termites, Reticulitermesluci fungus, live up to seven metres underground. *The Times June 3 1998*

WHERE'S ROD HULL WHEN YOU NEED HIM?

BURLINGTON, N.C. (AP) - Authorities have been on the trail of a big bird that's been seen wandering around town during the past two weeks. Three emu sightings have been reported to the Alamance County Sheriff's Department in the past two weeks, but deputies haven't found any loose birds, said Sgt. Ann Park of the department's animal control unit. The large, flightless birds have razor-sharp claws and are very dangerous, she said. *"It's still on the loose,"* said Burlington Police Capt. Steve Lynch, who saw the bird Saturday near a service station. Lynch said he thought the long-necked, long-legged, 4-foot tall bird was an ostrich, but a fellow officer told him it fit the description of an emu. The bird disappeared in a nearby field, he said. Later that day, a passerby tried to lasso a big bird seen near the former Shea's Restaurant building, Lynch said. The department received three calls about the creature Saturday, he said. Police haven't been able to determine who owns the bird or where it came from. No one has reported a missing emu, Lynch said.

NEWSFILE

ODDS AND SODS

WOLFTRAP, BEULAH AND OLD COURTHOUSE ROADS. About May 1, several sightings of an animal, described as a coyote or a cougar, were reported. Animal Control's wildlife biologist interviewed witnesses and examined the area of the sightings and found a footprint resembling a cougar's. The biologist and a representative of the Virginia Department of Game and Inland fisheries unsuccessfully attempted to photograph the animal with a motion-activated camera installed in nearby woods. There were no reports of threatening behavior by the animal.

NEW AND REDISCOVERED

NEW SPECIES?

HANOI, Vietnam (AP) -- The Vietnamese capital of Hanoi is buzzing with excitement following reported sightings of rare giant turtles in a downtown lake here thousands of pedestrians pass daily. And amateur video

ANIMALS & MEN # 17

footage purportedly of the turtles, long believed to be nothing more than myth and legend, now has skeptics wondering whether the giant beasts really do exist. For years, people have reported sighting three giant turtles in Hanoi's Hoan Kiem Lake. The latest sighting, and perhaps one of the most credible, came on March 24, when passers-by caught a glimpse of the turtles as they surfaced to take in the spring air. An amateur cameraman caught the creatures' appearance on video, which subsequently aired on Vietnamese television.

The station also claimed the turtles made a second appearance on April 5. Researchers who have been trying to get a glimpse of the turtles believe they could be the only ones of their kind in the world.

Stories about the mysterious creatures have been circulating for about 500 years, starting with the legend of King Le Loi and the giant turtle of Hoan Kiem Lake. According to legend, the gods gave Le Loi a magic sword, which helped him battle the Chinese invaders. Having freed Vietnam, the king and his courtiers were boating on the lake when a giant turtle arose, took the magic sword, then plunged to the depths and returned the blade to its divine owners. Since that time the lake's name has been "Ho Hoan Kiem, " which means "Lake of the Returned Sword. " The story is retold in thousands of schoolbooks, and in popular performances at Hanoi's water-puppet theatres.

Mythology and science mix in the work of Hanoi National University's Professor Ha Dinh Duc, the world's foremost expert on the turtles of the Returned Sword Lake. "The Hoan Kiem turtle is the world's biggest fresh water turtle. It can measure 2 meters (6 1/2 feet) long and can weigh as much as 200 kilograms," said Professor Ha Dinh Duc of Hanoi National University.

Professor Duc has been studying the turtles for the past decade, sometimes in conjunction with international reptile specialists. Some biologists feel these turtles could be the same as a rare species found near Shanghai, China, but Professor Duc disagrees. "I've compared these with other freshwater turtles elsewhere in the world and I see real differences. I hope further studies will show this is a new species, " he said.

NEWSFILE

A Hoan Kiem turtle, found and preserved 30 years ago, is now displayed at a small temple on an island in the lake. The plaque tells visitors it is thought to be more than 500 years old -- old enough, in fact, to be the turtle of the legend. A comparison of the preserved turtle with images of the Shanghai species shows clear differences in coloration and head shape, supporting Dr. Duc's thesis that this could be a new species. Much remains unknown about these ancient monsters living in the center of downtown Hanoi -- their number, reproductive ability, origins, and especially, whether or not they're unique to the Lake of the Returned Sword.

"If we have co-operation from international experts and they determine this is a new species, it will be a significant contribution to world biological diversity. And since the turtles are right here in the middle of urban Hanoi, many people can easily come to see them, " Professor Duc said.

Meanwhile, plans are afoot to clear the lake of pollution that could potentially harm the creatures, and the construction of an artificial beach has been proposed to facilitate breeding.

NEW BIRD FROM COLUMBIA
(OK **YOU** THINK OF A JOKE ABOUT AN ANTPITTA)

June 11, 1998 PHILADELPHIA (AP) -- Robert S. Ridgely was hiking down an Ecuadorean mountain path on atrip to record bird songs last November when he and a fellow ornithologist heard a strange sound --a call akin to an owl's hoot and a dog's bark. *"He and I recognized right off the bat that this was something very peculiar that we heard in the distance,"* recalled Ridgely, director of the Centerfor Neotropical Ornithology at the Academy of Natural Sciences.

What Ridgely, 52, and the young Ecuadorean Lelis Navarrete, heard and eventually saw high in the AndesMountains was the discovery of a lifetime - a new bird species. *"It didn't occur to me that something completely unknown was going toappear but in fact that's exactly what happened,"* Ridgely said. Once he saw the large bird with the unusual white facial markings, he knewright away that it was *"one of the most distinctive new birds to be found in a while."*

- 10 -

ANIMALS & MEN # 17 — NEWSFILE

It appears that this new species is the second largest known Antpitta, Ridgely said. Its most striking feature is a broad white facial stripe that arches below the eye, contrasting with a black crown. About one new bird a year is discovered. The find was unusual in that it occurred in a well-explored area near the Podocarpus National Park. "It's a remarkable bird and any discovery of a new species is truly remarkable these days. There just aren't many left to find," said John W. Fitzpatrick, director of the Cornell Laboratory of Ornithology in Ithaca, New York.

With some 9,000 species in the world, Fitzpatrick said, only about one new bird a year is discovered. About 40 minutes after Ridgely and Navarrete heard the call from about a half-mile away, the bird suddenly started to sing within 50 feet of them. Ridgely, who did not have a camera with him, made a quick tape-recording of the bird and played it back in hopes of eliciting a response. It worked. "The bird came crashing right back in front of me, right in the undergrowth."

In January, a team set up nets to photograph and capture birds. Four specimens were sacrificed for scientific study. New species usually are very similar to previously known birds, Ridgely said. "That's where this new Antpitta jumps out as being really stunning. Not only was it found in an area that is relatively well known, but it is so different," he said. Ridgely and other ornithologists have set up a foundation to raise money to buy land to protect the bird's habitat, much of which has been cleared for cattle grazing.

ANOTHER NEW SOUTH AMERICAN BIRD

RIO DE JANEIRO, Brazil (AP) -- The scientists said its song was unlike any they had heard before. And when they hung nets to capture the bird, they found out why - it was a species unknown to science.

Researchers at the Federal University of Parana said the tiny, gray-black bird that they captured in 1997 also had a unique habitat: a marshy area inside the city of Curitiba, 420 miles southwest of Rio de Janeiro. Marcos Bornschein, Bianca Reinhert and Mauro Pichorim named their new bird, a member of the Scytalopus genus, the lowland tapaculo. They said its scientific description and name will be published later this year. A similar bird lives in the forest only a few miles away from where the newly discovered bird makes its home, but that bird has a different song and never wanders to the marshes. Similar birds also live in the Andes Mountains, more than 2,000 miles westward. But closer study of the lowland tapaculo determined that 11 factors, from the shape of its feathers to its bone structure, were unique, Bornschein said. It measure about 4 inches long and weighs half an ounce. Jose Fernando Pacheco, an ornithologist with the Federal University of Rio de Janeiro, confirmed the finding. "The song is different and the type of terrain it inhabits is different," he said. The lowland tapaculo is the second new bird species that Bornschein and Reinhert have discovered.

TIE MY KANGAROO DOWN...

KAWAU ISLAND, New Zealand (CNN). A breed of Australian wallaby thought to be extinct for a century has turned up alive and well - in New Zealand. DNA testing by Australian researchers shows that a group of Tamar wallabies on Kawau Island, north of Auckland, are descendants of a wallaby population that vanished from mainland South Australia early this century. It turns out that the wallabies - which are similar to kangaroos - were shipped from South Australia to New Zealand in the late 1880s by New Zealand's governor, Sir George Gray. The discovery presents an opportunity to re-establish the breed in Australia. And some New Zealanders won't be sorry to see them go. "They look cute - they may be cuddly - (but) they've got a big strong kick, and they eat everything that grows," said Dick Vritch of the New Zealand Department of Conservation. Indeed, the more than 2,000 Tamar wallabies on Kawau Island are endangering several native species of birds.

(Internet: CZ OneList)

THE ONZA WHICH AIN'T

Finally the news that everyone has been suspecting for many years has been released. As predicted by Clinton Keeling (amongst others) in these very pages, the female onza shot in 1986 and examined by the ISC is no such thing - merely a malnourished female puma. Our standards of gentlemanly behaviour preclude us from saying that we told you so!

ANIMALS & MEN # 17
TERATOLOGY

ABNORMAL AMPHIBIANS (AREN`T THEY ALL)

The recent finding of abnormal frogs in many different parts of the USA and Canada spanned a wide range of amphibians and was not limited to species, geography or climate, according to James J. La Clair of The Scripps Research Institute in La Jolla, Calif. In a new report in the April 14 Web edition of Environmental Science & Technology, La Clair and colleague John Bantle offer an explanation for these findings by examining the effects of pesticide degradation in the early amphibian development. La Clair's group found that S-methoprene, an insect growth regulator that was introduced in the late 1970s to control fleas and mosquitoes, posed little risk to the development of amphibians. However, when exposed to sunlight, water and micro-organisms, La Clair found that S-methoprene breaks up into other products that dramatically alter embryo development. By adding minute amounts of these degradation products to developing embryos of the African clawed frog, *Xenopus laevis*, the Scripps group found that the embryo developed into a juvenile with deformations similar to those found in nature.

POLAR BEARS IN MIDDLESEX SHOCK!!!!

TROMSO. SCIENTISTS have discovered polar bear cubs with both male and female sex organs. The deformities are thought to be linked to the increasing pollution in Polar Regions. The four hermaphroditic bears were found in the Norwegian Arctic territory of Svalbard, where pollution levels are known to be high. Government officials and the researchers who found the newborn cubs on the islands of Edgeoya and Hopen suspect that the deformities are caused by polychlorinated biphenol chemicals (PCBs). The chemicals, which accumulate in fat reserves, are used in everything from electrical transformer fluids to degreasing agents in nuclear submarines, and are building up in the seals on which the polar bears feed. PCBs are among the thousands of man-made substances that scientists believe mimic animal and human sex hormones. Sex changes in fish have been monitored in Britain and in alligators in America,

NEWSFILE

but the polar bears are believed to be the first mammal to show such acute damage. Dagfinn Stenseth, the Norwegian Government's special adviser on polar affairs, said yesterday that the findings had implications for wildlife and human beings. *"The polar bear, like us, is at the top of the food chain. We are very concerned,"* he said. PCBs are banned in many countries, although Russia is believed still to use them. They are persistent pollutants that remain in the environment for many years.

The polar bear research adds to worldwide attempts to identify possible links between man-made chemicals and sexual deformities and diseases in human beings, as well as animals. Over the past 50 years, sperm counts have fallen in men living in industrialised countries. Some of the chemicals appear to mimic the female hormone oestrogen, while others appear to block or copy the male androgen hormones. A spokeswoman for the Norwegian Polar Institute, said researchers had studied 90 polar bears this season out of the territory's population of some 2,000. Andrew Derocher, the research scientist who made the findings, said yesterday that the bears were seen in April and May. The researchers had been discovering polar bears with both female and male characteristics for three years, he said, but this year's tally was the highest so far. It means that bears with both sex organs may make up nearly 4 per cent of the population, which is far higher than chance, and indicates that up to 80 polar bears in Svalbard may now be affected. *"What we don't know is if this phenomenon is circum-polar or just confined to polar bears in the Barents, which is more polluted,"* he said. Details of the findings have been published during the 22nd Antarctic Treaty Consultative Meeting, taking place in Tromso, Norway. Delegates from 43 nations that have signed the treaty, including Britain, are discussing how best to deal with a string of threats to the continent in the wake of the ratification of the Protocol on Environmental Protection earlier this year. The Norwegian findings relating to the Arctic, which is better studied, have strengthened moves to increase monitoring of wildlife and the environment in the Antarctic. Over the weekend, delegates agreed that a comprehensive report on the Antarctic environment, drawing on studies from countries such as Britain, was a priority. *The Times* 2.6.98

ANIMALS & MEN # 17

PULL THE UDDER ONE

WINTHROP, Iowa - A two-headed, four-eyed, three-eared calf born earlier this week turned an eastern Iowa farm into a magnet for the curious. News reporters, neighbors and visitors were trekking to the farm operated by Brian Slife and his father Gary for a peek at the animal, a Holstein named "Reflections" because of the matching white patches on its two heads. The calf probably has less than a 50-50 chance of surviving,"*but every day it lives those odds improve*," said Jim McMillan, a veterinarian who delivered the calf.

The calf appears to have one brain - both tongues move when it tries to lick - which could make walking difficult given the four eyes. It also has cleft palates in both mouths, a condition that canlead to pneumonia and other health problems in animals. McMillan said the family bought at an auction last week the heifer to which the calf was born. He said he was called out to help when the animal was having trouble with the birth. *"I examined the heifer and the feet were in a normal position. I went to find the head and it would not come up in a normal position for delivery,"* said McMillan. *"You have your arm inside the cow. I got to feeling around and there were two distinct noses. I knew then it could not be born in the normal way and performed a Caesarean section"*, he told Reuters. The family had no information on the parentage of the animal or what led to the malformations, McMillan said.

PIGS (TWO DIFFERENT ONES) - WELL SORT OF

May 3, 1998. LOS ANGELES (AP) - Even pigs with two snouts and three eyes have people who love them. Ditto the pig was born with those deformities at an Iowa farm and was to be sold to a circus freak show. But a group called Pigs Without Partners bought the animal for $5,000 and spent another $1,000 to ship Ditto to Los Angeles. Ditto currently has to eat from a tube because of his extra snout but planned surgery should allow him to feed like any other pig --except that Ditto will still have his unique features. Pigs Without Partners is now trying to find a surgeon close to Southern California since the group says it would be dangerous to ship the animal long distance after the operation.

NEWSFILE

RICHARD`S COMMENT: The birth of such disgusting malformed freaks is an obvious portent for the rising of Great Cthulu from his cyclopean tomb in slime drowned city of R'lyeh...

EDITORIAL COMMENT: I said SHUT UP Richard!!!

OTHER STORIES

GOODBYE ENGLISH DOG-ROSE (SNIGGER)

LONDON (Reuters) - Princess Diana is buried on land used for years as a pet cemetery and known to the staff at her childhood home as "Dog Island," a former housekeeper for her family said. The leafy Oval Island at Althorp, the Spencer family's rural estate, was used as a place to bury hunting dogs that belonged to Diana's grandfather Jack, Maudie Pendrey told The Daily Mirror.

"I cannot believe Earl Spencer could be so heartless as to bury his sister in a dog burial ground," she told The Mirror. *"It is a desecration."* Pendrey worked for the Spencer family into which Diana was born for more than 22 years, the newspaper said. She told the paper she had seen some of the dogs' gravestones on the island, but that the stones were removed to make room for Diana's memorial. *"I saw them. There were five dogs' gravestones with their names on them. They were about $2^{1}/_{2}$ feet high ... I understood there were other dogs buried there as well but without headstones."*

ANIMALS & MEN # 17

GOT MY MOTOR RUNNING GET OUT ON THE HIGHWAY.......

WASHINGTON (AP) — Climbing off his Harley Davidson Road King Classic, Wisconsin Gov. Tommy Thompson grabbed a toothbrush and some paper towels and prepared to wage war on the feathered foes of the Vietnam Veterans Memorial: pigeons. Joined by about 250 fellow hog riders, Thompson rode from Madison, Wis. , to Washington to celebrate his state's 150 anniversary. They came armed with supplies to clean pigeon droppings off the austere black walls and four granite stones to lay at the base of the monument. *"This is a very moving experience because so many of the riders are Vietnam vets and for some of them this is the first time back at the wall, "* said Thompson, a four-year Harley rider. Many of the delegates broke into tears as they sang "The Star-Spangled Banner" and read the inscriptions on the stones. *"Great many of us quit partying, don't drink or smoke. Haunting memories of the sights, sounds, stench of war tears at our frail spirit plus ravages our soul, "* Minneapolis resident Gerald "Mack" McDonel read from a plaque that he brought to Washington on the back of his motorcycle. Not everyone was pleased with the ceremony, however. Gentry Davis, deputy regional director of the National Park Service, said he was concerned about how the group was cleaning the wall. *"If we allow people to just come in and just clean the wall it could damage the names, "* Davis said. He said he wasn't offended at the implication that the park service doesn't keep the memorial clean, but did add that "if we see any major pigeon drops or bird drops, we try to clean it up. "

HOWL

A shop worker who is convinced he is a werewolf is suing his bosses in Romania because they will not give him time off when there is a full moon. The man says he feels restless and irritable even during daylight hours when the moon is at its peak. *Source unknown; June 1, 1998*

SPANK YER SKUNK

The following note was posted on an Interet Exotic Pets forum and I couldn`t resist including it! *"Have he ever hit or spanked the skunk for discipline? The skunk will remember that and always treat him like that. My friend spanked his wife's skunk and from* then on, the skunk would pee on his side of the bed whenever she got a chance.

NEWSFILE

HEART'S FILTHY LESSONS

SAN DIEGO (AP) — Ghost Boy, a rare albino koala, made his debut at the San Diego Zoo to oohs and aahs from adoring animal lovers. The only known albino koala in captivity, the tiny marsupial clung to its mother's back in its first public display Friday, showing off snow-white fur, a cute pink nose and matching eyes as it munched eucalyptus leaves. The koala — named Onya-Birri in Aborigine because of its unusual lack of pigment — was born in September, roughly the size of a jelly bean. Now about 2 pounds, it will reach 18 pounds when full-grown. Ghost Boy spent its first six months of life tucked safely inside his mother's pouch. When he first poked his nose out in March, zookeepers couldn't believe their eyes. *"There were three of us, and no one would believe it on their own, so we'd go and get the other one just to make sure,"* said keeper Chris Hamlin. Visitors to the zoo - young and old - gushed as Ghost Boy crawled atop his mother's head, using her ears as steps. As the mother, named Banjeeri, navigated a branch, the crowd gasped as one when Ghost Boy slipped briefly from her neck before latching onto her stomach. Albinism, or a lack of pigmentation, can be present in genes but not show up for generations, Hamlin said. Ghost Boy's mother has had other offspring - a koala baby is called a joey - but all had normal light gray fur. The animals native to Australia are known worldwide as the cute, fuzzy symbol of the country. Ghost Boy will spend his life at the zoo. Koalas usually stay with their mothers until they are about a year old, becoming solitary animals when full-grown. He will eventually be allowed in some of the outdoor enclosures, but only on overcast days. He's perfectly healthy, keepers said, but because he has no pigment his eyes are extremely sensitive to light and his skin could burn easily. *"We'll just have to keep him inside on sunny days,"* Hamlin said.

FOOTBALL CRAZY

The summer of 1998 has been centred, for many (including Graham, but not me and Rich), about football so it seems appropriate that A&M include a soccer story. It appears that Marc-Vivien Foe, a star player from The Cameroon was being courted by Manchester United....

Animals & Men Collected Editions Volume 4 **New Horizons**

ANIMALS & MEN # 17   NEWSFILE

"the deal, which will cost united upwards of £3 millionrn depends on the healing power of gorilla bones and hedgehog-hunting. Foe said: 'they are taking off the plaster on June 23, but in Cameroon, healers have said they will be able to cure me in three days by burying my leg in the ground and putting fire around it. They have also recommended massage with gorilla bones while invoking the spirits of my ancestors. physiotherapy would include going on a hedgehog hunt'." The Guardian 11.6.98

are "wrong" to gorge himself on human souls as the faithful sing hosannas of despair.

EDITOR`S NOTE: Any more of this crap, Richard, and not only are you sacked as Associate Editor but I`ll start charging you rent!

BIGGLES BREAKS HIS DUCK
LONDON - A duck that cannot swim has become an honorary flight lieutenant at a British air force station and, been outfitted with a life jacket.

The June edition of the Ministry of Defense's house journal reports that Jemima was found by airmen in the emergency water supply lagoon at the Royal Air Force's Marham base in eastern England. Suffering from a shortage of oil in her feathers, she was paddling furiously to try to keep afloat. The Aylesbury duck, which has now become a station mascot, is pictured wearing a bright red inflatable life jacket, designed to keep her head above water.

OLD WHALE TALE
ANCHORAGE - Scientists believe they may have found a way to determine the life span of the Arctic's largest inhabitant, the bowhead whale.

Biologists are putting the final touches on a study that shows bowheads may live more than 150 years. That could make them the world's longest-living mammal - longer even than elephants, which live to be 60 years old. Until early this decade, data suggested the 75-ton whales lived well into their 60s. But Native hunters began finding stone harpoon tips - a kind last used in the 1880s - embedded in the blubber of the bowheads they landed. After a half-dozen were found, scientists realized they had to do further research.

RICHARD`S COMMENT: Such a stomach-churning cavalcade of perversion and horror must surely mean that Great Cthullu has left the place where the angles

NEWSFILE
XTRA

KILLER BEES

STING SOMETHING SIMPLE
MEXICO CITY (AP) — A 39-year-old man was killed by a swarm of bees in northern Mexico after authorities failed to respond to emergency calls, the government news agency Notimex reported. Juan Manuel Alaniz Gomez died of a heart attack on his way to a hospital Tuesday in Cuidad Obregon, 420 miles south of Phoenix, Notimex quoted local police official Edgar Jacobi Noris as saying.

Jacobi Noris said the heart attack was caused by the bee stings, and that the swarm may have been Africanized killer bees, descendants of aggressive bees from Africa that escaped from breeding experiments in Brazil in 1956. Notimex quoted fire-fighter Sergio Martinez Silva as saying fire-fighters received an emergency call about an aggressive swarm of bees, and passed the alert onto the Secretariat of Agriculture, Ranching and Rural Development because fire-fighters didn't have the necessary equipment.

ANIMALS & MEN # 17

People at the secretariat never responded because it was nearing the end of their work day, Martinez Silva said. When fire-fighters responded to another call — this time about Alaniz Gomez — the man was covered in bees, and fire-fighters needed to turn their hoses on him to get the bees off. Africanized bees, which tend to attack in swarms, have been blamed for the deaths of more than 1, 000 people since 1956, including six from Arizona and Texas.

I GOT A BUZZ OUT OF THAT

California El Centro - Africanized "killer bees" may have claimed their first fatality in the state. A DNA analysis by the state confirmed that a pitbull chained in a back yard died last week when he was stung by a swarm of the honey bees. *USA TODAY - WEDNESDAY, MAY 20, 1998*

VIVA LAS VEGAS

Nevada Las Vegas - Two more swarms of Africanized "killer bees" have been found in southern Clark County, officials said. The bees were collected from trap sites near Davis Dam and Searchlight. Two swarms were discovered in May in the Laughlin area. Agriculture officials are setting more traps. THURSDAY, JUNE 11, I 998 - USA TODAY

NEWSFILE XTRA

REPORT ON THE PRESS LAUNCH (MIKE THOMAS OF NEWQUAY ZOO) OF BIG CAT V1DEO FOOTAGE
21.7.98

by PAUL CROWTHER,
Plymouth CFE Photographic lecturer.
(to be read in an American accent)

They say that the sun shines on the righteous. The problem: was the sun shining on me, or Mr Thomas? Mr Thomas is the curator of Newquay Zoo, and the man whose video footage of, quote, A Large Cat, I was driving to Newquay to see. As I drove I had a smirk on my face, a smirk bigger than the one Sean

NEWSFILE XTRA

Connery had as he watched Ursula Andress come out of the sea in Dr No. I was on a mission - I was a man with a question for Mr Thomas, and I knew the answer - because unbeknown to him, I had seen his video.

Two months earlier as part of a team of Beast Busters dubbed Mr Pompous and Mr Arrogant by the local press, I had seen his footage - footage which some how had got in the hands of a national newspaper. These press boys were no mugs; they had seen other newspapers make fools of themselves and these boys weren't about to do the same, so they called in the Beast Busters. I am the photographic expert and my partners the Biologist / Zoologist, but even I knew that Clive Lloyd did a better impression of an exotic cat as he walked to the crease for my beloved Lancashire, than the moggy we had watched (albeit possibly a big moggy). The clincher was when the moggy walked past a forestry-style bench: it didn't even make the height of the horizontal beam. At least my partner had had the decency to kept a straight face, even if I could not.

As I drove on, one thought crossed my mind over and over again. - Would he show the clip of the moggy with the bench? There were rumours that the tape had been re-edited and I know if I was him, I'd sure as Hell edit that scene out. Hence my question, is this the same footage as shown to a National newspaper reporter in June, or not?

11.30 Newquay Zoo, and the paving stones were cracking under the baking sun. I found myself amid honourable members of the press fraternity being ushered into of all places, the Zoo's Tropical House.

Mr Thomas began this five-act-tragedy by showing us some fancy pictures of African Cats .... mmmmm not bad. This was followed by some plaster casts of impressive paw prints... getting better. He then introduced two kids Daniel and Kieran ? they are Beast Watch! ....a nice touch. Kids: the aaah factor. Next, came Mr Thomas' rabbit from a hat, the anonymous cameraman - John. Unfortunately the six-foot blond haired John retold his story like a policeman giving evidence at the Old Bailey. Then the heat cracked the wrong man. John didn't want to give the footage's location away - and then promptly revealed that the site was not a million miles away from the Jamaica Inn on Bodmin Moor.

ANIMALS & MEN # 17

Then came the moment we had all waited for - the video.... all twenty seconds of it! To say the silence was deafening is an understatement. The silence was broken by a female member of our ranks murmuring "....it's a cat!" Mr Thomas was on the ropes and beginning to look like a man going into his tenth round with Mike Tyson, but, to give him credit, he still came out swinging. My sucker punch - the missing footage - was feebly countered by the old anonymity strategy; Mr Thomas had clearly forgotten that Anonymous John had already given the location away. The press sensed blood and were not about to let their prey loose.

A voice called out. "All those who believe they have just witnessed a video of a large cat raise their hand. None were raised. There then followed television interviews, analysis of the video footage, and the obligatory radio talk show. I was quite a popular chap for a while.

As I drove home one thought kept gnawing away in my mind: Why, Mr Thomas, why? To cap it all, half way home there was a torrential downpour. Even the gods were weeping. Mr Thomas you have set back the credibility of myself and others who believe in the beast, who are trying to find genuine footage or photographs, by years. Why, Mr Thomas, why? It wasn't even April the first...

A Chat with Lazarus

by Paul Crowther

(Still a Photographic lecturer at Plymouth CFE)

Twenty four hours earlier I had participated in the ritual slaughter of Mike Thomas of Newquay Zoo, after a trial by media. There was one troubling thought rattling through my mind, as I drank my evening Scotch between James Bond style smirks. Why Mr Thomas? Why?

I needed to talk to him, and I needed to talk to him fast. Surely a man of his intelligence would not

NEWSFILE XTRA

put himself through such treatment deliberately. How could I talk to him? Would he talk to anyone? Was he capable of talking after what BBC South West had done to him the previous evening?

In desperation I resorted to a modern mystic method of communication, ... I used the telephone! Surprise! He would actually talk to me. Like an impatient kid in a toy shop begging for a toy before its parents dragged him outside again, I blurted out my question - "Why Mr Thomas? Why? You must have realised that something like the murder of Caesar was going to take place at the Press Conference!" I didn`t give him a chance to question my parenthood nor to cut me off without first hearing my question.

For a man who had been sacrificed by the media twenty four hours earlier his voice was clear and calm as he told me what should have happened the day before.

Originally there were to have been five members of the local press in attendance by invitation only. (No, I was NOT on the list).

They were to view the video footage and then have a "gentleman's discussion " about the footage during which Mr Thomas would give his arguments for the footage being of a "wildcat" - not a beast, a puma or a panther or any other large man eating felid as the public imagined it to be. The results of this discussion were to be reported and any fears that the public might have had about man/child/large pet eaters would have been allayed.

Wildcats are fairly large aren`t they? They are also definitely not in the habit of revealing themselves in public", I chipped in. Not necessarily so, retorted the calm Mr Thomas.

They are in fact not that larger than a domestic cat, (I believe that this was his defence against my lack of park bench footage attack, (about which shall we say we agree to differ, seeing as Mr Thomas has more experience with these types of animals than I do!) Combine this with urbanisation, then perhaps the dietary needs of these animals outweigh their fear of human contact....mmmmmmm. Mr Thomas continued to outline his theories of wildcat populations and urbanisation and hybrids,

ANIMALS & MEN # 17 FEATURE

still in a cool, calm tone. "But! Mr Thomas!" I nearly screamed. "What was your reason for showing the video to the press like you did?

The answer - to show the general public what a Wild Cat looked like and hopefully more people would come foreword with sightings photographs and video footage. "But", I interrupted "After seeing what happened to you would you get in touch with you? The surprise is, it appears that Mr Thomas's gamble has worked. He said that he has received four phone calls in the last twenty four hours of a larger than normal black cat which is terrifying the moggy population of Liskeard. Members of his team were investigating these sightings as we spoke.

There was one point that Mr Thomas and I did agree on: until the general public sees either still images or video footage of "Wild Cats" in any shape or form in Cornwall to the quality that they see when watching Wildlife programmes on TV then unfortunately/ fortunately the sceptics hold the upper hand.

Conclusion: Reports of the demise of Mr Thomas have been greatly exaggerated. As you read this he is probably on a "wild cat chase". If he comes up with the goods, I for one will back him. If, however, there is any doubt in my mind, then.............

TYRANNOSAURS, TERROR BIRDS, TOURACOS AND TAMANDUAS:
THE HOTTEST NEWS IN VERTEBRATE PALAEONTOLOGY

By Darren Naish

Scarcely does a month go by without significant palaeontological news of some nature, and in this brief resume' I hope to bring you in on some of the most exciting of recent finds and theories. We start our rundown of news with arguably the most impressive of all animals ever, gigantic theropod dinosaurs, before moving on to the smaller, but no less impressive, bird-like dinosaurs and birds. Recent developments have also been made in the study of Cretaceous placental mammals, early anteaters, and carnivorous marsupials. In palaeoanthropology, a new paranthropine skull (*Paranthropus boisei*) has just been described - hot on the heels of the new species *Australopithecus bahrelghazali* and *Homo antecessor* - and a DNA study has shown that Neanderthals (*H. neanderthalensis*) were almost certainly not close relatives of modern humans. I also have some big news on coelacanths. Unfortunately, I don`t have the time or space to describe all of these discoveries at length, so I'll stick with the ones that interest me the most.

They Say Size Isn't Everything

Big news - in every sense of the word - is the recent discovery of an enormous *Tyrannosaurus* that apparently exceeds "Sue", previously the world's biggest tyrannosaur (at 12.5 m and 6-8 tonnes), by 15-20%. By playing with these figures, some newspaper journalists have made it known that the new specimen would be perhaps 21 m long and 9 m in height: I don't understand this, as 20% bigger than 12.5 is 15, still...

If any if this bears any semblance to the truth, then *Tyrannosaurus* may well be reclaiming its throne from the likes of Argentina's *Giganotosaurus* and Morocco's *Carcharodontosaurus*: theropod genera that, at least as far as the described material goes, do not definitely seem to have been truely bigger than "Sue" though both were initially claimed to be. The story of the therapods size war is a tangled one...

Prior to the giant tyrannosaur's debut, *Giganotosaurus carolinii*, described by Rudolfo Coria and Leonardo Salgado in 1995, was reckoned to be the biggest of the three with a 1.65 m skull and a 12.5 m length. The new *Carcharodontosaurus* material, described by Paul Sereno and eight other authors in 1996 - 71 years after material of this animal was first named as *'Megalosaurus saharicus'* (Deperet and Savornin, 1925) - also indicates an animal of about 12.5 m length. *Carcharodontosaurus* was supposed to have had a skull of 1.63 m, but Sereno`s reconstruction has an over-lengthened premaxilla, and a more realistic length is 1.52 m. Sereno *et al*'s new material, incidentally, shows that *Carcharodontosaurus* was emphatically not a giant marine theropodan cetacean analogue, as was suggested by. Bakker, Siegwarth, Kralis and Filla in 1992! *Giganotosaurus* was thought

ANIMALS & MEN # 17 FEATURE

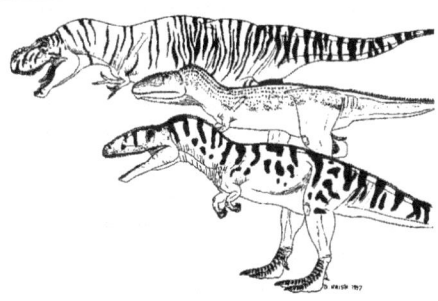

Fig. 1: The three biggest theropods compared. From top to bottom, *Tyrannosaurus rex* (Maastrichtian of western N. America), *Giganotosaurus carolinii* (Albian-Cenomanian of Argentina) and *Carcharodontosaurus saharicus* (Cenomanian of Morocco).

to be the biggest because, though its total length is the same as 'Sue', 'bigness' is a measure of weight to length, and the story **was** that *Giganotosaurus* was a real robust and thick-boned theropod that, when alive, would outweigh 'Sue'. Also, new skull material of *Giganotosaurus* discovered in March 1996 (unpublished as of writing) will allow revision or correction of the 1.65 m length given above - the rumours are that the true giganotosaur skull was bigger than 1.65 m (and therefore way bigger than 'Sue' and exceeding *Carcharodontosaurus*). Furthermore, at a talk he gave in 1996, Rudolfo Coria showed a slide of a dentary identical to that of the *Giganotosaurus* type, but 10% bigger! If the dentary scales in proportion to the total length in both the type and this 10% bigger specimen, and if the estimated 12.5 m length for the type is correct (note that there are too many 'ifs' for this exercise to be taken seriously), then the dentary might indicate a giganotosaur of 13.8 m. OK, but... even so, would a giant giganotosaur still be the biggest? Greg Paul, a renowned expert in the reconstruction and life appearance of dinosaurs, went and had a look at the giganotosaur type in 1996. Contrary to claims of it being a chunky heavyweight, he found that *Giganotosaurus* was less robust and with less massive proportions than big tyrannosaurs like 'Sue': if a giganotosaur and tyrannosaur of equal lengths were compared, the tyrannosaur would be heavier. So, despite all the hype generated by the new discoveries, it appears that 'Sue' was simply the biggest all along. Of course, the story doesn't stop there. A number of other theropods are even bigger - or at least longer - than 'Sue'. *Saurophaganax maximus* (Chure, 1995), a big Morrison allosaur named for the diagnostic components of the *nomen dubium Saurophagus maximus*, is estimated at total length 14 m. Other Jurassic allosaurs and the torvosaur *Edmarka* grew nearly as big. However, all are shallow-chested animals probably about half the weight of 'Sue'. *Bruhathkayosaurus matleyi*, a supposed gigantic theropod with a lower leg about 2 m. long (suggestive of a possible 20 m total length), turned out to be a titanosaurid sauropod (there was a suggestion that it could have been fossil wood, so bad was the state of preservation). *Kelmayisaurus gigantus* is a rumoured giant theropod with a vertebral column of 22 m length. Chinese dinosaur palaeontologist Dong Zhiming is supposed to be describing this one, but what the truthful situation is I don't know. There have also been persistent suggestions that *Spinosaurus*, a sail-backed elongate Egyptian theropod, could have been 15 m long. It seems to have been a comparative lightweight however, and probably did not exceed 4 tonnes. A specimen perhaps 20 m or more in length (therefore perhaps 6-7 tonnes or more) was displayed at 1996's Society of Vertebrate Palaeontology meeting - it's only a snout-tip though, and whether it was actually *Spinosaurus* or not seems problematic. Some workers think that *Baryonyx* - a 9.5 m long theropod from Surrey, described in 1986 (Charig and Milner, 1986) - is closely related to *Spinosaurus* (the snout-tip mentioned above is very like that of *Baryonyx*). Angela Milner has recently stated that the *Baryonyx* type specimen appears to be a subadult - an adult therefore could have been perhaps 15 m long. Again, such an animal would be longer, but not heavier, than 'Sue'. At the time of writing, it would seem that there is still uncertainty as to whether the new giant tyrannosaur is actually T. *rex*, or a new species. *New Scientist* has just reported that skull parts (about two-thirds of the left side) from this fossil have been stolen. Another T. rex specimen, dubbed 'Mr. Z-Rex', is going up for auction ('Sue', incidentally, has now been bought by The Field Museum, Chicago). With a femur only a few cm shorter than that of 'Sue', this animal is another biggie and as it's supposed to be a male, is particularly notable. The assumption at the moment is that female tyrannosaurs were bigger than males, but this needs further confirmation before it becomes fact.

ANIMALS & MEN # 17
Feathers and Furculae

And yet more theropod news (let's face it, most dinosaur news is theropod news) has recently been reported in *Nature*: it's *Velociraptor's* first preserved furcula. It's been said previously that a furcula is evident on the fighting *Velociraptor* (i.e. the specimen from Tugrugeen, near the Flaming Cliffs, Mongolia, preserved locked in combat with a *Protoceratops*), but Rinchen Barsbold, who has examined the specimen first hand, says this is incorrect. Furculae appear to be fused clavicles, though some ornithologists argue that they are actually a neomorph [brand-new structure not derived from pre-existing bits and pieces], and are now known for certain from a new allosaur-like theropod from Dinosaur National Monument, tyrannosaurids, oviraptorids and dromaeosaurids. What these furculae are doing in non-avian theropods is anyone's guess: the traditional 'explanation' for the presence of furculae is that they have evolved as a sort of spring to assist flapping flight. So, are all furculae-bearing theropods descendants of flying ancestors?

This is possible, and some workers consider it to be the most reasonable explanation: The school of thought propounding this view, dubbed 'BCF' (Birds Come First), has all dinosaur groups evolving from small, arboreal gliding ancestors (see *Omni* 16 (9): 34-86; *FT* 108: 34-37). The flightless dinosaurs, according to BCF, are dead-end relics that have branched from a lineage leading ever-more bid-like dinosaurs.. and eventually to true birds. BCF theory's leading advocate - George Olshevsky - was won increasing unofficial support, but most dinosaur palaentologists do not accept his views. To them, it is more likely, rather then being primitively present in early flyers, the furcula first evolved for another purpose (e.g. bracing of the sternal region) and was later adapted by flying theropods for use in flight

The abstracts from the 1997 Society of Vertebrate Palaeontology (SVP) meeting have just been published. As is to be expected, there was plenty to interest anyone interested in dinosaurs. 'Feathered' theropods continue to hog the limelight (see *A&M* 11: 10-11; *A&M 12*: 27-31). Having just appeared as resplendently fully feathered in Mike Skrepnick's cover illustration for Currie and Padian's new **Encyclopaedia of Dinosaurs**, it is fittingly ironic that the 'feathers' of *Sinosauropteryx* have apparently been debunked by Geist, Jones and Ruben - the three biologists best known as the scourge of all things Bakkerian. But they may have gone a step too far in suggesting that compsognathids were 'the first known semi-aquatic theropods'! I thought logic of this kind went out of the window with Bidar, Demay and Thomel (1972): they suggested that a *Compsognathus* specimen from Nice, France, had flippers and was an amphibious lagoon dweller, and they named it *C. corallestris* (distinct from the German *C. longipes*).

However, this idea was never reasonable. The French *Compsognathus* is still odd in being quite a bit larger than the German one though, and palaeontologist Mark Norell recently followed a long history of speculation in suggesting that it may be a separate species. Some Chinese palaeontologists do not deem *Sinosauropteryx* distinct enough for its own genus, and are calling it *Compsognathus prima* (I've heard that the etymology is incorrect, and the species

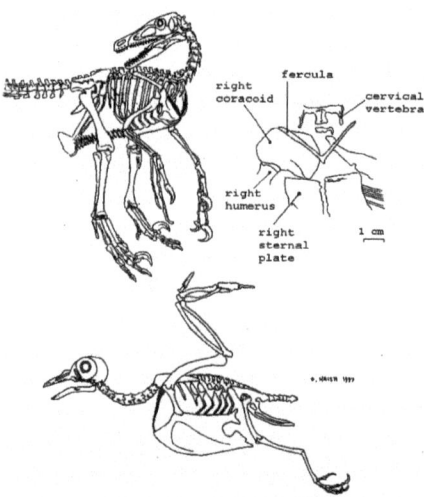

Fig. 2: Locations of wishbones (furculae) in *Velociraptor* (top left) and *Columba* (bottom), and as they looked when discovered in the sternal region of a fossil *Velociraptor* (top right), as seen in ventral view.

ANIMALS & MEN # 17　　　　　　　　　　FEATURE

Fig. 3: Diagrammatic representation of *Protarchaeopteryx* skeleton. The unusual structures in the top left are the tail feathers.

name should be spelt differently to match the gender of the word *Compsognathus*). Meanwhile, another Chinese 'feathered' theropod, *Protarchaeopteryx robusta*, is getting its share of attention. At least one specimen is reported as having large in-situ *Archaeopteryx*~style tail feathers, but the short forelimbs and large body size indicate that this animal was flightless. Kevin Padian reports that *Protarchaeopteryx*, despite its name, is not close to *Archaeopteryx*, nor even to maniraptorans in general [maniraptorans are all the descendants of the most recent common ancestor of dromaeosaurids and birds].

Terror-birds and Touracos: Turning Phylogeny on its Head

The phorusrhacoids were a group of large, mostly flightless, predatory groundbirds that lived in the forests and grasslands of the Americas, Europe and pre-glacial Antarctica from Palaeocene to Pleistocene times. The youngest phorusrhacoid known, the 3 m tall *Titanis walleri*, is from Florida (but there are rumours of specimens found as far north as Texas). Following the 1996 discovery of new Floridan *Titanis* material by Robert Chandler, it is now well known that, remarkably, phorusrhacoids did not have the small, stunted wings they used to be portrayed with - instead they actually had rather large stout arms with two clawed fingers (one of which was a mobile thumb).

It is also notable that some phorusrhacoids, such as the late Miocene *Psilopterus colzecus* described by Tonni and Tambussi in 1988, had a hyperextendable sickle-claw on their second toe. Some living seriemas do too, as did the dromaeosaurids and troodonts of the Cretaceous.

Chandler reported on his new *Titanis* 'hands' at the SVP meeting, but, of equal interest (to me), he also presented he tentative preliminaries for an amazing theory of phoruarhacoid affinity. Seriemas (Cariamidae) are evidently the closest relatives of phorushacoids, and it was not a surprise when Chandler reported that he believed this to be the case. Surprising to the extreme, however, is his contention that the next closest relatives of the seriema-phorusrhacoid clade are the touracos!! Yes, touracos (Musophagidae), those fruit-eating arboreal African forest birds traditionally allied with cuckoos.

The surprises didn't stop there - Chandler thinks that condors (Vulturidae [no longer known as Cathartidae, by the way]) are the outgroup to the touraco-seriema~phorusrhacoid clade. Obviously only a basic outline of his data was presented in his talk and abstract - I look forward to the doubtless controversial technical paper!

Incidentally, though Chandler's theory may sounds like a new one - it isn't. Palaeornithologist extraordinaire Storrs Olson - a man dedicated to the establishment of a bird family tree more realistic than the traditional one of Gadow (1893) and Wetmore (1960) - made similar enlightening suggestions back in 1985.

Olson speculated on evolutionary relationships between hoatzins (pronounced 'what-zins') and falcons, and thought that these groups, with seriemas (and therefore phoruarhacoids), formed an endemic South American radiation of primitive land birds. He furthermore found that touracos seemed to be the closest relatives of accipitrids (hawks, eagles and Old World vultures)! Add to this recently analysed morphological and genetic

ANIMALS & MEN # 17

Fig. 4: The phylogeny of phoruarhacoids and their relatives as recently outlined by Robert Chandler. Phorusrhacoids and cariamids form the crown group; musophagids are their sister-group; Vulturidae is the sister-group to Musophagidae + (Cariamidae + Phorusrhacoidea).

data which indicates that condors are actually short-legged storks (ciconuds): Sibley and Ahlquist (1990), the two authors who have recently reclassified all living birds on the basis of their studies on DNA-DNA hybridisation, even list condors as a stork subfamily. It should also be noted that Sibley and Ahlquist's scheme blatantly contradicts other theories mentioned here. For example, they saw falcons and accipitrids as true relatives and part of an extended Ciconiiformes that, while it includes waterbirds like grebes, pelicans, storks and albatrosses, is not close to primitive land birds like touracos or hoatzins. Touracos, in the Sibley and Ahlquist scheme, are close relatives of owls and nightjars, while hoatzins are cuckoos. And to return to falcons, Heinzel, Fitter and Parslow (1987) are among several authors who have proposed a close relationship between falcons and owls! If anything is clear from all of this confusion, it is that a lot of work remains to be done on the evolution of virtually all bird groups.

Migrating Marsupials

South American phorusrhacoids lived alongside another group of highly successful predators, the borhyaenoid marsupials - a diverse group that paralleled placental carnivorans in evolving mustelid-like, bear-like, dog-like and even sabretooth-like predators. Christian de Muizon (best known for his work on fossil seals and toothed whales), Richard Cifelli and Ricardo Paz have recently published new work on the affinities of early Palaeocene South American marsupials. Their aim was to resolve the affinities of the borhyaenoids. Borhyaenoids have previously been considered related to the Asian deltatheroidans, to the North American stagodontids (not to be confused with stegodontids, which are a group of fossil elephants), or to the Australian dasyuromorphs. The new work showed that borhyaenoids shared several unique features of the teeth and skull with didelphoids - the group that includes living didelphid opossums - and that the two should belong together as the Didelphimorphia. This group shares some odd dental features with the South American microbiotheres and the Australian dasyuromorphs: further, microbiotheres are evidently more closely related to dasyuromorphs than didelphimorphians as evidenced by their shared distinctive periotic bone in the skull, continuous lower ankle joint, and other features.

This anatomical data can be combined with biogeography: basically, marsupials originated in North America during the Cretaceous (the earliest known marsupial presently known, *Kokopellia*, is North American - there are suggestions now, however, that it is not a true marsupial but a very close relative) and moved southward. Didelphimorphians and microbiotheres evolved in South America - some didelphoid didelphimorphians then confused things by moving via North America into Europe, northern Africa (reported in 1983) and central Asia (reported in *1985*)*.

These migrating didelphoids had all gone extinct by Miocene times, but following the formation of the Panamanian isthmus about 3 Ma ago, South American didelphoids moved into North America once more. Presently, the Virginia opossum (*Didelphis virginiana*) occurs as far north as southern Canada, where it occasionally suffers from frostbite on its ears. Unlike didelphoids, the ancestors of all Australian marsupials moved southward and flourished in Antarctica (where they became extinct) and, their final home (for now!), Australasia. This model of Australian

ANIMALS & MEN # 17 — FEATURE

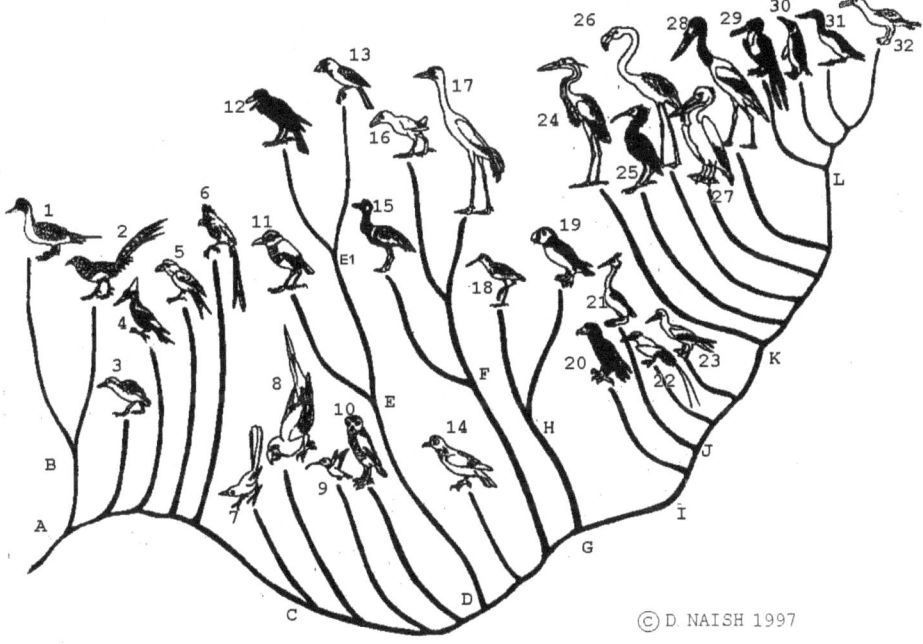

Fig. 5:-

The interrelationships of higher birds (Neognathae) according to the DNA-DNA hybridisation work of Sibley and Ahlquist (1990). Some of the more important or higher ranking clades are marked with letters instead of numbers.

A. NEOAVES. B. GALLOANSERAE.
1. Anseriformes. 2. Callomorphae.
3. Turnicae. 4. Picae. 5. Coraciae.
6. Colise. C. PASSERAE.
7. Cuculimorphae. 8. Psittacomorphae.
9. Apodimorphae. 10. Strigimorphae.
D. PASSEROMORPHAE.
E. PASSERIFORMES. 11. Tyranni.
E1. PASSERI. 12. Corvida.
13. Passerida. 14. Columbiformes.
F. CRUIFORMES. 15. Otididi. 16. Ralli.
17. Crui. G. CICONIIFORMES.
H. CHARADRII. 18. Scolopacida.
19. Charadruda. I. CICONII.
20. Falconides. J. CICONIIDES.
21. Podicipedida. 22. Phaethontida.
23. Sulida. K. CICONIIDA. 24. Ardeoidea.
25. Threskiornithoidea.
26. Phoenicopteroidea.
27. Pelecanoidea. 28. Ciconioidea.
L. PROCELLARIIOIDEA. 29. Fregatidae.
30. Spheniscidae. 31. Gaviidae.
32. Procellariidae.

Many of the relationships proposed in this classification are totally discordant with those indicated by morphological analysis and are not accepted by the majority of ornithologists.

ANIMALS & MEN # 17 FEATURE

marsupial origin is the 'Southern Dispersal Route': the opposing theory ('Northern Dispersal') used to be considered more likely, and apparently still is by some.

* A fossil marsupial has just been reported from Turkey, too (Maas et al., 1997). It is likely that it is a didelphoid, but it is probably unwise to make such an assumption at this stage.

To return to the borhyaenoids - whatever they are - it is interesting that *Thylacinus* has at times been considered to have been one of them. Such a view is nowadays discredited as thylacinids (including the recently described fossil species *Nimbacinus dicksoni* (Muirhead and Archer, 1990) and *Muribacinus gadiyuli* (Wroe, 1996)) are evidently dasyuroids related to the dasyurids. Work on thylacine immunology (Lowenstein, Sarich and Richardson, 1981), on RNA gene data (Thomas et al., 1989) and, most importantly, on mitochondrial DNA published this year (Krajewski, Buckley and Westerman, 1997) have also shown that *Thylacinus* belongs within the dasyuroids.

times, South America was an island continent. The other xenarthrans, the armadillos (Cingulata) and sloths (Pilosa), also appear to be endemic South Americans that only got to leave their home continent with the formation of the Panamanian isthmus. A supposed Asian xenarthran, *Ernanodon*, is controversial So what does *Eurotamandua*, an early European anteater, mean? *Eurotamandua's* original describer, Gerhard Storch, argued that *Eurotamandua* was an advanced anteater closely related to living tamanduas (Storch, 1981). This is a real dilemma, as it means that anteaters and all other xenarthrans would have had to have appeared much earlier than thought (say, in the Lower Cretaceous or even the Jurassic) and could have evolved, well, anywhere. And all of this without any fossil evidence other than *Eurotamandua*, and in contradiction to what is known of mammalian evolution. A dilemma. Of course, several possible answers to this dilemma have recently been made.

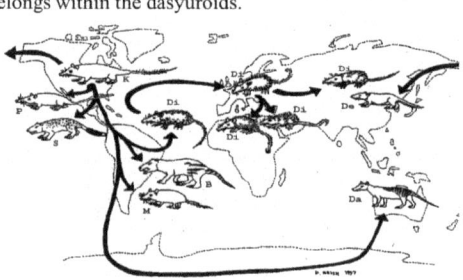

Fig. 6: Biogeography of carnivorous marsupials. K Kokopellia. P Pediomyidae.
S Stagodontidae. B Borhyaenoidea.
M Microbiotheriidae. De Deltatheroidea.
Di Dideiphoidea. Da Dasyuromorpha.
(See text for discussion.)

Out Of Place Anteaters, Or The First 'Walking Fircones'?

One of mammalian biogeography's greatest puzzlers has to be the presence of *Eurotamandua*, a supposed advanced anteater, in the Eocene Messel shales of Germany. Anteaters (Vermilingua) seem otherwise to be an endemic South American group that evolved there while, from Palaeocene to Pliocene

Fig. 7: From top to bottom, skeleton of *Eurotamandus joresi*; E. *joresi* restored as an anteater (based on earlier artistic restorations); life restoration of *Eomanis waldi* (the Messel pangolin). Note that, apart from the scales, the life restorations of *Eurotamandus* and *Eomanis* are actually not that different.

In a study of anteater evolution presented this year, Daniel Branham and Timothy Gaudin did not find that their data supported Storch's view of *Eurotamandua* as an advanced anteater - instead it might have been a primitive sister-group to all other anteaters. However, the characters that support this interpretation (including lack of teeth and lateral

- 24 -

ANIMALS & MEN # 17　　　　　　　　　　　　　FEATURE

process on fifth metatarsal) sound to me just like those that can easily be convergently evolved, so I don't buy it. A little better is Branham and Gaudin's other hypothesis that *Eurotamandua* is not an anteater at all, but the sister-group to sloths. So.. Eurotamandua is not an anteater? Well, if that's the case, we may as well go the whole hog and embrace Shoshani et al.'s (1997) work: they examined *Eurotamandua* in detail and showed that, in fact, it does not definitely have the xenarthrous vertebral articulations that are diagnostic for xenarthrans (hence the name). What's more, it shares more features with PANGOLINS than with any other mammals. So.. *Eurotamandua* is a pangolin? If correct, this resolves the dilemma of the out-of-place anteater and as we know from another Messel fossil, *Eomanis* (also described by Storch), that early pangolins were present in Europe, *Eurotamandua's* new identity is not a biogeographical nightmare.

And Finally...

Coelacanths (Actinistia) are an odd group of fleshy-finned fishes (sarcopterygians) related to lungfishes and tetrapods, represented today only by *Latimeria*. An old suggestion is that coelacanths are more closely related to chondrichthyans than to bony fishes and tetrapods, but the case for this really isn't good - the features cited (e.g. pituitary anatomy, urea retention, fatty liver) are almost certainly primitive ones widespread in vertebrates, or are ambiguous, and are in any case outweighed by many more features shared by coelacanths and bony fishes. Coelacanths are famous for being rediscovered, but it is not often recognised how odd their fossil record is. In fact, it's pattern is unique. Coelacanths were incredibly abundant and diverse in ecosystems of the Devonian and Carboniferous, became very rare in the Permian, peaked in diversity in the Triassic, and then gradually decreased in diversity through the Jurassic and Cretaceous. Until 1994 (when the North American *Megalocoelacanthus dobiei* -from the very latest Cretaceous - was described by Schwimmer, Stewart and Williams), the most recent known fossil coelacanth was Europe's *Macropoma*, a fossil of Campanian age (Campanian penultimate stage of the Upper Cretaceous: 83-74 Ma before present). These rare fossils show that, by the end half of the Cretaceous, coelacanths were becoming ever more reclusive from a palaeontological point of view. Not much longer, and they would disappear from the fossil record entirely.

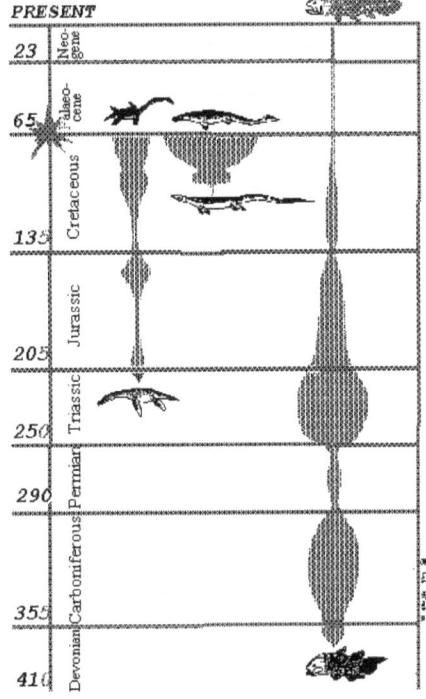

Fig. 8: The unusual fossil record of Actinistia (far right) compared to Plesiosauria (extreme left) and Mosasauroidea (middle), the two most important of late Mesozoic marine reptile clades. The star marks the KT event. Notably, plesiosaurs and mosasauroids thrive at high diversity before the KT event, and leave no post-Mesozoic record. Coelacanths dwindle out slowly as they approach it.

Well, almost entirely (read on). In every conceivable way, the coelacanth fossil record is utterly unlike that of marine reptiles - common, abundant, well represented and widely distributed right up to their end-Cretaceous mass extinction - so those writers who think that

ANIMALS & MEN # 17 FEATURE

Latimeria can serve as an analogue for post-Cretaceous marine reptile survival are in error. The dwindling fossil record of the last known, reclusive coelacanths shows that *Latimeria* is the ultimate in red herrings.

It's traditionally been thought that virtually all fossil coelacanths were freshwater animals, but this is an over-simplification often based on unreliable geological evidence. Nevertheless, Jurassic and Cretaceous coelacanths appear to have become successively more marine, with late Jurassic *Undina* being from shallow lagoons, early Cretaceous *Macropoma* being from continental, shallow seas, and mid and late Cretaceous *Axelrodichthys*, *Mawsonia* and *Megalocoelacanthus* being from open, offshore waters. Another myth, that fossil coelacanths were always smaller than Latimeria, is also incorrect: both *Mawsonia* and *Megalocoelacanthus* grew to lengths of 3.5 m!

A persistent problem, and one that some cryptozoologists have played to their advantage, is the 65 Ma gap in the coelacanth fossil record. Surely, if coelacanths can be totally absent as fossils from the end of the Upper Cretaceous onwards, similar possibilities for post-Cretaceous survival exist for other Cretaceous marine creatures (e.g. plesiosaurs). As argued above, the extreme rarity and dwindling diversity of Upper Cretaceous coelacanths is thoroughly unlike the high-diversity 'out with a bang' pattern for the last known marine reptiles (see diagram!). Furthermore, now - and this really is big news - fossil coelacanths from the 65 Ma gap are known. Naomi Goldsmith and Ilana Yanai-Inbar (1997) have just reported early Miocene coelacanth fossils from the Negev (south) of Israel. Their finds may be especially important as they imply that the fossils are very similar to *Latimeria*.

This provides further proof that plesiosaurs etc. were not present after the Cretaceous (some plesiosaur fossils are known from the Palaeocene, but they are from rocks only a few Ma younger than the end of the Cretaceous anyway, and are in any case almost definitely reworked [i.e. from older, in this case Cretaceous, rocks]), as, unlike coelacanths, there are no Cenozoic fossil plesiosaurs.

Incidentally, in a classic case of 'thunderbird syndrome', I have long recalled the description in the literature of another Cenozoic coelacanth ~ but have never been able to find the source. Recently, my misery was put to an end: the source is a 1986 paper by T. Orvig (published in that well-known geological journal *Geologiska Foreningens i Stockholm Forhand-linger*), and it described a Palaeocene coelacanth from Sweden.

STOP PRESS: UPDATES TO THE ABOVE

The above article was written early in 1997. Here are some of the latest developments relating to some of the stories covered above (as of July 1998).

Giant theropods

Claims that the new tyrannosaur specimen from Montana is 21 m long, and that it might belong to a new species, remain unsubstantiated. No data is forthcoming, but it has been asserted that there is no reason to think that the animal is not *Tyrannosaurus rex*.

In a 1997 analysis of variation within the genus *Allosaurus*, Smith did not find that *Saurophaganax maximus* was well differentiated from *Allosaurus*, and created the new species *Allosaurus maximus* for it. This is controversial.

Since the above article was written, the full descriptive monograph on *Baryonyx* has been published (Charig and Milner, 1997). More material both of *Baryonyx* and of *Spinosaurus* will be described in the near future.

Feathered theropods

The 'feathery' structures on the compsognathid *Sinosauropteryx* were not debunked by Geist, Jones and Ruben: their claim that the structures represented frayed collagen fibres from beneath the animal's skin is simply not correct as the structures are clearly not of dermal origin, and do not resemble frayed collagen fibres. A detailed examination of the *Sinosauropteryx* specimens and their integumentary structures (Chen, Dong and Zhen 1998) confirmed that the structures were coarse, pliable, and probably hollow strands covering the external surface of the animal. It could not

ANIMALS & MEN # 17

be confirmed that they were any sort of 'proto-feather', though this is looking increasingly likely. Feathers on *Protarchaeopteryx* have now been officially verified and were widely discussed in the media following their coverage in *Nature* of 25th June 1998. Another small theropod from the same site, *Caudipteryx*, also has feathers preserved on its tail and hand. Neither of these animals are birds as they do not possess the several distinctive characters all birds do (e.g. very elongate forelimbs, unserrated teeth, reduced fibula,) and they thus prove that non-avian theropods did indeed have feathers. Padian's argument (that *Protarchaeopteryx* is not close to maniraptorans) did not prove correct: both *Protarchaeopteryx* and *Caudipteryx* are maniraptorans. *Caudipteryx* appears to be the most closely related of all non-avian theropods to birds, while *Protarchaeopteryx* is more primitive, and perhaps closer to dromaeosaurids.

Wolverines or Muddy Badgers?

By Chris Moiser

(See Front CoverPicture)

Since the mid 1970s there have been numerous reports of the Wolverine (*'Gulo gulo"*) living wild in Great Britain. These reports have come from various parts of the country, and have been of differing degrees of accuracy. One recent newspaper report (Western Morning News 12.11.97) detailed four sightings in Devon in the previous twelve months. Other reports suggest that they are present in the Highlands of Scotland, and the Dyfed-Powys area of Wales as well. Despite the suggestion that there is a great deal of evidence to support the existence of a living and breeding population present, and that this population could be as high as 200 - 300 by 2010, (Hooper, T. 1998), convincing evidence is still absent. I would suggest that most sightings can be explained in a much more conventional way. Most sightings have been glimpses of animals at night; other suggested evidence includes sheep kills, footprints, and in

FEATURE

one incident loud snoring in a barn! (Hooper, T. 1997, 22). There is no record of the species having been recorded as indigenous in the United Kingdom, either in historic or prehistoric times. The likelihood of wolverines having been introduced, either intentionally or accidentally would appear to be slight for a number of reasons. Sir Christopher Lever, an acknowledged expert in this field, describes introduced species as having been introduced normally for one or more of three criteria. The animal must either be economic, sporting or ornamental, i.e. it was originally imported for commercial reasons, such as fur farming, for sport, such as shooting, or because it was good to look at. It seems highly unlikely that wolverines would have been imported for any of these reasons.

Fig.1. Badger (above) Wolverine (Below)

The only possible reason would have been for fur farming, however, although the fur has been used commercially, it has typically only been used in the arctic circle, on parkas. In this instance the fur is taken from trapped wild animals (Nowak and Paradiso 1983, 1005).The solitary nature and the habits of the animal, in conjunction with its reputation for ferociousness make it unlikely that it would be imported as a pet. Even if it was, this would be a solitary animal that had the potential to escape. Most authorities agree that the animals are entirely solitary in the wild, except when breeding. The animal is unlikely to have been imported

ANIMALS & MEN # 17   FEATURE

at any time for hunting, there would be too great an outcry from livestock owners, because of its reputation and the potential for losses of the smaller domestic livestock. It would not be a particularly good animal to hunt anyway in that it is, to all intents and purposes, inedible, and is likely to cause as much damage to hounds, as they are to it.

The nature and reputation of the animal then makes it much less likely to have been imported than many of the other species that are alleged to be living as introductions within Great Britain.

In addition its habit of caching food and feeding on carrion would be both likely to bring it rapidly to human attention.I would like to suggest that these alleged sightings of wolverines within Great Britain are erroneous and that the animals seen are in the main European Badgers (*'Meles meles'*). The reasons for this are several fold, and in part rely on some recent personal observations on wild Badgers. If we consider the size first of all.

In his Encyclopedia of Mammals, David McDonald quotes the Badger as having a head and body length of 67 - 81 cm., the Wolverine is "up to 83 cm." The badgers tail is 15 - 20cm., and the Wolverine, "up to 20 cm." The weights quoted are Wolverine, çÎ, about 15 kg., çÎ, about 10kg; the Badger is quoted at çÎ, about 12 kg., and çÎ, about 10 kg. The Wolverine of course has longer legs than the Badger, but otherwise has a very similar body-size. The Badger is also very widespread throughout Great Britain.

Whilst it might be said that under modestly reasonable light at night the Badgers' black and white face mask is still very obvious, there are several colour variations of the European Badger. Most authorities refer to an albino, a semi-albino (where the eye-stripes are still visible), erythristic (gingery), and a melanistic form (very dark).

Ernest Neal reported that albino badgers "are not extremely rare", in his book "The Badger" in 1948. Unlike many albino and near-albino wild mammals the colouration of white Badgers does not seem to affect their longevity. In his 1970 book, "The White Badger", Gordon Burness writes about Snowball, a white Badger, who lived for an unspecified time, as an adult and paired normally.

One local zoological garden has had a white Badger visiting the owners garden for several years running,

(Palmer, J. 1998). This apparently normal longevity may be because, other than man, there is no top predator that takes Badgers in Great Britain.

The lighter colour badgers are also prone to staining of the fur from the soil in which the setts are dug. If we then consider the albino, or semi-albino badger with dark soil staining, of the sort that might occur on a damp night, we have the appearance, to the lay person, or even a reasonable field biologist, of a Wolverine. Such animals could be seen sporadically, depending upon weather conditions, and once there is a suggestion, in the press, of a wolverine presence in one area, it supplies a rapid explanation for an animal not quickly recognised, either seen in that area, or elsewhere.

If the misidentification is taken up by the media and regularly propagated, then sightings become a self-fulfilling prophecy.

References and further reading

Burness, G. 1971. *The White Badger*. Carousel. London.

Corbet, G.B. and Harris, S. eds. 1991 *The Handbook of British Mammals*. Blackwell Scientific. Oxford.

Hooper, T. 1997. The Beast of Llangurig and others. *'Animals and Men'* '15" 22 - 24.

Hooper, T. 1998. *Preliminary notes on the numbers and types of exotic species currently in the United Kingdom and living wild*. Vale Wild Life Group. Bristol.

Macdonald, D. (Ed.), 1989 *The Encyclopaedia of Mammals* Unwin Hyman, London

Neal, E. 1948 *The Badger*. Collins New Naturalist. London

Nowak, R. M., Paradiso, J. L., 1983. *Walker's Mammals of the World*. Johns Hopkins. Baltimore.

Palmer, J. 1998. Personal communication.

******

EDITOR'S NOTE: In variance to how this article has been misconstrued in certain quarters, neither Chris nor the CFZ are stating that there are NO wolverines at large in the UK, merely that it is our opinion that many of the wolverines reported are no such thing.

This fascinating article gives ONE explanation which can account for SOME of the sightings

ANIMALS & MEN # 17

Turtle tales
by Dr. Lars Thomas

FEATURE

THE BIG ONES

REDISCOVERIES

The last couple of years in Denmark have been very much in the sign of the turtle, or tortoise if you like. All kinds of strange turtles have been cropping up all over the place. It started in 1996 with the rediscovery of the European pond tortoise. Last heard off in Denmark in the bronze age, it was found alive and well in several parts of Denmark, notably the central part of Jutland, but there has also been sightings in several marshes north of Copenhagen, on Funen and on the extreme eastern island of Denmark, Bornholm.

In the summer of 1997 some strange stories started coming in to yours truly about sea-turtles in western Denmark. Several people on the holiday islands Fanø, Rømø and Mandø claimed to have seen sea-turtles coming out of the water and climbing on to the beaches. Noone could produce any photographs or any kind of solid evidence, so all of these stories were discared as fruits of the silly season. At the end of November, things started to change.

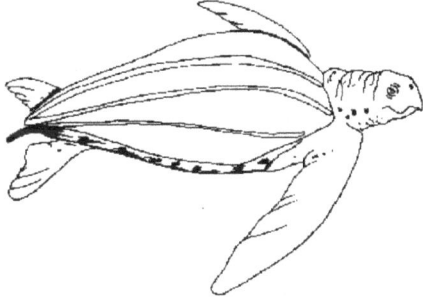

Later research showed, that the tortoise have actually been known for many years, but that most people have regarded them as released or escaped animals, which is unlikely as the pond tortoise is rather rare in captivity. We do have substantial population of red-eared terrapins though, so released tortoises can and do live in the wild in Denmark.

Two captured specimens of the pond tortoise have been DNA-tested, and althought he results are not conclusive, they indicate that the animals are closely related to the nearest wild population in Polen, but aso slightly different, which would indicate that they have lived in isolation for approximately 2.000 years.

People in southern Lillebælt (the narrow stairt between Jutland and the central danish island Funen) started seeing a very large dark brown creature swimming slowly just beneath the surface. Every now and then it would raise a large almost melon-shaped head take a few deep breaths, and disappear under water again. Danish newspapers had a field day on this one, but the mystery was solved about a month later. On December 23rd a fisherman found the creature, a leatherback turtle, floating south of the Als Peninsula, on the extreme southern east-coast of Jutland. He towed it in, and it was picked up by the Fishery and Sailing-Museum in Esbjerg, were it is still located.

EDITOR`S NOTE: As part of our ongoing researches we are especially interested in reports of marine turtles in European waters. On a related topic we are always interested in aquiring living specimens of soft shelled turtles of any species for our own collection. If anyone in the UK knows of any of these creatures either for sale in a pet shop or free to a good home through any other means, please would they let us know. We are also always interested in specimens of the larger aquatic salamanders such as mud puppies, sirens, etc.

ANIMALS & MEN # 17

THE ZIPHIIDAE, THE STATE OF THE ART, AND A POSSIBLE NEW SPECIES

By Darren Naish

It is cliché' nowadays to refer to beaked whales (Ziphiidae) as the most poorly known of large mammals: nevertheless, this is a description that still rings true. Of the 20 presently recognised species, eight were described for the first time this century, and two were described for the first time this decade. These two most recently recognised species are of special interest because they represent the largest of all recently discovered extant animal taxa.

Mesoplodon peruvianus, referred to as the Pygmy beaked whale (Rails and Brownell 1991, Jefferson, Leatherwood and Webber 1993), Lesser beaked whale (Carwardine 1995) or Peruvian beaked whale (Dalebout *et al.* 1998), was described in 1991 on the basis of 10 specimens which were captured or had beached on the Peruvian coast between 1975 and 1989 (Reyes, Mead and Van Waerebeek 1991). Since then, *M. peruvianus* specimens have also beached on the Mexican coast (Rails and Brownell 1991, Jefferson, Leatherwood and Webber 1993).

M. bahamondi, for which the common name Bahamonde's beaked whale has been proposed (Reyes *et al.* 1997), was described in 1997 on the basis of a single skull discovered on Robinson Crusoe Island off Chile (the journal issue it was published in was dated 1995 but this is evidently the planned, and not the actual, publication date). Cardenas, Yanez and Van Waerebeek (1988) first reported this species as *Mesoplodon* sp., and Van Waerebeek (1996) was prepared to announce it as a new species in a short note published in 1996. Naish (1996) was the first reference to this species in the cryptozoological literature. Evidence thus far unsupported by physical evidence suggests that other extant ziphiid species remain to be described. One officially recognised potential species, *Mesoplodon* ap. 'A', is only known from eyewitness and photographic evidence. It has been recorded from the eastern tropical Pacific (Pitman, Aguayo and Urban 1987, Jefferson,

FEATURE

Leatherwood and Webber 1993) and now the Peruvian coast as well (Van Waerebeek, quoted in Papastavrou 1997, Pitman in press). Naish (1996) and Reyes *at al.* (1997) propose that *M. bahamondi* and *M.* sp. 'A' are one and the same, but other identities, such as that *M.* ap. `A` is *M. pacificus* (Pitman, Aguayo and Urban 1987, Nowak and Paradiso 1991, Naish 1996), are possible. Eyewitness reports of what might be other ziphiid species, also as yet unrecorded by physical evidence, have been discussed in the cryptozoological literature (Heuvelmans 1968, 1986, Naish 1996, Shuker 1997). A number of others have yet to be bought to widespread attention (Naish, in prep.).

A study recently published by Dalebout *et al.* (1998) is the first to try to provide a database for species-level identification of ziphiids based on mitochondrial DNA. The authors took genetic samples from 15 species of ziphiid which had been identified to species by a ziphiid worker, and which were represented by diagnostic skeletal or photographic evidence. The species identity of these samples was therefore not in doubt and they were used as 'reference' samples to which others, less securely identified or identified without the presence of diagnostic morphological data (referred to as 'test' samples), could be compared.

A number of interesting discoveries resulted. Comparison of the 'reference' samples to 20 'test' samples taken from animals which had stranded on New Zealand showed that four of these had been misidentified. One such sample, coming from an animal previously identified as an Andrews' beaked whale (*M. bowdoini*) proved to be a Blainville's beaked whale (*M. densirostris*). This is the first record of this species from New Zealand and means that the specimen involved joins a long list of other mesoplodonts which have also been misidentified as *M. bowdoini* (Guiler 1967, Nishiwaki 1962, Moore 1963, Tidemann 1980, Mead 1989). Even the holotype specimen of Hubbs' beaked whale (*M. Carlhubbsi*) recognised by a new species by Moore (1963), was misidentified by Hubbs (1946) as a specimen of *M. Bowdoini*. The discovery of *M. Densirostris* on New Zealand. This is not surprising as this species already had the widest known distribution of any mesoplodont. Its occurrence round the shores of new Zealand had already been predicted

ANIMALS & MEN # 17 — FEATURE

by Jefferson, Leatherwood and Webber (1993) and hinted at in Watson s (1988) distribution map.

1. Peruvian Beaked Whale
2. Bahamonde's Beaked Whale (skull)
3. Andrews' Beaked Whale
4. Blainville's Beaked Whale
5. Hector's Beaked Whale

Another sample came from an animal identified as a Cuvier's beaked whale (*Ziphius cavirostris*), but which turned out to be from *M. bowdoini* (Dalebout *et al.* 1998). This is also an important discovery because *M. bowdoini* is very poorly known, represented by only about 20 strandings worldwide and as yet unreported as a live animal by eyewitnesses.

In conjunction with the history of misidentification referred to above, *M. bowdoini* has also been problematic because of its apparent closeness to *M. carlhubbsi*. Dalebout *et al.* (1998) found that *M. carlhubbsi* and *M. bowdoini* did not group together as close relatives however, calling into question previous suggestions that they are sister-species or even conspecific (Mead 1981, 1989).

Curiously, in Dalebout *et al.*'s (1998) analysis, *M. bowdoini* grouped with *Tasmacetus* as a sister-group to the rest of *Mesoplodon*, implying that *Mesoplodon* is paraphyletic or biphyletic.

A particularly intriguing result is an extremely marked genetic difference observed between two specimens referred to Hector's beaked whale (*M. hectori*), one from South Australia and the other from the North Pacific.

The large difference recorded by Dalebout *et al.* (1998) between the two specimens was far greater than that observed within any other ziphiid species, and when included in a phylogenetic analysis, the two specimens occupied markedly different locations on the mesoplodont tree. This strongly suggests that a new mesoplodont species has been discovered by way of its addition to the molecular database.

For more than a century subsequent to its discovery on New Zealand in 1866 (Gray 1871), *M. hectori* was assumed to be entirely austral in distribution. Then, in 1981, Mead (1981) published four stranding records, and referred to two sightings (both of which were photographed), which were of *M. hectori*, but were from the Californian coast.

These demonstrated *M. hectori* to be present in the northern hemisphere. Rice (1978) had already published one of these photographs, but the animal had been misidentified as *M. carlhubbsi*. Ellis (1980) also published one, but without a caption identifying the animal to species. More data on *M. hectori* in the northern hemisphere was published by Mead and Baker (1987).

All of these northern specimens may well pertain to the same species as *M. hectori* from the south (they seem to, as all share good, diagnostic morphological characters (Mead and Baker 1987)).

However, while both the northern and southern *M. hectori* specimens from which the samples used by Dalebout *et al.* (1998) were taken were reliably identified as having belonged to this species, it is evident that only one of them did.

Which one cannot be determined without comparison of samples from more specimens (Dalebout *et al.* 1998). Dalebout *et al.* (1998) state that neither specimens matched the morphology that would be expected from any of the five species they

ANIMALS & MEN # 17

were unable to obtain samples from (Northern bottlenosed whale *(Hyperoodon ampullatus)*, *M. bahamondi*, Ginkgo-toothed beaked whale *(M. ginkgodens)*, *M. pacificus*, and *M. peruvianus)*.

Based on their data then, the best conclusion at present is that a new mesoplodont has been discovered, and one that looks enough like *M. hectori* for it to be identified on morphological features as *M. hectori*.

References

CARDENAS, J.C., YANEZ, J.L. and VAN WAEREBEEK, K. 1988. Primer registro de delfin manchado *(Stenella attenuata)*, delfin comun *(Delphinus delphis)* y ballena picuda *(Mesoplodon sp.)* para el Archipielago de Juan Fernandez, Chile. *Abstracts, III Reunion de Trabajo de Especialistas en Namiferos Marinos de America del Sur* (Montevideo).

CARWARDINE, N. 1995. *Eyewitness Handbooks: Whales, Dolphins and Porpoises.* Dorling Kindersley (London).

DALEBOUT, N.L., VAN HELDEN, A., VAN WAEREBEEK, K. and BAKER, C.S. 1998. Molecular genetic identification of southern hemisphere beaked whales (Cetacea: Ziphiidae). *Molecular Ecology* 7: 687-694.

ELLIS, R. 1980. Beaked whales. *Sea Frontiers* **26** (1): 10-18.

GRAY, J.E. 1871. Notes on the *Berardius* of New Zealand. *Annals and Magazine of Natural History*, 4th series, 8: 115-117.

GUILER, E.R. 1967. Strandings of three species of *Mesoplodon* in Tasmania. *Journal of Mammalogy* 48: 650-652

HEUVELMANS, B. 1968. *In the Wake of the Sea-Serpents*. Rupert Hart-Davis (London).

_____ 1986. Annotated checklist of apparently unknown animals with which cryptozoology is concerned. *Cryptozoology* 5: 1-26.

HUBBS, C.L. 1946. First records of two beaked whales, *Mesoplodon bowdoini* and *Ziphius cavirostris*, from the Pacific coast of the United States. *Journal of Mammalogy* 27: 242-255.

JEFFERSON, T.A., LEATHERWOOD, S. and WEBBER, M.A. 1993. *FAO Species Identification Guide: Marine Mammals of the World.* FAO (Rome).

MEAD, J.G. 1981. First records of *Mesoplodon hectori* (Ziphiidae) from the northern hemisphere and a description of the adult male. *Journal of Mammalogy* 62: 430-432.

_____ 1989. Beaked whales of the genus *Mesoplodon*. IN RIDGWAY, S.H. and HARRISON, R. (eds) *Handbook of Marine Mammals Vol. 4: River Dolphins and the Larger Toothed Whales.* Academic Press (London), pp. 349-430.

_____ and BAKER, A.N. 1987. Notes on the rare beaked whale, *Mesoplodon hectori* (Gray). *Journal of the Royal Society of New Zealand* 17: 303-312.

MOORE, J.C. 1963. Recognising certain species of beaked whales of the Pacific Ocean. *American Midland Naturalist* **7a**: 396-428.

NAISH, D.W. 1996. Multitudinous enigmatic cetaceans, or 'whales in limbo'. *Animals and Men* **11**: 28-34.

NISHIWAKI, M. 1962. *Mesoplodon bowdoini* stranded at Akita Beach, Sea of Japan. *Scientific Report of the Whales Research Institute* **16**: 61-77.

NOWAK, R.N. and PARADISO, J.L. 1991. *Walker's Mammals of the World, 5th Edition.* John Hopkins University Press (Baltimore).

PAPASTAVROU, V. 1997. New south whale. *BBC Wildlife* **15** (3): 20.

PITMAN, R.L., AGUAYO, A. and URBAN, J. 1987. Observations of an unidentified beaked whale *(Mesoplodon sp.)* in the eastern tropical Pacific. *Marine Mammal Science* 3: 345-352.

RALLS, K. and BROWNELL, R.L. 1991. A whale of a new species. *Nature* **350:** 560.

REYES, J.C., MEAD, J.G. and VAN WAEREBEEK, K. 1991. A new species of beaked whale *Mesoplodon peruvianus* sp. n. (Cetacea, Ziphiidae) from Peru. *Marine Mammals Science* 7: 1-24.

_____ VAN WAEREBEEK, K., GARDENAS, J.C. and YANEZ, J.L. 1995. *Mesoplodon bahamondi* sp.n. (Cetacea, Ziphiidae), a new living beaked whale from the Juan Fernandez Archipelago, Chile. *Bolitin del Museo Nacional de Historia Natural de Chile* **45**: 31-44.

RICE, D.W. 1978. Beaked whales. IN HALEY, D. (ed) *Marine Mammals of the eastern North Pacific and Arctic waters.* Pacific Search Press (Seattle), pp. 88-95.

ANIMALS & MEN # 17

SHUKER, K.P.N. 1997. *From Flying Toads to Snakes With Wings.* Llewellyn Publications (St. Paul, Minnesota).

TIDEMANN, C.R. 1980. *Mesoplodon bowdoini* Andrews (Ziphiidae): a new whale record from New South Wales. *Victorian Naturalist* 97: 64-65.

VAN WAEREBEEK, K. 1996. New beaked whale off Chile. *Marine Mammal Society Newsletter* 4 (2): 3.

WATSON, L. 1988. *Whales of the World.* Hutchinson (London).

WATSON, L. 1988. *Whales of the World.* Hutchinson (London).

CLINTON'S COGITATIONS
by Clinton Keeling

Yes - Issue 16 of "Animals & Men" was belated, but only the churlish, insensitive and/or dim would dispute it was well-worth waiting for. Herewith random comments on it for your delight, edification or exasperation...

If a (seemingly) literate adult (p.6) cannot tell the difference between a Leopard and a Puma - "...what she believes may have been a Leopard or a Puma..." - I don't think any of their zoological statements need to be taken seriously, besides wasting our valuable time. I was most interested to read about the Tokoloshe on p.7, as although some declare it to be nothing more than a malignant spirit - something like the Scandinavian Troll - there are others who swear it's a flesh and blood hairy hominid, not unlike the Agogwe from further north, up Mozambique way.

Whatever it might or might not be, it plays such an important part in the live of so many Cape Africans that I was once told by an Afrikaans lawer that a native accused of quite serious crimes could probably be acquitted if he could convince the prosecution that he'd been told to do whatever it was a by Tokoloshe! And when it's borne in mind that this was a ruling dating from the old harsh days of apartheid it shows clearly how sincerely ingrained this aspect of Bantu folklore must be - and seemingly respected by others too.

Speaking for myself, I wouldn't leap a foot in the air in surprise if our old friend Australopithecus turned out to be at the bottom of it all...

Regarding "Lakeland BHM" (p.8) - forget it! In the highly unlikely event of your being taken in by it, the convincing sounding buildup, such as precise location, time, weather conditions and the like as this is easily done by any hoaxer in a few minutes if they are reasonably able with pen or typewriter.

I happen to know the area mentioned, and as the creature so carefully described is highly unlikely to be a result of the pure and immaculate conception, it's at least reasonable to suppose there are others of its large, conspicuous and singular-looking species shambling about there too. I don't think - as we used to say at school.

The only kind of person who would send dangerous muck of this sort to a newspaper is a) one sorely in need of psychiatric treatment (although as an ultra-reactionary I've not the slightest faith in it), or b) a pathological liar - which is more likely to be the case.

EDITORIAL NOTE:

I would agree with Clin that it is so highly unlikely as to be almost impossible that there is any FLESH AND BLOOD explanation for BHM sightings anywhere in the United Kingdom.

These `creatures` have been reported, however, for centuries and there must be some explanation for them. See the forthcoming paper by myself and Richard Freeman in *Fortean Studies Volume Five.*

ANIMALS & MEN # 17

COLUMN

Sorry, all noble and overworked members of the editorial staff, but interesting as they are I fail utterly to see how such articles as "But is It Art?" (p 10), "Who's Afraid Of the Big Bad.." (p.11), "Eastern Cougars" (pp.14-17) and all too many others, contrive to find their way into a publication specifically devoted to the study of <u>cryptozoology</u>. Perrhaps some kind person will take pity on me and explain matters.

EDITORIAL NOTE : essentially, whilst A&M is predominantly a magazine about Cryptozoology, it has always covered other aspects of the fortean universe whether because of their scientific interest or merely because they make me (and the gang) laugh.

I couldn't agree more with Graham Inglis that the new millenium (don't know about you, but I'm already sick of the sight and sound of that word) should really begin in 2001 - although I suppose the devotees of 2000 will argue that this would make the year neither one thing or the other... In short, the root of the trouble, or argument if you like, is the result of a monk named Dionysius Exiguus (Little Dionysius, Dionysius the Titch, Dionysius the Vertically Challenged) contriving to get hold of the wrong end of the stick back in the Sixth Century - but it's too long a story to attempt to go into here. Think yourselves lucky I've told you at least a bit of it!

Concerning the illustration of the Cat (ahem) on p.30 - offhand I'd suggest it's a Genet, which of course is one of the Viverrines. Interestingly, these were once kept to kill small rodents, like Cats (no - don't try to be funny, you know perfectly well what I mean), in various Mediterranean countries.

Regarding "Kent" coming from the Celtic word for "head" (pp.35-36), the word is Cainne (variously Cainn, Cann) and the origin of the Scots / Northumbrian "canny", meaning bright or perceptive or intelligent - literally "heady". "Kent" means "Land of the Canti" - a tribe of Celtic origin who may have been better endowed upstairs than most of the surrounding folk - or perhaps they weren't, with the appellation being bestowed ironically!

Ye ken (same root?), reading "A&M" does put the most esoteric information in the seeker after knowledge's way. you must agree...

On the same page Mr. Entertainment's cartoon forces me to the irreverent conclusion that he is badly in need of a few very simple lessons in elementary zoology - Camels are among the comparatively few mammals quite unable to swim.

EDITOR'S NOTE: Apologies all round are needed here. I am sure that Aberdeen's Mr Entertainment is perfectly aware that Camels can't swim; however, it wasn't him who drew the picture! I credited it to him by mistake, and it was actually by Dr Lars Thomas who meant it as an ironic illustration for his article about Moose in Lake Storjson a few issues ago...

p. 37 - and the paragraph about the Moon landing, back in 1969 when, you'll recall, the Americans just <u>had</u> to get there before the Russians did. I often wonder whether I'm the only person in the countxy who, from the word "go", has felt strongly that there isn't a scrap, shred, morsel or atom of <u>proof</u> - convincing as all the carefully set up "evidence" might be that Men has ever landed on the thing, or indeed got anywhere near it. I know I've upset more than one American on this issue, but "to thine own self be true". I once asked a colleague why he thought I might be the only doubter, when I'd have thought there'd have been many, to which he replied *"There you go, sounding your mouth off again: there are plenty of doubters, but most have the sense to keep that thing between the nose and the chin shut.'*

> **The editorial team of this magazine have done their best to ensure a smooth transition period to our new layout and format. However, there have been a few teething problems, and a few regular features, such as "Now that's what I call Crypto" and Mark North's cartoon are not in this issue. Be assured that they will be back as soon as possible.**
> **In the meantime, it's 11 pm at night, we're still working, still drinking white wine, and still listening to *The Clash*.**

ANIMALS & MEN # 17

I am reminded of what my headmaster wrote on my school leaving report: *"Must learn not to say what he thinks"*, while the form-master prophesised:

"One day this boy's tongue or pen or fists - or a combination thereof - will get him into very serious trouble".

which might surprise you....

****

I was interested to note the mention of the "Monster of Glamis" in the book reviews on p.4 as I've long been interested in this intriguing mystery. Forget the hairy egg shape; there's usually little or no smoke without fire and I've small doubt there's at least a sub-stratum of fact here. Particularly noteworthy is the "nearly limbless" bit, as this almost exactly describes the condition known as "phocomelia" (yes, it is from the same root as the generic name for certain seals) in which the rudimentary limbs (as per the Thalidomide cases) resemble flippers. It's said the "monster" lived to a great age, dying as comparatively recently as 1920 but most irritatingly I cannot find out who made this assertion, or gave the description. Surely some-one knows - or how did they get the information in the first place? In all seriousness, I feel this is interesting and important enough to justify an official commission to look properly into the matter - just as I do about the astounding, and seemingly authenticated, reports of "Spring Heeled Jack" during the last centuary. Regarding the "monster" I have a half-formed notion at the back of my mind that the Custodian of the Royal Archives at Windsor could shed some light on the matter - if he (or she in these crackpot days) had a mind or the permission to!

EDITOR'S NOTE (From our Files): Glamis Castle in Angus, which apart from being the ancestral home of the Queen Mother is also the site for one of Scotland's best known mystery humanoids; the monster of Glamis Castle. He is supposed to have been the hideously deformed heir to the Bowes-Lyon family who was, according to popular rumour, born in about 1800, and died as recently as 1921. He is supposed to look like *'an enormous flabby egg'*, having no neck and only minute arms and legs. His physical shortcomings are made up for by his immense physical strength, and according to some accounts his propensity for evil. There is a family `secret` concerning the monster, which is only told to the male heir of the Bowes-Lyon family when they attain majority. According to Peter Underwood, however: *"The present Lord Strathmore knows nothing about the monster, presumably because the creature was dead when he reached his majority, but he always felt that there was a corpse or coffin bricked up behind the walls".*

COLUMN

What's AFOOT

THE ANIMALS & MEN *"WHERE WE WENT AND WHAT WE DID"* COLUMN
EDITED AND COMPILED BY RICHARD FREEMAN

MYTHS AND MONSTERS: The Natural History Museum, London. 5th April 13th September, 1998.

After a cracking weekend at the Fortean Times Unconvention (described below by Nigel Wright), a

ANIMALS & MEN # 17 — COLUMN

visit to this exhibition was in order. The backbone of the exhibition is formed by six large anamatronic monsters, built by the Japanese company, Kokoro; who are responsible for many dinosaur exhibitions around the world.

The first one is the jewel in the crown a real showpiece. A 23 foot long green dragon with red wings stirs from its slumber, opening baleful red eyes at the visitor. The regally horned head, with its giant fangs has obviously been modelled on those at carnivorous dinosaurs. This is the finest model in the show; apart from its modest size, one could easily believe this was a real firedrake!! The accompanying text, however, falls far short of this magnificent mechanical reptile. The Museum play it ultra-safe and attempt to explain away dragons with such old chestnuts as monitor lizards, snakes, crocodilians and dinosaur bones. At the risk of being accused at narcissism, I would direct readers to my own article on dragons, (in issue 14 of 'Animals and Men') for a more in depth look at these most ancient of monsters.

Sadly, the quality of the other models do not even approach this dragon. For some odd reason, the visitor is compelled to view them through backlit muslin veils. Is this perhaps meant to make them look more mysterious? Why are the models displayed in this way? All that this achieves is to make looking at the models more difficult and extremely frustrating. The other creatures are a unicorn (narwhal and oryx are given as an explanation), cyclops (mastodon skulls), chimera (lion, serpent and goat haunted volcano!!), yeti (options kept open; Gigantopithecus, perhaps?), and an alien that looks like a cross between a Grey and a lizard man.

Apart from the dragon, the yeti stands out. It is 11 feet tall and is reconstructed as a giant bipedal, ground-dwelling orang-utan; which is what most people believe Gigantopithecus to be. Crunching on bamboo stalks, it makes a lifelike impression. Mermaids, kraken, lake and sea monsters are all tackled briefly and inadequately in the text. A small shop is situated close to the exit; which sells excellent bigfoot models.

It costs over £6 to get into the museum, but as well as the "Myths and Monsters" exhibition, the crypto-twitcher will find a whole host of other delights.

Britain's largest collection of dinosaurs is housed here; the sharp-eyed can also find a giant squid, ground sloths and a thylacine.

Far less fun is to be had in Bradford; where Cartwright Hall plays host to "The Unexplained, Part 2", a continuation of the exhibition at the National Museum of Film & Photography. Part 2 is by far inferior to part 1 (which was reviewed in the last issue). All this "exhibition" consists of is one room of photographs - all of which (bar one), I had seen before. They included unconvincing ectoplasm oozing from the mouths of mediums, a levitation (obviously someone jumping from a chair), the Cottingley Fairies, and some equally unconvincing fuzzy blobs also purporting to be pictures of fairfolk. In short, it was deeply and most profoundly crap! But what ot the one new photo? (Well, new to me). This was taken in 1995, at Traitor's Gate in the Tower ot London (Editor's Note - See the back cover of *Rum, Sodomy and the Lash* by The Pogues). It shows a black-sleeved hand, encased in a black glove, with a frilly, white cuff; which the photographer did not notice at the time. Rather than snapping a ghostly hand; I think that the person in question had been standing next to a Goth. Now did I visit Traitor's Gate in 1995?

ANIMALS & MEN # 17

A VIRGIN CONFERENCE-GOER BREAKS HIS DUCK!

a special report on the start of the conference season

by Nigel Wright

In thirty years of ufo interest, I had never attended a conference. This was the case until three weeks ago, when, much to my surprise and delight, Jon and Graham asked me to help out on our group stall, at the Dorchester UFO conference. And so it was, that on a rather dull and rainy day, I found myself sat in a crowded estate car, sharing the back seat with John's dog, Toby. (Thanks Toby; I'm still trying to get rid of the hairs!) On arriving at the venue, the corn exchange building, we spent the first half hour or so getting the stock for the stall out of the car, and setting the table up. The crew read the running order of lectures for the day, and picked out the ones each member wanted to listen to. A rota was then worked out, so that each person could hear what they wanted to.

The vast majority of stock that we were selling was cryptozoological in nature, and I must admit that I felt a bit of a fraud as I stood behind then stall, as the members of the public began to file in to the hallway, and took interest in our wares! As I prayed that no-one would ask me to complicated a question on the animal front, I was relieved when a young man asked me what my ideas were on the Roswell case. "I'm on my OWN ground!" was the first thing that went on in my mind!

And so, I found myself debating the finer points of this case, for twenty minutes or so, until Jon said I could go and look around the other stalls. During my wanderings I managed to have a very interesting talk with the writer Terry Walters. He struck me as a very sincere man, who really believes in his story. After this, I went on to have a talk with the English editor of "Nexus" magazine, Marcus Allen. It was then time for lunch, and, during this, I managed to glimpse the unmistakable form of Graham Birdsall, the founder and editor of *"UFO magazine"*. Chancing my luck, I stepped forward, and introduced myself. He turned out to

COLUMN

be a very pleasant man, and we talked about the wave of ufo activity over Exmouth, last year. Mr. Birdsall talked with me for about half an hour, then it was on with the business of selling wares from our stall.

Later on that day I managed to catch Mr. Birdsall's lecture, it contained some very interesting footage from Mexico which I found most convincing. The rest of the convention was spent selling goods on our stall and meeting various people from the UFO world. eventually, at about six p.m., we packed up and headed home for a well earned cup of tea...

The following Friday, and I was off again, this time to London for the annual UnConvention of the Fortean Times. This year it was held at the university of London, right in the centre of town.

We arrived at the venue late that night, and spent some two hours or so unloading stock and setting up our stall. It was then a trip out to the home of Emmet Sweeney, at Romford. He very kindly put us up for the two nights of the convention. Next morning, seven a. m., and we were off, across London to the venue. The doors opened at ten a.m., and the crowds rushed in. I have never seen so many people at one meeting!. So we had a very busy morning on the stall, and I was then off on my, by now usual, hunt for well-known faces.

Amongst my hunting trophies for that morning was a brief chat with Nick Pope. He struck me as a very strange man. Small in stature, he was surrounded by hangers-on, and thus was very hard to get to talk to properly. This was a great shame, because I particularly wanted to ask him a few questions about how a man who was still working for the government, could possibly be allowed to publish a book full of information from a highly placed government department, such as A52!! .Still, never mind: there is always next time! On day two, I managed to talk to Rev. Lionel Fanthorpe, of *Fortean T.V.* fame. He was a charming man, who's real life charm is every bit as nice as he appears on T.V.!

After our lunch, it was the turn of Colonel Blashford-Snell to be hooked by my one-man hunting expedition ! He was very polite and listened

ANIMALS & MEN # 17

to my points with great patience, before he had to go on with his book signing! The convention ended that night with a great party in the S.U. bar: here, our beloved leader Jon Downes really stood out as the fantastic party animal we all, who know him well, know him to be! I will not embarrass Jon with the details of his antics that night here - suffice to say that we who were there will never forget his glorious rendering of certain folk songs! Nice one Jon!

Weekend three, and this time the venue was to be Southend! At the magnificent hall, we went about the usual business of setting up the stall in the main approach to the lecturing centre. For me, the main coup of this particular weekend was that we shared our digs with Nick Redfern, the author of *"A Covert Agenda"*. Nick turned out to be a really great guy, and I'm glad to say that he and I have become mates since! He and I had several chats about the sightings over Exeter and Exmouth, in the 1950s, and he has promised to keep me informed of any papers that might pertain to these cases, that he finds. The other main event of the weekend was the first showing of new UFO footage from Lowestoft, filmed the end of last year. Now this film is really good - as good, in my personal assessment, as any from Mexico or Florida!

Then of the weekend: it was Jon and Graham's turn to speak. What followed can only be described as a truly enlightening experience! For a start, someone, I leave to your imagination to guess who, forgot to load the slides into the projector! Then both Jon and Graham took it in turns to explain the events of that memorable trip. At the end, they received a standing ovation, and then John performed a fantastic duet with the Rev. Lionel Fanthorpe. What a sight.

So, there you have it. My first convention xperience! Was it "good for me?", as the saying goes? Well, yes, it was: it really gave me the chance to hear and speak to so many of the main people in this business today. And, to be honest with you, it's hard work, but fantastic fun. Thanks Jon and Graham, and here's to the next!

P.S. Rule number One for all convention goers: never pack a Cortina estate with four or five hundredweight of stock - it handles like a pig!

LETTERS

LETTERS TO THE EDITOR

The Editor and his band of merry men welcome an exchange of correspondence on any subject of interest to readers of this magazine. We reserve the right to edit letters and would like to stress that opinions voiced are those of the individual correspondent rather than being necessarily those of the editorial team or the Centre for Fortean Zoology. Every attempt is made not to infringe anyone`s moral rights or copyright, and we apologise if we have unwittingly done so.

LAND WHERE THERE IS NO LAND......

Dear Jonathan

While I was on holiday in Salzburg in May I had the chance to finally read both "The Owlman & Others" and "The CFZ Yearbook 1998" (well, the weather wasn't that good), and I have a few

ANIMALS & MEN # 17   LETTERS

comments on the first and possibly a major issue arising from the second.

I should start by saying that I am a voracious reader with an encyclopaedic memory. This means that I can remember quotations and references with ease. I spotted one reference fairly quickly in *The Owlman*: on pages 211-212, you refer to Oscar Wilde devising a story about Jesus surviving the crucifixion and place this after his release from prison. I don't know if Eliman thus specifically dates the story, but if he does he is wrong. I read some years ago in one of Yeats's autobiographical pieces - I don't remember which one, but it was in the paperback selection of his prose published by Macmillan in the 60's - his account of visiting Wilde and finding a missionary consulting him on the colour of baptismal frocks; and when the missionary had gone Wilde said to Yeats, *"I have been inventing a Christian heresy,"* and told him the story which you quote. This belongs to the days of Wilde's respectability, before he went to prison.

Wilde had a wonderful attitude to religion. The story is that at Oxford, as part of his oral exam in Old Testament Greek, he had to translate the story of Christ's passion, and on being told to stop, replied, *"please let me go on. I want to see how it finishes."*)

The other thing I would say in respect of *The Owlman* is that at one point you commit, in my view, a literary libel. Your description of Daniel Mannix's *Those About to Die* (page 211) does not tally with my memory of the book - and I too read it in my early teens.

Mannix was exceptionally knowledgeable about the performing arts and wrote, in my view, an entertaining but solid account of the world of the Roman arena - a nastier place than modern circuses, but hardly recognisable from your description. Perhaps your Latin teacher was embellishing the text?

EDITOR'S NOTE: I would like to defend myself here, not as the Editor of this magazine but as the author of "The Owlman and Others". The passage to which Martin refers reads:

"When I was a first or second year pupil at grammar school in North Devon during the early 1970s, I went through a traumatic experience. I was in Latin class; and, for reasons best known to himself, the Latin teacher used to finish off every lesson by reading excerpts from a particularly gruesome book about the Roman arenas. He seemed, or so it appeared to me as an impressionable and admittedly rather immature twelve-year-old, that he took a salacious and almost perverted delight in reading descriptions of public crucifixions, burnings, disembowelments, dismemberments and ritual torture both of humans and animals to a class of about twenty small boys. I don't know what effect these stories had on the rest of the class, but they completely traumatised me, to such an extent that I feel very disturbed and upset even writing about it now, a quarter of a century later.

I started to investigate Phoenician mythology and found that there were links, many of them, to the subjects discussed in this book. They worshipped a corn deity, and more significantly sacrificed both animals and small children in horrific ways. I decided to dig deeper into the available literature on the subject, but found myself confronted with more and more graphic descriptions of ritual tortures, burnings and dismemberments on an enormous scale.~ My dreams, which had been relatively unfettered by visions of Owlmen, wizards and naked witches, became populated with ghastly visions of tortured children and I decided that here was where my research should end......"

My libel was perpetrated against my Latin teacher of a quarter of a century ago. I found the whole experience severely traumatic and indeed it is one which I still find difficult to write about. There is no doubt that Mannix wrote a well researched book, and I would not attempt to dispute it. However I did try to re-read it in recent years but still found it highly disturbing.

Anyway, getting to my real interest: the article on pages 35 to 47 of *The CFZ Yearbook* - I don't know where it comes from, but if you find out, please

- 39 -

ANIMALS & MEN # 17   LETTERS

please, please, please let me know); but I am fascinated by two sentences on page 38 which refer to:

"...the "great white whale" of the Greenland coasts, hunted for two centuries by the Scotch whalers, which they called Maby Dick, and regarded as the terror of the Arctic Sea. According to these mariners, it makes its appearance now at intervals; but is of so venerable an age that its body is completely covered by vegetation, algae, and marine mosses, in whose midst live attached to it, as to a rock, multitudes of shell-fish and polypi".

Now, by a fortean coincidence, while waiting at the Eurostar terminal to catch my train on the journey to Salzburg, I decided to buy some extra reading matter; and what book did I buy? None other than *Moby Dick*!

When I read that passage in the *Yearbook*, my first thought was that the author had lifted the legend from Melville.

Chronologically, it's feasible: *Moby Dick* was published in 1851, and the article is certainly later because it cites a publication of 1857-58 in the footnote on page 3.

However, there are two reasons to doubt that the author was simply cribbing from Melville:

• He (I guess in the mid-l9th century it would be a he) specifically attributes this whale to the Arctic Seas; Melville's was a Pacific whale (and a sperm whale to boot; Arctic whales were right whales).
• All the detail about the whale being covered in algae, etc, does not appear in Melville (though, if I recall correctly, some of it does in the John Huston film, which was scripted by Ray Bradbury).

I re-read *Moby Dick* on the journey back from Salzburg and confirmed that this was not a straightforward crib; and once back in London I consulted Harold Beaver's 1972 Penguin edition of *Moby Dick* and here things started to get really murky.

Beaver prints four sources for the *Moby Dick* story. One is Chase's narrative of how a sperm whale (non-white) rammed and sank the whaler *Essex* in 1820; the other three concern white whales. All three are sperm whales. More to the point, none is a first-hand story.

The white whale stories are, in chronological order:

• In his journal for February 19th 1834 Ralph Waldo Emerson (we're talking serious gossip here) records being told by a seaman of *"an old sperm whale which he called a white whale"* (interesting turn of phrase) *"which was known for many years by the whalemen as Old Tom"*. This whale's speciality was crushing the boats which attacked him; *"and he was finally taken somewhere off Payta Head by the Winslow or the Essex"* (the *Essex* which, you will recall was sunk by a whale in 1820).

• In 1837 Jules Lecomte published an account of a white sperm whale that was killed after a career of notoriety in 1828 by an unidentified Nantucket whaler. The story is that the captain of the *Oceania* offered his daughter in marriage to the harpooneer who killed the whale; the harpooneer in question turned out to be *"a tall Negro"* (but got the girl anyway). The whale was killed near the Falkland Islands.

• In 1839 J.N. Reynolds published *Mocha Dick or the White Whale of the Pacific*. This purports to be an account of an interview with the crew of the whaler *Penguin* at Mocha Island, which is situated *"upon the coast of Chili, in lat. 38.28 south, twenty leagues north of Mono del Bonifacio, and opposite the Imperial river, from which it bears w. s. w."*

Very precise; but I can find none of those names in my (admittedly not very large-scale) world atlas.

Accordingly to this account, Mocha Dick had haunted the island of Mocha since before 1810 (sperm whales, we now know, are very migratory). *"On the spermaceti whale, barnacles are rarely discovered; but upon the head of this lusus naturae, they had clustered, until it became absolutely rugged with shells"*. This version of the story had the *Penguin* kill Mocha Dick in the late 1830's.

• That story was published in *The Knickerbocker Magazine* in 1839; but in 1892 an article described the exploits of Mocha Dick from July 1840 to October 1842. Moreover, in 1846

- 40 -

ANIMALS & MEN # 17

Knickerbocker Magazine published another article on Mocha Dick which described him as *"a huge mountain-whale, that rises like an island every now and then from the bosom of the Pacific, trailing from his sides hundreds of slimy green ropes, that stream like "horrid hair" upon the waters"*.

So, what have we got? In chronological order, we have:

- the whaler *Essex* sunk by a non-white sperm whale in 1820 (as told by Owen Chase, who was on the ship at the time)
- a white sperm whale named Old Tom killed by the *Winslow* or the *Essex* some time before 1834 *(as* told to Emerson)
- an anonymous white sperm whale killed by a tall negro from Nantucket in 1828 (as told by Jules Lecomte, who was not there)
- a white sperm whale named Mocha Dick killed in the late 1830's by the anonymous mate of the *Penguin* (as told to J.N. Reynolds, who was not there and may not have been anywhere else)
- Mocha Dick surviving and wreaking havoc into the 1840's
- Hermann Melville's *Moby Dick* in 1851
- a whale (presumably a right whale) named Maby Dick who had, sometime after 1857-58, been around in the Arctic Seas for two hundred years or more (as recorded by anonymous, who got it from the Scotch whalers).

Put all these stories together, and you have a whale which is:

- definitely white
- almost certainly very old
- impossible to kill (reports of its death being consistently exaggerated)
- a sperm whale, except when it's a right whale
- found wherever there are whalers
- never actually reported by someone who has seen it.

What conclusion do I draw?

Well, on this limited evidence I am hesitant to reach a conclusion; but it looks to me as if the white whale is a nineteenth century whalers' foaf-

LETTERS

tale. Everybody's heard of it; no-one's ever seen it; and the harpooneer who's killed is always anonymous. If I am right, Herman Melville may have created the only major work of literature to be based on a foaf-tale. I probably need to do more research on this. The wisdom of doing so is questionable. As everybody knows, you never catch Moby Dick and look what happened to Captain Ahab. But never mind: having gone this far, I cannot not go further.

Call me Ishmael.

Martin F. Jenkins
London,

EDITOR`S NOTE: More discussion on this topic is welcomed. On the subject of semi-legendary cetacea does anyone have any knowledge of a famous dolphin called "Pelorus Jack" which once lived (I believe) near New Zealand?

Also, whilst on the subject of weird whales, Joan Aiken`s excellent children`s novel *"Night Birds on Nantucket"* features a PINK Sperm whale called "Rosy"....

FAIRY, MOTH OR WHATEVER

Dear Jon,

The individual who sent this to me is from Tennessee. Perhaps one of you entomology enthusiasts can provide an i.d.

"The insect that I saw was humming a song. I was on top of a hill and thought that I was hearing a radio or something like that but I noticed this little bug. The closer it got the more like a song it became. This little bug was flying upright like a ...fairy!

I was really excited because I thought what I saw was what people perhaps in earlier times might have mistaken for real sprites. This bug went from tree to tree and from flower to flower, stopping at each one.

I didn't see it eat anything - but, like I said, I was excited. It was about 2" tall and had blue eyes [which were] large almond shaped, and long antennae that hung like hair. It was really quite intriguing but as I moved to get a better look, it saw me and went

ANIMALS & MEN # 17

horizontal and was off like a shot. also the humming stopped when it saw me and it just buzzed away......

Adios. Chad Arment

INDIANA 'GATORS AND A WHALE

Thought I'd publish an account of some alligators, then the whale.

"Indianapolis Star, Dec 31, 1946" "Petersburg Lays Claim to Gator Killed Downstate"

Petersburg, Ind. Dec 30 - An alligator liberated in a government lake near here in 1900 is believed to be the one killed in Mariah Creek in Vincennes last week by two Pike County hunters, Ben Melvin and James Audear. It was recalled that a defunct road show in 1900 gave an alligator to John Eisert, an employe of the Petersburg Press, in payment for an advertising bill. Unable to sell the alligator, Eisert placed it in the lake where it remained until 1913 floodwaters carried down White River to the Wabash. There it apparently worked its way up the Wabsh and into Mariah Creek.

I think more than one 'gator is involved here

From an unnamed paper, same reigon (Knox County) paraphrased by my source

A alligator was said to be "cavorting" on Henery Deckers farm, in Decker township. (Note: There area is most likely the town of Decker, known as Deckers Chapple to some, and had several sasquatch sightings in late 70's, early 80's). Another farmer (Matthais Pickle) said the animal let a deep bass to the chorus of frogs.

It is unclear how familiar an Indiana farmer would have been with the groans of 'gators.

Whale time. This might be from Mt. Carmel, but it was listed with Knox County Folklore, no reference given. A possible clue was that the paper listed as the source was the "Western Sun". The 15 foot whale was seen in "Mauks Pond", which is possibly a medium sized lake. Could this whale be an Alligator? I think it was a newspaper hoax, maybe

REVIEWS

to counter the Sea Serpent report by another newspaper

Brad LaGrange

BOOK REVIEWS

The Owlman & Others

by Jonathan Downes.
(See back cover of this magazine for publisher and availability)

Guest reviewer Nick Redfern (author of *A Covert Agenda* and *The FBI Files*):

Although my profession is that of an author of books on the *somewhat* emotive subject of UFOs, only on seldom occasions have I ever reviewed *a* published work written by those with similar (or at least tangentially-connected) interests. In early 1998, however, a fascinating book caught my attention and prompted me to write my first book review in approximately a decade. Although my written output is indeed largely limited to the UFO controversy, I have a keen interest in an associated (or is it?) mystery - cryptozoology, and from an early age devoured the work of people such as Heuvelmans and Dinsdale.

One of my all time favourite books, however, was John Keel's *'The Mothman Prophecies.'* A dark and disturbing book, in which Keel chronicled the startling accounts of a number of people across the USA who had come into contact with a fearsome-looking beast dubbed 'Mothman' - primarily due to the fact that it appeared humanoid in shape; albeit with a pair of powerful-looking wings!

Coming across like a modern-day gargoyle, Mothman induced thoughts of horror and fascination in me when I read the book back in 1975 - at a mere ten years of

ANIMALS & MEN # 17

age! Indeed, I recall with fondness being castigated by one of my junior school teachers for reading such material when I should presumably have been followirig the exploits of the Secret Seven or the Famous Five! But now to the crux of the matter... Whilst Keel's book largely (although not entirely) dealt with sightings of Mothman within the confines of the USA, a very similar winged entity has been seen on a variety of occasions in the United Kingdom' That entity has become known in legend as 'Owlman'.

Indeed, references to Owlman have been reported in cryptozoological papers and manuscripts for a number of years; what was needed, however, was an in-depth, analytical look at the entire controversy. In 1998, that came to pass... I had for a number of years been aware of the work and written output of Jonathan Downes, and was delighted when in late 1997 Jon interviewed me for what was to be a first-class piece of work for 'Sightings' magazine in support of my book, *'A Covert Agenda'*.

In speaking with Jon, it transpired that we had many things in common (and most of them seemed to centre around wine, women and song!) and we thereafter became friends, liasing from time to time on matters of mutual interest. I was therefore most pleased when, in May 1998, I got to meet Jon in person when we both spoke before an audience at the Southend UFO Group's conference. The conference was a resounding success, and I was delighted to obtain a copy of Jon's then recently-released hook, *'The Owlman And Others.'*

I intended to sit down and read the book over the course of a few days; however, after having read the first couple of chapters, I found myself absorbed by its contents, and finished the book in one sitting.

But what does the book tell us? Quite simply, Jon presents us with a remarkable account of a series of incredible events which occurred in Cornwall in the blistering summer of 1976 (a year which, for me, was filled with scrumping, scrapping and thoughts of a certain girl in my class at school); events which centred around a series of sightings of the aforementioned Owlman.

REVIEWS

As Jon details with excellent clarity (not to mention a keen wit and fine story-weaving ability) the sightings of the elusive beast were nerve-wracking and awe-inspiring, to say the least. The book is filled with accounts of this particular winged phantom and its (his?) exploits in deepest and darkest Cornwall.

Whatever, Owlman was and still may be, Jon demolishes the notion that it was simply due to the misidentification of an everyday creature (such as an indigenous species of owl), and presents evidence of the presence in our midst of a truly creepy and darkly-evil creature which seems to take an inordinate amount of pleasure in scaring the living shit out of people whilst perching above them in trees like the godforsaken offspring between the devil himself and some mutated vulture!

To his credit, Jon works diligently to address the issue of whether or not the entire controversy was due to misperception and/or hoax; however, it is clear from Jon's exceptionally detailed investigations that such conclusions collapse upon carefully study. Moreover, Jon reveals that the sightings of Owlman only told part of the story: the book goes on to detail the many other bizarre events which were unfolding at the time in precisely the same vicinity, namely the sightings of sea monsters off the Cornish coast; the unusual activity of domestic and wild animals; and, most disturbing of all, the killing and mutilating of a number of animals under highly unusual circumstances.

In reading this particular aspect of Jon's book, I was fascinated to see that he had uncovered, a copious amount of data which had long been overlooked by previous investigators and which suggested that matters of both a serious and horrific nature were occurring throughout the Devon-Cornwall area in the late 1970's.

Certainly, sightings of man-like winged-entities; strange, sea beasts; shocking animal :nutilations; and remote areas of darkest Cornwall, all sound like the perfect ingredients for some long-gone 'Hammer' film; however, *"The Owlman And Others'* cannot be relegated to the realm of fiction.

It would be unfair of me to reveal Jon's conclusions on the entire affair; however, I found myself agreeing with his assertions and would implore anyone with even the remotest interest in reports of mystery beasts

ANIMALS & MEN # 17

roaming the wilds of Britain to secure a copy of Jon's book at the earliest opportunity. A must buy! And if you ever hear above you the beating of strange and powerful wings, tell Jon. He may put you in his next book!

RICHARD`S NOTE: *"HE LIKES OWLMAN, HE LIKES MORGAWR, HE LIKES WITCHES, HE LIKES SHIELS"*

Plants and Animals of The Gambia
by A.Barber and C.Moiser
(Plymouth College of Further Education)

An interesting little booklet for the travelling botanist or zoologist wishing more knowledge of the flora and fauna of this tiny West African country. Notes on all the major species and habitats to be found in The Gambia. This booklet (co-authored by our very own Chris Moiser) was originally produced to accompany the annual field trips to West Africa conducted by Chris and his colleagues at Plymouth College. One unfortunate ommission - no mention of Gambo (snigger). RICHARD F.

The Celtic Way - a long distance walk through Western Britain
by Val Saunders Evans
(Sigma Leisure)

Sigma leisure have produced a number of these invaluable little guide books but this one, with its slightly new-age and neo-pagan slant is really to be reccomended to students of folklore and weirdness along the Celtic Fringe. It not only tells you how to get to some of the most beautiful parts of the United Kingdom but also details some of the more obscure pieces of folklore (including much of interest to the Cryptozoologist and fortean).

An excellent little book and one which for only £9.99 we can recommend reasonably highly. JON D.

REVIEWS

WEB SITES
by GRAHAM INGLIS

The Internet is a dynamic (or even chaotic) entity: people can change servers and web addresses can be, as they say, subject to alteration.

Got a site that should be listed here? - tell us about it!

Our site -The CFZ - website address is
http://www.eclipse.co.uk/cfz
and now includes a news service and an embryonic picture gallery.

The English version of Michel Raynal's Virtual Institute of Cryptozoology service at
http://perso.wanadoo.fr/cryptozoo/welcome.htm
is now being developed - with text and pics

The news section on the Earthly Delights site at
http://www.planet13.co.uk/earthly/EarthlyDelights.htm
looks at Bodmin Moor: its terrestrial zodiac, big cats and celtic stones

Brian Goodwin's site at
http://freespace.virgin.net/brian.goodwin/index.htm
covers big cats, serpents, dragons, Nessie, and news from Fortean Cumbria

Ben Roesch's site is at
http://www.ncf.carleton.ca/~bz050/

Chas' Loch Ness site is at
http://website.lineone.net/~chas.sweeney/ness.htm

and includes an opportunity to get "Loch Ness in a bottle" - not the whole loch, however... only some of it.

- 44 -

ANIMALS & MEN # 17

PERIODICAL REVIEWS

by GRAHAM INGLIS

We welcome an exchange of publications with magazines swimming in the same ballpark as our good selves...

Bigfoot Record

Bigfoot Research Center, Apt F, 21 Benham St,, Bristol, CT 06010, USA.
A wealth of sightings, book reviews and information on the Sasquatch / Bigfoot entity, including reproductions of newspaper articles. The supposed photographs of the thing don't exactly carry conviction, however, due to degredation in the copying process.

Animal News

NAPAK, 57 Marlboro Ave, Goole, E. Yorks, DN14 6JB. A5 magazine: 22pp.
NAPAK aims to present a united and informed front to prevent unreasonably restrictive "anti-keeping" legis-lation , and to educate the public in animal keeping.

Dead of Night

Lee Walker, 156 Bolton Road East, New Ferry, Merseyside, L62 4RY. A4 60pp £2
"Animals & Men" is a magazine of *fortean* zoology, rather than the narrower field of *crypto*zoology. "Dead of Night" covers fortean matters right across the board, such as ghost stories, conspiracy theories, strange news, UFOs, and religious / ritualistic / cultist / bizarre behaviour. And fortean zoology of course.

REVIEWS

Merseyside's "only publication dealing with all paranormal phenomena" is a very entertaining and substantial read.

Parascience

Domra, 65 Constable Rd, Corby, Northants, NN18 0RT. £2.50 A5. 42pp. Issue 1 - Autumn 1998.
Articles from the fringes of science. Issue 1's subjects include thoughtforms "psychodemiurgics"!), dowsing, Velikovsky's Comet, mystery animals in south-west England, and the much-maligned (or sometimes just cribbed) work of Nikola Telsa who researched unconventional means of propagating energy through the atmosphere. A good and very interesting read.

Cryptozoologia

Belge Protection des Animaux, Sq de Latins, 49/4 B-1050 Bruxelles, Belgium. A4 16pp
French mag with a contribution team including Michel Raynal, Franois de Sarre and Dr Lara Palmeros.

Herp Life

Karen Tucker, 14 Shrubbery Close, Barnstaple, Devon, EX32 9DG. 4-Sided (2pp) newsletter of the South-Western Herpetological Soc., England.

Mainly About Animals

13 Pound Place, Shalford, Guildford, Surrey, GU4 8HH. A5. 4 per year costs £5 in UK.
Clinton Keeling is never shy of expressing a strong opinion and this magazine has the gravitas one might expect when edited by the sort of man who'd probably abhor the mixed metaphor near the top of this page.

How do gulls decide to spend their day? Why do so many domestic dogs walk "off-square"? The July issue delves into these matters, and also includes pieces on the Bali tiger, tree monitor lizards, and zoological news.

- 45 -

Animals & Men Collected Editions Volume 4   New Horizons

ANIMALS & MEN # 17

ANIMALS & MEN
BACK ISSUES: £2 each

Back issues are available from the editorial address. Please see "methods of payment" on p.47.

CONTENTS (all issues also contain news pages, reviews and letters) :

1 Relict Pine Martens, Giant Sloths, Sumatran and Javan Rhinos, Golden Frogs, Frog Falls.
2 Mystery bears in Oxford and The Atlas Mountains, Loch Ness reports, Green Lizards, Woodwose, The Tatzelwurm.
3 Giant Worm in Eastbourne, Lake Monsters of New Guinea, Giant Lizards in Papua, Mystery Cats, Black Dogs on Dartmoor, Scorpion Mystery.
4 Manatees of St Helena, Migo: The Lake Monster of New Britain, The search for the Tasmanian Thylacine.
5 Mystery cats, Loch Ness, More on the "Migo Video", Boars and Pumas, The Hairy Hands of Dartmoor.
6 The Owlman Special; also the Humped Elephants of Nepal, Mystery Cats, Sabre-toothed cats, Mysterious hominids of Africa, The British Nandi Bear?, Bibliography of Cryptozoology books part 1 (by Dr Karl Shuker).
7 Mystery Whales, Strangeness in Scotland, On collecting a cryptid, Bodmin Leopard Skull, Shuker's Cryptozoological Bibliography pt 2.
8 Green Cats and Dogs, Mystery Whales, Quagga Project, Bibliography of Cryptozoological books (3rd & concluding part), Malayan Man Beast.
9 Hong Kong Tiger, Horseman of Lincolnshire, Scottish BHM, Congo Peacock, Mystery Whales.
10 Mystery Moth of Madagascar, Bengal Leopard Cats, The Derry, Wild Boars in Kent, a new Irish lake monster, mystery whales and the truth about the Essex Beach Corpses.
11 The "Walruses Special", also: Feathered Dinosaurs, Ground Sloth Survival in North America, Mystery Whales, Initial Bipedalism.
12 Lions: The Barbary Lion, etc. More Feathered Dinosaurs, Chinese Crabs in the Thames, Mystery Animals of Germany, News from New Zealand.

13 Pangolins; also Moby the Sperm Whale, Barking Beast of Bath, Yorkshire ABCs, Molly the Singing Oyster, Leatherback Turtles, Walruses.
14 The Dragons of Yorkshire, Irish mystery animals, In Search Of "Gambo", Charlie Fort and the Vampire Sheep Slayer - and Jackals; and the first of Clinton's Cogitations (Clin Keeling looks back on and comments on the previous issue).
15 Lake Dakataua "Migo" monster update, The Weird Warbling Whatsit of the Westcountry, The Beast of Llangurig, The Waspman, The Bigfoot "Murders", and three articles on Beavers.
16 Expedition Report: The Search for the Chupacabra; Quagga Project update; Bestiary #1 (by Ade Dimmick); Snakes with Legs; Eastern Cougars; Giant Lizards in the English Countryside? (Darren Naish)

BACK ISSUES

THE GOBLIN UNIVERSE
BACK ISSUES: £2 each

Back issues are available from the editorial address. Please see "methods of payment" on p.47.

CONTENTS (all issues also contain news pages, letters, and record, magazine and book reviews) :

Issues 1-3 were freebies brought out mainly to publicise the activities of a band called The Amphibians from Outer Space. They also contained dodgy poems about postmen. They are no longer available

4 St Neot: Weirdest Village in the West? Naked witches, hellhounds and Capel's tomb. The Vampire of St Leonards (Exeter). Cattle Mutilation. Psychic Detectives.
5 Crop Circles & Animal Mutilations. Ghosts of Glamis Castle. Communication with UFOs,. The "nooshpere" / text semantics.
6 Jon and Tina are shown the Rendlesham UFO crash site in Suffolk. Mystery Planets (Karl Shuker). Cannibalism in Scotland. Create your own country.

Animals & Men Collected Editions Volume 4 **New Horizons**

ANIMALS & MEN # 17

THE CFZ YEARBOOK 1998

edited by
Jonathan Downes & Graham Inglis

200pp. £12.50

Published by and available from the CFZ

Contributors:

Tom: Anderson, Neil Arnold, Richard Freeman, Mike Grayson, Martin Jenkins, Roy Kerridge, Chris Moiser, Nick Molloy, Richard Muirhead, Darren Naish, Michael Playfair, and Emmet J. Sweeney.

Subjects:

Giant crocodiles, cryptozoological films, African Stories, Nessie - asking the right questions, Nessie - diary of a hunt, Ichthyosaur evolution, Mammoths and the Comet, Sea Serpents, Amerindian icons, Strange Snake stories, an alphabetical guide to water monsters, the Fortean Fauna of Percy Fawcett, and The Zambesi River God.

THE OWLMAN AND OTHERS

by Jonathan Downes

NEW UPDATED EDITION

See back cover of this issue for more information...

and p.42 for an independent review of the book, by NICK REDFERN.

OUR OWN PUBLICATIONS

MORGAWR:
THE MONSTER OF FALMOUTH BAY

by
A. Mawnan-Peller

HOW TO ORDER and METHODS OF PAYMENT

Subscription rates INCLUDE postage. On other orders, postage and packing is extra: please add 25p (£0.30non-UK) per magazine and 75p (£0.90 non-UK) per book.

Payment can be made in UK cash, by IMO (an international money order), Eurocheque, or by a cheque drawn on a UK bank. Please make all cheques payable to Jonathan Downes.

Please send all orders to

CFZ, 15 Holne Court, Exwick, Exeter, Devon, EX4 2NA, England.

Britain is one of the few countries of the world where US dollars do **not** circulate. If making payment in US$ then please add $14 to cover the currency exchange fee.

As explained in the editorial on page 3, for various reasons there have been problems or delays with the mailouts of some books and magazines. These problems should be sorted by the time you read this...

With a new introduction by Tony Shiels, this booklet is available for £1.50 from the CFZ.

by
Jonathan Downes

£12.95 from
Domra Publications, 65 Constable Road, Corby, Northants.

"Anomalist" award winner 1997

ISSN 1354 0637   TYPESET BY THE CHEEKY COCKNEY CULTISTS

"My Old Man said Worship Great Cthullu"

Issue 18

Christmas 1998

This issue was important from a historical point of view, because it was the first edition to be published after Richard F came down to Exeter to join the CFZ full time in the summer of 1998. It took a long time to produce, because I spent much of the intervening months writing *The Rising of the Moon* for Domra publications. As you can see from the typographic quality, we were beginning to learn what we were doing, but there was still a long way to go. One of the features of these early publications was a long, rambling and often vicious column by veteran zoologist Clinton Keeling. I found out afterwards that `Clinton's Cogitations` appeared in several different magazines, where he would use the space allotted to him to praise, or condemn bits of the previous issue that had moved him for good or ill. I was only in my late thirties at the time, and in awe of Clin, so I put up with it for far longer than I should have. It is certainly not something that I would accept now..

Animals & Men Collected Editions Volume 4 　　　　　　　New Horizons

Animals & Men

The Journal of the Centre for Fortean Zoology

The Mysterious Lamprey of Puerto Rico

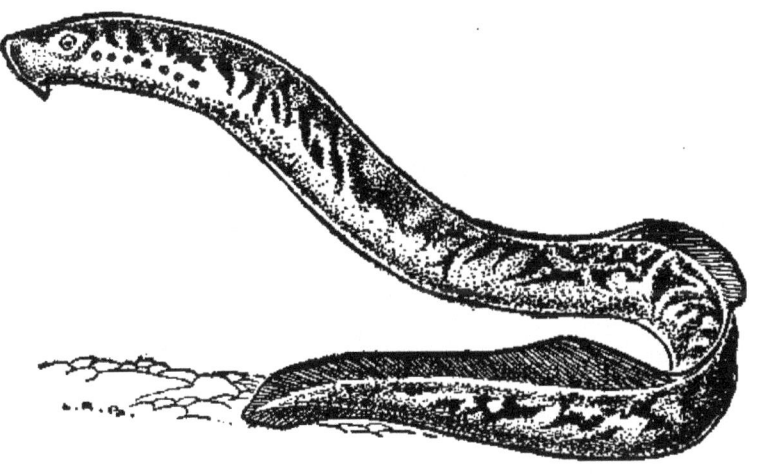

GUST '98 expedition report; out of place animals in Kent; mystery sharks; the wolverine "strikes back".......

Issue 18 　　　　　　　　　　　£2.00

Animals & Men Collected Editions Volume 4 — New Horizons

ANIMALS & MEN # 18

WHO'S WHO & WHAT'S WHAT

THE CURRENT CREW OF THE CFZ MOTHERSHIP ARE:

Director: Jonathan Downes
Deputy Director: Graham Inglis
Assistant Editor: Richard Freeman
Toby the CFZ dog
Magazine cartoonist and artwork: Mark North
Newsagent from nowhere: Richard Muirhead
Maxine Pearson: "blondes have more fun."
Paranormal research: Gill Bennett
Associate founding editor: Jan Williams
Tour Manager: Nigel Wright
Hedge-Witch: Joyce Howarth

CONSULTANTS
Consulting Editor: Dr Bernard Heuvelmans
Cryptozoology: Dr Karl Shuker, Dr Lars Thomas, Loren Coleman
Zoology: Clinton Keeling, Chris Moiser
Cetology and Palaentology: Darren Naish

REGIONAL REPRESENTATIVES
Scotland: Tom Anderson
Surrey: Nick Smith
Somerset: Dave McNally
West Midlands: Dr Karl Shuker
Kent: Neil Arnold
Sussex: Sally Parsons
Gtr Manchester & Cheshire: A E Munro
Hampshire: Darren Naish
Leicestershire: Alistair Curzon
Cumbria: Brian Goodwin
Yorkshire: Steve Jones
Tyneside: Simon Elsdon

USA: Loren Coleman
Denmark: Dr Lars Thomas, Erik Sorensen
Republic of Ireland: Daev Walsh
Spain: Alberto Lopez Acha, Angel Morant Fores
Germany: Hermann Reichenbach, Wolfgang Schmidt
France: Francois de Sarre
Mexico: Dr R A Lara Palmeros
Canada: Ben Roesch

"In her abnormalities, nature reveals her secrets"
(Goethe)

CONTENTS:

3 Editorial
4 Newsfile

17 GUBU Norge: The G.U.S.T. Expedition, by Daev Walsh.
22 The Return of *Gulo gulo*, by Terry Hooper
24 Cryptozoological Sharks, by Allan Munro
26 The Mysterious Puerto Rican Lamprey, by Jonathan Downes
29 Equus Wild and Brown, by David Barnaby
32 Putting in an Appearance, by Neil Arnold

34 Clinton's Cogitations, by Clinton Keeling
36 Letters
40 What's Afoot? - by Richard Freeman

42 Reviews: books, websites, periodicals
44 Cartoon - by Mark North
46 Back issues and CFZ publications

ANIMALS & MEN

CFZ, 15 Holne Court, Exwick, Exeter,
Devon, EX4 2NA, England

http://www.eclipse.co.uk/cfz

SUBSCRIPTIONS:

For a 4-issue (one year) subscription:
£8 UK   £9 EC
£14 US/Canada/Oz/NZ (airmail)
£15 Rest of World.

Please see METHODS OF PAYMENT on p47

ANIMALS & MEN # 18
THE GREAT DAYS OF ZOOLOGY ARE NOT DONE...

Dear Friends,

Welcome to another issue, and the end of another year. It has been a momentous year for all at The CFZ for a number of reasons, and I am sure that next year will also have its fair share of triumphs and disasters. That is what life, and especially the tiny microcosm of life that is The Centre for Fortean Zoology is all about.

The keen eyed amongst you will notice that the cover of this issue ain't in colour. This is simply because although we now have the facilities to print in colour, there is no real point in doing so unless we have a suitable pic for the front cover. We do not want to use colour printing merely as a gimic to sell more copies of the magazine. When there is something deserving of being immortalised in colour, believe me, we shall do so.

What would an editorial of this fine publication be without an apology? This ish is no exception. On October 31st our friend and colleague Darren Naish got married. The three core members of the CFZ posse were invited to the ceremony and to the meal afterwards, and we were drivingt happily towards Southampton when the trusty CFZmobile broke down and we had to be towed home with our figurative tails between our legs.

Although we made our excuses via the telephone we have not, until now, been able to present our apologies in an acceptable form, so here goes:

Darren and Toni. All three of us are greatly sad that we missed your big day, and we all wish you all the best for your life together - a sentiment that I'm sure will be echoed by your many friends and admirers within the fortean, cryptozoological and palaentological communities.

EDITORIAL

On a different note - the 1999 CFZ Yearbook is now complete and will be available in mid January priced £10.75 (including p&p). Those people who have an outstanding order for one of the Doc Shiels books which we were due to publish during 1997 or one of the new books from American publishers that we are no longer able to supply will get a free copy.

For some reason Richard Freeman has an ongoing fascination with depicting my in various crypto-zoological poses with my long suffering girlfriend in the role of my hapless victim. Gawd knows why, but this ish I am King Kong and the Divine Ms M is Fay Wray - It seems appropriate somehow...

All things being equal we will have taken delivery of our new laser printer within the next week or so, and although the next issue of A&M will not be until the spring, due to filming committments, we shall be resuming normal service again as of April.

Until then, our best wishes for Christmas and the New Year, from all at the CFZ

Jonathan Downes

NEWSFILE
Compiled and edited by Graham Inglis

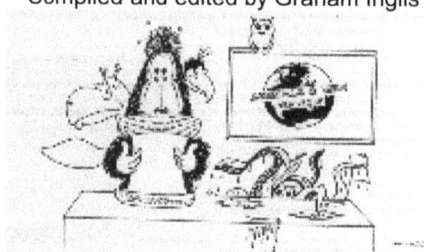

REINTRODUCTIONS

SCOTLAND AWAITS THE BEAVER'S RETURN

The prospect of the beaver again being seen on the backwaters of Scotland's rivers increased yesterday with a declaration of support from the WWF (World Wide Fund for Nature) - a body closely involved in the hefty rodent's successful reintroduction elsewhere in Europe.

Hunted to extinction in the British Isles more than 400 years ago, the beaver has become the favoured candidate of those who want to turn back the wilderness clock in Scotland. However, not everyone is happy with the idea of the beaver's return. Anglers in particular think the dam-building creature could be the last straw for salmon populations already seriously depleted on many rivers.

WWF, in its submission, says there is abundant scientific evidence that the beaver can help improve the conservation value of sites. The otter, water vole, trout and salmon can all benefit from beavers' coppiceing of trees, small-scale dam building and grazing of aquatic vegetation. It generally only builds dams when suitable river bank sites have been used up - to keep the water level above the entrance to its lodge home - and even then the dams are only about 12-18in high, and easily jumped by a salmon.

Beavers weigh up to 20kg and each one is estimated to fell two tons of timber a year in its hunt for food - the bark of birches and aspens in winter, and grass, herbs and shrubs in summer. - *The Independent - 14 July 1998*

ORANG-UTANG RE-RELEASE

Thirty-six orang-utans rescued from devastating forest fires last year have been released back into the wild.

NEWSFILE

Workers at a primate refuge center said they reintroduced the apes into unburned jungle habitat in East Kalimantan province. The orang-utans were flown in from a refuge, said veterinarian Amir Ma'arif. The apes were brought to the refugee over several months last year after fires forced them to flee their old habitats. About 1.2 million acres of forest were burned by the fires. The number of orang-utans living in Borneo has dwindled from an estimated high of 20,000 to around 2,000 because much of their habitat has been destroyed by development and fires. - *A.P. 20-9-98*

EURO-BISON

European bison could be soon back in the English countryside, 400 years after they died out. Biologists believe the 1,800lb, 6ft high animal could be used to clear scrub and undergrowth, recreating a more 'natural' flora. Unlike its American cousin, a separate species, the European bison tends to browse rather than graze. It is mainly found in the wild in forests on the Poland-Russia border.

Simon Wakefield from Marwell Zoo, near Winchester, Hants, said: 'One problem we do have is that bison are considered dangerous under the Dangerous Wild Animals Act and you can only put them in places where they do not come into contact with the public.' The final decision will rest with local authorities, who are likely to be wary. In Yellowstone, the American national park, bison roam free but tourists who have approached too close have often been gored.

CONSERVATION

TROUSER SNAKES THREATEN AUSSIE WILDLIFE.

Smuggled green pythons intercepted at Cairns airport in May were carrying a new virus that may have had the

Animals & Men # 18

potential to devastate Australia's native reptiles, fish and amphibians. The 10 smuggled snakes were being brought into the country hidden in a man's trousers. After two died, scientists isolated a virus from both snakes that belongs to a group of viruses that cause disease in Australian fish and amphibians. 'It's possible that this virus, which hasn't been identified in Australia before, could have seriously affected Australia's valuable aqua culture industry as well as our wildlife,' said Dr Deborah Middleton.

PEREGRINE FALCON

Peregrine falcons, under US federal protection for 8 years, "are back": 1,600 pairs are in the country and may even come off the endangered list. Since the American alligator was the first to be removed from the endangered list in the late 1970s, only six other species have recovered enough to be taken off. Peregrines would be the first recovered species to be removed since the gray whale and Arctic peregrine falcon in 1994. - *St. Louis Post-Dispatch, Sep 1998*

POOL FROG

The pool frogs of Norfolk may be a British species with a lineage back to the Ice Age. It is about the size of a common frog but has bronze colouring on its back and gold or green eyes. Only one specimen, a male, is known to survive and he is under guard at a secret location in Norfolk. Nine closely-related female frogs has been flown from Sweden to Britain in an attempt to save him from being the last of his line - to 'back breed' the offspring to get back to almost pure British stock.

"PROTECTIVE ACTIONS" ROUNDUP:

Oregon coastal coho salmon - to be US-listed as a threatened species.
Texas Prairie Dogs - might be US-listed, to the incredulity of some ranchers.
Turtle eggs: 5 arrests and 26,000 turtle eggs siezed in Oaxaca, Mexico.
Koala: U.S. proposes listing, citing habitat destruction as the primary threat to this Australian icon.
Condor - 9 raised in captivity in Idaho will be released in Utah.
Hawaii's bottom fish (red onaga, ehu and opakapaka) population is reportedly on the verge of collapse due to over-fishing.

NEWSFILE

Panda - Cheng Cheng, 13, has given birth to twins in a Chinese breeding centre. Only 1,000 pandas are believed to be left in the wild.
Brown Bear - Autumn (fall) hunt in Kenai, Alaska was cancelled for 4th year running because too many females were killed in the Spring hunt. Black Bear: Vermont numbers rise to 3,000 after fall hunting season "adjusted".

TIGER FEET

WWF slams Japanese TV cookery show for cooking tiger meat: Three Japanese entertainment personalities shown dining on the tiger at a restaurant in Shanghai described the meal as delicious and showed no remorse when they learned what they were eating.

ALLIGATORS AND CROCODILES

FLORIDA CROC

A llicensed alligator hunter may have broken Florida's record for the largest alligator caught. This gator is close to 14-feet long, and weighs-in at more than 1,000 pounds. On Tuesday, someone turned him in to a licensed processor who plans to make leather goods out of the gator's hide. Alligators may only be harvested during very limited, control led hunts. If someone is lucky enough to win one of 500 annual alligator hunting permits issued through a lottery, and then actually capture an alligator, it has to be turned over to a State-licensed alligator 'processor' who prepares the skins for sale.

Today, alligators are classified as a *threatened* species because of their similarity in appearance to the American Crocodile, an *endangered* species. Prior to their legal protection, alligators were sold in pet stores & souvenirs shops as novelty items. - *A.P. 18 Sep 98*

CROC TAMER DEATH

Thailand's famed crocodile hunter and tamer, Yuen, has died of lung disease at the age of 84. Hundreds of thousands of tourists had witnessed his shows since

ANIMALS & MEN # 18

he began performing in 1973. He thrust his head inside a crocodile's jaws in each act. - *A.P.*

NEW YORK SEWER ALLIGATORS ARE ON ENDANGERED ANIMALS LIST!

Florida alligators that wound up in the sewers hereafter being flushed down toilets as babies are dying out, experts say. The large reptiles - which were brought back by vacationers in the 1960's - have been having difficulty reproducing in New York's sewer system, an increasingly hostile environment.

Alligators like to nest in mounds of decaying vegetation exposed to the sun, and this is impossible beneath the city streets, according to zoologists. The sewer gators have also been falling victim to disease. In the wild, their ancestors basked in the sun and this helped control parasites.

Another problem: Rising levels of sewer gas, hydrogen sulphide and volatile industrial chemicals have made survival for second- and third-generation 'gators difficult. 'Alligators and even rats would have difficulty surviving in New York's sewers today,' said a leading herpetologist. 'I very much doubt that there are more than 20 alligators left.' *"Weekly World News", 29 Sept. 1998*

Following this 'news item', Loren Coleman commented on the Internet: "I see this tabloid is having fun at the expense of facts again. The sewer alligators, which really date from the 1930s, not the 1960s as per this 'article', probably died out long ago. Much enjoyment in seeing this piece of the lore..."

THE IMPORTANCE OF BEING ERNEST..

A San Francisco woman called the Animal Care and Control Center to complain that an iguana was 'staring' at her cat. The officer who responded to the call discovered the lizard was a 3½-foot-long crocodile. Capt. Guldbech said a man called the Center claiming to be the owner of the 6-year-old crocodile, named Ernest. The man said Ernest disappeared a few weeks ago during moving home. The man refused to give his name and has not collected the animal - because owning a crocodile is illegal, punishable by up to six months in jail.

CROCODILES SURPRISE TOURISTS.

Two stray crocodiles caught bathers by surprise in Guadalajara, a Mexican seaside resort: they crawled out of a river onto a beach and took a swim in the ocean, officials said. About a meter (3 ft) in length, the reptiles sent beachgoers fleeing and provoked a major hunt by authorities. They later returned to the river. - *27 August 1998 Reuters*

OUT OF PLACE

MINK STINK

Thousands of mink caused havoc in Finland after they were released from a fur-farm. No one immediately claimed responsibility, but police believe that animal rights activists were behind the action. 'Many of the freed minks were run over by cars or killed each other because they are predatory animals even though they have lived in captivity,' said Police Chief Inspector Rune Swahn. 'Many will also disturb the wildlife in the forests and many won't survive because they are used to being fed.' - *A.P. Sept 9, 1998*

RAPA WHELK

Marine scientists have concluded that a type of predator sea snail that was accidentally dumped into the Chesapeake Bay, Virginia, is breeding and is more widespread than expected. The veined rapa whelk,

ANIMALS & MEN # 18

native to the Sea of Japan, is considered a threat to native shellfish. It has been found at 19 locations. - *USA Today 23-9-98*

EMU RUNS WITH CATTLE

Home, home on the range, where the deer and the emu play. - Emu?

Edward Hastings and his sister were repairing a water tank last week when their cattle plodded into the field with an odd escort - an emu.

The five foot tall (1.5 meter), 100-pound (45 kg) flightless Australian bird ran to them for water. 'It was pretty strange seeing this emu running with our cows,' said Hasting's sister, Roberta Schuchard. 'He was crazy that day.'

Since then the emu has spent its time peacefully eating grass and roaming between Hastings' pasture and a neighbour's. Hastings checks in on the bird daily while harvesting.

Ms.Schuchard said she doesn't know of anyone in the area who own emus or similar-looking ostriches. She called the sheriff's office Friday in hopes of finding the owner. 'It wasn't a nuisance or anything. The cows aren't too upset about it,' she said. 'But if it were my animal, I'd want somebody to turn it in.'

Ted Funyak, a county animal control officer, planned to capture the emu and take it to a local ostrich farm until someone claims it.

'It's not going anywhere right now,' he said. 'It just wanders right up to you, but whether it'll do that when we grab it will be another story,' he said. - *Montana (USA) 28-8-98*

Other stories on the CFZ website or in the CFZ newsletter:

Rare Mexican Gray Wolf Pup Seen in Arizona - A.P., Phoenix, 18 July 1998
Chicago: new infestation of the Asian long-horned beetle has been found in. 3-8-98
Red fire ant, a bane of agriculture, has been spotted in New Mexico. 4-8-98

NEWSFILE

Nematodes (microscopic worms) found in Kentucky water supply, triggering a boil-water alert. 11-9-98

Chipmunks get loose at Hong Kong Airport: one woman scratched. - Sep 98

Stingrays attack 100 beachgoers in Florida after being driven to shore by hurricane - Oct 98

Minnesota (US) and Frankfurt (Germany) on alert for escaped kangaroos - 8-9-98

Hawaii Mobilises Against Brown Tree Snake - an "environmental enemy" - 24-7-98

GREY WOLVES

Biologists who spied a pair of Mexican grey wolves wandering a remote Arizona national forest got a pleasant surprise when they took a closer look. 'They saw two wolves emerge from some trees with a puffball following them,' said Wendy Brown, a wolf recovery biologist for the U.S. Fish and Wildlife Service in Albuquerque, New. Mexico.

The puffball was a pup, apparently the first born to gray wolves in the wild to survive for any real length of time in nearly 50 years. 'The parents crossed a creek, but the pup stopped and whined,' Brown said. 'Then the parents coaxed it across.'

The pup, which was spotted in the Apache-Sitgreaves National Forest, is believed to be 9 to 11 weeks old and about 20 pounds. The news came only two days after backers of the wolf reintroduction effort said they had given up hope that any of the pups born this spring had survived. The last Mexican gray wolf seen in the wild was shot to death near Alpine, Texas, in 1970. They had been all but gone from the area since about 1950, many of them killed by ranchers who saw them as a threat to livestock.
A U.S.-Mexican captive breeding program has brought their numbers to about 175. - *(Associated Press 18 July 1998)*

Animals & Men # 18

ATTACKS, EPIDEMICS AND ANOMALOUS DEATHS

newsfile

SCORPIO RISING

Scorpions are the fourth major cause of death in Iran's southern province of Khuzestan, the daily newspaper Q'ods reported on Saturday. Quoting a report by state veterinary researchers, it said that after respiratory, infectious and digestive diseases, scorpions cause the greatest number of deaths in this humid, oil-rich province. The report did not give any figures on those killed, but said some 25,000 people were treated for scorpion stings in Khuzestan every year, adding that some 60 different varieties of the deadly arachnid could be found in Iran. 'Population growth and urban development have brought the residents in closer contact with scorpions,' the report said. - *8-8-98 Reuters*

THREE DIE AFTER ATTACK BY RABID BATS IN MEXICO

Rabid bats have prompted a health alert in northern Mexico's scenic Copper Canyon, where three people have died from bat bites and eight others recently were attacked. A 40-year-old Tarahumara Indian man and his two teen-age sons died after a group of bats attacked them while they slept in the village of Batopilas, a popular tourist stop.

The deaths occurred two months ago, but Mexico City health officials couldn't confirm the cause was rabies-induced encephalitis until now, newspapers reported Friday. Bats attacked eight other people last month. - *A.P. Oct 2, 1998*

TOXIC MICROBE

Researchers reported the first scientific evidence of a human health threat from a toxic microbe that has killed millions of fish along the U.S. East Coast, saying it was responsible for a new neurological syndrome.

Maryland researchers blamed the single-cell microorganism Pfiesteria piscicida for problems discovered among 24 people exposed to contaminated water on Chesapeake Bay's Eastern shore last year. The syndrome, though temporary, was marked by several disturbing symptoms including impaired memory, disorientation and learning difficulties.

Operators of so-called factory farms, which raise poultry and other animals, have come under fire from environmentalists who say nitrate-rich runoff from the huge operations has allowed Pfiesteria to flourish.

BEARS

Montana - Increased grizzly bear sightings suggest the bears are expanding out of the Bob Marshall and Scapegoat wilderness range, officials say. Bears are being seen about five miles south of previous boundaries. People are calling for officials to hire a bear specialist. - *Aug 4, 1998 - USA Today*

TIGER

A rare white Bengal tiger being walked on a leash in Florida killed its trainer after it was startled by construction workers. - *A.P. 8-10-98*

PET PYTHON PUTS THE SQUEEZE ON HER OWNER

A 260-pound Burmese python was shot three times with a shotgun and beheaded after ripping a toilet out of the floor and trying to swallow her American owner.

When police arrived at Christopher Paquin's home, Squeeze, his 19-foot pet snake, was coiled around the 27-year-old with her jaws locked around his forearm. 'I was calm until I couldn't get her off me, ' Paquin said. 'Once she got down to the bone it really started hurting.'

Paquin's rescuers finally separated man from beast. Officials stunned the snake by spraying it with a fire extinguisher and then shot it three times with a shotgun. 'The damn thing was still moving, ' said Paquin. His hand, which now features 35 snake-tooth marks, is in a cast.

ANIMALS & MEN # 18

NEWSFILE

The snake was loose because Paquin was cleaning its cage. When he tried to put her back in the cage, she attacked. 'I'll never get another one, ' he said. - *A.P. 13-10-98*

growing that the secretive cougar is getting too comfortable around the booming human population that now shares its habitat. - *A.P. 8-8-98*

MYSTERY CATS

COUGAR ATTACKS INCREASING IN AMERICA...

When concerns about marauding cougars rise, wildlife experts offer reassurances: The typical cougar (a.k.a. mountain lion, puma and panther) is a shy creature that avoids people and prefers to eat deer rather than pets or children.

Wastington State game warden Rocky Spencer and a hunter arrived with two hounds to track a cougar after it savaged a family's dog. The hounds came across it just 100 yards into the woods, and the snarling cougar turned on the dogs with a fury that sent both back to the truck to lick their wounds.

'I've had dealings with upwards of 100 mountain lions, and that was the most aggressive I've seen, ' Spencer said.

Once hunted nearly to extinction, cougars are on the rebound around the West. It's an ecological success story that's causing both celebration and nervous glances over the shoulder. Worries are

COUGAR WANDERS INTO DOWNTOWN BUILDING IN CANADA

VICTORIA, British Columbia (Reuters) - Authorities hope to return a cougar to the wilderness after the big cat was discovered wandering inside a downtown building in British Columbia's capital city.

'It scared the crap out of me, ' said Craig Grebicki, an employee of Scott Plastics, who managed to trap the cougar in a room by throwing a chair against a door.

Conservation officers shot the cat with a tranquilliser dart and captured it without incident. It was unclear what prompted the cat, a three-year-old female, to enter the building, but officers described it as 'extremely malnourished. ' 'She walked in right by one of our sales reps. He just saw the tail and at first he thought it was a dog, ' said Sheila Simpson, a company employee.

British Columbia has had a very dry summer this year, making it difficult for animals including cougars and bears to find enough food in the wild. A cougar was also recently captured prowling in a park in a Vancouver suburb. - *Reuters 09/16/98*

PANTHERS? - MAY BE RIVER OTTERS!

If it's black as a panther and looks like a cougar, it could be a river otter, according to Wastington State officials.

'Otters are definitely cat-looking in appearance,' said Curt Wood, state Fish and Wildlife Department officers in Lincoln County. In addition to a flat head and a whiskery face, river otters have long tails and dark fur that, when wet, can appear jet black - just as a number of credible witnesses here have described recently - *The Spokesman-Review 2 Oct 1998*

Animals & Men # 18

FIERCE PANTHER TURNS OUT TO BE REAL PUSSYCAT

A large, mysterious black beast that fearful Novato residents believed to be a panther was videotaped yesterday on a hillside looking suspiciously like a fat cat. A well-fed house cat is, in fact, what state Department of Fish and Game officials concluded the animal was, but at least one resident refuses to believe them. 'I've had cats all my life, big and small and this is not a house cat, ' said Brooke Toothman, 45. 'What I saw was a huge animal.'

Nonetheless, teenagers at an orientation barbecue yesterday at Sinaloa Middle School didn't seem to be worried. 'A panther, here?' said Casey Arnold, 14, as he stuffed a hot dog in his mouth. 'That would be the day.' - *August 22, 1998*

DARTMOOR 'LION' SOUGHT

Two reports of a large cat with a mane on Dartmoor, S.W. England, sparked a major operation on 18 Nov 98, with convoys of up to 20 vehicles, comprising police and journalists, driving through various small villages and country roads. Armed police and tracker dogs scoured fields and woodland. No zoos or wildlife parks have reported a missing lion, and the favoured explanation is that, if the sightings are genuine, it is an escaped or released pet that was kept illegally.

Roundup of other 'beast' alerts:

Colorado: Wheat Ridge - mountain lion on loose; police says there were 2 sightings - 18-8-98.
California: Jarrahdale - cougar-like cat blamed for for unexplained livestock killings. - 1998.
Maine: Fryeburg - reports of mountain lion. (Last confirmed sighting was 1938) - 15-8-98
New Mexico: Las Cruces - mountain lion in back yard captured by tranquilliser darts - 21-8-98.
Texas: Colleyville - panther? Traps baited with meat are being set out - 25-8-98 .
Washington: Davenport - sightings of cougar-like black cats may be river otters. - 2-10-98
Wisconsin - 'mountain lion' reported wandering in woods west of Interstate 90-94.

NEWSFILE

British Columbia: Victoria - cougar wanders into downtown building. - 1998.

UK: Herts - 'puma-style animal' seen roaming in the north London suburbs... 27-9-98

LAKE & SEA MONSTERS

SEARCH FOR ELUSIVE REPTILE TAKES NEW TWIST

Wildlife experts from Florida and Texas have been asked to help city officials catch a mysterious reptile swimming in a park lake. An anonymous group says don't bother, as it prompted the reptile sightings last week by placing an inflatable toy alligator into Washington Park's south lake.

'The timing of the Washington Park caiman story is no coincidence,' the group said in a fax sent to Denver media outlets. 'That this hoax would share headlines with the crisis in the Clinton White House only serves to underscore the real crisis confronting America - the trivialization of the media.' - *A.P. 20-8-98*

ANIMALS & MEN # 18

NESSIE FOOTAGE

Experienced Loch Ness Monster spotters described the latest video footage apparently showing the head of the elusive underwater creature as the most exciting breakthrough of recent years. Gary Campbell, from the Loch Ness Monster Fan Club, believes a film taken by a family on holiday at the loch is the best footage of 'Nessie' he has ever seen.

But wildlife watchers have poured cold water on the theory, claiming the pictures just show an inquisitive seal.

LOREN INVITED TO LOCH NESS

The pursuit of one of this century's most enduring mysteries, the Loch Ness Monster, may be closer to being solved. Dan Scott Taylor, Jr.'s minisub expedition has picked internationally known cryptozoologist Loren Coleman to come along for the ride. Taylor, who built the original 'yellow submarine' to seek Nessie, in 1969, is building a bigger mini submarine to 'finish the job he set out to do in 1969'. And he has invited Coleman along as a technical observer. The NESSA Expedition plans to launch the minisub in June 1999.

CHINA

A Chinese scholar says the monsters that have been reported several times in Tianchi Lake in China's Jilin Province are recorded far back in Chinese history. Gong Yuhai, 69, who studies early Chinese culture, says that the Shanhaijing, a collection of fairy tales, contains many accounts of turtle-shaped animals with a pig's head and black skin, which are quite similar to monsters in the Changbai Mountains, where the lake is located. *28/5/98 China Daily*

Giant softshells? - Richard Freeman

CADDY COMES IN FROM THE COLD?

Ted Bousfield, lake monster researcher, suggests that Cadborsaurus and Ogopogo may be related and might have arrived 10,000 years ago. Thus Ogopogo, so the reasoning goes, could have become landlocked in the Okanagan where Columbia River dams have blocked direct access to the ocean for both salmon and serpents. A rash of Caddy sightings followed the appearance of a newspaper article in which Caddy hunter Bousfield remarked that the creature seemed uncharacteristically coy this year. - *Victoria (BC) Times-Colonist, 21 July 1998*

NEWSFILE

BHM's

SKUNK APE PROTECTION

A bill making it illegal to molest a skunk ape has been passed by a Florida legislative committee. Last session, the bill passed committee but never reached the floor. - *Aug 1998*

THE YETI

An American climber said Tuesday he had seen the Yeti, or the Abominable Snowman, while on a skiing expedition on the Chinese side of Mount Everest. Craig Calonica said he saw two Yetis together 'around Sept 17' with thick shining black fur walking like men except a little hunched over at the shoulder. 'Their arms were very long and their hands were very big.' - *Oct 13, 1998 Reuters*

Tyrolean adventurer Reinhold Messner says the 'Yeti' is not a humanoid ape but a large bear, and there are about 1,000 roaming Nepal and Tibet, usually at night. Messner said, after examining its footprints, 'It's clearly a Tibetan bear, similar to a grizzly but with longer hair.' - *Reuters 6-10-98*

Bipedal bears are more unlikely than giant apes - Richard Freeman

ANIMALS & MEN # 18

I WISH THEY COULD ALL BE CALIFORNIA BIGFEET

A 9-foot-tall, yellow-eyed beast making bloodcurdling screams turned a group of campers as shaky as the marshmallows they were roasting when they decided the creature must be the legendary Bigfoot. Tim Ford, 22, told California Department of Fish and Game officials Thursday that he's convinced he saw the elusive man-beast, who he claims left tracks 6 inches wide and 20 inches long in remote Hayfork, about 200 miles north of San Francisco.

'You could see his arms hanging way past his knees,' one camper said.

NEW AND REDISCOVERED

KOKAKO MAY BE OK

Hopes that New Zealand's South Island's kokako may still be alive were raised when two hunters reported a possible sighting. A brief search for the supposedly extinct bird, with steel-grey plumage, was mounted but was called off because of bad weather. A more detailed search will start in two weeks.

The kokako, believed to have been extinct for 30 years, is about the size of a magpie and has distinctive orange-coloured wattles at the base of its beak. The North Island kokako has blue wattles and is not extinct.

MUTANT MOSQUITOES

Biologists say a new species of mosquito is evolving in the tunnels of the London Underground. Researchers at the University of London believe the insects are descendants of mosquitoes that colonised the tunnels a century ago when the railways were being built. Originally bird-biters, they apparently evolved new feeding behaviour, dining on rats, mice, and maintenance workers. 'It looks as if there has been a unique colonisation event,' says biologist Richard Nichols.

THE MOUSE THAT ROARED

British scientists have discovered a mouse in Ecuador that catches fish. The Andes rodent is almost blind; however, it locates fish with its long, sensitive whiskers and drags them from the water with its front paws. - *Globe & Mail 21-8-98*

NEWSFILE

TERATOLOGY ETC

WHERE THE BUFFALO ROAM

Michigan Hanover - A genetically rare baby white buffalo born on a Jackson County ranch three weeks ago has died. The female calf contracted pneumonia, owners said. One of every 40 million buffalo are born white, statistics show. - *USA Today - Aug 19, 1998*

ANIMAL MUTILATIONS

A grisly animal mutilation at a County Down [Ireland] farm is being connected with UFO sightings in the area. Several people in South Armagh and Omeath have reported seeing a large circular ball of light in the evening sky. At the same time the UFO research group QUEST was contacted by a farmer in Carnlough who reported the mutilation of one of his cows. Miles Johnston from Quest said: 'The cow carcass had been drained of blood, the flesh had been removed from its head and its vital organs were gone.

This is the first known case of its kind in Northern Ireland but it has happened to thousands of animals in the US and Britain.

ANIMALS & MEN # 18

NO IVORY

Nature is fighting back against Uganda's ivory poachers by dramatically increasing the number of elephants born without tusks, scientists say.

Dr Eve Abe, a Cambridge-educated elephant specialist at the Ugandan Wildlife Authority, said: 'A survey I conducted found that up to 30 per cent of a sample of adult elephants in the Queen Elizabeth Park do not have tusks. ' Dr Abe's latest report found that 15.5 per cent of the whole female population were tuskless. In the male elephant population the level was 9.5 per cent. A study of the same area in 1930 found only one per cent of elephants were without ivory, due to rare mutations.

INSECT EXPERT: 'BUGS CAN READ YOUR MIND'

Be careful what you say in front of a cockroach - it may be able to read your mind. That's a according to environmental educator Joanne Lauck of San Jose, California, who claims insects have feelings, and avoid humans who are bugged by bugs. Lauck says she came to the conclusion with the help of a giant Madagascar hissing cockroach named Cedar. When she invited elementary students to pet the bug, one boy made a joke about squashing Cedar. The cockroach then happily crawled around the arms of every student except the boy who wanted to crush the roach.

PALAENTOLOGY:

WORMS TURN EARLY

Worms may have lived on Earth a billion years ago, Yale University researchers say. They discovered fossilised tunnels that may be burrows left by ancient worm-like creatures that lived in sandbeds beneath a shallow sea that covered what is now central India. Scientists previously thought multicellular animals originated 500 million to 6 00 million years ago, in a sudden explosion of diversity during the early Cambrian period. *30-9-98*

NEWSFILE

LARGEST GROUP OF DINOSAUR PRINTS FOUND

The world's largest group of dinosaur footprints have been discovered at a site near the Bolivian town of Sucre, a Swiss palaeontologist, Christian Meyer, has announced.

Footprints up to 3 feet long were found in the area, which includes prints of several dinosaur species, making it one of the rarest finds in the world. 'There is no comparable site in the world,' said Meyer. Two weeks later, another discovery was announced by Meyer: 'We found two eggs that could be from dinosaurs,' - adding that the eggs dated back some 68 million years. 'They were found in green limestone and there may be more in other layers.' *Reuters 1-8-98, 13-8-98*

OTHER PALAEONTOLOGY NEWS ON THE CFZ WEBSITE:

World's smallest mammal fossil found in Wyoming tree stump. Sept 30, 1998
Dinosaurs ruled every continent, looked more bizarre than popular images. Oct 1, 1998
Royal Tyrrell Museum, Alberta, Canada: more details of feathered, turkey-sized theropods. Aug 31, 1998
Andaman Islanders "descended from the first modern humans to migrate across Asia." Sep 98.
New Zealand Maoris Came from Taiwan, DNA analysis suggests. Sep 98.
Dendrochronology (wood dating) could rewrite ancient history in the eastern Mediterranean. 27 Sep 1998
The L.A. "Tar Ranch" (La Brea Tar Pits) discoveries. Sep 1998.

WILD CHILD

Misha Defonseca survived the Europe Holocaust as a seven-year-old Jewish girl by fleeing into the forests to escape from the Nazis and was adopted by a family of wolves. Years later, as a teenager, "for me men were prey. When I needed them, I took them," Misha recalled. "It was the law of the wild - the law of the wolves. I enjoyed men. When I met my husband, I wasn't an angel. I punched people in bars. But he was so patient and I told him everything ... I have the social graces, but I don't trust humans like I trust animals - they're less likely to stab you in the back.' - *The Times (UK) July 21 1998*

ANIMALS & MEN # 18
OTHER NEWS

TIGER-MEAT GOURMET SHOW

A leading Japanese television network has provoked outrage for showing its entertainers eating and enjoying tiger meat in a cooking program filmed in China. The Worldwide Fund for Nature said the program set a terrible example for viewers.

Three Japanese entertainment person-alities, shown dining on the tiger at a restaurant in Shanghai, described the meal as delicious and showed no remorse when they learned what they were eating. - *Sept 1998*

REPTILE TRADE ARRESTS

A five-year undercover U.S. Fish and Wildlife Service investigation that succ-essfully infiltrated the illegal reptile trade ended with the arrest of an international wildlife dealer and 2 couriers.

'Reptile smuggling is a high-profit crim-inal enterprise, and the US is its largest market,' said Service Director J. Clark. 'Sacrificing the world's legally protected rare species to meet the demand for reptiles prized as exotic live collectibles will not be tolerated by this country...' - *A.P. Sept 1998*

GALAPAGOS TURTLES TO BE RESCUED

The Galapagos islands' giant turtles will be evacuated from the archipelago's largest island, Isabela, to get them out of the way of lava from an erupting volcano.

Head of the national park, Chavez, said the turtles were currently nesting, meaning their colonies were dispersed throughout the islands, 600 miles west of the South American mainland.

The islands were visited by English naturalist Charles Darwin in 1835 - *A.P. Sept 1998*

NEWSFILE

DARWIN'S FINCHES GET BOOST FROM EL NINO

The El Nino weather phenomenon may have wreaked havoc around the world, but for the famed Galapagos finches that clinched for Charles Darwin the truth of evolution it came as a blessing in disguise.

The heavy rains that El Nino brought caused vegetation and insects to flourish all round the archipelago, and this led the finches that feed on them to breed like mad,' scientists at London's Natural History Museum were told. By the time the phenomenon's latest cycle had died out by May this year, the small birds had produced so many offspring that they stopped breeding early. 'They were probably worn out...' - *Reuters 17-9-98*

SLOTH DUNG YIELDS SECRETS

A pile of dung from an ancient sloth has yielded up secrets from the creature that left it 19,000 years ago, in the form of DNA, researchers from the Max Planck Institute have announced.

The team used a new technique to tease the DNA out of the dung, something no one else had been able to do - it shows the long-dead animal ate plants such as capers, mustard, mint and lilies.

The nearly-fossilised faeces were found by Hendrik Poinar of the Institute in a cave 18 miles east of Las Vegas, Nevada.

The cave is full of dried-up animal poop, which researchers have been trying to analyse.

Now, a technique known as polymerase chain reaction (PCR), which makes trillions of copies of tiny gene fragments, making enough product to look at, enabled identification of the animal as a member of the sloth family, 'presumably Nothrotheritops shastensis, whose bones were found in the cave.'

This giant sloth has been extinct for 11,000 years. But there was DNA in its stool from plants. *Science - July 10, 1998*

Animals & Men Collected Editions Volume 4   New Horizons

ANIMALS & MEN # 18   NEWSFILE

WEIRD SCIENCE

WHY DO THEY PIG OUT ON STONES?

An animal behaviour expert has been given £5,000 to find out why pigs chew stones after eating. Ian Horrell, an animal psychologist from Hull University, will spend the next few months studying the behaviour of Britain's eight million pigs in seven different locations around the country. - *The Times, Sept 24 1998*

TEXAN PAYS LAB $5 MILLION TO CLONE PET DOG

A Texas millionaire is paying a cloning laboratory $5 million to produce a living replica of his pet dog Missy. The cloning laboratory of Texas A & M University at College Station had been given two years to produce a clone. Laboratory Director Mark Westhusin said he thought other millionaires would be keen to follow suit. Other laboratories and companies were hoping to move into commercial cloning of pets and racehorses. - *BBC Newsnight 24-8-98*

BILLIONS OF BLEEDING BACTERIA

THERE are five million trillion trillion bacteria on Earth, give or take a handful, according to a census that confirms that they are the planet's dominant life form. The study has revealed a far greater number than previously thought, 'a five with 30 zeroes after it,' according to Professor William Whitman, a microbiologist at the University of Georgia.

AH!!! THE CHILDREN OF THE NIGHT...

A Spanish neurologist, proposing a novel genesis for one of the most feared ghouls in Western culture, says the tale of the blood-sucking predator may have originated with a major rabies epidemic in Europe in the 1700s. Gomez-Alonso said he had always assumed vampires were fictional creatures from Europe's superstitious past.

'Then one day I saw a classic Dracula film, ' he said. 'I watched the film more as a doctor than as a spectator, and I became so impressed by some obvious similarities between vampires and what happens in rabies, such as aggressiveness and hypersexuality.'

He said even the vampire's fatal kiss, the bite itself, could be traced to rabies. 'Man has a tendency to bite, both in fighting and in sexual activities, ' Gomez-Alonso says. 'The intensification of such tendency by rabies increases the risk of transmission, as the virus is in saliva and other body secretions.' - Sep 1998

EXTRATERRESTRIAL LIFE?

Scientists are becoming more optimistic that life exists elsewhere than Earth. 'There have been key discoveries that suggests life is simple, straightforward and easy if you have the right conditions, ' Bruce M. Jakosky, a University of Colorado planetary scientist, said at a meeting of the American Astronomical Society. 'There is a remarkable change among scientists from just 20 years ago. 'In this solar system alone, there are at least four places besides Earth where life could have evolved. And beyond the sun, untold numbers of stars could be shining on planets teeming with life of some form. 'There has been a revival in the serious search for life.' *A. P. - Oct 14, 1998*

ANIMALS & MEN # 18

DEFORMED FROGS

In a deepening ecological mystery, state scientists have plucked four deformed frogs from a tiny wetland in Norfolk in north-western Connecticut - the opposite corner of the state from a pond where numerous frog deformities have been documented since last year.

The Connecticut survey is part of a nation-wide search by scientists for answers to a 3-year-old mystery. They are trying to find what's causing the deformities and are concerned about the implications for people. If the culprit is a manmade chemical or natural substance, they wonder whether it could someday cause harm in humans.

Frogs are considered a 'sentinel species,' - succumbing early to threats that may later affect humans. Because of their permeable skin and because they live both on the land and in the water, chemicals and pathogens can affect them easily.

This year since July 1, almost weekly sampling surveys at the pond have shown that between 10 percent and 30 percent of frogs caught by volunteer teams had deformities. A sampling usually entails catching at least 50 frogs for observation. The nation-wide search for answers is a loosely co-ordinated scientific effort. Scientists at state and federal agencies, universities, conservation groups and even some individuals report their findings to the North American Reporting Centre for Amphibian Malformations.

Other species of frog are just vanishing; so vexed are the experts that a supermarket tabloid ran a story headlined 'ALIENS STEALING OUR FROGS!' - *The Hartford Courant / A.P. 18 Sept 98*

ROADRUNNER ADAPTS TO DOG FOOD

A study of roadrunners by University of Arizona biologists has determined the desert bird is adapting well despite urban encroachment. The foot-tall creature feasts on unguarded dog food and has territorial spats with rabbits. About 1,200 have been sighted inside Tucson. - *USA Today, July 24, 1998*

NEWSFILE

PIGEON FLIGHT HAS MYSTERIOUS 90% FAILURE RATE

Some 2,200 homing pigeons competing in two races along the East Coast of the USA never made it home, leaving their handlers wondering if somehow, some way, the birds' legendary instincts went south.

'I've never seen anything like this,' said Earl Hottle, who has been racing pigeons for 37 years. 'Nobody can explain it.'

About 1,600 pigeons vanished out of 1,800 competing in a 200-mile race from northern Virginia to Allentown on Monday. And 600 out of 700 birds were missing after a 150-mile race on the same day from western Pennsylvania to Philadelphia.

Ordinarily, the swift birds should have been back in their lofts in a matter of hours.

'Apparently somewhere they got sidetracked,' said Ron Lizcz, who lost 14 birds.

Each weekend in the spring and fall, thousands are trucked up to 600 miles away and released. Relying on their homing instinct and incredible stamina, the pigeons fly directly to their lofts. The ones with the fastest times are the winners.

'Is it unusual? Yes. Is it unprecedented? No,' said Rick Phalen, executive director of the American Racing Pigeon Union in Oklahoma City. 'But I don't have a recent recollection of this big a loss in the country.'

The National Weather Service all but ruled out weather. It said there was a drastic change in wind direction Monday at 3,000 feet, but racing pigeons usually don't climb higher than 250 feet, and fly low on windy days.

Birds of prey? 'The chances that 2,000 hawks would get 2,000 pigeons are pretty unlikely,' racer Dennis Gaugler told the newspaper. 'The birds would scatter when attacked.'

'The truth is that nobody knows what happened,' racer Robert Costagliola told the Morning Call, 'and probably never will.' *Reuters 10-9-98*

ANIMALS & MEN # 18

GUBU NORGE
(The 1998 GUST Expedition)

by Daev Walsh

'Merdre!' - "Pere Ubu" (Alfred Jarry)

'They sought it with thimbles, they sought it with care;
They pursued it with forks and hope;
They threatened its life with a railway-share;
They charmed it with smiles and soap.'

"The Hunting of the Snark" (Lewis Carroll)

Laden with misgivings, I trundled myself and my luggage through Oslo's Fornebu Airport. It was August 3rd, 1998, and I was there to meet the rest of the GUST (Global Underwater Search Team [2])

contingent, with whom I was to travel to Lake Seljordsvatnet, some 130km or so (as the crow flies) west of Oslo. Once there, we were to investigate 250 years of lake monster reports. Before leaving Ireland, I perused Michel Meurger's findings concerning Seljordsvatnet, in particular his references to Halvor Sandsdalen's book on the subject [3]. The creature seemed to be a hybrid of the "Havhest" - half horse-half fish, usually shown with a curling fishtail - and the lindorm, or Scandinavian dragon, traditionally portrayed as a serpent with a horse's head, once a huge land snake, later demoted to murky lakes. Our "sjøormen", or serpent, apparently began its earthly days in a smaller lake, from which it

FEATURE

migrated, to Seljordsvatnet. It transpired that quite a few members were hesitant about committing themselves to the expedition - some of us had even left it to the last moment to pay for our flights. These doubts were not so much based on the idea of looking for a lake monsters, but rather the eccentric behaviour of Jan-Ove Sundberg, the leader of the expedition. One Swedish team member told me that he had been accused of being a spy for a Swedish UFO magazine. I veered close to being told to stay at home because Sundberg felt I came across as too sceptical in a Sunday newspaper interview, and I had gotten wind of some pretty odd shenanigans in which Sundberg was involved, near Loch Ness in 1971 [4].

Nevertheless, whether it was the taste of adventure, sheer devilment, or perhaps a genuine "quest" for The Serpent, ten of the twelve team members convened in the arrivals hall of the airport around 1640, and subsequently made for our transport.

The expedition was to turn into one of the most hilarious farces I've ever had the pleasure to be implicated in, and as I write, more than a week after its apparent conclusion, the dust is still rising. A 52-minute Discovery Channel documentary on GUST is due in the autumn, and a BBC series on 'science mysteries' is to feature footage, and will be shown next spring. Kurt Burchfiel's article on the shenanigans will appear on the *Strange* magazine website [5], and my own is appearing in *Fortean Times*. And then there's the mini-war that Sundberg himself has waged on several of the expedition members, and our very own Mr. Downes!

EDITOR'S NOTE: I have never made any secret of the fact that since the break-up of my marriage I have been receiving psychotherapy. Indeed it is one of the minor themes of my new book *The Rising of the Moon*.

I have also made no secret of the fact that I have been known to hoist a wee dram on occasions. Sundburg, however, decided

- 17 -

ANIMALS & MEN # 18 — FEATURE

that I was a psychotic alcoholic who, in his words had *"brought shame upon my country"*. He made these accusations about me over the Internet, and to my pleasure, large portions of the international Cryptozoological community came to my defence and NO-ONE backed up his extraordinary claims.

However, after the expedition he sent me `doctored` e-mails purporting to be from Daev Walsh claiming that Daev himself held me in extremely low esteem and that I was essentially a dangerous lunatic. As this article proves, this is far from being the case!

In the light of the revelations included in this article I feel that anything Sundburg says should be taken *cum grano salis*, and essentially neither I, nor anyone else involved in the **Centre for Fortean Zoology** wish to have anything more to do with him. However, we have decided to eschew any further mud-slinging with someone whose behaviour has been, at best, unwise, and at worst libellous and unpleasant!

Lake Seljordsvatnet, is something of a paradise - squeezed in by 1500m high mountains, it's some 14km long, and a kilometre or so wide. According to the apparently official chart, it's 138m deep - there were reports of an area of 157m, and one day we found a depth 147m - if our echo sounder was truthful. Seljord - which has adopted The Serpent as its coat-of-arms - is an attractive scattered community of 3,000 or so, and has just one main drag of businesses housed in wooden buildings.

The local council had put some effort into GUST, as part of a tourism campaign, and various technology companies sponsored our equipment. During the two weeks I spent in Seljord, we used two different Simrad echo sounders, a side-scan sonar, a GPS hooked into a Konmap moving map system, and a couple of remote-control submarines.

I wasn't the only one to be quite surprised by the huge emphasis put on the equipment, much of it for the benefit of the media, who came in their dribs and drabs. We had no more than a perfunctory lesson on the sounders and sonar, and using the submarines seemed to be a mite premature -- yes, there were reports of underwater caverns, but I felt the chances of any anomalous creature strutting its stuff in front of an underwater camera to be rather remote.

Our one chance to send a sub down to the deepest part of the lake had to be abandoned, due to a heavy swell. As for our collective inexperience in using the other equipment, this led to much disagreement later on -- we all pretty much agreed that we were using it incorrectly, but there was little agreement on the nature of the misuse. This was not helped by problems with generators, and the regular breakdown of equipment.

On the first day of 'shift' - we split into teams of four, and mounted three shifts spanning 24 hours in the home-made "Mother One" (built by Norwegian team member Arne Thomassen). There was a lot of excitement over a few of the echo-sounder traces, and one report of a visual sighting from the road by Ulf Burman and Peter Caspersson - my notes read:

'7 August 1998 1140 sighting by Peter C and Ulf 75-100m north of Hugsdalen, momentarily seen thru trees from the road, partially obscured. 3m long black object breaking surface, not a wave. South-north alignment. Conditions, water choppy, SE wind, bright sunny day, with light cumulous clouds.'

Later in the expedition, this sighting seemed to be forgotten about, in favour of 'evidence' that Jan himself had been involved in gathering. Dr. Jason Gibb had made some interesting bacterial finds while diving, leading to further speculation on the 'exploding log theory' [6], and Ulf Burman "filmed" lengthy footage of apparently live objects moving just below the surface of the lake, leaving light ' v ' wakes - all of this was practically ignored by the team leader, Jan.

Reports of 'tracks' - footprints in the silt on the bottom of the lake - had been claimed by a local man, seen when he was diving a "year" before. Jan went hell for

ANIMALS & MEN # 18   FEATURE

leather on this, regardless of the testimonies of our scuba divers that the bottom was loose sediment. Any mark in that kind of bottom would be gone in a few hours, but Jan still insisted that we go looking for them.

In an email to me after the expedition he said, "I think that the man fooled us, that the tracks was a practical joke that went too far," and later that "*I, Peter and other Swedes and also Arne -- sensed there was something wrong here and we did all we could to get our hands on [the witness], to have him show us exactly where the tracks were supposed to be. But the man avoided us at all costs, making up stories that he was on vacation, on the harvest, here and there and everywhere and at the end we just knew he was laying* (sic) *to us.*"

In the course of the expedition, this certainly wasn't communicated to either Dr. Gibb or myself, in fact I went out of my way to emphasise the uselessness of the information given to me by the witness by phone, but was badgered instead for my scepticism. After a spate of large echo soundings - some up to a couple of metres long, Jan began telling the press, and anyone who cared to listen, that we had had contact with an object 5m long (the size seemed elastic). I mightn't have had much experience with echo sounders, but at least some of us understood that echo sounders -- and sonars -- don't draw 2D pictures of 3D objects, they merely detect differences in density. They do not give any kind of conclusive evidence of size or nature of an object.

Things began to get really silly when Jan decided that he had taken photos of the alleged beastie. He told me that he was alone on the deck at the time, and didn't want to disturb the film crew, who were at work in the cabin. I got a different version from "several" others present, who maintained that he wasn't on his own, and that what was seen, and photographed, was merely a series of waves or boat wakes. Nevertheless, Jan told us that he intended to "sell" the photos to none other than the *Daily Express*, for the princely sum of 60,000 Norwegian Crowns - 6,000 Irish pounds (USD8000) or so. And so,

before they were actually developed, Jan was planning to sell them.

On August 13th, he had Arne drive him to Oslo, where Kodak developed his slides. On his return, he maintained that he had something very interesting to show us, which he did, in the form of an after-dinner slide show. Unfortunately, where Jan could apparently see a 'serpent' in the photos, no one else could -- a couple of people said 'well maybe', while marine biologist Jason Gibb and I voiced our opinions that the photographs "showed" nothing other than, well, waves. We didn't discount the fact that Jan had seen something anomalous, or that there was anything big and wriggly under the surface of the water, but we emphasised that the photographs "displayed" only waves.

A vote was called -- who wanted to sell them? There was a 10-2 vote against. Jan was surprised, as he thought we would like the money. None of us needed it quite "that" badly, so Jan said he would sell them for himself -- '*what about the contract?*', was the bemused response. Jan suggested that 'Well, we can change the contract', which gave rise to laughter of disbelief.

Obviously feeling cornered, he then attempted to put the team on a collective guilt trip -- after telling us that he thought "we" could do with the money, he changed tack, telling us that as Arne had paid for boat fuel from his pocket, it was necessary to sell the photos to cover costs, or else pay 500Kr (IR50, or USD62) each. Jason reasonably pointed out that he would be happy to pay that amount if it saved his integrity, and I added my opinion that people don't forget these photos, they would show up in coffee table books for eternity, with "our" names attached.[7]

The meeting broke up, leaving a definite rift in the camp. This was the evening of Thursday 13th, and until the afternoon of the 15th, Jan not only sulked, but declined to speak English and was rather curt to any of the Swedish or Norwegian team members who he felt had thwarted his plans. The whole shebang was getting far too silly. I was getting tired of the lack of proper research -- here we were looking for a flesh and blood creature, without so much as a cursory glance at the local food chain. Jason and Kurt Burchfiel were of a not dissimilar opinion, as Jan's dismissive attitude towards any of our constructive suggestions was really starting to grate.

ANIMALS & MEN # 18 — FEATURE

And so it came to pass that Kurt and I decided that we no longer wished to have our names attached to the burgeoning circus that GUST had now become. At a briefing on the afternoon of Saturday 15th, we calmly explained our reasons. Kurt explained how he felt that Jan had gathered together a bunch of genuine people -- who were seriously interested -- and used them in his quest for money and notoriety. I finished off by how I found it unacceptable that the members of the team who were unable to speak Swedish or Norwegian had been cut out of the information loop, when English was supposed to have been the official language of the expedition. We rose, and left the room.

Jan has since accused me of looking at him with *'cold staring, murderous eyes'*, and having directed our resignation in 'an aggressive manner'. I would like to ensure the reader, that no such behaviour was forthcoming from this rather mild-mannered writer.

Kurt and I spent the next day winding up some of the parts of the documentary that needed to be finished -- 'perception tests', using floating logs. Jan, aboard "Mother One", hung about offshore from where we were filming, taking photographs of us. Those interested can see the use to which such photos are put by ambling along to my *GustUp* page where they can see my very own contribution to Jan's rather surreal campaign against me(he seems convinced that I have some hidden agenda) [8].

Apart from the general accepted opinion -- as voiced by Kurt, that Jan's main motives were money and fame etc., I spent much time considering *"other motives"*, and I quote here from Patrick Harpur's wonderful book *"Daemonic Reality"* [9] :

'A quest, can perhaps be imagined as an extroverted version of the shaman's introversion - perhaps they are the outside and the inside of the same Way. Unlike the shaman, who is passive in the face of the dismembering otherworldly beings, the quester is active, singleminded, even obsessive. To draw mythological analogies, he is less like Orpheus, the archetypal shaman, than like Odysseus, Jason and Aeneas, whose journeys took place through this world while beset at every turn by intrusions from the other. (In Christian terms, the quest becomes the pilgrimage while the shaman's journey becomes the mystic's ascent to God.) The danger for the shaman is that he might travel too far or too badly prepared into the Otherworld and so lose his soul; the danger for the quester is just the opposite - the Otherworld is too close to him, threatening to overwhelm and possess him. Even as he clings to his this-worldly perspective, which the shaman is compelled to give up, he is bombarded by the otherwordly. The song of the Siren lures him towards the mind-wrecking rocks. Paranoia is always just around the corner.'

In my opinion, Jan's quest seems to operate on two levels, as apart from the money and fame quest, he seemed to be following the path of the classic quester, in pursuit The Serpent (note capitals and singularisation),whatever it may be -- the Nemesis of the quester, a form of self-sacrifice? Even the search plan had a heading, *"The Search for The Serpent"*. Jan's confirmed this in an email this week: 'internally we were taking about the serpent or the serpents but to the media I said we weren't sure there was unknown animals in the lake'.

If I may be allowed to quote selectively from "Brewer's Myth and Fable", under the heading of 'Serpent':

'In Scandinavian myth, the Nidhogg, the Dread Biter, is evil as living at the root of the Yggdrasil and trying to destroy it.' (The Yggdrasil is the 'world-tree' is the connection between heaven and earth, and it is 'the tree of life and knowledge, and of time itself'.

If I'm right, and Jan is something of a 'serpent quest', it's rather ironic that after he returned to Sweden, he decided to accuse me of "Satanism". This is apparently due to my devil's advocation, my occasional habit of signing my emails in Irish, i.e. 'is mise le meas' (which translates as 'yours respectfully'), and my also occasional use (when the whim is upon me) to sign myself as 'Daithí Breathnach'. Jan wondered if I was 'speaking in tongues', and whether I'd changed my name for membership of a 'satanic sect'.

I was tossing around such serpentine ideas in my head when I found myself, on August 18th, in Vigeland Park in Oslo, designed by sculptor Gustav Vigeland. 'Guarding' the park's bridge were four pillars, each depicting a human, in the nasty process of being savaged by weird beasts, in three cases "serpents". Old Gustav seemed to have a whole primeval Human versus The Serpent thing going on, as depicted in his sculpture and metalwork --such as the Park gates [10].

ANIMALS & MEN # 18 — FEATURE

To conclude this little diatribe and fly on the walls report, I would like to emphasise that despite all the craziness listed above, much of our stay in Norway was quite enjoyable, and have some great friendships have been forged. I'm only sorry that the situation did not lend itself to a serious study of the area - e.g. witness reports and local tales were regarded as "actual fact", whereas anyone who cares to approach the problem from an inclusionist point of view will realise that there are huge coatings of "recurring motifs" which need to be stripped off lake monster reports, myths and tales before anything useful can be derived. A good read of Michel Meurger's *"Lake Monster Traditions"* [11] should elicit some enlightenment with regard to the proliferation of such motifs. As Harpur says:

'In the case of lake monsters, Meurger established that the following motifs - he calls them 'folklore beliefs' - are pretty much universal. Beginning with the lake itself, it is "bottomless"; it "interconnects" with other lakes or the sea; it is the scene of anomalous "luminous phenomena"; it is impenetrably "dark"; it has submarine "caverns"; it has strong currents and eddies or whirlpools which are caused by (or sometimes synonymous with) serpents; it is prone to unexpected "squalls"; it has swallowed up "divers who never return".'

Until these motifs are weeded out - not discarded, just separated out from the usual speculation surrounding lake monsters - expeditions such as GUST will be stuck in the mire of pseudo-science, and will hinder rather than help cryptozoology and fortean research.

A Snark? We didn't get a chance to find a Boojum.

* * * * * *

The Team. L - R: Davy Russell (USA), Kurt Burchfiel (USA) Arne Thomassen (Norway), Dave Walsh (Ireland), Ulf Burman (Sweden), Jan-Ove Sundberg (Sweden), Eric Joye (Belgium), Peter Caspersson (Sweden), Magnus Backlund (Sweden), Peter Lakbar (Sweden), Vemund Bjorge (Norway) and Jason Gibb (UK)

REFERENCES/NOTES:

1. GUBU: 'Conor Cruise O'Brien invented the term GUBU in 1983, after [Charles J.] Haughey [former Irish prime minister] had called the discovery of a young serial killer hiding in the flat of the government attorney general he had appointed "grotesque, unbelievable, bizarre, and unprecedented." The term GUBU stuck, and stayed, and finally outlasted Haughey's career itself. It will be the epitaph of a man who saw himself as both a Tammany ward-boss and the Soul of the Nation.' - Kevin Myers

2. Official site: http://www.bahnhof.se/~wizard/gust/

3. HJ Sandsdalen - *"Seljord's Ormen"*, Seljord Kommune ISBN 82-992140-0-9

4. The *Sunday Business Post* (Ireland) June 28 1998, Page 11, TW Holiday - *The Goblin Universe* pages 174-177

ANIMALS & MEN # 18

The Return of *Gulo gulo*

by Terry Hooper

(Terry Hooper runs EAR - the Exotic Animals Register)

EDITOR'S NOTE: The subject of whether or not wolverines are living wild in the United Kingdom is one which we have covered on several occasions in recent issues.

Terry Hooper has always been adamant that they are here, other contributors to *Animals & Men* have equally adamantly taken the opposite view. In Issue 17 Chris Moiser presented a workable hypothesis to explain SOME sightings of creatures reported to be Wolverines. Clinton Keeling has made comment on his suggestions in his regular column, Tom Anderson's comments are in the letters pages and Terry Hooper has submitted this lengthy reply.

In issue 19 Chris will be replying to both Clin and Terry......)

Chris Moiser's article (A&M17) on dirty albinistic badgers (or even erythristic ones) sparking off wolverine reports was very interesting and I'm sure

RIGHT TO REPLY

there are quite a few people awaiting a heated debate on the possibility of wolverines living in the UK. [1] Well, there isn't going to be one.

Ernest Neal's book on badgers is, of course, a classic. Neal notes that some badgers are greyer than others, in fact, some may be described as *"really silvery"*. He also refers to photographs of a badger cub he took in 1944 in Conigre of a cub *"with a black velvet-like coat yet its companion of the same was quite normal in colouration"* [2]. There was some white visible *"so it is not a true melanistic variety, but it approaches this condition."*

Neal does indeed point out that albinos, off-white or slightly yellow like a ferret, and with pink eye, are not rare. In fact, Phoebe Cooper who covers an area of West Wales for the EAR, has noted albinos in her area. I can add other instances to this which shows that Neal's work, even fifty years later, is still the best reference source.

The erythristic form is a more usual variation according to Neal. The dark parts of the coat are replaced by a sandy-red; Neal reports that a "fine specimen" of the red form was to be found in Taunton Museum - it was killed on the Blackdown Hills. I am still waiting to hear if this specimen has survived. Reports of this type came from a number of counties in Neal's day and still do today. Add to this Neal's notes on yellow badgers and the will understand that not everything about badger colouration is - dare I say it - black and white.

So, despite 55,000+ being killed by cars each year and a further estimated 16,000 shot, snared and baited each year (that's *71,000* dead each year), the colour variations are still there.

- 22 -

ANIMALS & MEN # 18 — RIGHT TO REPLY

E.Kay. Robinson and many other naturalists have stories to tell which all compare in details. Usually a person or a couple will rush out of woods and in a rather panic-stricken state, will report having seen or been approached by a bear. On each occasion investigations have proven the Bear to be a badger. It is almost impossible to believe that anyone brought up in England would not recognise old Brock but it still happens.

I suppose that, at the risk of being boring, I'll repeat my old adage; "people see woodlice and report armadillos".

I have immense respect for Chris and his expertise and knowledge but I would certainly not mis-identify the badger on last issue's cover an a wolverine. But, it must be said, I have been studying wolverine photographs and footage a great deal. Peter Public night well do so, however.

The people I deal with are usually all very knowledgeable about native and non-native wild life.

One forester went to investigate a report of an animal attacking a domestic cat and found the cat looking "as though it had been through a meat mincer". He followed a trail and found the culprit a few yards ahead; it was without doubt a wolverine and was followed some distance.

As this animal was heading for a built up area (which it gradually moved away from) the forester called the police and a dog handler was on site in six minutes - because he had just investigated another incident involving the same animal.

This area also saw a sheep attacked and killed in front of four witnesses during good daylight - and their descriptions could not be faulted. A farmer also had a sheep killed in another incident and the RSPCA Inspector involved had seen big cat kills in north America and ruled this out. He also ruled out dogs, foxes or any other regular predator. However, when he learned that his predecessor and three others had been investigating wolverines in the area, his response was; "Ahh. Now, yes, that does make sense..."

We call this area of the English-Welsh border 'Area A'. We literally know where the wolverine came from, how many got away, in what areas they were heading and how widespread they are now. The origins of these wolverines in the area go back as far as 1969.

North Wales, Area B, has a suspected small wolverine population.

Area G covers yet another part of Wales where tracks were found, sheep killed, and a number of very credible people saw and described wolverine.

Area D covers parts of Devon and Cornwall and the most notable sighting here involved naturalist Trevor Beer and his daughter who saw two wolverines in daylight. Both are fellow members of the British Naturalist Association (f, 1905). Neither would mis-identify badgers as wolverines in those conditions. In the Cornwall area in 1980 two RSPCA inspectors looked into unusual animal deaths for which a wolverine turned out to be responsible.

Area E is the North-west Somerset area where there have been a number of close proximity wolverine sightings. Police tell me they have had no reports further north of the county yet.

Area F is the North-east Coast of Scotland where a possible pair of wolverines were known to exist in the 1970s. This area is still under investigation.

Area G is in a part of Kent where one naturalist believes he quite clearly saw a wolverine but we've had no other reports so far.

Police, foresters, farmers and some animal welfare groups only pass information on to the AP in strictest confidentiality With some we have a two way written confidentiality contract. As soon as big cats or exotics are reported we get the "loony fringe" driving around farmland and housing estates in four wheel drive vehicles and with, illegally, high powered weapons and certain other individuals we know of pop up as "hunters for hire".

The police, farmers and others do not want this. Besides which we need to study reports and, if possible, the animals in question. Yes, it upsets certain naturalists but **that's** just tough!

ANIMALS & MEN # 18

Wolverines are, like many other animals that make "good hunting", much maligned and have over-exaggerated reputations. They are as elusive as the wolverines in their overseas habitats, and they display the same shyness here in the UK. While attempts by hunters and farmers in northern Europe to exterminate wolverines continues, in the UK they are doing quite well.

In a year or so we ought to have the information that people like Chris require but we will not endanger any animal. The British Naturalist Association seem to accept that we have new, introduced native species in the UK -including wolverine- and in 1999 my paper on the subject will be published in its esteemed journal, Countryside.

Chris' article is based on solid data he has and his point of view, as far as certain cases are concerned, is one I agree with. But I will. not be shaken from the stance that wolverines are here and are breeding well.

REFERENCES

1. I have covered the subject of wolverines a couple of times in the EAR Bulletin and ought to note that even the MAFF and Dept. of The Environment admit that wolverine are in the UK.

2. NEAL, Ernest, *The Badger*. (Collins, London. 1971): pp 8-12

I invite correspondence on wolverines or any exotic living wild in the UK. Write to me at: 85 Risdale Road, Ashton Vale, Bristol, or telephone me on: 0117 955 0932

EDITOR`S NOTE: We must apologise for not having printed the correct credits to the picture used in the last issue - our front cover photo-graph was not, as implied, either copyrighted to us or to Chris Moiser but to Porfell Animal Land in Cornwall where the picture was taken. Many apologies to all concerned.

FEATURE
CRYPTOZOOLOGICAL SHARKS

by Allan E. Munro

Much considered among marine cryptozoologists are the possible existence of giant seals, basiliosaurs and plesiosaurs. Much less attention is placed on the possible existence of unknown species of sharks, despite the discovery of the megamouth. Here I have collected a few cryptozoological sharks, and I have placed them into four categories.

SHARKS AS SEA SERPENTS

Often commented upon is a shark caught by Captain S. W. Hanna at New Harbour, Maine and reported in an American journal known as the Sea Side Press in 1880, that was described as a young sea serpent, that was about 25 feet long and only 10 inches in diameter, shaped like an eel. The animal, dead when found, had a flat head and a snout that projected and was noted to overhang the small mouth, which contained small teeth. When naturalists enquired, Captain S. W. Hanna gave more details.

The skin was not like a scale-fish, but more like a dog-fish or shark, though a great deal finer in quality. I did not save the fish for the reason that I did not know what I had caught. In fact, I considered it a streak of ill-luck rather than good fortune, having torn my nets very badly and otherwise bothering me in my business. The body was round or very near that form ... the colour of its back was of a slate or fish colour; belly, greyish-white ... The head did resemble that of a shark, only more stunted, i.e., it did not lengthen out like those of a sharks. The mouth was very small, not any larger than the mouth of a good-sized dog-fish, with fine teeth, located at the extreme end of the head or nose.

Captain S. W. Hanna`s animal has been likened to a frilled shark, but the frilled shark does not have a typical shark snout, and this animal cannot be a species of frilled shark, but an unrelated lineage of elongated sharks. The sighting of an unknown animal in the Kyle of Lochalsh by Dr., Farquehar Matheson and his wife in 1893, however, is possibly a frilled shark. What was reported as a long, thin

ANIMALS & MEN # 18

straight neck as tall as the boat's mast rose out of the water ahead. This was described as being brown, with a ruffle at what was described as the junction between the neck and head (which was said to join the neck from behind rather than underneath, as is how the head of an elongate shark would join the spine). Although Dr., Farquehar Matheson believed this to be the head and neck of a reptile, no body could be seen underwater. It could be that the ruffle of what was described as the neck was the gills of a shark, with part of the body raised out of the water. More like the animal caught by Captain S. W. Hanna is a report from the south-western Chinese coast in 1861, reported in the log of Captain Boyle of the Beaver, that featured a stranded snake-like shark that reached 24 metres long. Boyle requested that the head be cut off, and that the lower jaw cut off so that he could see the inside of the mouth. This was likened to a snakes, but with three rows of soft teeth and a vertical gridiron-shaped feeding apparatus at the back of the mouth. The snake-like head had a snout that was noticeably flat, and this is also noted in the catch of Captain S. W. Hanna, and this hints at a shark identity. Yet another elongate shark was reported in the Shipping Gazette for 1886, at Carabelle in Florida. The animal was said to be 49 feet long and 6 feet in circumference. The animal had a shark-like head and also had a tail with what the report described as formidable fins. The animal was caught from a fishing boat with a shark hook, and was towed wildly until it was tired out then was shot.

THE GIANT SHARK

The oceans were once home to a giant shark known as Carcharocles (not Carcharodon) megalodon. This animal, was over twice as long as the unrelated great white shark but was similar in habits, being an inshore surface dweller. It has been suggested that the C. megalodon survives today. In 1918, icthyologist David G. Stead was told by fishermen at Port Stephens N.S.W. that heavily weighted 3.5 foot long crayfish pots had been effortlessly towed away by what was described as a white shark estimated to be 115 to 300 feet long (up to more than five times as long as megalodon), although this is almost certainly an exaggeration. Author Zane Grey was sailing off Rangiroa, when he saw a shark that was longer than his boat (which he measured as 35 to 40 feet long) that was yellow or green, unlike a great white shark. Five or six years later, about 100 miles to the northwest of Rangiroa, his son Loren Grey had a similar experience with a yellowish shark. This shark had a brown tail, and Loren could estimate the head as 10 to 12 feet across and the body as between 40 and 50 feet long. The Zane Grey sighting was in either 1927 or 1928, whilst the Loren Grey sighting was in 1933. The Polynesians who are fishermen in N.S.W. believe that the sea is home to a fish known as the lord of the deep. This animal is said to be twice as long as the upper size estimate Loren Grey gave for his Rangiroa sighting, and nearly twice as large as megalodons were. It has been suggested that they are megalodons that live in the deep sea and eat squid. However, megalodon was a shallow water animal, and no remains of Megalodon have been proven to have been later than Pliocene.

TIMOR SEA CARPET SHARK

It is possible that giant versions of the sea-bottom sharks known as the wobbegongs or carpet sharks exist in the Timor Sea. These animals are vertically flattened and rather slow moving, being camouflaged and waiting for prey to swim close enough to attack. This prey does not include swimmers, for wobbegongs do not feed on mammals and are too small to bite unless provoked. However, the natives of the Timor Sea tell of the ground shark, a man eating shark that, rather than give chase, attacks swimmers who approach the sea bottom. The ground shark seems to be a giant form of wobbegong.

THE TADPOLE-LIKE SEA ANIMALS

Photographer Robert le Serrec was near Hook Island when he spied and photographed in shallow water a large injured animal of a rarely reported type of water animal on the 12th of December 1964. The animal was similar in shape to a giant tadpole, but Robert le Serrec said that it was 70 feet long. Such sea animals are occasionally reported, on three occasions by more than one person (such as on the 11th of September in 1876, when Captain Webster of the Nestor, together with passengers and crew, saw such an animal in the

ANIMALS & MEN # 18

Malacca Straits). One account comes from Captain Brockhurst in 1880.

Sitting alone on poop of steamer Oceanic at noon, looking at flying fish, saw a long serpent in water 1 or 2 feet below surface, alongside the vessel, thought length 40 feet, circumference 2 to 4 feet, pale yellow colour, dark line on back and on ribs, head a little larger than body, could not see any fins, saw it for 5 or 6 mins and then mentioned it to friends on board.

This type of animal, which is yellow with black stripes, has a shape like a giant tadpole, 18 to 60 metres long, and has a head that merges into the body and a pointed, whip-like tail. The animal is probably a member of the sharks. Although the upper end of the range of sizes reported is probably inaccurate, there is room in the sea for undiscovered planktonivorous sharks and rays.

I recommend for those interested in mysterious sharks, "From Flying Toads To Snakes With Wings" by Karl Shuker. "In Search Of Prehistoric Survivors" contains material on the lord of the deep. Books on general marine cryptozoology sometimes contain material on mysterious sharks.

THE MYSTERIOUS PUERTO RICAN LAMPREY

by Jonathan Downes

EDITOR'S NOTE: it is quite peculiar - as I have noted before - to be writing an 'Editor's Note' to something which you, yourself have written but on occasion it is the only logical thing to do. I have been a professional fortean zoologist for many years now and I have written many hundreds of thousands of words on the subject. As regular readers will know, together with my colleagues at the Centre for Fortean Zoology I have conducted a number of investigations into mysterious animals around the world.

One of the problems with Cryptozoology *per se* is that in many cases there is very little evidence other than anecdotal for the existence

RIGHT TO REPLY

of a particular creature. In the tale I am about to relate, which is, by the way, taken from my forthcoming book *Only Fools and Goatsuckers* I tell the sad story of how, one Friday evening on the Caribbean island of Puerto Rico, I held an unknown animal literally in the palm of my hand without actually realising it!

About an hour before dusk we managed to get back to some "on the ground" (or in fact "in the water") investigating. Several researchers, including those cited by Scott Corales in his excellent *"Chupacabras and other Mysteries"* had noted that the food chain upon the island of Puerto Rico had appeared to have gone completely awry.

We have already seen how both Graham and I were disappointed at the lack of small fauna in El Yunque. Although certain folk within the ufological and paranormal research communities will no-doubt have blamed this natural imbalance either on the arcane experiments of the darker side of the United States security forces, or indeed upon the Chupacabra itself, we felt that it was far more likely that these depredations are the result of indiscriminate use of pesticides and artificial fertilisers on the lowland farms.

There was, however, one reasonably foolproof way that we could check this hypothesis, and this was to examine the zoofauna of one of the lowland rivers that flowed directly from El Yunque itself. As anyone who has known me for any length of time will tell you, there is an innate attraction between me and running water which has taken up large parts of my life since I was a small child. I have never been able to pass a river or stream without investigating its depths, net in hand, in search of whatever fauna and flora lurk within. This little river was no exception.

As the AVP posse interviewed Graham I went off to do what I do best - I rolled up my trouser legs and went paddling. Unlike the situation in the rain forest high above us there was no shortage of small life in the water. I noted at least three species of fresh water shrimps and several species of tiny armoured catfish. Most interestingly from my point of view - I caught a lamprey.

ANIMALS & MEN # 18   FEATURE

Lampreys have always been of particular interest to me. They are amongst the most primitive of vertebrates and have fascinated me now for nearly three decades. The Encarta Encyclopaedia describes them:

"Lamprey, common name for any of about 40 species of smooth-skinned, eel-like, jawless fishes. Lampreys are widely distributed in the streams and seas of temperate and subarctic regions worldwide, except for waters off southern Africa. Adult forms of parasitic species live on the blood of fishes and sometimes devastate fisheries. Like the related hagfish, the lamprey has a pistonlike tongue that creates suction when the mouth is placed against an object. Numerous small teeth on the mouth and tongue pierce the flesh of fishes. The animal has no bony skeleton, its chief support being a flexible cartilaginous rod.

All lampreys breed by ascending freshwater streams to spawn once before wasting away and dying in two to three months. Eggs hatch in two to three weeks. The blind and toothless larvae burrow in the mud, straining water through their mouths to capture small life forms for food. The larva is so unlike the adult that scientists formerly believed it to be a member of a special genus (Ammocoetes). It remains in the mud for at least four years before undergoing a metamorphosis and departing for its adult habitat. Adults are about 91 cm (about 36 in) long."

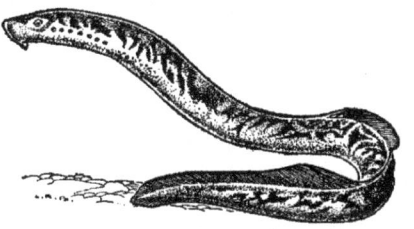

The problem is that like any cursory description this one leaves out more than it includes. I find these tiny creatures fascinating and their macabre zoology perfectly mirrors the lifestyle of the more esoteric paranormal entities which I have also dedicated much of my life to searching for. I seem to have an innate fascination for blood suckers (whether they be of the undead or the parasitic type), and the fact that I found a well grown lamprey in a stream in chupacabra country seemed like a good omen for the next part of our journey.

I watched it for about ten minutes. It was about eight inches in length and an olive grreenish colour. It hung on to the algae covered rocks with its sucker, and moved like a tendril of some bizarre water weeds in the current of the stream. It was perfectly adapted to its environment and I wished that I could have stayed there longer to observe it. It is one of the worse parts of going on expeditions is that whilst you are in a certain place your time is so limited that you are unable to carry out all the tangential investigations which tempt you at every term. One such tangential investigation that I was forced to forsake was that of the musical aspects of the Santeria cults on the island and another (and probably more important) was the ecology of this peculiar little jawless fish.

It was only when I returned to the United Kingdom that I realised quite how important my sighting had been because, search as I did, I was unable to find any references to Puerto Rican lampreys in any of the available literature either in zoological libraries or on the Internet. I spoke to some of the local people on the subject but none of them had more than the slightest inkling what I was actually talking about. This shouldn`t really have surprised me because as I have noted already in these memoirs the people of Puerto Rico are not noted for their zoological knowledge.

I contacted Dean A.Hendrickson, Curator of Ichthyology at the Texas Natural History Collection (a division of Texas Memorial Museum) to see if he could help me solve the mystery of the Puerto Rican lamprey:

"Dear Sir,

I am a zoological researcher from the UK. I was in Puerto Rico earlier this year and I caught a lamprey in one of the lowland streams near Canovenas. I was unable to identify the species.

I have been unable to find a species list of Puerto Rican fishes, and I would be grateful if you could tell me what species of lampreys live on the island.

ANIMALS & MEN # 18

Yours sincerely,

Jonathan Downes
The Centre for Fortean Zoology"

One of the most fantastic things about the advent of e-mail for the fortean (or indeed any other sort of) researcher, is that it gives you almost instant access to information.

When I was writing *"The Smaller Mystery Carnivores of The Westcountry"* (1996) I was reliant on writing letters and sending them the `old fashioned way`. In many instances this would mean a delay of two or three weeks in order to gain even a tiny and relatively unimportant piece of information. When you consider that this was usually when the letters were written to people who were not only living in the same country as me but often only within thirty miles of my house you can imagine my frustration.

The advent of The Internet has allowed almost instant access to information.

I e.mailed Dean Hendrickson at lunchtime, went out to do my weekly food shopping, and had the spark plugs on my car changed, and by the time that I returned his reply was awaiting me. It was, however not as helpful as I had hoped:

"I too don't have ready access to any "fishes of" publications for Puerto Rico, so can't help with the lamprey (I'd be interested to learn what it turns out to be, however).

I then contacted another renowned American Ichthyologist, Karsten Hartel, who replied to me:

Dear Jon:

There are no records of lamprey from the Caribbean that I know about, especially in fresh water. Was the specimen an adult? If so how big? Did you save the specimen? I'm quite sure the specimen must have been an eel of some kind.

I'm sending a copy of this to Dr. Hensley at UPR.

My reply was simple:

Hi

The lamprey was an adult rather than an ammocaete. It was very similar in appearance to the European *Lampetra planeri* although a little larger. It was about seven inches in length and about half an inch thick, and olive green-brown with black eyes, a sucking, circular mouth, black eyes and a row of gill slits. I observed it sucking onto a rock in the strong current in the middle of the river.

Unfortunately I did not secure the specimen, as I did not realise that it was anything unusual. I was making a documentary for British TV on a completely unrelated subject.

I would, however, be interested in descriptions of whatever freshwater eels there are in the area, but I am certain that it was not an eel.

Jon Downes

In the absence of any other information I have to therefore conclude that the CFZ may indeed have come across a new species of animal during its sojourn on the Island of Paradise - a hitherto unsuspected species of petromyzonid. However the search amongst the internecine archives of the sacred groves of academe continues and we hope that the mystery will soon be solved. If not, it will be one of our first priorities on our return to the island, for return we are most definitely going to do.

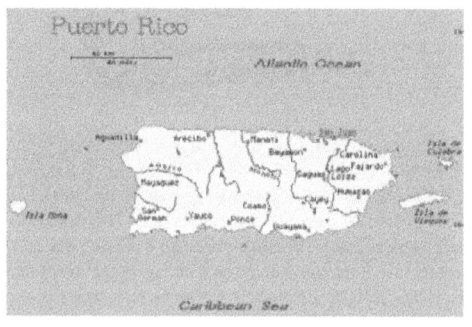

ANIMALS & MEN # 18

EQUUS WILD AND BROWN

by David Barnaby

Very soon after the television broadcast of the BBC programme 'Quest for the Quagga' Reinhold Rau received an E-mail communication fron a man in England. In fact, Reinhold received quite a few communications after the broadcast. This communication was slightly different from the usual in that the writer of it thought he might have photographed a Quagga in 1975.

1975; that was one startling bit. Photographed; that would be another. The Quagga had indisputably disappeared just about one hundred years before. Reinhold knew that; he is the world's Quagga expert.

The Quagga was a zebra of the extreme south of the African continent. It was one of the first big mammals to receive the impact of gun-bearing Europeans with serious intentions of staying in Africa and doing things their way.

One hundred years after it was shot into extinction, Reinhold Rau, another European and long-term resident of South Africa, was doing his best to repair some of the damage. By "doing his best" I mean devoting a major part of his life to the Quagga Project. The Quagga Project is a breeding programme based at the South African Museum whose aim is to reconcentrate those Quagga genes which remain in the animal's near relatives into New Quaggas. The Quagga Project has herds of real zebras living on real African soil and

FEATURE

producing foals by perfectly natural means, but the fact that the Project was mentioned in *Jurassic Park* and that the Quagga itself did actually disappear gives it a certain surreal quality to those who seek only the newsworthy. Reinhold, therefore, regards the media with a certain wariness and treats claims to have seen twentieth-century Quaggas with some suspicion.

There have been quite a few such claims over the years, and one, at least, was treated seriously enough to cause an exploratory expedition to be mounted. Quite reasonably, Mr Rau told the writer of the B-mail letter that what he had photographed was unlikely to be a Quagga.

The writer, a Mr Silvester, nevertheless had three photographs of an Equid which seemed to resemble quite closely the picture of the Knowsley Quaggas (c.1850) which appeared in the Radio Times, advertising the television programme. He was naturally curious to know what it was he had photographed and justifiably excited by the thought that it might be an individual Quagga throwback of some sort. The latter was unlikely but not impossible.

Mr Silvester did not claim to be an animal expert but he had lived in South Africa for fifteen years. He had had much pleasure from animal watching and had visited many game parks with his own family and visitors and with visiting businessmen whom he had taken there. It was perhaps remarkable in itself that he remembered from twenty years before taking photos that were recalled by the Radio Times picture. He remembered the incident well. In fact the three photos were divided

ANIMALS & MEN # 18 — FEATURE

between himself and his father-in-law. Not only that, he remembered fairly precisely where and in what conditions the photos were taken. Such information is always crucial.

Reinhold could not help much but he passed my address to Mr Silvester. At least I lived in England. As it turned out I lived only about half an hour's drive away from Mr Silvester.

Mr Silvester's story was perfectly convincing, and by the time we had arranged to meet and project the slides, my own curiosity had been raised to a high pitch.

Mr Silvester came to my house and was immediately attracted to a large chart on the wall, showing the twenty-three existing Quagga skins, all mounted as full animals. He was anxious for me to see the pictures and I was equally anxious to see them, but we were very balanced about the whole thing. First we talked and had a cup of tea. Mr Silvester wanted to give me some background before I saw the photos; an excellent idea. He told me that the pictures were taken in what was Rhodesia at the time; in the the Kyle River district. The animal was alone at the time and living wild in a small nature reserve. He remembered that the owner of the reserve had had something to do with the training of wild animals for film appearances and the like.

We projected the first slide. There was a wild brown equid with some stripes visible. It had an alternately-coloured zebra mane and an unstriped brown rump. Those indeed are Quagga charac-teristics. The first photo showed the animal in full profile. The others showed it from the back. All were clear pictures taken fairly close to the animal. What was quickly clear to me but understandably not clear to someone who, unlike me, did not suffer from Quagga obsession, was whereabouts on the animal the stripes appeared. The stripes were most obvious on the legs. Striped legs on an equid showing all those other characteristics said to me in fairly clear language; "hybrid".

At first sight, I was not willing to say whether it was a *horse x zebra* hybrid or a *donkey x zebra* hybrid, but I was fairly sure it was one of the two.

Somewhat naturally, my opinion was disappointing news to Mr Silvester. However, he himself was seeking the truth and not trying to create news I explained the reasons for my thinking and we looked at some photos of the donkey-zebra hybrids at Colohester, and at the photo of a horse x zebra hybrid living with a wild zebra herd in Namibia, in Lutz Heck's book. Between us, we even came to the conclusion that the animal was a donkey hybrid rather than a horse hybrid. Such hybrids give no indication of which parent is the zebra and which the domestic animal. We might guess, however, that since the animal was living wild it was born in the wild and so its mother would be wild, i.e. the zebra rather than the domestic.

It also occurred to me later that since the reserve owner was involved in some aspect of animal training, and therefore animal keeping, there might have been a little human influence in the breeding between the equid's parents.

ANIMALS & MEN # 18

I did promise to send copies of the photos to Reinhold Rau so that at least there would be a second opinion.

Reinhold found three photos interesting. Hybrids, ethically desirable or not, are always of interest to anyone interested in breeding. When he wrote back to me he said he was of the firm opinion that the animal was a donkey x zebra hybrid, with no clue as to which parent was which. Zebra hybrids, he said, were not all that rare and he knew of a few at the moment in the Cape Town area.

Horse x zebra hybrids have existed in the wild, as we have seen. Chester Zoo had a couple not all that long ago. Tim Kniveton tells me that these two were extremely spirited animals, difficult to manage. His photos of them confirm this.

So was it all for nothing? No, not really. Mr Silvester discovered what he had really photographed. The very existence of a wild-living hybrid is automatically of some zoological interest and a clear photograph of the animal is truly a bonus. Another bonus is the verifiable information about the time and location of the sighting. If only we had such information about some of the real Quaggas.

The Quagga itself has frequently been described as half horse and half zebra - which it certainly is not - and when we find an animal that really is half-and-half it is an easy step for a non-expert to think of the Quagga. Zebra hybrids in nineteenth century American circuses were actually called Quaggas.

In nineteenth-century Europe, zoologists and breeders were much more interested in breeding Quagga hybrids than in breeding Quaggas, for reasons which were economic rather than conservational. Quagga hybrids also have their place in the history of British art, genetics and the herds kept on the estates of the British aristocracy.

When Gmelin reported his contact with the Tarpan in the late eighteenth century, he described it as half horse and half ass. The confusion of unfamiliar wild animals with half-and-half creatures has a long, almost respectable, history.

* * * * * * * * * *

FEATURE

A story of conservation reparation, travel and art in Europe and Africa.

The book that inspired the BBC-TV programme

Quaggas and other Zebras

by David Barnaby Price £9

Basset Publications, 18 Pasiey Street, Plymouth PL2 1DP

ANIMALS & MEN # 18

Putting In An Appearance

by Neil Arnold

This is a brief file, in reference to a few appearances, they could be deemed, ".. a turn up for the books!"

Although many strange, and out-of-place animals have showed up in the rural shroud of Kent, there are just a few that I have not covered, and I'm pretty sure that this will always be the case.

Most of these 'animals' seem to be of this plain and these include big cats, large insects and others which I have mentioned in previous articles, most of these having been featured in *Animals & Men* I have felt, or believed, that in the past there may have been a misidentification between the spectral black dogs and the out-of-place big cats. Of course, it sounds as though I am questioning the witnesses awareness, but I often think that as the big-cat situation was not as widespread in the '60s, '70s and even early '80s, especially in Kent, that maybe folk were seeing big cats but putting it down as giant hounds.

I know that a majority of people know what they are seeing an in the '70s a phantom black dog was sighted, on a dark lane at Sevenoaks. However, I wonder how many people have actually mistook large 'hounds' ? Who knows, maybe nowadays people are still seeing these enormous canines but instead are labelling them as big cats. Whilst hunting for the local beastly big cat I accidentally caught another out-of-place creature on film, without even realising it.

In January of '98 I dodged the divots at Blue Bell Hill and tried to hold my camera steady, hoping to catch a glimpse of a mystery predator. Instead, I captured, and very shakily (rather Roger Patterson-like) a peculiar green bird. It fluttered from nowhere, about twenty-five metres away and settled on a dirt path, between two thickets. I walked towards it, almost breaking my ankle, and the bird remained in view. Although it seemed an unusual bird I was not excited about it, but I filmed it because I'd not seen one before.

FEATURE

A few days later an article appeared in a local newspaper asking, 'HAVE YOU SEEN THE GREEN ALIEN?' The feature was in reference to the unusual bird I'd actually filmed. Apparently, the birds are parakeets, originating from West Africa and India, the size of collared doves and enjoy screaming like children in a playground. The birds are also known for their acrobatic flying and of course, their colour.

I immediately contacted the local paper, which I'd already been in touch with regarding the big cats.

There are indeed a few thousand of these 'foreigners' fluttering around Kent, a majority of them preferring to roost on shopping centres, probably mistaking them for the Taj Mahal.

Since my original sighting, I have twice more seen the birds, proving that they are probably the most common out-of-place animal to roam this county.

The flying squirrels of Kent have to indeed be one of the most fascinating, yet elusive creatures. My most detailed account, which also appeared in an issue of *Fortean Times*, occurred in Tatsfield. It was here that a motorist, upon coming around a bend of a country lane , saw a grey creature fly across in front of the car and land on a tree opposite.

The witness thought it was a bird until he approached.

He describes it; "The front and rear limbs of the creature appeared to be joined by a flap of skin and it floated and clung to the bark. I couldn't believe what I was seeing but I actually saw the animal again, although on the other side of Tatsfield. I don't know if it was the same creature. "

In Pakistan these creatures have only been rumoured to exist. *Eupetaurus cinereus* was originally discovered the Himalayan regions in 1888, and one of the last official sightings occurred in the mid 1920s. In 1994 researchers believed they had found a front paw of the creature but the rumours were confirmed when a female was allegedly captured in the Sai Valley, in Pakistan. It

- 32 -

ANIMALS & MEN # 18 — FEATURE

was apparently let go after examination. It measured two-feet in height, bore a two-foot long tail and has a piercing scream.

For a creature to be so scarce in its 'native' country is an enigma itself, but to appear in a place such as Kent is a bewildering mystery, and yet the witness, who saw the creature twice, can not be questioned. There are certainly not many British animals that can be mistaken for a flying squirrel. Any theories ?

Another case concerning rare creatures of their homeland turning up in equally strange places, occurred in the early '70s when a 'Tasmanian wolf' was sighted, on a couple of occasions around the Lympne area.

The beast was seen in car headlights and described as being, *". . . bigger than a dog, yellowish in colour and bearing stripes."*

Maybe the beast was a tiger, but there were, and have not been any reports of escaped tigers, or captured tigers and considering this sort of game is more of a threat to man, I find the story somewhat strange.

However, the striped creature was seen again in the '70s and again described as being *"...grey and yellow and striped."*

The RSPCA were called out to examine foot-indentations and confirmed the presence of a mystery creature. An animal that has failed to appear again, some twenty-years later.

We can not rule out the possibility of bizarre cases of out-of-place animals, but the likelihood of such an existence seems frail, in comparison to other creatures. Of course, big cats do roam Britain, but the few cases of mystery bears, bison, tigers and alligators seem to fade. Many of these files remain unsolved but attract more scepticism due to their brief appearances and lack of consistency.

Not anywhere near bizarre is the re-emergence of the Maid Of Kent beetle, which Dr. Karl Shuker reported on in Fortean Times. The one-inch long beetle was last officially reported back in 1950 but in 1997 made an appearance at an Isle Of Sheppey sanctuary lavatory. The creature, which resembles a golden-haired bee was thought to have become extinct in the mid-'60s, but I have obtained a handful of reports of these insects since then. However, insects are not as easy to find or see, even if they are native to this country. Big cats may be elusive and not of this country but there is more chance of seeing one of them, even if a Maid Of Kent beetle lived in your garden. The insect world hides a billion secrets, many will remain untold forever.

However, in the case of the 1997 find, the warden who spotted the creature, reared it in the winter months before letting it go. My final two cases are of contrasting emotion, one being rather mysteriously sad, the other uplifting in an adventurous way.

The local Wildlife Trust has become alarmed at finding a small number of dead otters in the county, particularly in Sevenoaks. One of these corpses being found near the railway line.

The strange thing, or even stranger should I say, is the fact that otters are increasingly rare in Kent, even to the extent where investigators have almost dismissed their existence. So , where are they coming from and how are they dying ? Well, I plan to investigate the mystery further, hoping to find out cause of death.

If these animals have not come from far, then there is proof that Kent does have a minor population, or as the case may be... **did** have a population.

I don't think there is even a one-in-billion chance that a mammoth could be lurking in Kent's wild Weald. However, it seems as though many of the creatures remains are entombed in the bed of the River Medway. Indeed, the Medway area holds many secrets just waiting to be discovered.

I contacted the Maidstone Museum who believe that many Ice Age mammals await discovery. *"It is a rich area for many remains, especially those of the mammoth"*, said a spokesman. *"It is a huge valley. The sea level was lower 13, 000 years ago than it is today and since it has risen remains have been buried. "* There is a geology group currently scouring the area in search of remains, many of the members have hunted for fossils for more than twenty years.

ANIMALS & MEN # 18

One said: *"If you know where to look there are many remains to be found, just beach combing proves to be productive."*

In the past Kent has revealed many startling discoveries, one of these being a fossil skeleton of an iguanodon, which was found in a Maidstone quarry. The discovery was the only one of its kind in England and the bones are now on display in London's Natural History Museum.

Other expeditions and fossil-hunts have also been of great worth. In 1911, a 50, 000 year-old elephant was discovered at Upnor marshes, near Ohathams historic Dockyard. The Royal Engineers were practising digging trenches when they found the twelve-foot skeleton.

Rather oddly, the prehistoric iguanodon appears as one of the creatures displayed on Maidstones coat of arms

So, if the mammoth remains are being dug up so many years later, what are the chances of someone finding remains of a big cat? 'Experts' often find it strange that remains of big cats and Bigfoot are not found, however, imagine how confused researchers would be now if in prehistoric times there had been 'out-of-place' creatures? Just think, way ahead in the future some poor expedition is going to find a puma skeleton in Kent and be extremely baffled.'

And finally. . . an unusual piece of nature, which may have appealed to Charles Fort, took place in 1948 when South Kent was besieged by an unusual large number of rooks. Many fields of crops were damaged, especially on the Romney Marshes, when the descending black hordes invaded from France.

The plague was increasingly bizarre , almost abnormal , as it took over the area. The National Farmers Union assembled to organise shooting parties, but such was the number of the enemy, that they gave up without any knowledge of how to combat them.

The ravaging rooks came over daily from their native land and the scenario probably made Hitchcock`s "The Birds" seem cute in comparison.

Much weirdness in the Weald.

CLINTON'S COGITATIONS

BY CLINTON KEELING

Yes, I know - criticising the work of others can be equated with destroying an instrument one hasn't the skill to use, but I'm not criticising - I'm making comments. In any case, from the now far-off days of my childhood, the value and importance of "how others see us" was firmly instilled into me.

Right, here goes...

I was going to congratulate all concerned on the new appearance and production of "Animals and Men" - but then I found a word missed out and three spelling errors in my own "Cogitations". Come on, gentlemen, you can do better than that.

I've always had a high degree of respect for Chris Moiser, but this time he's really excelled himself, with his photograph on the cover as he's achieved one of two remarkable feats - either a) that the camera can indeed lie, or b) he not only came face to face with but for once got a good photograph of an unknown animal. I mean look at it: the "British Wolverine" be damned - any twelve year-old interested in animals could see it is a Badger with the head of a Lemur: go on, look at it again...

I was sorry to read, in the account of the Giant Squid (p.4), that damned word "transportation" - I mean, what the blue blazes is wrong with just "transport" in that context?. It's on a par with talking about water being "acidic" when acid is meant, or "causation" for cause or going on about "a garden situation" or "a class-room situation" - when all is really necessary is just "garden" or "class~room". It's just pointless affectation and I believe, of trans-Atlantic origin.

On the following page the "Lake Iliamna Monster" sounds rather like a Pilot Whale (<u>Globiocephalus</u>). Certainly the "water squirting" suggests a Cetacean.

ANIMALS & MEN # 18

Most interesting, by the way, to hear it was reported in the "Bristol Bay Times", as here's an extra bit of Forteana for you. This bay in Alaska is so-called because very occasionally a mirage is seen far out to sea of some large city and it's believed to be Bristol, here in England. Say what you like about Keeling - he might be an egotistic braggart (although, to be fair, someone once said it was justified) but he does come up with some interesting things.

I wouldn't get too upset about there being only an estimated five hundred New Guinea Singing Dogs left, as - aberrant cries apart - physiologically they are one and the same as the Dingo of Australia. I kept the latter species, and bred it, for many years, and when some N.G.S.D.s were brought into this country in the 1960s I had the chance of examining them closely. There's no difference, believe me.

On p.9 someone is confusing the blundering, harmless Emu with the Cassowary - the only bird potentially dangerous to Man. Why oh why, I continually, and pointlessly, ask myself will people persist in showing their ignorance by making erroneous assertions of this sort, rather than ask someone who <u>knows</u>?

Regarding "The Onza Which Ain't" (p.11), our revered and respected (the two are not necessarily synonymous) Editor virtually apologises for having said words to the effect "I told you so" - although I cannot think why, as the only people likely to take offence at this extremely mild admonition are those who've been stupidly obstinate and wouldn't be "said", to use a very apt northern term.

I <u>do</u> think that's a bloody silly term - "not a million miles from..." (p.16) as it might come as rather a shock to Mr. Crowther to learn that nowhere on earth is a million miles from anywhere else - or indeed anything like it.

I nominate the comment on p.35 - "The present Lord Strathmore knows nothing about the monster presumably because the creature was dead when he reached his majority" - as one of the daftest

CLINTON'S COGITATIONS

that's ever appeared in "A&M" - and that's against some pretty stiff competition.

I mean, dammit, the English Civil War took place before I reached my majority, as also did the Black Death, the opening of the Stockton and Darlington Railway and the Jack the Ripper murders - but I could write a lengthy article on any of them. Sorry, but I just don't see the "reasoning" behind this outlook. Do you?

On the previous page, headed "The editorial team...have done their best" (in fact it should be "<u>has</u> done <u>its</u> best!) there's a lovely bit of tautology in "11 p.m. at night". Come on, wake up at the back there - why add "at night" to 11 p.m.? I'm beginning to think it's time I was on the board too.

Thank you, most sincerely, Nigel Wright, for putting "rendering" on p.38 and not this horrible, damnable, Yankee "rendition" that everyone (apart, seemingly, from thee and me) uses now.

Jonathan, old son, why didn't you drop me a line or give me a ring when you were working on Issue 17, and tell me you wanted some information on "Pelorus Jack" (p.41) - which would have saved you all the trouble of putting the matter out to tender in the way you did. He was a Risso's Dolphin who, in the closing years of the last century, seemed to take a delight in swimming and leaping in front of steamers going through Pelorous Sound, New Zealand as though acting as a pilot. After several years of never failing to do this he suddenly disappeared - officially he'd been injured and subsequently died, after being hit by a ship's screw - although this doesn't sound very likely as he always leaped along by the bows.

There is still a story that someone went aboard a ship as a passenger but with the intent ion - either for a wager or for "sport" or out of sheer criminal tendencies - of killing Jack when he appeared, by shooting him. Which is what he did - although I'm pleased to say that afterwards the crew didn't exactly say to him "good shot, old chap", if you get my meaning.

ANIMALS & MEN # 18

LETTERS TO THE EDITOR

The Editor and his band of merry men welcome an exchange of correspondence on any subject of interest to readers of this magazine. We reserve the right to edit letters and would like to stress that opinions voiced are those of the individual correspondent rather than being necessarily those of the editorial team or the Centre for Fortean Zoology. Every attempt is made not to infringe anyone's moral rights or copyright, and we apologise if we have unwittingly done so.

A NOISE ANNOYS

Dear Jon,

Richard King forwarded this to me today, can any body help? It kind of sounds like rifle fire at first, but then he seems to know about the outdoors, and describes it as electrical. It sounds like it is coming from an animal, as it does move. Here it is:

LETTERS

Several years ago, probably around 1990 in February, very cold weather, I came home from work after midnight (I often work as the night librarian here). I parked my car in front of my house, which is in a very rural area with a six acre woods about 50 feet from the front door.

There are fields around the woods and no houses for about a ¼ mile or so. My dog kept barking, which is strange for him, and barking at the edge of the woods. I thought nothing of this, and walked from my car to the house when I heard the sound. All I can say is that is sounded like a very amplified electronic noise, and it went like this, phonetically: "BZZZ-SSSSSS-TTTT BZZZ-SSSSS-TTTT BZZZZ-SSSSS-TTTT CLACK CLACK CLACK!"

This repeated about every minute or two and the dog went nuts. At first I thought an electric transformer had blown or something like that, and it sounded amplified because it came from far away, like one hundred yards or so.

I thought of everything, like could this be some teenager coyote hunters (at midnight!) trying to call them in with some strange device, I thought of animals, like buck deer fighting or a buck knocking his antlers against a tree; perhaps a bizarre water bird off course.

Well, I got my wife and she heard it, too, and it seemd angry at the dog's barking and the sound seemed to move around the woods gradually in a small area. I didn't have a flashlight that worked. After an hour I heard it no longer; it made the noise about every minute to about every 5 minutes and gradually stopped and we went in. The next day, in daylight, I checked around the area for tracks, etc., but found none. It was rather frightening and strange, and no one has ever been able to tell us anything.

If you have any suggestions or have heard of anything like this, please give me your ideas. UFO? Who knows? This is a quick description of the noise, and I'd appreciate any help on your part and am interested in your comments. Have you heard anything like this?

BradLaGrange

- 36 -

ANIMALS & MEN # 18
Ain't life a bitch: just when you think you have discovered a means of making pots of money your, goose goes and buggers off!
Or,
Your "golden cat" goes walkabout.

Dear A&M,

As I reported in the last edition of A&M, I was involved in the trial by media of Mr. Mike Thomas of Newquay Zoo and his video footage of the "Beast" of Bodmin (NOT).

Several days after the event I got a very strange phone call from Anonymous John, (video camera operator extra-ordinaire) he was not a happy bunny. The feeling I got from analysing his vitriolic attack, was, not that he was upset over the mugging that Mr. Thomas had received, no, but that it was entirely my fault that he had not made any money out of his video footage. Not a brass farthing let alone the many thousands of pound that the had anticipated.

An hour into the two hour phone call Anonymous John started to ask questions, dealing with his quest to capture the elusive "Beast" on film. Then he came out with the most astounding statement I have ever heard: "expenditure is no problem". It appears that Anonymous John was/is convinced that he will be able to recoup any expenditure through sales of his pictures, and still make a handsome profit. (So much for his statements at the press conference about helping Mr. Thomas in his "non" money-making quest for the Beast.)

If he follows my advice as to what photographic hardware to buy, I don't think Anonymous John will be making much of a profit, as he would have to pay at least ten grand for the camera kit I described to him as 'minimum' requirements ! Ha ! Ha !. Somewhere in Devon or Cornwall there is a Nikon or Canon retailer who thinks that Christmas came in the middle of July this year.

LETTERS

For those of you who follow the Beast of Bodmin stories you may know that myself and Mr. Pompous or Mr. Arrogant (depending on your point of view), scragged the *Cornish Guardian* and their Beast pictures at the beginning of the year. Well, this month there was a letter from the Anonymous "snapper" of those pictures, defending Mr. Thomas against those doubters, and attacking horrible people who don't believe in the beast.

Anonymous Snapper pledged himself to obtaining photographic proof of the Beasts existence and backed his statement by writing that he had obtained far superior photographic equipment than he had previously used, with this new equipment he was convinced that the proof needed was imminent.

It is ironic to say the least, that these two independent Anonymous Gentlemen with their new expensive, better cameras have now had, in the case of one ten months and in the other three months to come up with the goods, and, we haven't seen a single new image published!

Perhaps the Beast is having the last laugh and definitive proof of its existence will come in the shape of a photograph taken on a 1970's Kodak Instamatic, by a little old biddy who has been feeding "The Beast" cod heads at her farm in the back of beyond for the last twenty years!

PS If you want to make money in Cornwall - open a Camera shop that sells top of the range Nikons or Canons and the most expensive telephoto lenses they make, I'll send these would be "Beast" snappers to you. As Barnum said - "There is a sucker born every minute"

PPS - An interesting development, in the new intake of students this year one of them has a friend who "knows where the Beast is"!!

Keep snapping, who knows one day your Beast may come.

Best wishes

Paul Crowther

ANIMALS & MEN # 18

FLEXING YOUR MUSSELS

Dear Jon,

You all recall what a horrible time we of the Great Lakes region are having with this zebra mussel problem. You may all also recall that I live near Lake Winnebago which in Indian means "Lake Stinking Waters." Apparently some of the little critters have been found in this wonderful lake I have the pleasure of living near. Well, my next door neighbor, who happens to be the big DNR water guru around here, has announced that should the zebra mussels take hold in Lake Winnebago, we can expect it to "improve" the water quality. So ain't that a slick twist?

PS...Lets hope the sturgeon like em.

Felinda Bullock, Wisconsin

THE WORM TURNS

Dear Jon,

I have never put this story in print, but have discussed it with several biologists of whom I have worked with, and none could come up with any definition of the animal I am about to describe. Personally I believe it may be a known species, but I have dug through lots of books trying to find it, to no avail.

During the Spring of 1978, Corey Rudolph and I were camping out in the mountains dividing the Mojave Desert and Los Angeles, and following up on Sasquatch reports nearby. One morning, as we were walking around in the high desert which was still slightly snow covered, we came upon something wiggling in the snow near a little creek. Upon closer examination we saw that it was a worm of some sort, and we began to dig it out of the snow. Once in hand, it immediately coiled up into a tight ball, and now appeared more like some sort of wire. As we felt it we noticed it was very stiff, and could not be forced to re-coil. Its body was maybe 5 mm in diameter and about 9 inches long when fully outstretched. It was brown in color, and its head was an abrupt stump with what looked like the ball from a ball pen at the end. It had no eyes or anything, just a wire-like body with a ball-pen mouth. In fact, we weren't even sure it was a mouth at all. It also had no apparent anus. I took it home and kept it in a small tupperware bowl of water for about 3 months, and fed it nothing. It remained alive, and would stretch-out in the bowl, but coil again if touched. After three months we decided to take it back to the same area, and release it. We searched the libraries and called several "worm" experts, none of which had ever heard of this species. All books on worms were without this one.

Whatever it was, it never died in our captivity, without food of any sort. It was released in a small creek and simply drifted away in the current. To this day, I have no idea what it was, but we decided to name it the "Rudolph-Trapp Snow Worm." I don't expect any of you to have heard of such a thing, but if you have, I'd like to know about it.

Sincerely,
Douglas E. Trapp - Dallas, Texas

LETTERS

GULO AND GULLIBLE

Letters to the Editor.

At first glance at the cover of A&M17 I thought, "muddy badger". Reading the caption, I thought, "No, it damned well isn't". Given the indistinct nature of the print, undefined depth of field, perspective, etc it was still a muddy badger, no question.

The lack of evidence for the wolverines existence in Scotland and probably also Wales is overwhelming.

The numbers required for a viable population composed of solitary animals would seem to preclude the escapee theory. It is not impossible that some misguided control freak, finding his Barratt semi inadequate for, say a Bengal tiger, downsized to a wolverine. Possible, yes. Likely, somewhat less so. To extend Lever's idea that its most likely purpose here would be as a pet, limits its presence here even more. Ferret fanciers apart, the mustelidae does not possess the "*aaah* factor" to such an extent to make it appeal to humans. Even hand-reared wolverines tend to revert rather dramatically. Next door's poodle could be put own to natural wastage. a shortage of primary school children would be less easily explained.

But its main failure factor as a pet is its intrinsic lack of "glam". It's one thing exercising the clouded leopard on the common, but there is little kudos being seen leading something that brings forth cries of "Hey mister, that's an ugly bugger of a dog you've got." As a fashion its sadly lacking. As an exercise in machismo it's a disaster, as hardly anyone would know what it was, thus missing the point of the studded collar and its owner's plethora of tattoos. This would lead to the owner being ambushed by small boys and "badgered" with mammalian-related questions.

Which brings us back to the reason for all this demented supposition, wishful thinking and general myopia from a thankfully miniscule minority of the cryptid orientated population. Possible litigation prevents me "outing" these sad souls, but if ever there comes a petition to provide nest boxes for tooth fairies, just check the first few names. Despite its enormous implications I can exclusively reveal that muddy badgers do exist. I have seen them. Red badgers also exist, these I have also seen, admittedly rarely.

On a windswept clifftop on the northeast coast of Scotland stand the ruins of Dunnotar Castle where once was hidden the crown jewels of Scotland. (Yes, we have a set as well.) The ground surrounding this stately edifice looks like any arable farmland, until you plough it. It comes up brick red and so do the local badgers. given the requisite rainfall, more than adequate hereabouts. This is not a sub-species, this is mud we're talking.

The landed gentry of Kincardine were (perhaps still are) the Arbuthnotts. In common with other younger sons of the nobility, knowing his elder brother would inherit, George John took himself off to Canada around 1850 to work for the Hudson Bay Company.

As was common for the time, on his return home he wrote his memoirs, the usual sort of Victorian colonial jingoism that should be shunned like the plague. Apart from one small paragraph. G. J. was a "sportsman" - that is he killed for pleasure, so he had a basic knowledge of natural history and game.

His "Notes and Observations gathered in Our North West Territories" mentions an encounter with what he thought was a badger, shot by his guide. This was, of course the first "glutton" he'd encountered and he explained his mistake by the corpse being almost the same colour as his native local badgers back in Scotland.

Always hard to disprove a negative, it's even harder to deal with the awesome gullibility that leaves you shaking your head at the shortfall in rationality on seemingly obvious explanations of natural phenomena.

Chris Moiser was mouthing logical, reasoned sense. The utterances of some others emanated from an orifice facing a different direction. entirely.

Yours,
Tom Anderson - Aberdeen

SCIENCE: THE BIG STICK?

As well as being interested in the discovery of new species, I support organisations that seek protection of currently-threatened ones - like Minke whales.

Japan has an active whaling fleet and has been hunting and killing Minke under the guise of "scientific research" for years - although most of the meat ends up in restaurants rather than test-tubes.

A large area around Antarctica was designated in 1994 as a whale sanctuary, by the International Whaling Commission It now appears that Japanese whalers have extended their "research" programme to this area too! The pro-whaling organisation *Breach* say that the Japanese whalers often try to avoid "quick kill" explosive harpoons, and prefer traditional lances, to avoid destroying valuable flesh

Additionally, *Breach* have alleged that some of the whale meat is used in school catering, to foster the taste for whale meat amongst the kids, in the hope that they will become paying consumers later.

I wonder if these children will grow up with the notion that "scientific research", wanton inflicting of pain, and gratuitous self-indulgence of desire are all synonymous? Such notions are not unknown in human history. A *new* New World Order beckons?

Steve Johnson, Wolverhampton.

ANIMALS & MEN # 18

WHAT'S AFOOT?

by Richard Freeman

In the last issue, Nigel Wright reported on the Fortean Times Unconvention. Whilst mentioning our editors' talk he didn't mention mine! Well, since this is my column, I'll just have to blow my own trumpet: I lectured about dragons at the '98 Unconvention and it went down a storm, so there!

Cryptozoology certainly seems to be the flavour of the month with TV producers; and the long-awaited *X-Creatures* finally appeared. I was expecting a *Life on Earth* style series with a huge budget and immaculate research - God, was I ever wrong! Let's take an episode by episode look at this series....

* One of the most likely cryptids, the yeti, featured in the first programme. After briefly interviewing a few native witnesses and walking a few hundred feet up a mountain presenter Chris Packham concludes that there is not enough food above the snowline to sustain a giant ape. Yetis live in the mountain heights - *ergo*, no yetis. Anyone with even a passing interest in the yeti will know they live in the valleys below the snowline, in forests of bamboo, rhododendron, and assorted semi-tropical plants..

Other areas with recent sightings such as western China are totally ignored. The main thing that sticks in my mind is the Sherpa woman's tearful recount of a yeti that killed her yaks and tossed her into a river in 1974. The animal was probably more interested in her livestock and she was merely in the way

WHAT'S AFOOT?

(genuine unprovoked yeti attacks are very rare: see my article "The Bigfoot Murders" in *A&M14*) but the incident still obviously frightened her 24 years later! What did Packham think she saw, a monkey?

When he is talking to a white person with a few letters after their name, Packham's attitude seemed to change to one of fawning acceptance. A case in point was his behaviour towards Debbie Martyr (I actually believe that Debbie saw an unknown primate, but that is not the point). Because she is a professional he was willing to accept *her* testimony but not that of natives who live cheek-by-jowl with the animals in question,.

* The next programme featured the giant squid, no longer a cryptid but definitely still a monster. The main problem I had with this episode was the recounting of the sighting of J.D.Starkey from an Admiralty trawler off the Maldives. In his original testimony Starkey matches the kraken's length to that of the ship: 175 feet +. In the show, the ship's length is cut to 60 feet ! Why is this? - did the natural history unit balk at the idea of a 175 foot squid?

* The Loch Ness monster programme was probably the high point of the series. Sightings are, they say, natural phenomena misinterpreted due to expectation, coupled with sightings of giant sturgeon. I agree up to a point, but there is a hardcore of sightings less easy to dismiss. In particular the very clear land sightings. Packham's dismissal of the Spicer case as a couple of otters is pitifully inadequate.

Megalania prisca survival is also dismissed after a brief talk with one palaeontologist and an interview with a couple who saw a big "goanna" (much too small to be *Megalania*). The Frank Gorden encounter is not even mentioned - is the great dragon of Oz too contentious, even when a qualified herpetologist sees it?

Bigfoot was the episode that caused the biggest kerfuffle: Sasquatch groups the world over raged at Packham's dismissal of their icon. His attempt to recreate the Patterson footage is laughable, with a costume that would shame Star Trek, as was his assertion that the animal behaved unnaturally by calmly walking away from two very close hum Actually I

Animals & Men # 18 — what's afoot

have seen film of wild gorillas acting in exactly the same manner. Native testimony was once again tossed aside in a cavalier fashion!

* British big cats were next up, even the *X-Creatures* couldn't deny these. The assertion that they are not breeding however is highly questionable. Given a puma's lifespan in captivity is around 17 years and considerably less in the wild, they and other species must be breeding. They have been seen consistently since the sixties so unless there is a mad animal-releaser turning them free every few years, this is a foregone conclusion.

The reconstruction at the start of this episode was highly alarmist, showing a man being killed by the beast of Exmoor. This tone continues through out the programme commenting on attacks by pumas in America. The area of California in question has had an explosion in puma numbers coupled with human encroachments on their habitat. This is not a concern in Britain where there are probably only 200 or so at large.

* The final programme dealt with an animal that I am 100% sure still exists: the thylacine. Film taken in 1973 on mainland Australia was shown, which I had not seen before - but despite looking convincing at first, it was almost certainly a feral dog or fox with mange. Packham concludes that thylacines might still exist on Tasmania but not on the mainland. Most promising mainland areas like Queensland were ignored as were the compelling accounts from New Guinea. It was speculated that a thylacine pup preserved in alcohol may one day be used to clone new specimens.

In conclusion: cringe-inducing pap! From start to finish, this whole series of *The X Creatures* was a cavalcade of base errors and appalling arrogance, which I would sum up as pitifully bad film-making.

* * * * * *

National Geographic ran a far superior documentary on the giant squid: after examining the legends and historic accounts it followed Dr Clyde Roper's attempt to film the squid by attaching a "crittercam" to the back of a sperm whale, his target's only predator. Sadly, the lord of the deep remained elusive, but new insights into whale behaviour, such as vertical sleeping, were discovered.

MAMMOTH RE-CREATION

Equinox recently ran a programme about a Japanese scientist hoping to re-create the mammoth. Having perfected a technique of fertilising eggs with dead sperm, he now hopes to use mammoth sperm on a female Asian elephant. The odds seem stacked against him. Firstly he must find a male mammoth with intact genitals. Then, there is no guarantee the sperm and egg will be compatible. Elephants don't sexually mature until around 17 and are very slow reproducers - hence even with exceptional luck it could take 50 years of back-breeding to get one specimen. Still, I wish him all the luck in the world.

LINKS

Web Sites of cryptozoological or fortean interest

Our CFZ web site can be found at http://www.eclipse.co.uk/cfz and is currently undergoing some pretty hefty reorganisation to give it a properly professional appearance. By the time you read this, the new version should be up and running - and well worth checking out!

As always, feedback is always welcome - say, if you spot a typo. Or, if you want to send £10,000 as a token of your esteem...

OTHER SITES

The information below is for guidance only: web-sites may change or close without our knowing!

www.planet13.co.uk/earthly/EarthlyDelights.htm (Earthly Delights) looks at Bodmin Moor: its terrestrial zodiac, big cats and celtic stones

Brian Goodwin's site at http://freespace.virgin.net/brian.goodwin/ includes big cats, serpents, dragons, Nessie, and news from Fortean Cumbria. (cont'd)

ANIMALS & MEN # 18

The English version of Michel Raynal's Virtual Institute of Cryptozoology service at http://perso.wanadoo.fr/cryptozoo/welcome.htm is now being developed - with text and pics

Ben Roesch's site is at http://www.ncf.carleton.ca/~bz050/ which includes the "Cryptozoology On The Internet" list of sites, a sub-page of Ben's, which can be found at http://www.ncf.carleton.ca/~bz050/HomePage.czlinks.html

-----

BOOK REVIEWS

BOOK REVIEWS

The Flight of Dragons
Peter Dickinson. Paper Tiger £13.99
Large format, 134pp. ISBN 1 85028 411 3

A soft-back re-print of the original 1979 classic of cryptozoology. Dickenson's theory runs that dragons were a direct descendent of *Tyrannosaurus rex*, that flew and spat fire by manipulation of hydrogen gas. Sumptuously illustrated by Wayne Anderson, this is a totally captivating book. I think dragons were supernatural creatures rather than flesh & blood but this is still one of my all-time favourite books.

- **Richard Freeman**

This book combines fact with fantasy and science with romance, and looks at the folklore aspects as well as discussing a possible mating and evolutionary cycle. Some of the suggestions are pretty bizarre, eg, "flight was achieved by a controlled digestion of parts of the bone structure." An entertaining read, though

- **Grham Inglis**

Weird World 1999
(Fortean Times) John Brown Publishing, London.
£8.99 96pp

This large format book is colourful in both senses of the word. Divided into sections, it contains mini-features and news round-ups in various categories of "weirdness" - the human world, animals, paranormal, and the natural world, and also has "shorts" from various geographical regions - eg, the Strange Asia map with little boxes of text scattered around it. The subjects cover the normal *Fortean Times* gamut, and include Lionel Fanthorpe's Top 10 Mysteries (including the haunted Ford Capri), the "blobs" washed up on the Tasmanian coast, the CFZ's Chupacabra hunt in Mexico, a gallery of nice crop circles, how to make your *own* crop circle, that Martian "face", tales of inept crime (some really are extraordinarily inept), and strange deaths. A fun read.

And, may I take this opportunity to say that the current "CFZ-mobile", a Ford *Cortina,* is haunted by nothing more than bits of rubbish like old Coke cans and empty cigarette packets... - **Graham Inglis**

- 42 -

ANIMALS & MEN # 18

MAGAZINES

DEAD OF NIGHT

A4 62pp £2. Lee Walker, 156 Bolton Road East, New Ferry, Merseyside, L62 4RY

Masses of info including strange news stories, superstitions and conspiracy theories. probably in pole position as a worthy rival - or complement - to *The Fortean Times*...

THE CRYPTOZOOLOGY REVIEW

166 Pinewood Ave, Toronto, M6C 2V5, Canada

Summer 1998's Review includes crypto news (somewhat obscurely described by Ben Roesch as "all the latest cryptozoology news fit to print"), and three articles: how big does the Giant Squid get, underwater panthers - what the Mississippi "piasa" pictographs depict, and part 3 of sea serpent carcasses. The next issue should be out by now.

EXOTIC ZOOLOGY

3405 Windjammer Dr., Colorado Springs, CO 80920, USA. Quarterly. $10 US, $13 non-US.

Matthew Bille's 8pp mag looks at the more prozaic end of cryptozoology (rather than the fortean and "ghost animals" area).

The Nov/Dec issue looks at reports of coelacanths in the Indian Ocean, debunks Packham's *The X Creatures* Sasquatch treatment in much the same way as Richard does in *this* magazine (p.40), and has a brief roundup of news and comment.

MAINLY ABOUT ANIMALS

A5 32pp Quarterly. Subscrip: £5 per year. C. Keeling, 13 Pound Place, Shalford, Guildford, Surrey, GU4 8HH.

Zoological articles and news, edited by Clinton

MAGAZINES

Keeling, also a contributor to *Animals & Men* - see pp 34-35 of this issue for his latest "Cogitations"...

COVER UP

SUPR (Scottish Unexplained Phenomena Research) A4 magazine 12pp £1.25 from David Colman, 49 Limefield Cres., Bathgate, WL, Scotland EH48 1RF

Scottish ufologists co-operate (or sometimes don't) to find out who's covering up what.

PORCUPINE!

Kadoorie Farm, Lam Kam Road, Tai Po, New Territories, Hong Kong.

40pp A4 newsletter from the Dept of Ecology and Biodiversity, University of Hong Kong. Covers South China as well as HK, with news on animal conservation / distribution studies / rehab programmes / rescue, roundups of sightings, and book reviews. Issue 17 also features South China's three shrews.

ERAS NEWSLETTER

Essex Reptiles & Amphibians Society, 1 Thyme Rd, Tiptree, Essex.

A monthly 24pp "member's newsletter" in A5 booklet form. The intro, by 'snakecharmer', comments, "I have never known such a quiet month. You really are being either very careful or very secretive." However, there *are* articles, ads for exotic pets - and their food ("cheap squeaks!" proclaims one ad...), breeding reports, and forthcoming shows and events.

MAGONIA

£1.25 John Rimmer, 5 James Tce, Mortlake Churchyard, London SW14 8HB

Magonia's been running for nearly 30 years now, and is still seeking to "interpret contemporary vision and belief", mainly in the UFO/Fortean areas. A mag that doesn't pull its punches.

Animals & Men # 18

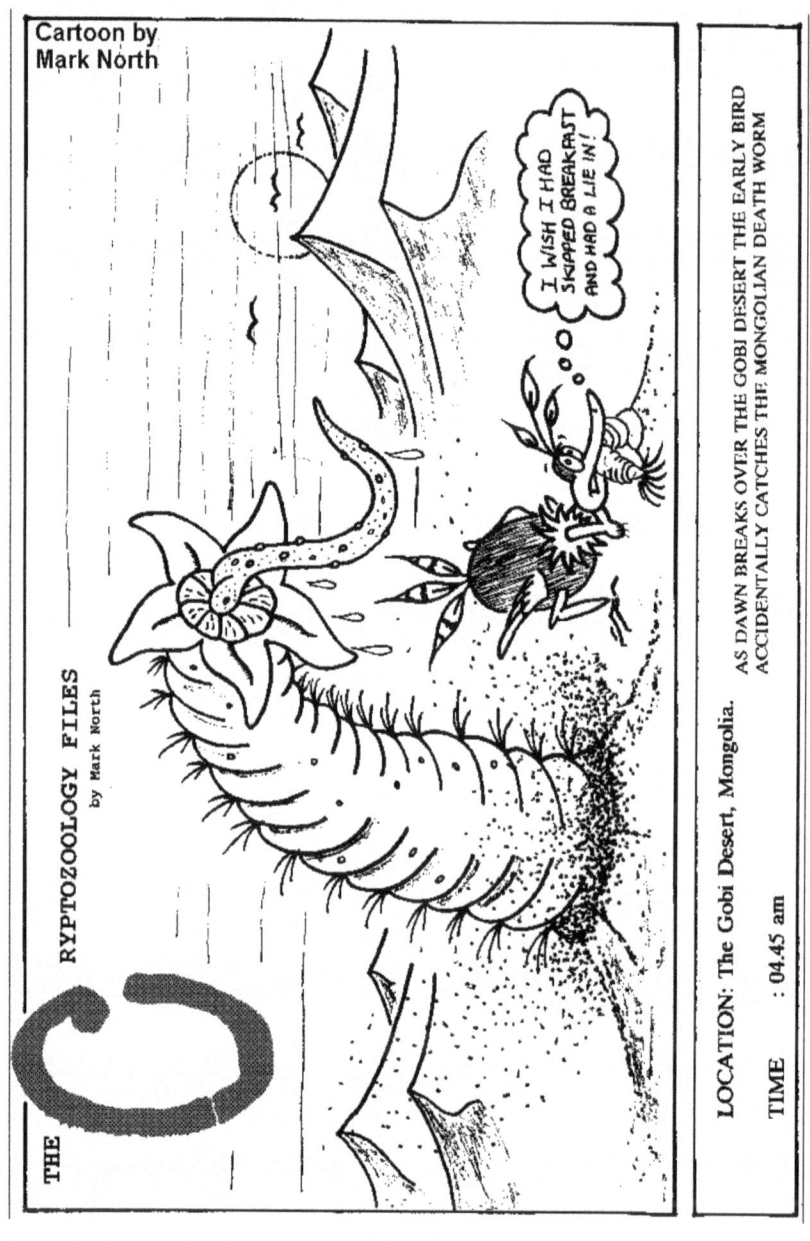

Animals & Men # 18

ANIMALS & MEN
BACK ISSUES: £2 each

Back issues are available from the editorial address. Please see "methods of payment" on p.47.

CONTENTS (all issues also contain news pages, reviews and letters) :

1 Relict Pine Martens, Giant Sloths, Sumatran and Javan Rhinos, Golden Frogs, Frog Falls.
2 Mystery bears in Oxford and The Atlas Mountains, Loch Ness reports, Green Lizards, Woodwose, The Tatzelwurm.
3 Giant Worm in Eastbourne, Lake Monsters of New Guinea, Giant Lizards in Papua, Mystery Cats, Black Dogs on Dartmoor, Scorpion Mystery.
4 Manatees of St Helena, Migo: The Lake Monster of New Britain, The search for the Tasmanian Thylacine.
5 Mystery cats, Loch Ness, More on the "Migo Video", Boars and Pumas, The Hairy Hands of Dartmoor.
6 The Owlman Special; also the Humped Elephants of Nepal, Mystery Cats, Sabre-toothed cats, Mysterious hominids of Africa, The British Nandi Bear?, Bibliography of Cryptozoology books part 1 (by Dr Karl Shuker).
7 Mystery Whales, Strangeness in Scotland, On collecting a cryptid, Bodmin Leopard Skull, Shuker's Cryptozoological Bibliography pt 2.
8 Green Cats and Dogs, Mystery Whales, Quagga Project, Bibliography of Cryptozoological books (3rd & concluding part), Malayan Man Beast.
9 Hong Kong Tiger, Horseman of Lincolnshire, Scottish BHM, Congo Peacock, Mystery Whales.
10 Mystery Moth of Madagascar, Bengal Leopard Cats, The Derry, Wild Boars in Kent, a new Irish lake monster, mystery whales and the truth about the Essex Beach Corpses.
11 The "Walruses Special", also: Feathered Dinosaurs, Ground Sloth Survival in North America, Mystery Whales, Initial Bipedalism.
12 Lions: The Barbary Lion, etc. More Feathered Dinosaurs, Chinese Crabs in the Thames, Mystery Animals of Germany, News from New Zealand.

BACK ISSUES
13 Pangolins; also Moby the Sperm Whale, Barking Beast of Bath, Yorkshire ABCs, Molly the Singing Oyster, Leatherback Turtles, Walruses.
14 The Dragons of Yorkshire, Irish mystery animals, In Search Of "Gambo", Charlie Fort and the Vampire Sheep Slayer - and Jackals; and the first of Clinton's Cogitations (Clin Keeling looks back on and comments on the previous issue).
15 Lake Dakataua "Migo" monster update, The Weird Warbling Whatsit of the Westcountry, The Beast of Llangurig, The Waspman, The Bigfoot "Murders", and three articles on Beavers.
16 Expedition Report: The Search for the Chupacabra; Quagga Project update; Bestiary #1; Snakes with Legs; Eastern Cougars; Giant Lizards in the English Countryside?
17 British Wolverine - or muddy badger?, Turtle Tales, Killer Bees, The Ziphiidae - possible new species, Vertebrate palaentology, Video: the Beast of Bodmin press conference.

THE GOBLIN UNIVERSE
BACK ISSUES: £2 each

Back issues are available from the editorial address. Please see "methods of payment" on p.47.

CONTENTS (all issues also contain news pages, letters, and record, magazine and book reviews) :

4 Naked witches, hellhounds and Capel's tomb. St. Leonards Vampire. Cattle Mutilation. Psychic Detectives.
5 Crop Circles & Animal Mutilations. Glamis Castle ghosts. Communication with UFOs.
6 Rendlesham "UFO crash site" in Suffolk. Mystery Planets (Shuker). Cannibalism in Scotland. DIY countries.
7 The Terror of Gloucestershire. Telpas. Barnum & Tom Thumb. The Making of "The Owlman" film. KKK operations in Scotland?

ANIMALS & MEN # 18

CFZ Yearbook 1999

edited by Jonathan Downes, Richard Freeman and Graham Inglis

Includes

Surviving Neanderthals - a search for man's closest relatives
- by Jonathan Downes and Richard Freeman.

The Beast of Bluebell Hill - by Neil Arnold

Sightings of a mystery animal in Kent.

Wolverines in Wales? - by Roy Kerridge

Wolves may no longer live at Wolf's Castle Crag in Pembrokeshire, Wales, but at least one man believes that the fields and woods below the hill are home to an equally fearsome animal, the Wolverine.

Waitoreke: The Enigma from New Zealand - by Craig Heinselman

Reports of a mammal living in the mountain lakes and rivers of New Zealand has been reported over the years, with varying descriptions from otter-like, beaver-like and seal-like. Craig looks at the etymology of the name of this animal, the diversities of life on and around New Zealand, its habitat, the theories (through behavior, anatomy and habitat) and the evidence thus far.

Folk tales involving were-beasts from Ghana - by Louis Baba

Pelorus Jack

The text of the 1911 booklet by James Cowan on "Pelorus Jack", the solitary white dolphin which met coastal steamers plying between the two main islands of New Zealand.

Chance would be a Fine Thing - by Graham Inglis

Life on other planets? Silicon lifeforms? A look at some of the possibilities.

The 1999 Yearbook will be available from the CFZ in mid January 1999

£10.75 (UK)

£11.50 (overseas) - (prices inclusive of postage & packing)

ANIMALS & MEN # 18
THE CFZ YEARBOOK 1998

edited by
Jonathan Downes & Graham Inglis

200pp. £12.50

Published by and available from the CFZ

Contributors:

Tom: Anderson, Neil Arnold, Richard Freeman, Mike Grayson, Martin Jenkins, Roy Kerridge, Chris Moiser, Nick Molloy, Richard Muirhead, Darren Naish, Michael Playfair, and Emmet J. Sweeney.

Subjects:

Giant crocodiles, cryptozoological films, African Stories, Nessie - asking the right questions, Nessie - diary of a hunt, Ichthyosaur evolution, Mammoths and the Comet, Sea Serpents, Amerindian icons, Strange Sea Snake stories, an alphabetical guide to water monsters, the Fortean Fauna of Percy Fawcett, and The Zambesi River God.

MORGAWR:
THE MONSTER OF FALMOUTH BAY

by
A. Mawnan-Peller

With a new introduction by Tony Shiels, this booklet is available for £1.50 from the CFZ.

OUR OWN PUBLICATIONS
THE OWLMAN AND OTHERS

by Jonathan Downes

NEW UPDATED EDITION

See back cover for more information...

For more information on CFZ projects and publications, visit our website at:
http://www.eclipse.co.uk/cfz

HOW TO ORDER and
METHODS OF PAYMENT

Subscription rates INCLUDE postage. On other orders, postage and packing is extra: please add 25p (£0.30non-UK) per magazine and 75p (£0.90 non-UK) per book.

Payment can be made in UK cash, by IMO (an international money order), Eurocheque, or by a cheque drawn on a UK bank. Please make all cheques payable to Jonathan Downes.

Please send all orders to

CFZ, 15 Holne Court, Exwick, Exeter, Devon, EX4 2NA, England.

Britain is one of the few countries of the world where US dollars do **not** circulate. If making payment in US$ then please add $14 to cover the currency exchange fee.

Animals & Men Collected Editions Volume 4 — **New Horizons**

by
Jonathan Downes

£12.95 from
Domra Publications, 65 Constable Road, Corby, Northants.

"Anomalist" award winner 1997

ISSN 1354 0637   TYPESET BY THE CHEEKY COCKNEY CULTIST
                   "My Old Man said Worship Great Cthullu"

Issue 19

Spring 1999

It is about time that I made a long-overdue apology. In 1999 a nice bloke called John Tait offered to do full colour covers for us. He did a couple, and they were magnificent—probably my favourite covers that we ever did. However, for various reasons that I cannot even remember twelve years later (although I have a vague suspicion that they were our fault) we let the arrangement lapse.; John, if you are reading this, I offer my heartfelt apologies. I think that we treated you fairly badly, although I hope that you realise that this was by no means intentional.

On other fronts, this was the time that the magazine was beginning to get a little formulaic, although that was by no means necessarily a bad thing. It was about then that the concept of regular columnists took hold, and although many of the original columns no longer exist, it is a conceptual ideal that we have stuck with until the present day..

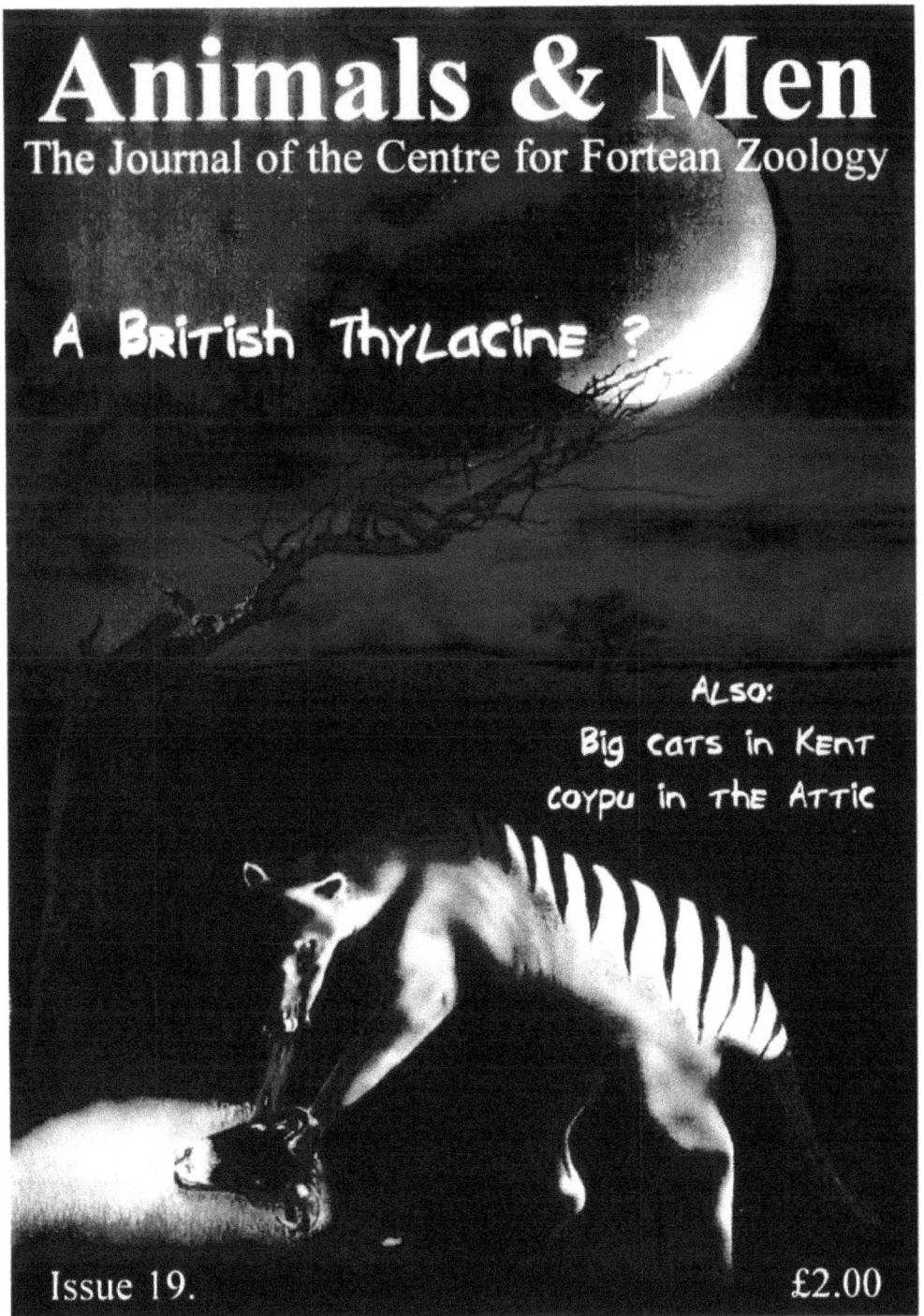

ANIMALS & MEN # 19

THE CURRENT CREW OF THE CFZ MOTHERSHIP ARE:

Director: Jonathan Downes
Deputy Director: Graham Inglis
Assistant Editor: Richard Freeman
Toby the CFZ dog
Magazine cartoonist and artwork: Mark North
Newsagent from nowhere: Richard Muirhead
Associate founding editor: Jan Williams
Tour Manager: Nigel Wright
Hedge-Witch: Joyce Howarth

CONSULTANTS

Consulting Editor: Dr Bernard Heuvelmans
Cryptozoology: Dr Karl Shuker, Dr Lars Thomas, Loren Coleman
Zoology: Clinton Keeling, Chris Moiser
Cetology and Palaentology: Darren Naish

REGIONAL REPRESENTATIVES

Scotland: Tom Anderson
Surrey: Nick Smith
Somerset: Dave McNally
West Midlands: Dr Karl Shuker
Kent: Neil Arnold
Sussex: Sally Parsons
Gtr Manchester & Cheshire: A E Munro
Hampshire: Darren Naish
Leicestershire: Alistair Curzon
Cumbria: Brian Goodwin
Yorkshire: Steve Jones
Tyneside: Simon Elsdon

USA: Loren Coleman
Denmark: Dr Lars Thomas, Erik Sorensen
Republic of Ireland: Daev Walsh
Spain: Alberto Lopez Acha, Angel Morant Fores
Germany: Hermann Reichenbach, Wolfgang Schmidt
France: Francois de Sarre
Mexico: Dr R A Lara Palmeros
Canada: Ben Roesch

"In her abnormalities, nature reveals her secrets"
(Goethe)

WHO'S WHO & WHAT'S WHAT

CONTENTS:

3 Editorial
4 Newsfile
16 The Case of the British Thylacine, by Richard Freeman.
19 Bestiary: The Rukh, by Ade Dimmick.
20 Coypu in a Yorkshire Attic, by Andrew Scott
20 Sweet Wallaby of Mine, (Chuck Leonard - *Mojo* Magazine)
21 Sipandjee - An Unidentified Ape, by Allan Edward Munro
22 Clinton's Cogitations, by Clinton Keeling
24 Ayrshire Tales, by Mark Fraser.
28 Curiosity Killed the Cat, by Neil Arnold
35 North of the Border, by Tom Anderson
36 Letters
38 Book Reviews
42 Ground Sloth Survival, by R Freeman
45 Back issues and CFZ publications

ANIMALS & MEN

CFZ, 15 Holne Court, Exwick, Exeter, Devon, EX4 2NA, England

http://www.eclipse.co.uk/cfz

SUBSCRIPTIONS & PAYMENTS:
PLEASE SEE PAGE 47

This issue is dedicated, with love, to the memory of Lee - the best neighbour the CFZ ever had - who lost her battle with cancer on 20th April 1999.

We ask for your good wishes, and prayers to whichever god you believe in, for her and her bereaved husband Roly

Animals & Men Collected Editions Volume 4 — New Horizons

ANIMALS & MEN # 19
THE GREAT DAYS OF ZOOLOGY ARE NOT DONE...

EDITORIAL

Dear Friends,

As I sit here typing this editorial it seems only too amazing that it is five years to the month since I started this magazine, and in the words of Robert Hunter, "What a Long, Strange Trip it`s been!"

Looking back at the last five years, and glancing over to the list of people involved in creating this present issue of Animals & Men, it is good to note, not only how far we have come in the last five years but how many of the people who were with me at the beginning in the first few issues are still around now.

It`s also sad to remember those stalwarts of the A&M editorial posse who are no longer with us. I would particularly like to thank Jan Williams, who, although she is not presently an active contributor is still a valued friend and colleague. If it hadn`t been for you, my dear, this whole thing would never have started in the first place! Really!

I`d also like to take a few moments to remember our two departed cartoonists, Jane Bradley and Mort, both of whom who are now dead and both of whom are still sadly missed.

In recent years, much of the day to day running of the CFZ has devolved upon the broad shoulders of Graham Inglis and Richard Freeman (who for reasons best known to himself has depicted me as Godzilla this issue) who have both brought their own inimitable styles to the Centre for Fortean Zoology, and without whom I think that I can safely say that the CFZ would no longer be in existence.

I owe them both a personal debt of gratitude for helping me through my divorce and the period of illness which followed. Thanx should also go to Chris Moiser, Tom Anderson, Mark North, Darren Naish and Clinton Keeling who all in their own ways not only helped me through some of the worst times in my life but also helped define the magazine that you are now reading. Thanx Guys.

OK, enough of the maudlin stuff already! We`ve completed five years, what are we gonna do in the next five? The answer can only be that we shall continue to strive to get bigger and better and do our best to find out (in out own little ways) whether (at the risk of sounding like something from a well known TV show), the truth is indeed out there. Five years down the line we ain`t doing too bad, and things can only get better.

Slainte

Jonathan Downes (Editor)

ANIMALS & MEN # 19

NEWSFILE
Compiled by
Jonathan Downes

NEW AND REDISCOVERED

NEW LIZARD SPECIES

According to our old pal Chad Arment, an American herpeticulturist suggests he may have acquired an undescribed species of tegu. Those jolly nice people at the Copyright Liberation Front managed to get hold of a picture, but we have no other details. Richard Freeman, a seasoned herpetologist confirms that with

NEWSFILE

the markings similar to those of a European wall lizard, this is not a species he has seen before.

REDISCOVERY OF THE CARIBBEAN MONK SEAL?

According to the Marine Mammals Conservation list on the Internet (marman@uvvm.uvic.ca) which quoted Boyd, I. L., and M. P. Stanfield. 1998 , *Circumstantial evidence for the presence of monk seals in the West Indies*. Oryx 32:310-316.

Based on interviews with 93 fishermen in northern Haiti and Jamaica during 1997 an assessment was made of the likelihood that monk seals survive in this region of the West Indies. Fishermen were asked to select marine species known to them from randomly arranged pictures: 22.6 per cent (n=21) selected monk seals. This number was significantly ($P < 0.001$) greater than the number who selected control species (walrus, harbour seal, and sea-lion) that they were unlikely to have observed.

However, it was not significantly different (n=19, $P > 0.1$) from the number who selected manatees, which are known to occur in the region in small numbers. More than 95 per cent of respondents also identified species that are known to occur commonly in the region. Further questioning of the 21 respondents who selected monk seals suggested that 16 (78 per cent) of them had seen at least one in the past 1-2 years. Those fishermen that were able to provide further descriptions gave information about size and colour that was consistent with many of these seals being

ANIMALS & MEN # 19

monk seals. It is possible that the Caribbean monk seal is not extinct.

Last seen in 1952, the Caribbean Monk Seal is usually considered to be extinct. However, it should possibly be pointed out that according to many authorities if it weren't for their geographical separation, Caribbean Monk Seals and the endangered Hawaiian Monk Seals would be charted as the same species.

PAINTED POOCHES?

We were recently e-mailed these pictures of some rather jolly looking puppies to us...

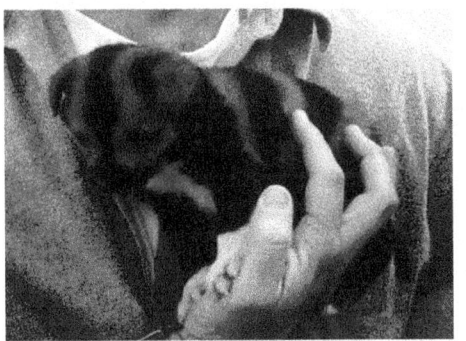

The pictures were accompanied by the following text:

...a young man was visiting China. These puppies were being sold by a street vendor for twenty dollars apiece.

NEWSFILE

The vendor spoke little or no English and therefore could not explain where these dogs came from or what they were. To date, their breed identity is a mystery."......

Our thoughts are that these dogs are almost certainly ones that have been dyed to make them more saleable, but we are intrigued enough by the mystery to throw it open to you, the reader. Answers and ideas please.......

FRESHWATER FUN

Regular *Animals & Men* readers will know that I have a sneaking fondness for freshwater crabs, and so I was particularly pleased when the *Sydney Morning Herald* of December 15, 1998 announced the discovery of a new species from Australia. They report:

"Freshwater crabs are one of the most mysterious and little known of bush creatures. Since the 1970s scientists have thought there were only two species of freshwater crab in Australia, and that these - which had lost the ability to survive in salt water - had evolved when the country was part of the super-continent Gondwana. But crustacea expert at the Australian Museum, Mr Shane Ahyong, has discovered new species of freshwater crab in Sydney pet shops which are making their way into the aquarium trade years before they are being described by science. He has traced back one, apparently a new species, to a particular stream in Cape York. It does not yet have a common name but is similar in appearance to another recently described freshwater species known as the wine glass, deaths head or jolly roger crab because of the black skull and crossbones-like mark on the top of its carapace (shell). It seems Australia has at least seven species of freshwater crabs, ranging from the pygmy crab whose carapace is less than 2.5 centimetres wide to possible freshwater wine glass crabs reportedly with shells 10 centimetres across. Aquarists are attracted to the crabs because they are easy to breed and keep. Mr

ANIMALS & MEN # 19

NEWSFILE

Ahyong said. *The freshwater crabs have made a number of adaptations to amphibious life including giving birth to fully formed miniatures of themselves and being able to move their internal organs from side to side in order to force oxygen through their gills.*"

REDISCOVERY OF THE JAVAN TIGER

The Javan Tiger (Panthera Tigris Sondaicus) was last seen alive in 1972 and is generally considered to be extinct. In January 1999, however, an Indonesian magazine called *Tempo* made some extraordinary claims. *"At the very least, there are five individuals,"* the article quotes Wayhu Giri P. as saying. Wayhu is identified in the piece as a member of a team of naturalists who found suspicious footprints, claw marks, and scat in the 58,000-hectare Meru Betiri national park on the island of Java. The article also quotes Indra Arinal, identified as the Head of Meru Betiri National Park, as reinforcing Wayhus assertion by proclaiming, *"Sightings by locals prove that the Javan Tiger is indeed still around."*

Perhaps so, but other claims of lurking Javan tigers have been made as recently as 1997. Rumors then circulating through the international media alleged that forest fires raging in Indonesia at the time were flushing surviving members of the subspecies from their smouldering habitats. In all cases, however, those reports were found to be inaccurate; the cats observed were leopards, not tigers. *"Reports like this article in TEMPO are sensational,"* says Cory Meacham, author of the book *How the tiger lost it's stripes*, which details the endangerment of the animal.

"They would shake the world of conservation if they were true. For a split second, we all want to believe that we have another chance to save the Javan tiger. But the odds are very, very long. Incontestable proof has yet to be supplied by any credible source. I`m afraid that in all likelihood these will once again be found to be some other type of forest cat, not tigers."

The Meru Betiri team, however, is evidently convinced otherwise. The article in TEMPO explains that the scat they found, according to researchers they asked to examine it, contains hair, splinters of bone, and claws from prey, which are found, the researchers assert, in the scat of tigers but not of other cats. Johannes Subijanto, identified in the article as the Head of Sub-Directorate for the Conservation of Flora and Fauna in the Department of Forestry, hopes to settle the matter once and for all. "There must be a DNA test done on the spoor which was found," the piece quotes him as saying, noting that a sample of the scat has been sent to the United States for further analysis (no mention of where, specifically). For more information, consult the TEMPO magazine website at www.tempo.co.id. The complete text of the original article, which appeared on page 38 of the January 12-18 1999 issue, can be found there.

RHINO RESUSCITATION

The Sumatran, a.k.a. hairy, rhino (*Dicerorhinus sumatrensis*) is probably the most endangered of all rhinoceros species. Numbers have declined by 50% due to poaching over the last 10 years, leaving fewer than 400 Sumatran rhino surviving in very small and

ANIMALS & MEN # 19

highly fragmented populations in Southeast Asia with Indonesia and Malaysia being the only significant range states.

It was very important news, therefore when Associated Press reported on March 8th 1999 that:

"Villagers on India's border with Myanmar have reported sighting the rare two-horned Sumatran rhinoceros, a species once believed extinct in the Indian subcontinent.

Recent sightings in the far eastern Indian states of Manipur and Nagaland suggest the hairy Sumatran rhinoceros are surviving on the subcontinent, said Anwarudding Choudhury, chief executive of the Rhino Foundation. "Going by reports received from tribal villagers in Manipur and Nagaland, there could be at least 10 to 15 Sumatran rhinos in India," Choudhury said.

The Sumatran rhinos once roamed the wet savannah grasslands from the foothills of the eastern Himalayas in Bhutan and northeastern India to Indonesia. But with poachers killing the animal for its horn, believed to have certain aphrodisiac properties, the species reportedly became extinct in the early 1920s."

THE NAME GAME

The Texas Audubon Society plans to sell the rights to name a new species of bird that was recently discovered to the highest bidder next month. The group will use the money for bird conservation efforts in Texas and Brazil.

Bret Whitney, a bird expert and co-owner of an Austin-based nature tour company, discovered the new type of bird during a recent expedition in the Amazon region of western Brazil. According to tradition, Whitney has the right to name the species.

Instead, he donated that right to the Texas Audubon Society, which is auctioning the right on March 5 at its 100th anniversary celebration in Fort Worth.

NEWSFILE

Organisers don't believe any species name has ever been bought or given away. "I'd say that as long as the person who discovered the thing is agreeable, there doesn't seem to be anything wrong with it," said Dr. Eugene Hargrove, director of the Center for Environmental Philosophy at the University of North Texas in Denton. That is, he added, "unless it produced a really stupid name."

I think that the folks at The Centre for Fortean Zoology would probably use this historic occasion as a chance to vent their stupid senses of humour to the full, but as we haven't got any money to spare for frivolities like that, we shall never know....

BUDDY CAN YOU SPARE A PARADIGM?

Animals & Men subscriber C. G. M. Paxton, a marine biologist at the Oxford university, has just published in the Journal of the Marine Biological Association of the United Kingdom, what Michel Raynal has described as "a remarkable contribution to "mathematical cryptozoology".

By plotting on a graph the descriptions of large marine animals (more than 2 m long) from 1830 to 1995, Paxton obtains a curve almost hyperbolic which has not yet reached its asymptote (the limit value corresponding to the knowledge of all the large marine animals).

Through extrapolation, Paxton can calculate the number of large animals remaining to be discovered in the oceans :

"This suggested a total of approximately 47 species awaiting description [...] with an instantaneous rate of description in 1998 of 0.189 per annum [...], suggesting one new large open water species is discovered approximately every 5.3 years."

Paxton is now studying the possibility of extending his method to large freshwater animals.

ANIMALS & MEN # 19

BHM

NEWSFILE

The tourism department in Shennongjia is issuing a special card at home and abroad which reveals the secrets of "Big Foot" in a bid to promote local tourism. It said that anyone who purchases this card will be provided with a tent, camping equipment, food and other daily necessities.

The sponsor announced that anyone snaring a live "Big Foot" will be awarded 500,000 yuan; if a dead body is found, the discoverer will be rewarded with 50,000 yuan. Those who take photos or videos of "Big Foot," or collect its fur or excrement will also win prizes ranging from 10,000 to 30,000 yuan, the sponsors said.

IF YOU DON`T WANT TO FOUKE ME BABY

On Tuesday, December 1, 1998 the *Arkansas County Gazette* published an article in which it claimed that *"The Fouke monster, a legendary bigfoot look-alike, still stalks the lowlands of Miller County, according to local residents"* It claimed over forty sightings in the preceding year including *"22 sightings in one day. ...There's even one guy who swears there's a family [of monsters] who live behind his house."*

The most recent sighting was on July 17 *"when four people purportedly saw the creature walking along a dry creek bed about 5 miles south of town."* The newspaper article admitted however that since the creature was first reported in the 1940s no-one has actually managed to capture a specimen on film and that *" For a time, the only evidence of the creature was a plaster cast of a 13½-inch footprint taken from a local soybean field."* In true fortean zoological traditions *" The cast was destroyed in a service station fire in the late 1970s "*.

YEREN WIN PRIZES (ALL WE NEED NOW IS DALE WINTON)

According to the *Xinhua News Agency* on December 1st 1998, authorities in Shennongjia in central China's Hubei Province, has announced that any tourist or adventurer who catches a yeren or Chinese wild man will be eligible for a prize of 500,000 yuan (60,240 U.S. dollars).

LAKE AND SEA MONSTERS

A six foot three inch sturgeon which weighed 105 pounds was washed up on the shores of Lake Harriet near Minneapolis in October 1998. Although this is by no means the largest fish of this species ever discovered it is interesting to note that there have been reports of `sharks` and even lake monsters from the lake for many years

ANIMALS & MEN # 19

and that this fish was probably the cause. Some ichthyologists have estimated that this fish could have been seventy or eighty years old. Had the fish been caught by an angler, it would have been a state record. Minnesota's record lake sturgeon, caught in 1994 in the Kettle River in Pine County, was 70 inches long, with a 26½ inch girth. It weighed 94 pounds. *Animals & Men* salutes the local entrepreneur who immediately rushed out the following postcard....

Meanwhile a sturgeon measuring over seven feet long was caught last summer in Lake Erie (home of more `monster` sightings over the years) and a "record breaking" sturgeon of unspecified measurements was caught in Iranian waters. Just how big do these fish get? Does anyone know the real records for the biggest sturgeon ever? There are several species and it is usually said that the beluga sturgeon (which produces the finest caviar) is the biggest but we have been unable to get hold of properly verifiable records.

If anyone in the A&M readership happens to know please tell us and we shall print it in the next issue.

MYSTERY CATS

United States

Although the Eastern Cougar is still officially extinct there is a burgeoning amount of evidence to suggest

NEWSFILE

that it does indeed still exist. *The St. Louis Post-Dispatch* [Illinois] reported on December 30, 1998 that although Pumas have not been recorded in Missouri since 1927, researchers at both ends of the country are *"studying hair and muscle samples from a mountain lion pelt found by a deer hunter* [on] *Nov 13 beside a road in Texas County in south-central Missouri. The pelt still had the feet and head attached, as if it had been skinned for mounting."*

Mountain lions once roamed throughout Missouri but were largely wiped out by shooting by the 1860s. The last documented report of a wild mountain lion in the state was an animal killed in 1927 in the Bootheel. In recent years, two mountain lions were videotaped in Missouri, one in Reynolds County in the Ozarks and another near the Springfield area.

Meanwhile in Rhode Island the *Providence Journal* reported in December 1998 that:

"He says he got a very clear look at the tawny-coated cat, larger than his 80-pound German shepherd and with a tail as long as his arm-span, rummaging through trash barrels in his front yard on Dec. 16. As he raced toward it, he said, it leaped across his entire front yard in just two bounds.

I called DEM, [Department of Environmental Management] *and right away they're telling me it's a bobcat. But I know what bobcats look like, and this was no bobcat,"* said Supinski. Michael Morrissey, an officer with, DEM agreed. After looking at the eight-

ANIMALS & MEN # 19   NEWSFILE

-inch tracks, he wrote in his report that they seemed to originate from "a large cat, larger than a bobcat." And the large cat that best fits Supinski's description -- since a typical bobcat or lynx weighs less than 30 pounds -- is the Eastern mountain lion, according to a DEM book on Rhode Island mammals."

The most recent proven sighting in Rhode Island occurred when a lion was killed in West Greenwich in 1847 or 1848. Its remains are kept at Harvard University's Museum of Comparative Zoology.

The *Chicago (Illinois) Sun-Times* reported on November 24, 1998 that

"Authorities are suspending their search for a mysterious catlike animal that has been spotted in Will County. The hunt will resume if the elusive feline is spotted again, said animal control officer Brian Vanek. ``Right now that animal - if there is an animal - could be anywhere," he said.

The search Monday focused on an area near Monee between Interstate 57 and Illinois Route 50. Animal control officers, local police, volunteers and a State Police helicopter, using infrared equipment, have had no luck finding the animal after three days of searching underbrush and wooded areas.

A dark brown animal was seen Friday near Parkview Elementary School in Steger. Later, there was another sighting in Crete. A search near Steger turned up some mysterious paw prints, but nothing that conclusively proves a lynx, bobcat or other large animal is roaming the countryside of Will County.

However, in CONCORD, N.H. on January 11, 1999 http://www.nandotimes.com) - reported that a video taken on Christmas Eve 1998 suggests that the Eastern Cougar is alive and well.. "There are people out there who believe that wolves would come back on their own and mountain lions would come back on their own," said Rosemary Conroy of the Society for the Preservation of New Hampshire Forests. As for herself, Conroy said she believes cougar sightings are more likely a rural myth but added that *"as long as there are large blocks of land out there, it's possible."*

The most recent sighting came on Christmas Eve morning. Maureen Clark, a photographer and bear trainer in Lincoln, said she and a nephew saw the small, rusty coloured, long-tailed animal clearly in her backyard. However, by the time she grabbed her camera, the animal had wandered away.

"It's not like it was a monster, but it wasn't a house cat," she said. Fish and Game biologists have studied the 6-second tape but reached no conclusion because the view of the animal is largely blocked by trees and leaves. Spokesman Eric Aldrich said some believe the animal could be a mountain lion, but Gustafson and biologist Mark Ellingwood are more skeptical. Gustafson and Ellingwood pointed to what seems to be a striped tail and pointed ears on the cat in the video.

They said mountain lions normally are solid coloured with rounded ears. Gustafson speculated that it could be a large feral cat or the much more common bobcat with an unusually long tail.

Ellingwood said biologists would love to confirm sightings, but they must rely on hard evidence such as tracks, scat, hair or photos.

"It's like chasing ghosts," he said.

A more tangible encounter took place in Pittsborough when, according to *the North Carolina Headlines* on Thursday 19 November *"A volunteer at the Carnivore Preservation Trust who was attacked by a 150-pound cougar has been reunited with the animal. Mark Kostich suffered bites and puncture wounds on his neck, shoulder and legs Sunday... and nerve damage has left one arm partially numb. Yesterday, the 37-year-old Kostich paid a visit to Cooper the cougar... but he didn't get too close. Kostich says he will still volunteer at the sanctuary for endangered animals, but he won't go in any cages again. Meanwhile, board members and employees plan to review safety procedures this weekend.*

The News and Observer says the attack on Kostich was the second this year involving a Preservation Trust animal worker. "

The misidentified moggy which turns out to be the TRUE (whatever that means) identity of a mysterious

ANIMALS & MEN # 19

ABC is a common motif within fortean zoology, but it is unusual to find a Transatlantic version of the story.

On the 5th January 1999 *Associated Press* in Oregon reported that:

"Police rushed to the scene when a caller said a cougar had been spotted in a field near Oak Elementary School, and the two officers took up a position on the perimeter. Peering through binoculars from a distance of six to seven city blocks, they spotted the ferocious feline a domestic house cat, probably a calico. Cougars don't usually have orange faces with white chests, the officers noted.

They cleared the incident with their dispatcher at 10:15 a.m. Monday with one notation: Sure, it was just a calico, but it was a really big one."

OUT OF PLACE

MONKEY BUSINESS

On October 20th 1998, *The Associated Press* reported that workers in Covington, were setting fruit traps and searching through woods for the last of two dozen rhesus monkeys that had escaped from a Louisiana primate research centre, which is supposedly the world's largest.

NEWSFILE

The monkeys broke out of their cage at the Tulane University Primate Centre startling suburban New Orleans residents who happened across the small creatures on the following day. Fred Drought was driving to work when he thought he saw a dog run across the road. Then he realized he was looking at a monkey. *"It looked kind of lost,"* Drought said. *"Like it didn't know which way to go."* The Tulane center has more than 4,500 monkeys. It uses the animals to study cancer, malaria, leprosy, and other diseases. In a scenario reminiscent of one of the crappier science fiction movies Richard Freeman likes to torment us with at the CFZ, the Centre Manager, Astor Bridges reassured the public with an announcement that "the escaped monkeys were used only for breeding and had not been infected with diseases"

Yeah, right!

SEWER SNAKES

As the controversy regarding alligators in the sewers rumbles on (see *Clinton`s Cogitations* this issue) it is heartening to note that at least one species of reptile has been salvaged from the sewers of the Land of the Free. *Associated Press* (who seem to have a monopoly on these sorts of stories - at least they seem to post more of them than *Reuter*s - announced on the 20th October 1998 that a seven foot python was found in North Bergen, New Jersey, just across the river from New York City. Police say it wasn't bothering anyone. In fact, one officer said the snake was just "sunning itself." Nevertheless, they tossed it in a garbage can and held it for the Humane Society. A teenager who noticed the commotion admitted to being the owner. He says he tossed the snake down a sewer a few hours before because it was too expensive to feed. Experts say it costs between five and ten dollars a week to keep a python full.

STREWTH!!!!!!

On December 21, 1998 *Associated Press* (again!!!) reported that Kevin Fisher of Tanworth in the West Midlands swore he hadn't been drinking when he told police he spotted a wallaby under a lamppost in his home town.

ANIMALS & MEN # 19

"Mr. Fisher couldn't believe his eyes and sounded quite shaken. He swore blind he was still sober," an unidentified police spokesman told reporters.. "Luckily, we took him seriously," the spokesman said. "Though at first we were tempted to tell him to hop it." And we haven't heard THAT joke before!!! The wallaby was apparently called 'Willy' and had escaped from a nearby zoo.

WIL-E-COYOTE

The St Louis Post Dispatch on Tuesday, December 8, reported that residents of Chicago's south suburbs say hungry coyotes are roaming their neighborhoods and attacking pet dogs and cats. One resident, Linda May said that she had watched in horror two weeks before as her 5-month-old cockatoo, Cheli, was snatched off his tether by a large animal that loped out of the darkness. "It was strong enough to break the chain," said May, who lives in Lemont Township.

"I think it was a coyote." She isn't the only one in the area who believes at least one coyote ismaking the rounds looking for something to eat.In the last two years, Jill Nicholson said, four of her family's animals have disappeared.

"Two cats and a big duck that we used to take care of in a pond on our property (vanished)," said Nicholson. *"Then in the middle of September, our dog disappeared."* Nicholson suspects the dog was killed by a coyote she's seen around the neighborhood on and off for years. In recent years, coyotes have been spotted throughout the south and southwest suburbs, from Harvey to Joliet to Evergreen Park.

CAYMAN GEDDIT.......

At last *Reuters* have come up with a story, even though their taxonomy is a little awry. On the 4th March 1999 they announced that a 7-foot, 175-pound (79 kg) alligator that was pushed out of its natural feeding grounds by development in Rio de Janeiro resorted to dining on local pets.

The story continued in this vein, describing how "the ravenous reptile" had invaded a home near a swampy nature park and gulped down the owner's dog along with four chickens that were in the yard.

NEWSFILE

Apparently it took four officers from Rio's environment patrol squad 30 minutes to subdue the alligator.

They were able to wrestle the reptile onto a stretcher and ship it unharmed to a zoo. At the risk of being labelled as annoying pedants, can we point out that there aren't any alligators in Brazil. Either it is a true cryptozoological oddity or (as is more likely) it was a Caiman....

MEET THE BEETLES

The Associated Press ushered in Samhain by announcing that a species of black and orange ladybug (probably one of the *Cocchinella* spp but we can't be sure) is reaching plague proportions across Missouri.. Exterminators had been flooded with calls over the past week as the unusual Asian beetles squirm their way into homes across the state for the winter.

- 12 -

ANIMALS & MEN # 19

But Mike Brown, state entomologist for the Missouri Department of Agriculture, urged home owners not to overreact.

The lady beetles won't injure people, pets or plants, they don't carry disease, and they can't structurally damage a home. Besides, he said, gardeners and farmers will come to appreciate their presence in the spring.

One lady bug can consume 50 to 60 aphids a day while munching on a variety of other insects including scales, mealy bugs, mites, leaf hoppers and various types of soft-bodied insects - the kind that infest trees, bushes, herbs and small grains. Missouri agricultural experts, from gardeners to golf course superintendents, started importing the beetles about five years ago for the purpose of fighting aphids, Brown said. "Probably the one negative aspect of this beetle is its behavior in trying to find shelter," he said.

The typical ladybug burrows into the ground for the winter, but the orange and black Asian ladybeetles are natives of Japan and China and live a very different lifestyle. About two weeks before Halloween, the beetles leave the woods and fields in search of a place to hibernate for the winter.

FEARFUL SYMMETRY

On January 27, 1999 *The Associated Press* in Jackson, New Jersey reported a 600- to 800-pound tiger that was on the loose in a densely wooded area was shot and killed by authorities. Police and state Division of Fish, Game and Wildlife officials had tried to tranquillise the animal with drug-filled darts but when that didn't work, they shot the tiger. The irony was that they were unable to determine who owned the unfortunate beastie.

The Police said that officials at Six Flags Great Adventure & Safari Park, a nearby tourist attraction, *"believe they have all theirs."* It wasn't a good time for big cats because only six weeks before on 7 December 1998

The Electronic Telegraph reported that a cheetah had mauled to death a three-year-old boy after it escaped from its enclosure in a zoo near the city of Saumur, in the Loire Valley, police said.

The accident occurred on Saturday when two five-year-old female cheetahs that had dug a trench under the fence

NEWSFILE

surrounding their enclosure at Doue-la-Fontaine broke loose and headed for a group of visitors. One animal attacked the boy and mauled his father, who had tried to beat it off. He was taken to hospital with cuts. The zoo was closed pending an inquiry.

Meanwhile about a month previously in India on the 28th *The Associated Press* (Gad bless `em). reported that a leopard sauntered into a house and lolled on a bed for four hours, watching television and napping, before being packed off to the zoo, newspapers reported Thursday. Bim Devi bolted the bedroom door and ran out screaming to call the police, in Panchkula, a town about 250 kilometers (155 miles) northwest of New Delhi, after her four-year-old son saw the leopard stroll into the driveway and break open the bedroom door, *The Asian Age* reported. No-one was hurt.

Officials said the animal had either escaped from the local zoo or strayed from a dense forest near the town, and entered the house to escape morning traffic. *"It watched all the morning (television) programs,"* Devi was quoted as saying by *The Hindustan Times. "It tampered a little with the children's books and school bags but did little other damage to the house."*

ANIMALS & MEN # 19

Tired by then, it took a nap sprawled on the bed.

The Centre for Fortean Zoology will confirm that daytime TV has that affect on *people*, so why not on leopards?

BIRD BRAINS

The Shetland News (http://www.shetland-news.co.uk) reported on the 18th February 1999 that as heavy snow showers batter Shetland, many islanders will feel jealous to see a Mediterranean cattle egret bird leave the snow-covered far North for the much kinder climate in southern Portugal. After having been in the care of local SSPCA officer Ron Patterson for the last three weeks, this lucky bird is getting a free lift from British Airways back to where it is supposed to be, theAlbufloa Marsh near Faro in Southern Portugal.

The heron-type bird was found exhausted and near starvation at the end of January when it made an emergency landing on one of Shetland's inter-island ferries, at least 2,000 miles from its natural habitat. Sincethen Mr Patterson has looked after the bird at the SSPCA Wildlife Centre, Tingwall. Mr Patterson said yesterday (WED) the cattle egret had recovered well, but it was time for the bird to get back to the wild.

However, this was not the only exotic visitor to our shores this winter. On the Isle of Man according to the *Manx Independent* of Friday 19 March 1999 a spectacular frigate bird, the first ever to survive after reaching the British Isles, will soon be flown to its native sea to be released back into the wild. Only a handful of people know where the bird has been recovering since it was found on a Castletown beach in February. The bird was exhausted and injured when found, but was soon in the capable hands of experts. It was feared the adult female, with a wingspan of eight feet, would attract thousands of birdwatchers eager to see the unique sight.

Elizabeth Charter of the Department of Agriculture, Fisheries and Forestry said the *fregata magnificens* could have come from the Azores or Central America. Manx squid has proved popular with the bird, which has regained lost weight and strength and should soon be ready for a return to its native clime. When it is ready, Mrs Charter said the bird would be flown by willing airlines and conservationists to the Florida Keys, where it will bereleased into the hands of more experts. The only other frigate bird to have landed in the British Isles was found in the Scottish Isles but died, she added.

And on the other side of the Atlantic the *La Crosse Journal Sentinel* of November 7, 1998 reported that Lars, a green, violet-ear hummingbird, native to Central America, had died at a rescue centre in central Wisconsin. *"What he was doing in Edwin and Marcella Larson's backyard in this Mississippi River town, thousands of miles from his home,is anybody's guess. Blown badly off course by a hurricane? His internal compass completely out of kilter? What is certain is this: The little guy was adored.* "He really touched a lot *of people,"* Marge Gibson, a noted wildlife rehabilitator *from Antigo who nursed the bird, said Friday.* "How so much energy could have been packed into one teeny little guy really captured people's interest. People took the little sprite to heart."

NEWSFILE

CLINTON HAS LONG HORN?

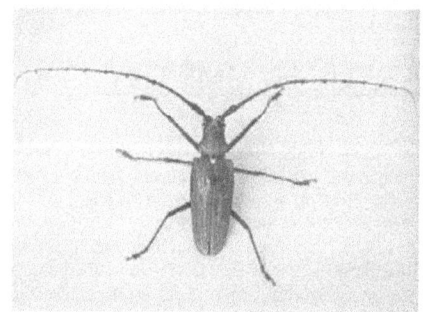

On the 3rd February *Associated Press* announced that the man who has already said that smoking dope is OK if you don't inhale, and that oral sex ain't adultery (and that starting a war in the Balkans might save his political arse) had declared war on "Troublesome alien species such as the Chinese mitten crab and the voracious Asian long-horned beetle" which are costing Americans tens of billions of dollars and threatening entire ecosystems. I thought you didn't approve of ethnic cleansing, Bill?

ANIMALS & MEN # 19

TO BE SURE

There seem to be several interesting visitors to Irish waters in recent months. According to *Science Today* on Monday 11th January 1999 large numbers of jellyfish *(pelagia noctiluca)* have been stranded over a three-month period along the west coast. This is an exceptional event, according to Marine Institute scientists, and it is the first time they have been recorded in such numbers in Irish waters. They were first detected in Donegal in August and spread to other parts along the western coast during the following months. This species, noted for its physical beauty, has amber brown to red-brown patches and sometimes flecks of pink with trailing mouth parts and tentacles. It can grow to about 12 cm in bell diameter. Dr Dan Minchin of the institute's fisheries research centre in Abbotstown, Co Dublin, would like sightings of the species to be reported to him (email: dminchin@frc.ie).

A fortnight later *The Irish Times* reported that Lough Swilly in Donegal is experiencing a starfish population explosion but it could tackle the problem with a technique developed in Clarinbridge, Co Galway. This is one of the main findings of a study carried out by Galway student, Niamh McKeown, which took a Marine Institute award in the recent Young Scientists' Exhibition. Ms McKeown (13), who is a second-year student at Salerno Secondary School in Galway, recorded 2,040 starfish per hectare in Lough Swilly, where there are significant shellfish beds. This compares to only 30 or fewer starfish per hectare in Clarinbridge, near the lucrative oyster beds.

Starfish can have a devastating impact on shellfish. One of the techniques used against them involves adding lime to the water. However, the use of "hairy ropes" in Clarinbridge is far more successful and more environmentally friendly, she says. The ropes are hung from a boat and used as a dredger to snag the starfish, she explains. *"It only needs to be done once or twice to clear the area."* Disappointingly, she found that the starfish have no economic value. *"I thought they might have a medicinal use but unfortunately not,"* she said. Niamh McKeown took a joint first place in the junior category for biological and ecological sciences at the exhibition and was also given a prize by Dr John Joyce of the Marine Institute for the best individual project with a marine theme.

NEWSFILE

IT'S ONLY METAL; WHAT A BOAR......

The Independent on 23 October 1998 reported that "Wild boars of Kent cause havoc in the hop gardens " with a dramatic piece of journalism which began.....

"A CHILL wind whistled through the trees, whipping up the autumn leaves carpeting the forest floor. In the dense undergrowth, rustling noises could be heard. Was that a faint grunting in the distance? Here, deep in woodland on the Kent and East Sussex border, lurks a colony of wild boars that has become the scourge of farmers. The boars are blamed for ravaging fields and wrecking crops in search of food. Some say that they even snatch lambs by moonlight....."

A local farmer was quoted as saying that if she had her way they would all be machine gunned (what a nice lady) *because "they've rooted up our hop garden; it looked like the Somme,"* she says. *"And they've taken lambs in the night. All you find in the morning are little hooves."*

Beckley Garage is regularly called upon to repair vehicles damaged by boars that can weigh up to 300lb. *"If a car is in collision with a boar, the car comes off worse,"* says Mrs Farrant. Down the road, John Taylor, of Little Farm, is dejected. *"They rooted up a six-acre maize field,"* he says. *"There's no point replanting it because they'll just come and dig it up again."*

The National Farmers' Union wants the ministry to order a cull of the boars, which were hunted to extinction in this country in the 17th century. The current population originates in the 40 or so commercial farms that rear them for their succulent meat. Many scampered to freedom when the 1987 hurricane flattened fences. *The Times* got in on the act on January 26 1999 when it announced that *"Wild boars 'should be eradicated'.* The Game Conservancy Trust, which advises the Government on countryside issues, said there would be a growing risk of people being injured or killed if boars were left to breed unchecked. The trust also gave warning the animals could damage crops, kill lambs and ground-nesting birds, and pass on diseases to

ANIMALS & MEN # 19

free-range pigs. Up to 300 wild boars are at large in Kent, East Sussex and Dorset after escaping from commercial farms. Each female can produce two litters of up to nine piglets each year.

The trust's recommendations came in response to a Ministry of Agriculture, Fisheries and Food consultation document published last year. Dr Stephen Tapper, who wrote the trust's Wild Boar Consultation Report, said yesterday: *"It would be irresponsible to do nothing . . .These populations will increase and could get out of hand."* He said that trained marksmen should be hired to eradicate the animals, and that tighter controls should be imposed on farms.

Keith Taylor, of the Wild Boar Association, supported the trust's call for eradication.

A spokesman for the ministry said that the trust's report echoed the recommendations made by the Central Science Laboratory, and that eradication was one option that ministers were studying.

WHO'S AFRAID OF THE......

On March 21, 1999 the *Seattle Times* reported that B-45F, an independent, elk-eating gray wolf on the verge of adulthood, has journeyed alone from Idaho to seek a home in the meadows and the snow-capped mountains of northeastern Oregon. But as she does her "wolfy thing," as one fan puts it, B-45 (the F is for female) has triggered a range of intense reactions: naming contests and an ad campaign from wildlife enthusiasts captivated by her solo odyssey; angry phone calls and threatening e-mails from cattle ranchers who want her removed or shot. In a debate that had been raging for a month, the wolf is cast as both hero and villain:

She is a pioneer who may lure male wolves into the state, establishing a resident pack there, or she is a menace to livestock and tourism, the region's economic mainstays. Wildlife authorities consider B-45 an environmental success story, proof that attempts to restore endangered species to their native territory is working....

* * * * * * * * * *

FEATURE

THE CASE OF THE BRITISH THYLACINE

by Richard Freeman

In the spring of 1810, a bizarre series of livestock killings began. Over the next six months, a mystery predator cut a bloody swathe through Cumberland. This creature was never identified, but became known as the Girt Dog of Ennerdale. Though often quoted this chapter In British animal mysteries is one of the most cryptic and obscure. Un re-reading the tales recently, I found a strange thread that no-one (to my knowledge) has picked up on before. The saga of the Girt Dog may be even odder than anyone has ever realised; and the 'Dog' itself may be a doubly Fortean beast.The tale began when the corpse of a half-eaten ewe was discovered on the fells above Ennerdale Water. The victim was soon followed by others,

ANIMALS & MEN # 19

this makes the event even more extraordinary. as the culprit killed every night. Farmers and shepherds patrolled the hills, but the creature remained unseen. Such was the quantity and ferocity of the attacks; that natural predators, like foxes were discounted. As local farmers became worried; posses of men and dogs scoured the area, but the beast evaded them. It never attacked the same flock on consecutive nights. Its uncanny elusiveness caused superstitious ramblings among the villagers. More fuel was added to this growing fire; when the beast began to show some disturbing eating habits. Many carcasses were left mostly uneaten, but the blood had been drained from their wounds, as a vampire would do. Finally, someone caught a glimpse of the creature. A shepherd watching his flock at dawn saw the killer, but its description brought even more confusion. It was like a tawny-coloured dog, with dark, tiger stripes, quite unlike anything he had ever seen before.

Ennerdale today - still one of the most remote parts of the Lake District

the Dalesfolk argued over the identity of this strange beast; as to whether it was a wolf, or a lion, or a tiger? Some even believed it to be a supernatural entity, touting its love of blood as 'proof'. Around this time the name 'Girt Dog' was coined. Another queer attribute of the 'Girt Dog' was its effect on normal dogs. Fell sheepdogs would cower in its proximity, and refuse to follow its spoor. More proof of its diabolical nature, whispered the locals. Hunting dogs were brought in to replace *the* sheepdogs and a pack was collected to hunt down the killer. After days of hunting, the pack finally tracked down the 'Girt Dog' and forced it to break cover. It tried to run, but the hounds soon caught up with it. the 'Girt Dog' turned on its pursuers with unbelievable savagery, killing several hounds swiftly.

The rest at the pack scattered in terror and the monster escaped. Obviously no normal dog could have caused such a bloody rout. The farmers changed tactics and littered the hillsides with poisoned sheep cadavers. The 'Girt Dog', however, disdained carrion, preferring to rend and slay amidst the living flocks. As the bodycount rose, rewards were offered for anyone who could end this reign of terror. Once a group of armed men had the beast encircled. The creature charged at one of the men, who lost his nerve and threw himself aside.

Unfortunately, an elderly man, Jack Wilson, who was also quite deaf, was collecting firewood close by. The 'Girt Dog' ran straight through his legs and bowled him over. Jack swore that it was more like a girt lion than a girt dog. Professional huntsmen were called in, but had no more luck. The 'Girt Dog' led many on a wild goose chase. Up to 100 mounted men with packs of dogs failed to catch it. Finally, on September 13th 1810, the 'Girt Dog' was surrounded and shot. Incredibly it escaped, despite its wound and ran towards the River Enen. Here it was found cooling its injury and ran once more to Eskat Wood, where it made its last stand. Flushed from cover, mortally wounded, the huntsmen's dogs closed in and tore it to shreds.

ANIMALS & MEN # 19   FEATURE

What little was left at the bizarre predator was sent to Keswick Museum, and mounted as a specimen. Sadly, Keswick Museum closed in 1876 and no record was kept of what happened to the exhibits. So ends this weird tale. What are we to make of it? Well, we have some intriguing clues. The 'Girt Dog' displayed some characteristics which were very unlike any dog. All the witnesses described it as being striped.

There are no striped dogs; but this animal must have sufficiently resembled a dog to have been given the name 'Girt Dog'. The animal drank its victim's blood, while often leaving the flesh untouched. All canids eat the meat at their prey. It terrified ordinary dogs, and easily killed hunting dogs, even when outnumbered. Only one animal could account for these descriptions -- the Thylacine. the striped coat and blood-drinking behaviour at the marsupial wall is well-known. Tasmanian hunter described how it could bite through a dog's skull with ease and Sir Richard Owen described it as "the most fell beast ol prey". This hypothesis may seem fantastic at first, but let us examine some facts.

The thylacine did not suffer from serious persecution until the 1860s. In 1810, it was still a common animal, in Tasmania, where many were kept in captivity. there were no laws governing zoos at the time and although there were only a few sedentary zoos in Britain in the 1800's; there were many travelling zoos. These appalling institutions consisted of caged animals being carted around Britain by horse-drawn carriage. This must have been a terrible ordeal for both the exhibits and the horses.

Perhaps the best known of these was the infamous Wombwell's travelling Menagerie. As well as the stock-in-trade such as bears, lions, tigers and monkeys; Wombwell's also exhibited rarer animals, such as snow leopards. It is even thought that they possessed a gorilla, without even knowing it!. Apparently mis-labelled as a chimp, it would have been the first gorilla in Britain, (gorillas were as unknown as yetis until tile 1840's). Zoological accuracy was not a high priority in these establishments. I refer readers to Clinton Keeling's article *"The British Nandi Bear"* in issue six of *"Animals and Men")*.

Therefore, it is not out of the question that a travelling zoo had thylacines in its collection, and that one of them had escaped in the Lake District in 1810.

Remember there was no television or radio then and many people were illiterate, especially in the countryside. Most people know nothing of natural history beyond their own country, hence the confusion the 'Girt Dog' caused.

Enquiries at the new Keswick Museum drew a blank, as did those at other Lake District Museums, Libraries and Historic Societies. No records of the whereabouts of the stuffed specimens were kept. One hopes that the museum's stock was sold on, rather than just thrown away. Very little of the 'Girt Dog' would remain now; but it isn't beyond all hope that somewhere, in some dusty basement or attic, is a skull labelled 'wolf' or 'dog', which has too many incisors and opens far too wide to be either species.

- 18 -

BESTIARY: THE RUKH
by Ade Dimmick

In this issue I would like to look at the Rukh or Roc. Another fabulous creature that, although a creature of considerable mythological pedigree, may have actually existed in a less-exaggerated form.

The Rukh was a giant bird-like creature which featured prominently in Arabian myth and legend.

Its roots however, can be traced back to much earlier Persian sources. In fact the words Rukh and Roc are said to be related to the Persian names for the Bird of Immortality. The Rukh was a 'Storm Bird' - the movement of its wings created the winds and it flight path created lightening. (Many Rukh-like creatures have assumed this role in the mythology of the world, as well as representing the Bird of Immortality.)

Sinbad the Sailor had a number of encounters with the Rukh on his voyages. On one particular occasion he was actually carried off and deposited on a rocky eyrie atop a Rukh egg. Sinbad measured the eggs circumference as fifty paces - described by one source as resembling the white dome of a mosque. As one can imagine, a bird that lays such an egg must itself be of gigantic proportions. So large in fact, it was said to be able to carry off elephants and block out the light of the sun! It's feathers were also said to be the size of a palm frond. Some sources state that it resembles a giant eagle or a griffin in appearance. Others refer to it as having two horns on its head and four humps. Legend maintains that the Rukh only ever lands on Mount Qaf, the *axis mundi* or centre of the Earth. However, some stories do refer to it landing occasionally in isolated places. In the 13th century Marco Polo wrote of the Rukh, which he believed originated on the island of Madagascar, he also believed that the Rukh was a type of griffin. Many centuries earlier the historian Herodotus (c.BC480) referred to stories told by Egyptian priests, of giant birds which would carry off both people and animals. These 'birds' originating from a 'land east of the mainland'. (Possibly Madagascar?)

The reference to Madagascar is important as it may lend a degree of authenticity to the Rukh legend. Giant birds have existed in the not-too-distant past on the island of Madagascar. Related to the ostrich, Aepyornis Maximus, stood at ten feet and weighed in at 990lbs, a formidable bird by any standards! It also laid king-size eggs, not quite Rukh-like dimensions, but never-the-less measured 15 inches in length and 3 foot round. Interestingly enough, the Aepyornis itself was considered to be a mythological creature by western zoologists until bones and eggs (containing half-developed chicks) were discovered, and there is apparently evidence to support their existence up until the mid 1800's.

Is it possible that the giant birds of Madagascar were actually the legendary Rukh, having become assimilated with earlier mythology and bold seafarers tales - ultimately exaggerated to mega-proportions by story-tellers down the centuries?

ANIMALS & MEN # 19
COYPU IN A YORKSHIRE ATTIC.
by Andrew Scott

During the early eighties (1981) my family moved into a converted barn in a village called Horsehouse in Coverdale. The barn was being rebuilt after a fire and a new roof had to be built.

The barn was in a field away from the river cover and the environment was fairly damp. Anyway when the barn was completed we moved in. Over the next few weeks however there were strange scratching noises emanating from the attic at night, although we put it down to being mice or rats, we eventually had to investigate it as the noises were becoming louder.

My dad climbed into the attic and shone his torch around. As he shone his torch into the attic, two big eyes reflected back in the darkness. When my dad came down he was very pale and he exclaimed that there was something in the corner with great big eyes.

The next day we contacted the local environmental pest control who came over to investigate. After going into the attic he announced that we had a Coypu up there. Well fortunately he had the appropriate equipment to catch it, which he managed to do and put it in a cage, where upon he whisked it off in his van. I can only guess it sought shelter in our attic whilst the roof was being built, during the winter

FEATURE

Sweet Wallaby of Mine

(Written by Chuck Leonard for, and taken verbatim from, *Mojo* Magazine)

Few people know that Axl Rose is one of rock 'n' roll's greatest animal lovers. The Guns N' Roses lead squealer adopted several cuddly creatures over the course of his career, but the pride of his collection was acquired on a 1988 Australian tour: a wallaby.

An implausibly cute, floppy-eared bundle of fun, it became Axl's favourite pet. Axl settled on the name Ozzie, a hilarious pun on the creature's Antipodean origins, and sly dig at The Sabs' lead singer. Axl spent many happy hours frolicking with his friendly marsupial, taking it with him as Guns N' Roses crisscrossed the globe. Ozzie even had his own luxury flight case, complete with hidden airholes, which eased his passage through customs.

If questioned, Axl's plan was simply to assure officials that the animal must have made its own way into an unattended equipment case, and become trapped. Sadly, Ozzie's convincing disguise as a package of electrical equipment led to tragedy. It was during a string of tour dates in Alaska that one roadie left what

ANIMALS & MEN # 19

he thought was a surplus case in the band's U-Haul while Axl and friends soundchecked. When Axl emerged, demanding the whereabouts of his furry friend, the band's road manager rolled out Ozzie's flightcase. Exposed to sub-zero temperatures in the van, Ozzie was frozen solid.

Guns N' Roses mythology has it that another faithful roadie attempted to assuage Axl's grief by taking the unfortunate marsupial home and preserving it in his chest freezer, in the hope that cryogenic advances would allow Ozzie to be resuscitated. There are no reports as to whether leading veterinarians are nearing a remedy for Axl's deep-frozen friend.

* * * * *

FEATURES

SIPANDJEE - AN UNIDENTIFIED APE
by Allan Edward Munro

In 1993, in Gabon, Steve Holmes was working at an isolated oil facility. One day, a few kilometres inland and 200 kilometres south of Port Gentil, he was driving to lunch at around noon when he glimpsed for a few seconds an ape that ran into the road 10 metres away, and which caused him to break sharply before running with arms raised high through long grass and into the forest.

The 1.5 metres tall Primate was running bipedally and was built like a man except for the fact that the arms were longer and that much of the animal had reddish brown hair the same colour as the laterite rock used locally for road construction. The local name for this reportedly aggressive animal is sipandjee, but other cryptozoological primates are known throughout Africa under different names, and probably incorporating more than one species. The waterbobbejan (South Africa) type, therefore, is probably what would be described as a robust australopithecine, whilst the agogwe (East Africa) is presumably a species of gracile australopithecine. The sipandjee may be congeneric with the agogwe.

This is based on information given to me by Steve Holmes, and for further reading on the subject, I recommend Fortean Times issue 111 (June 1998). The cryptozoological Primates of Africa are often overlooked, as discussion usually centres on areas like the Himalayas or the Cascades, and material on the subject is hard to come by, compared to Bigfoot etc....

ANIMALS & MEN # 19 — FEATURE

CLINTON'S COGITATIONS
by Clinton Keeling

Greetings, gentlefolk, and herewith the above - based on "A&M", issue 18. I've for long had a high regard for the Scots, and still retain two legacies of having spent part of my schooldays in their country - a) a preference for porridge made with salt rather than sugar, and b) the ability to spell correctly. Consequently I was rather surprised to read (p.4) that there are plans to re-introduce the Beaver to Scotland, as I'd have credited the Scots with more sense than to allow this. Before we go any further it might not be out of place here to mention that I spent over three years with the Canadian Wildlife Service.

Have you ever seen a Beaver dam, and lodge? It resembles a cross between a flood (which, of course, it is) and a battlefield - furthermore on which the said battle has been lost. Not only that, but the water in the dam is always opaque and muddy - while I've known of at least two occasions (where it was necessary for the dam to be reduced) when the only means of destroying the lodge was with dynamite, literally. I think it isn't unreasonable to ask ourselves whether we really want this sort of imposition on our overpopulated little country with its ever-diminishing unspoiled areas? Admittedly the European Beaver isn't as bad in this direction, but there's really no room now for an introduction of its size.

Incidentally, someone is talking baloney when they assert the Beaver became extinct here a mere four hundred years ago. Eight or even nine hundred years since would be nearer the mark. Why, oh why, will those who set themselves up as pundits not make sure of their facts?

EDITOR'S INTERJECTION: As the `pundit` in question, I feel that I must step forward here to defend my honour. Herewith a quotation from J E Harting's *British Animals extinct within historic times* (1880):

"After stating that the Teivi was the only river in Wales, or even in England, that had Beavers, Giraldus remarks: *"In Scotland they are said to be found in one river, but are very scarce-"* Hector Boece (or Boethius), that shrewd old father of Scottish historians, writing in 1526, enumerates the *Fibri* or Beavers, with perfect confidence, amongst the *ferae naturae* of Loch Ness, whose fur was in request for exportation towards the end of the fifteenth century, and he even speaks of *"an incomparable number,"* though perhaps he may be only availing himself of a privilege which moderns have taken the liberty of granting to medieval authors when dealing with curious facts. Bellenden, in his vernacular translation of Boethius' *"Croniklis of Scotland,"* which he undertook at royal request in 1536, while omitting stags, roe-deer, and even otters, in his anxiety for accuracy, mentions *"Bevers"* without the slightest hesitation; and, though exception may be taken to the first clause of the sentence, yet the passage is worth quoting:

"Mony wyld Hors and amang yame are mony Martrikis [pine martens], Bevers, Quhitredis [weasels], and Toddis [foxes], the furrings and skynnis of thayme are coft [bought] with

ANIMALS & MEN # 19   CLINTON'S COGITATIONS

great price amang uncouth [foreign] merchandis." Harting goes on to refute claims that it existed into the sixteenth century in Scotland and even later in Wales.I rest my case. On the same page there's also the old (and daft) mis-spelling of Orang Utan - Orang Utang. As is well known, Orang Utan is Malayan for "Man of the Woods". Orang Utang is still Malayan but means "Man in debt"!

EDITOR'S NOTE: So when folk tell me that I look like an orang utang it is a comment on my finances rather than my beard. Cool!

I wouldn't dispute that tuskless Elephants are on the increase in Uganda (p.13) - but if you seriously think it's nature's way of "fighting back", as per the text, I assume you also believe in the 'wee folk' (well, as a subscriber to A&M, perhaps you do...)

.....ermm yes we do in fact (Richard and Jon)

Far more likely, I'd say, is the fact that the big ivory-carriers have been harried and shot for so long there are comparatively few of them left, with the result the small-tusked or the tuskless are now more in evidence, if not the majority, and their genes are being carried on. So, on the same page, "Bugs can read your mind". What sheer, utter, bloody rubbish; what puerile, insulting tripe. Where did it originate? Oh, I see - California... I don't know whether I'm becoming crotchety in my old age, or whether I'm just finding it harder to grasp things, but after reading "Gubu Norge" (pp17~21) I felt obliged to read it again, as I had the uneasy feeling I might have missed something in it, but seemingly I hadn't. I know what I have to say may offend some people, but I honestly believe it ought to be said, as it involves a trend definitely on the increase in journalism and it isn't a good thing. In a way I congratulate the author, as it's taken him a solid five pages in which to next to nothing. Should you consider this a harsh judgement, I seriously suggest you read it again, objectively. I could have written it in perhaps a page and a half.

EDITOR'S NOTE: Here, again, I must come to the defence of Daev Walsh (who wrote the article in question) and indeed me for approving it. The GUST expedition to Norway in search of a legendary lake monster had achieved so much media coverage, and there was so much misreporting about what really happened that we decided to cover the expedition in depth. Jan Ove Sundburg had made (and continues to make) so many extraordinary claims about his findings (and other subjects) that he deserves the scrutiny given to his expedition by Daev and us.......

You know, although I haven't the pleasure of knowing the gentleman, I've come to have quite a high regard (and by my standards that's ecstatic praise) for Tom Anderson, who has always struck me as writing sound sense. He seems to have had a couple of lapses in his letter "Gulo and Gullible" (pp 38-43). First, I must make it clear I wholeheartedly agree with the basis of his point - that the belief that this large, diurnal, noisy species, with its characteristic gait and destructive habits is not only living but also breeding in this country should be relegated to the realm of Cloud Cuckoo Land, as the only zoological collections to have kept the species this century are the Zoological Society of London and Norfolk Wildlife Park - neither of which had any escapes or disappearances. This then, leaves us with the private sector, as it might be called, but only a very few Wolverines have ever graced private collections here for the simple reason the species has always been very difficult to obtain. Where I disagree with Tom Anderson is in his very common and completely misguided assumption, to judge by what he wrote that every non-domestic animal in private hands must automatically be no more than just a "pet". He should just try telling, for example, Raymond Sawyer who has just achieved breeding Giant Tortoises in his splendid collection at Cobham, or Christopher Marler who, at Olney, has the country's only Gayal (Bos frontalis) and breeds the Bald Eagle annually, or Martin Bourne who has the country's only privately-owned Tapirs and has bred Chevrotains at Middleton, near Manchester, that they are "pet-keepers:' On second thoughts, as I wish Tom Anderson no harm, I wouldn't advise it..

EDITOR'S NOTE: Having re-read Tom's letter. I would like to add my ha'porth. Firstly, neither Tom nor anyone else at *Animals & Men* would wish to denigrate any of the fine work being done by people keeping exotic animals in what Clin calls 'The Private Sector'. The CFZ have a small collection of exotics as, I know, does Clin himself.

ANIMALS & MEN # 19

However this does not detract from the undoubted fact that in my opinion at least, the vast majority of people who keep exotic animals do so for the wrong reasons and have insufficient knowledge of the species they have taken on. I've been guilty of that in the past, (and when necessary I have always shouted for help to Clin!!) Pet shops are notorious for selling people animals with insufficient or completely erroneous instructions as to how to look after them . Our files are full of horror stories which suggest that prior to the Dangerous Wild Animals Act of 1976 all sorts of people were being sold all sorts of animals that they were completely unsuited to keep. These included several species of felid, and even bears. However I have to agree with Clin, Chris and Tom that the evidence for anyone ever having kept Wolverines as pets in this country is scanty in the extreme............

The other point? Well, Mr Anderson apparently disapproves of "Victorian colonial Jingoism" - and it must be admitted he might have a point.

I mean, not only did we inflict on many other countries, particularly in Africa, so many horrors during our occupation, but when we departed, instead of immobilising them or taking them with us, we just left them.

Things such as railways, roads, schools, colleges and universities, hospitals and clinics, successful agricultural systems, democratic government, airports, daily papers, law and order, home industries..

Small wonder the French and Portuguese, being more humane than us, fought like fury to hang on to their colonies and their subdued peoples. Kind you, there's still hope - many parts of Africa are showing their yearning for the good old days by going back to incessant inter-tribal warfare and genocide and torture and not coping with famine - keep it up lads and lasses, this way you'll soon be back to your old average lifespan of thirty years. Sic transit gloria mundi...

FEATURE

Ayrshire Tales

By Mark Fraser
Editor of *Haunted Scotland*

While chatting to an acquaintance, Mr. Jack Dunlop, who has worked on the land day and night for practically all of his forty years or so, around the area of Maybole in Ayrshire, I asked if he had ever seen or come across any signs of 'Big Cats.' Alas he had not, but he never dismissed the idea as he knew others who had found remains of lizard-like creatures, the largest being around two feet in length, one he found partially skinned. Jack firmly believes that these lizard-like animals now live in the countryside. maybe once they were pets, he muses, but they must now have established themselves in the countryside.

Another odd tale he told me was concerning 'chicken mutilations.' He returned one morning to his yard to find fifteen dead chickens were heaped in a neat pile together at the end of the row of bodies. Somewhat shocked and rather distraught at loosing so many fowl, Jack eventually packed them away in a black bin liner and dumped them for the time being unceremoniously in the corner of the yard.

Again on returning from the fields later in the day he was somewhat dumbfounded to find that the black bin liner had been ripped open and the chickens along with the heads displayed in exactly the same manner as he first found them, were lined in a row. Now Jack being a no-nonsense down to earth sort of chap did not think of aliens but went for his shotgun and positioned himself by his back scullery window which overlooked the scene of the crime. After about a quarter of an hour a weasel or ferret (I cannot now remember which it was he said.) came running across the yard toward its trophies from its hiding place in the grass. 'Bang' the animal was shot dead, which is a shame because I personally would liked to have known what it would have done next

ANIMALS & MEN # 19 FEATURE

with the dead chickens. I mention this because I have come across a couple of old stories recently of alleged 'animal mutilations' involving farmyard animals being lined up in this manner, maybe this is a possible explanation. But I stress it does not take away the fact that animals which have been operated on, rather then mutilated, (Which I feel is a misleading description but one I will continue to use anyway) have been found across the globe in mysterious circumstances.

Incidentally as an interesting aside while talking to Gary Campbell of the Official Loch Ness Fan Club, he told me of a game-keeper friend in Sutherland who had witnessed an otter attack and kill a lamb. It stripped its skin bare and proceeded to feed on its carcass!

William O'Neil spotted a large animal early Wednesday morning (9th of August.) around 3 am. It crossed the road and was carrying what he thought was a rabbit in its mouth. It was dark in colour and around the same size of a rottweiler dog.

He switched on his main beams and was sure it was not a fox or a dog. He was driving back from Inverness and the sighting occurred on the Blair Atoll - Pitlochry Road.

October 3rd, 1997. Mrs. White was doing her house work when she noticed an animal that somehow seemed out of the ordinary to her - it reminded her of a puma. She took a couple of looks and then decided to film the animal which was sat at rest, not moving at all. After a minute of filming she continued with the house work, when she returned the animal had gone.

She never saw it arrive or leave. The animal moved only once during filming and that was to look directly at Mrs. Whites bungalow. She describes it as being black with a large head and a kind of square maybe snub kind of face. The animal was sat against wire fencing, it is not known if it was behind or in front of it. The height of the fencing from the ground is:

- Ground to top fence post = 4 inches.
- Ground to top wire = 37 inches.

The ground behind the fence is consistent with the above measurements. The ground in front of the fencing is not level and in some places is 49 inches to the top fence post and 37 inches to the top wire. Depending on whether we can find out if the

ANIMALS & MEN # 19

animal was behind or in front of the fence we may be able to estimate its height and size.

A copy of the video is in my possession.

A Strange Bird. May *1995*, Ayrshire.

The creature was seen on the *A76* approaching the roundabout at Irvine coming from Kilmarnock. David Berryman saw a large bird which he estimated to be three feet in length with a large wingspan. It followed parallel to the male driver of a car. The bird remained at the car's side and seemed to glide effortlessly as the car reached speeds in excess of 70 mph. It was dark in colour

ANIMALS & MEN # 19 — FEATURE

and had a strange "square shaped mouth or beak. It also seemed to have tufts of fur instead of feathers."

The witness was alone and as he turned into Irvine and headed towards Harbourside the bird carried on straight ahead, although it must have followed the car, or seemed to have for over a mile. The bird obviously made a great impression on David Berryman in order for it to stick in his mind and ring me.

Pike & Sheep.

David Currie, is in his late 40's, and after spending fifteen years in the Australian outback he thought he knew all about animals and their strange behaviour. That was until he and his wife took a stroll in the grounds of Kildrurn Castle, an old Campbell stronghold. They had to walk across a field to reach the castle and as they passed a small river they both saw a huge pike laying motionless just below the surface of the water. Its huge eyes stared at the couple, "seemingly taking everything about them in,"

Mr Currie mused later. Then, with an inexplicable seizure of fear, the couple suddenly became rooted to the spot for a few moments. They then quickly walked up-stream with the pike following them until they moved away from the waters' edge.

Almost at once the couple were surrounded by sheep and they stood in the middle of them.

The sheep closed in, prodding and nudging the now terrified couple who "began to believe that nature had turned against them". After several minutes of jostling the sheep then made a pathway for Mr and Mrs Currie who were now completely shaken. They headed for their car, abandoning all ideas of visiting the castle.

Incidentally Kildrurn has a notorious past connected with black magic and witchcraft. Today, negative vibrations and energies are said to be still present, especially in the ground and trees.

ANIMALS & MEN # 19   FEATURE

Curiosity Killed The Cat

By

Neil Arnold

In the 1930's a hunt ensued. A pursuit like no other. And yet an action taken, that faded into obscurity from the day it proceeded.

In 1963, Shooters Hill near East London, was to be the site where the search for the Surrey Puma began. Meanwhile, in the '80s on the West Country quagmire known as Exmoor, the Royal Marines were tracking The Beast. Another mystery felid. However, some sixty years previous the first big cat hunt took place. An event forgotten like any normal day. A moment of great significance, yet never to reach the cryptozoological heights that the Exmoor and Surrey hunts had touched. For in the '30s there was no media attraction and certainly no big cat flap. Or was there?

During the latter part of the '90s Kent has become a hot-spot for big cat sightings. Although a number of large felines roam the Weald, the main cat sightings have caused local newspapers to give birth to the legend of the Beast Of Blue Bell Hill.

It is not clear as to what species of large cat is stalking the rural valley, but there is enough evidence to suggest that a number of predators stalk by day and night. This enigma has received a great deal of coverage, this causing argumentative theorising between myself and the few other people who have an interest in the phenomena. However, debate is now over for over the past few months and weeks I have gained information that finally sheds light onto the moggy mystery. I have discovered the root, the one seed from which the puzzle stems.

Leonard Cuckow has seen big cats in Kent on three occasions. His most recent sighting occurred whilst he was strolling with his wife Marjorie, near their home in Strood. The couple are both in their eighties and have many tales to tell. I met up with the charming couple after I contacted them in regards to a 1998 Easter sighting. They were walking down a disused lane to view local roadworks. This particular lane is flanked on the left by an orchard, and on the right a football-pitch sized bramble site.

It was late morning and as they walked Leonard knelt down to tie his shoelaces. As Marjorie continued she noticed, on the left bank, a large sandy-coloured cat. Alarmed by the couple's presence it sprang, from a sitting position, some fifteen-feet clearing the lane, and landing on the opposite bank before scurrying away into the undergrowth. Leonard caught a fleeting glimpse of the creature as it leapt so close to his wife. It was around four-feet in length, muscular and cheetah-like in its appearance. Leonard marked the area, rang the local newspaper but asked for anonymity. Unfortunately the newspaper gave full details, but this proved to be a blessing for me. I contacted Mr. and Mrs. Cuckow who proved to be very warm. I gained hordes of information during a three-hour chat and Leonard told me things the newspapers knew nothing about.

I never once doubted the couple's experience and after tales of angling, farming and nature I explored the area where the big cat was spotted.

ANIMALS & MEN # 19

Stonehorse Lane is about fifty metres long, running off a main road. It is brought to an abrupt end ~ major roadworks as a bypass is currently being built. However, the wild 'field' on the right, although being low in its cover and lacking in actual woodland, is an undisturbed patch. In a way it is an odd area and quite out-of-place against the hum of the busy High Street and noisy estates. And yet it is perfect habitat for a big cat.

I roamed the thickets during the warm May day. With my still camera at the ready I threw small stones into nearby brambles, hoping to alarm any large feline, although I must admit that in the lonesome silence I was incredibly unsettled.

A fox would raise its curious head but no feline would show its face. However, I believe that this particular area may well be a stop-off for the cat. There is much prey for the predator, and although building work progresses only fifty-feet away, the foliage is a distant world. In fact, many years ago a convicted murderer settled in the Stonehorse Lane thickets whilst he was on the run. Forr three weeks he eluded capture, and only when he emerged from the brambles was he caught

Leonard saw another big cat whilst fishing in the '80s. He was with friends at Snodland Lakes when they spotted a large cat that was drinking from the lake. Leonard is adamant to this day that the creature was no dog. He knew by the way it 'went down' that it was a huge feline.

In the '30s Leonard was in his 'teens'. His father owned a pub at Halling, an old fashioned pub built up high and from its windows the kids would stare across the landscape of the Downs. During his childhood there he'd heard many tales of ramblers spotting puma-type cats and other out-of-place cats. And then, one day in Wouldham Leonard had his first, and most significant big cat sighting. In fact it is Kent's most significant big cat event.

Leonard was playing shove ha'penny (a game involving a slate board with chalked horizontal lines, participants would 'shove a half-penny' with

FEATURE

the heel of their hand in order to nudge the coin over the lines. Certain lines would represent points) with a few friends. A number of others were viewing the rolling fields where a steam-engine would often pull a plough to furrow the land.

About a dozen boys, including Leonard were alerted by one fellow that something black and strange was prowl mg about 'up there'. The creature they all watched mooched about before strolling into undergrowth. The creature was then seen again over the next few days by different people.

Drastic action was taken as apparently big cat sightings were quite frequent in them days, according to Leonard. And so, the Royal Engineers were called in. Some sixty men who combed the Downs, banging pieces of metal as their rifles hung over their shoulders. Soon after the commotion began, the black feline was sighted. Eventually it was shot in the Downs at Burham, where some sixty to seventy years later, big cats are still seen.

According to Leonard, everybody knew where the cat had come from and it was certainly not the only cat. And so the police approached the local zoo, Garrard Tyrwhitt-Drake Zoo, owned by Sir Garrard Tyrwhitt-Drake. A man of some importance within the community, but a man who admitted that the dead feline was indeed his. It had been a 'black leopard'.

Leonard recalls many incidents in the '30s and '40s when big cats were seen escaping from the inadequate captivity. It also seems as though Sir Garrard had his dark side, despite being Mayor and member of

ANIMALS & MEN # 19   FEATURE

various zoological societies. Being such a distinguished gentleman often disguised the fact that he inter-bred animals as well as provided poor security for his animals. And believe me, the zoo was rich in exotic animals, all reared as his own collection. Hugh William Tyrwhitt-Drake bought Cobtree Manor House, its surrounding land and several farms from the Brassey family of Preston Hill, Aylesford in 1904 after originally leasing it to them previously. Eventually, the estate was inherited by his son, Sir Garrard.

The grounds were enlarged to maintain Garrard's collection of wild animals and from the '30s to the '50s much of the estate space became a zoo. Sir Garrard lived in Cobtree Manor with his wife and he died in 1964 aged 83. He is remembered as being an active man, owning his own circus, being known in the community and often seen riding his coach and horses. However, his deeds of generosity and his general appearance hid the fact that his mis-use of nature still causes people to speak of such acts.

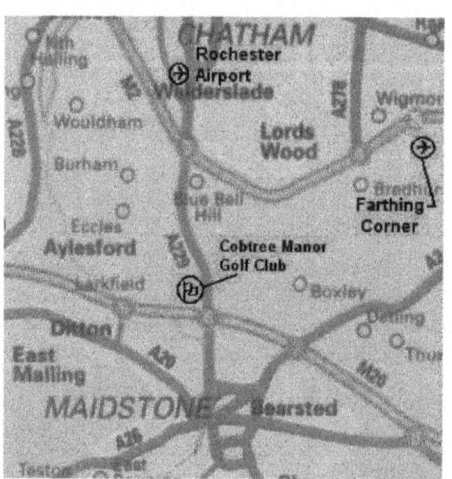

Whilst there have been no bizarre reports of five-legged creatures in Medway, I have gained information from people who experienced, first hand such techniques. In fact, Leonard Cuckow was often allowed deep into the zoo, where many visitors were not welcome. His father was a friend of Sir Garrard's, as well as being 'in' with local gamekeepers, farmers and the like. This vein continues to this day as Leonard is very friendly with local people of importance. The thousands of yearly visitors to the zoo never heard about the frequent escapes which caused such big cat flaps and they certainly never knew about the cross-breeding of species, those unfortunate animals locked in the dingy basement beneath the zoo.

The zoo closed in 1959 due to rising costs, labour shortages and the fact that Drake was ageing. It seems that a majority of the animals were sent out to other zoos, one of these being in the Bronx, New York. However, I do not believe that all were dispersed legally. Of course, not all of today's big cat sightings can be put down to Sir Garrard's poor system as I have no doubt that people, to this day release large animals. However, the big cats of Kent now have a history to their mystery.

Drake began to build his collection of wild animals in 1900 and he had one of the largest collections in the country. His possessions began to attract townsfolk and around 1912 his shows aided local charities. By 1913 he had acquired bears, kangaroos and many birds and he moved his collection of two-hundred and fifty to Tovil.

The zoo's opening was successful but it only lasted a year due to the war. Soon after though the collection was rebuilt and after mini-tours and exhibitions a permanent zoo was set up at

ANIMALS & MEN # 19 — FEATURE

the Cobtree estate. It was opened in 1934 and in two seasons it attracted over 150,000 visitors. My Grandfather vouches for the fact that show business people were invited to the zoo as were Royalty. They all experienced the miniature train which took visitors from the entrance to the actual enclosure.

The zoo struggled through the Second World War although locals feared that bombing raids would release the hungry lions. ' And then it faded into nothing, the site now enveloped by a green golf course. The only remain being a restored elephant house.

The zoo was nothing in comparison to todays enclosures at Howletts and Port Lympne but it was something different for the families at war time. Maybe Drake took advantage of his high profile for we must remember that his exhibition was an enjoyable distraction, so did anyone care about a strewn puma or two ?

I never knew the man but through sources it would seem that his zoo was often approached by the local authorities in regards to escaped animals. Indeed, judging from a 1939 programme we could take a pick from any number of creatures. Drake may not have logged his entire collection and also may not have missed the few that went astray.

I needed to spotlight Sir Garrard and his zoo due to the fact that I 'd been fortunate enough to be in contact with people who actually saw cats escaping from his cages. Indeed, Sir Garrard may not have been aware of insufficient security and by the time something had been done it was too late.

I feel entitled to point a finger at Drake, as well as various other rich families in Kent who kept large cats in their mansions. It is even known that various rock stars around Kent and Sussex kept large creatures but what happened to those is another story. There is also the possibility that Sir Garrard knew animals had escaped but turned his nose up for not wanting his reputation dented. If his zoo had been examined it would no doubt have been deemed unsafe and suffered a premature collapse, thus draining him of his wealth.

For the record, Sir Garrard collected the following animals over twenty years of his zoo time: Bears, bison, baboon, camel, cheetah, chimpanzee, deer, dingo, elephants, foxes, gnu, hyena, jackal, kangaroo, leopard, lion, llama, monkey, porcupine, racoon, rats, special sheep, wild swine, wolves, yak, zebra, many birds, reptiles, horses and fish.

Indeed, here we may have the answer to Kent`s crypto riddle.

Did escaped creatures from sixty years ago spawn the cycle in effect today? Whilst a majority of the animals, as far as we know, were kept in captivity successfully, there must have been escapee' s.

This has to be fact, otherwise an eighty-year old gentleman would not bring it up. Indeed, the big cat sightings of the '90s are triggering memories of past occurrences. In many cases, from years ago, people often do not think about what they've seen, until years later when a similar incident causes them to.

I often ask myself though, how come other out-of-place animals are not seen in the area? If a variety of species did escape from Drake's Zoo then I can only assume that they died shortly afterwards. I've no hard reports of sightings involving any of the listed zoo creatures, except for the big cats.

ANIMALS & MEN # 19 — FEATURE

Judging by what Leonard Cuckow saw in his teenage years, I would have to say that a handful of escapes would be sufficient enough to spawn todays local flap of feline sightings. However, I do believe that some of the big cats have come from other sources, such as private collections. I certainly do not believe that the Kent cats are the same cats that roamed the areas of Surrey, Sussex and Essex. Maybe one may have prowled this far but I immediately dismiss the possibility. The fact is, the Kent cats have only hit the headlines in the latter part of the '90s. This fact must surely dismiss the possibility that cats from neighbouring counties, in the '70s and '80s have reached Kent. I have no doubt in my mind that the recent spate of sightings are, in some way caused to the intervention of the 1976 Dangerous Wild Animals Act.

The strange thing is, if so many cats escaped from Drake's Zoo, why weren't they seen in the '50s, the '60s, the '70s and the '80s like they are now ? Well, I do have sightings which stretch back to those years, but they were not frequent, or at least they were not reported. Of course, this immediately alters the situation. At the moment the local newspapers are covering the cat situation very often, yet in the past the media may have only featured a cat sighting once a year. Straight away this changes the phenomenon.

Meanwhile, Mr. Cuckow does not recall the newspapers in the past featuring such tales. And, Leonard never reported his cat sightings until now, due to the fact that the local paper was actually covering the flap.

I am aware of a number of livestock kills in Kent that point to big cats. Mr. Cuckow pointed me to Islingham farm, a small holding with a pond, a few miles away from his home. The farm is near Wainscott, an area not far from other big cat sightings and flap areas such as Cooling, covered in other articles.

Apparently one of the farmers at Islingham Farm had lost a few lambs and dismissed the idea of foxes.

He openly spoke to Leonard about the kills but when I contacted the farm I was basically snubbed by the farmer. He simply told me that he had had lambs killed but it was done by a fox, he also believed that the cat-flap was due to drunken witnesses. If bizarre hallucinations causes people to see large felines in Kent, then the woman in the following case must have taken the largest tab of acid known to man:

Marilyn Dorrell had the sighting of her life towards the end of April when she apparently saw two big cats and a domestic cat, all in the same vicinity and only yards apart. Of course, upon hearing about the incident I began to question the reliability of detail but Marilyn was positive of what she saw. She said: "Some people asked me if it was a fox but it definitely wasn't - it was a puma."

I hear you ask me, 'What is so bizarre about a routine big cat sighting?' ; here is my answer. All of the sightings of Kent big cats have occurred in rural areas such as fields, woodland and undergrowth, even big cats seen near buildings have emerged from. woodland. However, Marilyn Dorrell spotted the mystery cats in the local High Street, albeit at night. Marilyn was on her way to a show at Chatham's Central Theatre, a building that lies on a busy, shop-filled street. There is no woodland near-by.

ANIMALS & MEN # 19 — FEATURE

She was with members of her family on the April evening and upon nearing the theatre car-park (situated at the back of the building) she noticed a crowd of people looking up at a domestic cat which seemed to be stranded on a roof of a building. The bizarre thing about this was the fact that a lynx was present too.

Marilyn, and the crowd watched for some time before going on to the show. However, after the programme Marilyn decided to go back to the area. Upon arriving she saw the domestic cat again, as well as the lynx. Even more strange was the even larger cat she spotted walking on a higher ledge. It was a Puma!

She said: *"It started walking up and down the ledge looking down at the other two cats on the roof - I was just amazed by it"*.

Marilyn then staged an early morning vigil in the car park to see if the puma was going to go any further and although she saw it again it never ventured to the ground. Even more bizarre is the fact that the next day the fire brigade were called out to rescue the domestic cat, and when they got to the spot they were surprised to see a lynx spring out and bound off, but there was no sign of a puma!

The sceptical perception of such an incident would obviously question the witnesses accuracy in identifying an animal. Even I first thought about the possibility of misidentification but the witness managed to pin-point the various species of feline from puma to lynx to domestic cat. If there was to be any element of exaggeration then surely Marilyn would have 'seen' three big cats.

At least one big cat was seen, this can be backed up by the firemen who disturbed the creature. Of course, this particular event is quite bizarre and quite extraordinary as it is a very different big cat sighting. However, although the flap is quite rich at the moment, I do not see any need for Marilyn to have fabricated the story. There may be a few holes in the tale, but there are also points which harden its truth. I do not know if the crowd of people actually saw any big cats but they obviously saw the domestic feline. It would seem strange if Marilyn was the only person to see the bigger cats because surely the people never moved on once Marilyn had joined them find it strange that Marilyn seems to be the only witness and even the newspaper report stated that Marilyn 'seemed' to be the only witness.

I never jump to conclusions in assuming that all big cat sightings are genuine, this can also be said for experiences with UFOs, other beasts and ghosts. However, all cases must be looked into and analysed and with Marilyn's incident I must simply look at what is there. Indeed, she is positive of what she saw and if we come to doubt her then we must say that the firemen never saw a lynx. A Puma, being three times the size of a lynx, may well have pursued the smaller big cat. In turn, the lynx may well have been tracking the domestic cat. These theories offer a number of confusing Possibilities. For one, if the lynx was on the same ledge as the domestic cat, why didn't it attack it at all ? In fact, they seemed to keep each other company for more than a day without any friction: Also, if the puma was hungry, why didn't it venture further ? Of course, it may not have been able to find a way down but it seems awfully peculiar to hear of such company. There did not seem to be any vicious commotion between the felines and this brings me to question Marilyn's descriptions. Is there a Possibility that she did see a puma, as well as two cubs ?

ANIMALS & MEN # 19 — FEATURE

If this is the case, maybe the roof of the building was their unusual habitat. However, the more I think about the event, the more confused I become. Of course, there is the Possibility that Marilyn did see one big cat but maybe she'd read about the cats in the paper and decided to exaggerate the incident for the gain of five minutes of fame. This seems unlikely too, although it is bizarre as to why no puma emerged when the firemen moved in to rescue the domestic `moggy`.

There is no woodland directly near Chatham's busy High Street. The big cats must have been released in the vicinity by someone or they travelled from woodland by night. However, would a domestic cat attract them to such a concrete jungle ? Indeed, cats can be curious creatures and big cats have been known to travel along the town rail-road lines in order to venture into more busy areas. However, no other sightings emerged from this period and so it remains one of the most mysterious big cat sightings that I've ever heard about.

It seems impossible that all the big cats were stranded on the building of the roof. If this is the case, we must still ask why a lynx ? Why a puma?

Since this incident the Beast Of Bluebell Hill.....

EDITOR`S NOTE: See Neil`s article in the 1999 Yearbook

.......and other local big cats have quietened down. The sightings are still occurring but I guess there is always the fear that some stories are either exaggeration are complete fiction. There are many reasons as to why people 'make up' experiences, but the case I have just mentioned almost seems too strange to be unreal. I say this because, let's face it, if you are going to make up a story regarding a big cat sighting, surely you would go for something a little more believable. The fact is, some kind of cat was seen on a roof-top in Chatham High Street, however, I do believe the 'cats' were of one species.

I certainly believe that a domestic cat was present and certainly a lynx-type feline, but I also believe that maybe the 'puma' was a lynx too. I would have suggested that the 'puma' and lynx were one, but Marilyn claims to have seen three separate felines.

I am quite baffled by the case. Unfortunately, apart from the newspaper report, much detail on the incident has faded into obscurity.

This may be due to the fact that the local authorities do not want to alarm local 'shoppers' who would obviously be put off by the existence of a big cat, or cats.

The 'puma' creature was not seen again as in the case of the lynx and the domestic cat.

If the 'puma' had scampered off in the day, it would most definitely have been spotted, for the area which surrounds the 'sighting place' consists of car-parks, extremely busy town roads, shops and many housing estates. The nearest woodland would only provide temporary cover, for it is only of small size.

So, some sixty years ago, a handful of big cats escaped from a local zoo, and in some cases have spawned a phenomenon. I'm pretty sure that many big cat sightings of today have stemmed from zoo escapes that may well have occurred over fifty years ago.

ANIMALS & MEN # 19

If the cats were in abundance then, and able to breed then the population of today seems quite unsurprising. However, in some cases it would appear that such felines have caused almost a degree of supernatural confusion in their ways.

Although there are many zoos littered throughout Britain, not all stock a variety of big cat. More recently Kent has become more populated by zoos inhabited by big cats, however, any escapes that have occurred have been dealt with.

Big cats sightings date back to the 1700's, but the 1900's has most certainly brought the mystery to even more prominence.

However, I don't think anyone or anything can explain as to why such creatures should mysteriously vanish as well as appear in extraordinary places.

NORTH OF THE BORDER
by Tom Anderson

Illegal eagle

It is notoriously difficult to breed golden eagles in captivity. Recent claims from Moscow Zoo that their captive breeding programme is a spectacular success were therefore met with some scepticism.

As yet there is no evidence that Scottish eggs or chicks have been smuggled into Russia but assuming someone is telling porkys, (or is it Gorkys ?) they must be coming from somewhere illegally.

FEATURE

Once a species is represented in a collection it is easy to produce paperwork proving it to be captive bred. Should this nefarious trade be Russian-run, we need look no further than the current boom in organised crime thereabouts.

Around twenty billion roubles worth of illicit goods enter Moscow annually and some of it, it has to be said, with official sanction. A favourite method is the use of large wicker baskets, purportedly full of vegetables etc, but ideal for secreted wildlife due to the ventilation advantages of basketry. This is known as Mafia Raffia.

ANIMALS & MEN # 19

The ingenuity of animal smugglers surpasses even that of drug couriers. During the Tour de France of `89 a PR man for a tyre company was suspected of border crossing with rare snakes inside his Michelin man costume. Customers at Ecuador's Quito immigration noted a disproportionate number of hunchbacks in transit and found people were carrying tortoises in shoulder harnesses of ex Argentinean army webbing from the Galapagos islands, an national reserve, it's ecology threatened by rats and goats. You are probably familiar, gentle reader, with the quaint Spanish custom of hurling latter omnivore from church bell towers. This is not, as you may have thought, to test its suspension system, but originated in Navarre, famous for the bull running of Pamplona. The story goes is that a local cleric, confronted by his bishop for stealing holy relics, inserted a necklace into an unfortunate kid and tossed it to the starving peasants below, proclaiming his affinity with the common people. This is one of the few instances where the animal was the vessel of the contraband, rather than vice versa.

LETTERS

LETTERS TO THE EDITOR

The Editor and his band of merry men welcome an exchange of correspondence on any subject of interest to readers of this magazine.

We reserve the right to edit letters and would like to stress that opinions voiced are those of the individual correspondent rather than being necessarily those of the editorial team or the Centre for Fortean Zoology. Every attempt is made not to infringe anyone`s moral rights or copyright, and we apologise if we have unwittingly done so.

WOLVERINE WEIRDNESS

Hi Jon,

Just a quick note re Animals & Men #18.

Enjoyed the Wolverine story. It reminded me of a time when I was in about 6th grade (around 11 years of age) when we had a "wolverine scare". Supposedly wolverines had come to town and were being vicious. We were warned to stay away from woods and fields, and to go straight home from school. It had us pretty scared. Being 11, I believed it all, so did no other research, so do not know if a wolverine was actually spotted or not. As for the lamprey......was it possible that a lamprey from another area could have survived in this stream? I ask because my sister and I

- 36 -

ANIMALS & MEN # 19

came upon two lampreys at a beach near our cabin.

They were not indigenous to the area, but are great bait, although illegal as far as I know to use. From their location we surmised that they had been used for bait, then dumped by some asshole. They were about 7 inches long unstretched, and quite a bit longer when fully extended. We tried pulling them off of the rocks to destroy them, and wound up smashing them there.

I am not an advocate of killing things as you well know, but the thought of the lampreys getting a toe-hold in that swimming lake was not very attractive. My question then is..... do you think it could have been an introduced species?

- Felinda Bullock, Wisconsin

JON REPLIES: the most interesting thing about `my` lamprey is that (although I didn't know this when I caught the creature or when I wrote the article in the last issue) there are at present no known species of warm water lampreys in the world. This creature is therefore something particularly special. As to whether or not it could have been an introduced specimen: as always, one has to ask the question `why`. The only introduced fish that I have managed to find from Puerto Rico is the Mosquito Fish *(Gambusia affinis)* which was introduced (as the name implies) to control mosquitoes. More details will be released on the Peurto Rican lamprey in due course...

Pelorus Jack

Dear Jon:

Concerning your enquiry in the last issue of A&M about the dolphin 'Pelorus Jack', the following is from Rudyard Kipling's "Something of Myself" about his visit to New Zealand in October 1891:

LETTERS

"...at Wellington I was met, precisely where warned to expect him, by 'Pelorus Jack', the big, white-marked dolphin, who held it his duty to escort shipping up the harbour. He enjoyed a special protection of the Legislature proclaiming him sacred, but, years later, some animal shot and wounded him and he was seen no more".

The editor of the book adds that the dolphin's territory was not Wellington but French Pass, across the Cook Strait from Wellington.

A query for Richard Freeman:

I found an account in a history of the Knights of St John of how a future master of the order killed a 'dragon' on the island of Rhodes in the fourteenth century. The creature did not breathe fire, fly or otherwise behave flamboyantly; were there still crocodiles in Egypt at that time, and could one have got across to Rhodes? If he is intending to hunt 25 ft monitors, would he be interested in the knight's technique?

- Chris Clark
Walton on the Hill (Tadworth), Surrey

RICHARD REPLIES: Certainly there were crocodiles in N. Egypt at that time. They were probably still found as far north as Turkey in the 14th century. However, the Nile crocodile *C.niloticus* dislikes salt water and would have to have been taken to Rhodes by boat. Both the Nile crocodile and the Nile monitor (another contender for the Rhodes dragon) are still found in Egypt south of the Aswan Dam. And yes, Chris any dragon hunting tips from days of yore (especially those involving virgins) will be gratefully appreciated.....

ANIMALS & MEN # 19

BOOK REVIEWS

Richard Freeman, Zoologist and *Animals & Men* editor, ruthlessly finds out what's afoot in the world of fortean-related books.

The search for the Giant Squid
Richard Ellis.   Hale   *****

Mr Ellis is an eminently readable author who previously distracted us with the excellent *Monsters of the Sea*. In his new tome Richard turns to a cryptid who made the leap into reality, *Architeuthis dux* - the giant squid. This is *the* book on giant squid being by far the most detailed and authoritative work on the animal to date.

The book traces the squid through ancient legends of the old Norse Kraken to early naturalists like Erik Pontoppidan who grasped for the truth to his 19th century counterparts who unmasked the monster. He looks at how we have portrayed it in literature and on screen and details the (so far fruitless) expeditions to film this colossus alive. The most fascinating part of the book is the chapters on human encounters with the Kraken. Many of the tales of giant squid attacking and sinking ships seem to be apocryphal but the myths are enhanced with biological riddles. Far more enthralling: what do they feed on? What is their breeding cycle? How big do they grow - 60, 80, or 100 feet?

The complete list of strandings from 1545 to the present day makes compelling reading as dose the list of all the full sized models of the giant squid displayed around the world (including one at the historically named town of Dildo in Newfoundland). No one has ever seen Architeuthis alive and well in its true habitat. Even this book with its wealth of information cannot capture the essence of this living legend. As Ellis puts it himself....

"We know we are supposed to believe in it, but still we doubt. Can there really be a 60 foot long creature with unblinking dinner plate eyes in the unknown vastness of the icy depths? The existence of Architeuthis only confirms our fears and inadequacies; despite our puny efforts to find it the monster perdures....We need to find the giant squid, but we also need not to find it." Miss this book at your peril. - RF

In the Domain of the Lake Monsters
John Kirk   Key Porter $24.95   *****

Unfortunately this book is currently only available in America. Hopefully it will be

ANIMALS & MEN # 19

released in Britain, as it is a fantastic read. The book is broken into several sections. The first and perhaps the most interesting charts John's own involvement with Ogopogo, the monster of

Lake Okanagan. It tells of his move to Canada and his discovery of the lake's strange inhabitants. Mr Kirk has been lucky enough to have seen Ogopogo on several occasions, some of them quite close. Far from being a lay man John was once producer and master of ceremonies at Ocean Park, Hong Kong, which makes his testimony compelling. This part of the book put me in mind of the very personal writings of the greatly missed Tim Dinsdale, the original lake monster hunter. This is a touch that has been missing in many recent books on the subject in their rush to be ultra-scientific.

REVIEWS

The next part looks beyond to lake monsters world wide dealing with them continent by continent. These include some very obscure cases from lakes of which I have never heard. It is these ill-known lakes that are the most compelling read due to the new data Kirk has uncovered. Finally there's a comparison between Ogopogo and Nessie, looking at morphology and behaviour. This seems to indicate the two are different species.

The book is slightly marred by lack of illustrations, references and an index but these are minor gripes. Overall the book makes an excellent addition to any cryptozoologist's collection. - RF

Fortean Studies Volume 5
Steve Moore (editor)
John Brown Publishing £19.99
*****

The latest and best in the distinguished annual collection of papers on all manner of fortean subjects. There is much here for the cryptozoologist. Gary Mangiacopra, Michel Raynal, Dr Dwite Smith and Dr David Avery look at early evidence for giant constricting snakes in South America. Unfortunately the two cases they concentrate on the most, I believe to be hoaxes. The celebrated Fawcett case is narrated by the Colonel like an extract from a poorly written Edgar Rice Burroughs novel and the width he gives for the snake is ridiculously small. Algot Lange's story is even more silly. He gives the snake the power of hypnotism that only he (being a white man) can resist. The skin of the 52 foot snake that he supposedly took back to New York never materialised. I wonder why? This said, I actually believe in the existence of the *sucuruju gegante* - and Gary's writing is always a joy to read. Pity he picked two duff cases.

ANIMALS & MEN # 19

Our old mate Karl Shuker provides an insightful supplement to Bernard Heuvelman's checklist of cryptozoological animals. This spectacular tour of the menagerie of the dammed ranges from giant pangolins in Indonesia to marsupial "apes". Some, like mainland thylacines, are more probable than others such as surviving pterosaurs, whilst others, for example - the waheela (modern descendent of the bear dogs?) are so ill-known we can but guess. One wonders which of these absentees from the ark will be discovered first.

Andy Roberts, a writer more usually associated with ultra-skeptical ufology, provides a thought provoking article on the infamous big grey men of Ben MacDhui in the Cairngorms. After much digging Andy shows us this celebrated classic of forteana is no such thing.

Together with your editor, yours truly's humble offering was an examination of dog/anthropoid hybrids. Looking at case histories and folklore we found werewolves and dog-headed people scattered throughout many cultures from the giant "baboons" of Africa to a dog-headed saint!

For me, the collection was slightly marred by the inclusion yet again of insufferable drivel by Michel Meurger. Quite what the fascination the F.T. posse seem to have with this no-hoper and his intelligence-insulting pap is beyond me. Let's hope he will be absent from next years' volume! - RF

REVIEWS

Strange & Unexplained Phenomena
Jerome Clark and Nany Pear
Visible Ink   *****

General books on forteana are two a penny and go from utter tripe to classics by Karl Shuker or Francis Hitching. This book belongs firmly to

ANIMALS & MEN # 19

the latter category and is a pleasure to read. Just about every crypto critter going is covered with old cases, cheek-by-jowl with brand new material. An original idea was to show how forteana has been represented on the big screen by detailing films of each subject in the margins. Though far from exhaustive this is an interesting addition. With lively illustrations smashing cartoons and biographies of leading lights in each subject this is a must read book How can it fail? - after all, pears are the most fortean of fruits. - RF

Strange Beasts - Creatures that both Terrify and Intrigue.
Orbis Publishing   99 pence   **

A shop checkout style book that consists mainly of reprints from the old Unexplaned magazine of the late 70s. A mixed bag of subjects British big cats, Neanderthals, Minnesota ice man, vampires, mermaids, thunderbirds, Irish lake monsters, dinosaur extinction, the devil's hoof prints, dragons, surviving mammoths, toad folklore and werewolves, quite a mix! It's only 127 pages long and won't tell you any thing you don't already know but it's a good book for children with an interest in the subject. RF

REVIEWS

The Butterflies of Papua New Guinea: Their systematics and biology by Michael Parsons.
Academic Press *****

Do you like butterflies? Do you like Papua New Guinea? Then you will love "The Butterflies of Papua New Guinea"! Unfortunately it is priced at £185, which makes it way beyond the budget of the casual buyer. This is the ultimate guide to northern antipodean lepidoptera. At nearly 1000 pages long and with over 3000 colour plates it not only includes an exhaustive species list but notes on the systematics, phylogeny and habitats of these exotic and beautiful insects. An essential purchase for the serious student of the subject.

ANIMALS & MEN # 19   FEATURE

Giant Ground Sloth Survival

by

Richard Freeman

Richard Freeman, zoologist, looks at giant ground sloth survival in South America, with first a short overview; he then concentrates on sightings from Venezuela.

Ground sloths were terrestrial edentates found throughout South America. They ranged in size from *Megatherium*, that was as large as an Asian elephant, down to species no larger than domestic cats. They were all herbivores, browsing foliage that they pulled down with their spectacular claws. Ground sloths were capable of bipedal movement that helped them reach high growing vegetable matter. The scythe like talons also doubled up as defensive weapons against contemporary predators like *Thylacosimilus*, a marsupial sabre toothed "cat". It is believed that the whole group became extinct about 10,000 years ago at the end of the Pleistocene epoch due to climate change and human predation. However many cryptozoologists, myself included, believe that at least one species has persisted till the present day.

A medium sized group of ground sloths were the *mylodonts*, about the size of a gorilla. These possessed a singular feature, skin that was studded with bony nodules (dermal ossicles) that effectively acted like chain mail. These seem to be the animals reported today .In 1558 French explorer and priest, Farther Andre Thevet was told of a Patagonian animal called the *su*. This was said to have a short face, long tail, and powerful claws, all features possessed by ground sloths. The su also carried its young on its back as all sloths do.

Ramon Lista, Argentina's Secretary of State, saw a specimen in the 1870s, whilst exploring Santa Cruz in southern Patagonia. Lista and his companions saw a large animal they described as resembling a pangolin (a group of scaly ant/termite eating mammals from Africa and Asia) but with reddish grey hair instead of scales. The men fired on the creature several times but it escaped unscathed into the undergrowth. The failure of the bullets to harm the beast may have been due to its dermal armour. The Tehuelche Indians said this area was inhabited by an ox-sized animal with dense fur and huge claws. It was famed for its invulnerability to arrows and bullets.

In 1932 a British Museum expedition searched Central America for surviving mylodonts. Led by Dr Thomas Gann it concentrated on the Yucatan and Honduras. In a marsh close to the Rio Hondo border with British Honduras (now Belize), Gann briefly spotted a ground sloth. He describes it as trotting on all fours like a large ape. It had a sizeable body covered with black, shaggy fur and a white mane obscuring the face. Richard Greenwell, secretary of the International Society of Cryptozoology, was told by a colleague that he had seen a ground sloth in a cave in Ecuador.

ANIMALS & MEN # 19 — FEATURE

Picture: Richard Freeman

More recently Dr David C. Oren of Brazil's Goeldi Natural History Museum has been investigating reports of ground sloths in the Matto Grosso area of the Amazon. Indians speak of a creature they call *mapinguary*.

The greatly feared beast has red fur, is invulnerable to arrows (except on the stomach, the only place mylodonts were not armoured), has backwards pointing feet and a second mouth in its belly from which it spews forth a noxious breath.

These last two features seem odd but Oren thinks he can explain them.

Ground sloths had incurving claws that left tracks that looked as if the feet were pointing back to front. The second mouth Oren believes is a gland that emits a foul-smelling gas as a defensive measure.

The Indians say it feeds on a diet of berries and bacaba palm hearts, leaving droppings resembling those of a horse. Oren has yet to lay eyes on the mapinguary but he has collected horse like droppings that are currently being analysed.

In Venezuela these creatures are known as *mono grande* or *di-di*. The natives believe them to be huge apes but this is almost certainly incorrect as

(cont'd)

ANIMALS & MEN # 19

there are no apes in S.America (or any fossil precedent for them). It is more likely that what is being reported are ground sloths. These animals are superficially similar to apes, with their short faces and partially bipedal stance.

Roger Courteville was a civil engineer who led an ethnographic expedition into S. America and in 1926 became the first man to cross the entire continent by car. He twice encountered ape like animals in 1938 and 1947. One of these occurred on the Colombo-Venezuelan frontier. He described it as follows...

"A prominent brow overhung its very soft grey-blue eyes. A dark hairless face rose above its receding chin. It had a tuft of thick hair on the crown of its forehead; a powerful neck towered above its broad v-shaped thorax; long reddish hair covered its limbs and body."

There is nothing in this description that cannot be reconciled with a ground sloth. Courteville continued... *"Its upper arms seemed longer than its forearms, just as its thighs seemed longer than its shins. The footprints left in the fine sand showed me that it walked on the outside edge of its feet, as chimpanzees do"*

Ground sloths also put their weight on the outside of their feet; this we can see from fossil tracks. Apes however put the weight on the whole foot. He approached to within a couple of meters of the animal before it bared its teeth and fled back into the jungle.

Dr Charles Barrington Brown, Government Surveyor in British Guiana heard rumours of hairy "men" living on the Upper Mazaruni on the Venezuelan frontier in 1868. He himself heard the alleged cry of the di-di, a whistle beginning in a high key and slowly dying away in a low key, repeated three times. Brown was told by the Indians....

"The di-di is said by the Indians to be a short, thick set, and powerful wild man, whose body is covered in hair and who lives in the forest. A belief in the existence of this fabulous creature is universal over the whole of British, Venezuelan, and Brazilian Guiana. On the Demera river some years after this, i met a half-breed woodcutter, who related an encounter that he had with two di-di,- a male and a female-in which he successfully resisted their attacks with his axe. In the fray, he stated he was a good deal scratched"

The question of ground sloth survival is not as controversial as one might at first think. These creatures are thought to have disappeared only ten thousand years ago at the most. This is an eye-blink in the geological time scale and far more recent than many other touted prehistoric survivors such as plesiosaurs and none avian dinosaurs.

We must also remember that ground sloths have been seen by some very respectable witnesses such as Dr Gann. This lend credence to the stories. Other likely cryptids have been seen by zoologists and biologists and include thylacines, Megalania prisca (the 30 monitor lizard of Australia), and the Orang-pendek, Sumatra's ape man. I would personally list these three animals together with the Asian yeti, Delcourt's gecko and the giant ground sloth as the cryptids most likely to actually exist and the most likely to be found in the next century.

Finally we must consider the terrain in which the ground sloth lives. The S. American rain forest is some of the least known territory on the planet. In Venezuela there is a forested plateau the size of Wales that rises out of the jungle on sheer cliffs hundreds of feet high. It was the inspiration for the "Lost World".I doubt if there are any dinosaurs up there, but there might be ground sloth

ANIMALS & MEN # 19

ANIMALS & MEN
BACK ISSUES: £2 each

Back issues are available from the editorial address. Please see "methods of payment" on p.47.

CONTENTS (all issues also contain news pages, reviews and letters) :

1 Relict Pine Martens, Giant Sloths, Sumatran and Javan Rhinos, Golden Frogs, Frog Falls.
2 Mystery bears in Oxford and The Atlas Mountains, Loch Ness reports, Green Lizards, Woodwose, The Tatzelwurm.
3 Giant Worm in Eastbourne, Lake Monsters of New Guinea, Giant Lizards in Papua, Mystery Cats, Black Dogs on Dartmoor, Scorpion Mystery.
4 Manatees of St Helena, Migo: The Lake Monster of New Britain, The search for the Tasmanian Thylacine.
5 Mystery cats, Loch Ness, More on the "Migo Video", Boars and Pumas, The Hairy Hands of Dartmoor.
6 The Owlman Special; also the Humped Elephants of Nepal, Mystery Cats, Sabre-toothed cats, Mysterious hominids of Africa, The British Nandi Bear?, Bibliography of Cryptozoology books part 1 (by Dr Karl Shuker).
7 Mystery Whales, Strangeness in Scotland, On collecting a cryptid, Bodmin Leopard Skull, Shuker's Cryptozoological Bibliography pt 2.
8 Green Cats and Dogs, Mystery Whales, Quagga Project, Bibliography of Cryptozoological books (3rd & concluding part), Malayan Man Beast.
9 Hong Kong Tiger, Horseman of Lincolnshire, Scottish BHM, Congo Peacock, Mystery Whales.
10 Mystery Moth of Madagascar, Bengal Leopard Cats, The Derry, Wild Boars in Kent, a new Irish lake monster, mystery whales and the truth about the Essex Beach Corpses.
11 The "Walruses Special", also: Feathered Dinosaurs, Ground Sloth Survival in North America, Mystery Whales, Initial Bipedalism.
12 Lions: The Barbary Lion, etc. More Feathered Dinosaurs, Chinese Crabs in the Thames, Mystery Animals of Germany, News from New Zealand.

BACK ISSUES

13 Pangolins; also Moby the Sperm Whale, Barking Beast of Bath, Yorkshire ABCs, Molly the Singing Oyster, Leatherback Turtles, Walruses.
14 The Dragons of Yorkshire, Irish mystery animals, In Search Of "Gambo", Charlie Fort and the Vampire Sheep Slayer - and Jackals; and the first of Clinton's Cogitations (Clin Keeling looks back on and comments on the previous issue).
15 Lake Dakataua "Migo" monster update, The Weird Warbling Whatsit of the Westcountry, The Beast of Llangurig, The Waspman, The Bigfoot "Murders", and three articles on Beavers.
16 Expedition Report: The Search for El Chupacabra; Quagga Project update; Bestiary #1; Snakes with Legs; Eastern Cougars; Giant Lizards in the English Countryside?
17 British Wolverine - or muddy badger?, Turtle Tales, Killer Bees, The Ziphiidae - possible new species, Vertebrate palaeontology, Video: the Beast of Bodmin press conference.
18 GUST expedition; Wolverines; crypto sharks; Puerto Rican lamprey; Out-of-place animals in Kent; Quaggas and hybrids.

THE GOBLIN UNIVERSE
BACK ISSUES: £2 each

Back issues are available from the editorial address. Please see "methods of payment" on p.47.

CONTENTS (all issues also contain news pages, letters, and record, magazine and book reviews) :

1 Witches, hellhounds and Capel's tomb. St. Leonards Vampire. Cattle Mutilation. Psychic Detectives.
2 Crop Circles & Animal Mutilations. Glamis Castle Ghosts. Communication with UFOs.
3 Rendlesham "UFO crash site" in Suffolk. Mystery Planets. Cannibalism in Scotland. DIY countries.
4 The Terror of Gloucestershire. Telpas. Barnum & Tom Thumb. The Making of "The Owlman" film. KKK operations in Scotland?
5 Kent witchcraft; Nick Redfern interview; King Arthur; Dorset Hellstones; The Poultrygeist; Whales.

- 45 -

ANIMALS & MEN # 19

THE CFZ YEARBOOK 1999

Includes

Surviving Neanderthals - a search for man's closest relatives
- by Jonathan Downes and Richard Freeman.

The Beast of Bluebell Hill - by Neil Arnold: Sightings of a mystery animal in Kent.

Wolverines in Wales? - by Roy Kerridge

Waitoreke: The Enigma from New Zealand - by Craig Heinselman

The evidence thus far; varying descriptions from otter-like, beaver-like, or seal-like. The theories (through behaviour, anatomy and habitat).

Folk tales involving were-beasts from Ghana - by Louis Baba

Pelorus Jack

The text of the 1911 booklet by James Cowan on the solitary white dolphin off N.Z.

Chance would be a Fine Thing - by Graham Inglis. Life on other planets? It's certainly a possibility...

£10.75 (UK).   £11.50 (overseas) - (prices inclusive of postage & packing)

THE CFZ YEARBOOK 1998

edited by Jonathan Downes & Graham Inglis

200pp. £12.50
Contributors:

Tom: Anderson, Neil Arnold, Richard Freeman, Mike Grayson, Martin Jenkins, Roy Kerridge, Chris Moiser, Nick Molloy, Richard Muirhead, Darren Naish, Michael Playfair, and Emmet J. Sweeney.

Subjects:
Giant crocodiles, cryptozoological films, African Stories, Nessie - asking the right questions, Nessie - diary of a hunt, Ichthyosaur evolution, Mammoths and the Comet, Sea Serpents, Amerindian icons, Strange Snake stories, an alphabetical guide to water monsters, the Fortean Fauna of Percy Fawcett, and The Zambesi River God.

ANIMALS & MEN # 19

OUR OWN PUBLICATIONS

THE OWLMAN AND OTHERS

NEW UPDATED EDITION

by
Jonathan Downes

£12.95 from
Domra Publications,
65 Constable Road, Corby,
Northants.

"Anomalist" award winner 1997

SUBSCRIPTIONS

For a 4-issue (one year) subscription:
£8 UK   £9 EC
£14 US/Canada/Oz/NZ (airmail)
£15 Rest of World.

HOW TO ORDER and METHODS OF PAYMENT

Subscription rates INCLUDE postage. On other orders, postage and packing is extra: please add 25p (£0.30non-UK) per magazine and 75p (£0.90 non-UK) per book.

Payment can be made in UK cash, by IMO (an international money order), Eurocheque, or by a cheque drawn on a UK bank. Please make all cheques payable to Jonathan Downes.

Please send all orders to

CFZ, 15 Holne Court, Exwick, Exeter, Devon, EX4 2NA, England.

Britain is one of the few countries of the world where US dollars do **not** circulate. If making payment in US$ then please add $14 to cover the currency exchange fee.

For more information on CFZ projects and publications, visit our website at:
http://www.eclipse.co.uk/cfz

"Not JUST a UFO Book - this is a major investigation into the links between UFOs, animal mutilations, Mystery Creature Sightings, and other fortean phenomena..."

£12.95 from
Domra Publications, 65 Constable Road, Corby, Northants

Also available from Domra: *The Owlman and Others* by Jonathan Downes - Winner of the 1997 *Anomalist Award*.
£12.95

Animals & Men ISSN 1354 0637

TYPESET USING FAMILY VALUES

'Up here, I feel so big and mighty...'

Issue 20

Christmas 1999

1999 was a very strange year. In the early summer I accepted the editor's job on a magazine called *Quest* which was published by a complete shyster called Roy Bird. I did my best to produce a creditable magazine, and I think that I succeeded, but I became embroiled in a horrible financial mess which ended up in me, and many of my associates (including my own father) being owed considerable sums of money, and my reputation being sullied for several years. It was not a pleasant time, and I think that my general bad feelings about life in general are mirrored in this particular edition.

Nick Redfern arrived on the scene as well during this period, and as regular CFZwatchers will know, like me, Graham and Richard he is still very much part of the scene now, even though he has been living in Texas for the best part of a decade..

ANIMALS & MEN # 20

THE CURRENT CREW OF THE CFZ MOTHERSHIP ARE:

Director: Jonathan Downes
Deputy Director: Graham Inglis
Assistant Editor: Richard Freeman

Toby the CFZ dog
Magazine cartoonist and artwork: Mark North
Picture Editor: Phil "Jester" Williams
Associate founding editor: Jan Williams
Tour Manager: Nigel Wright
Hedge-Witch: Joyce Howarth

CONSULTANTS

Consulting Editor: Dr Bernard Heuvelmans
Cryptozoology: Dr Karl Shuker, Dr Lars Thomas, Loren Coleman
Zoology: Chris Moiser
Cetology and Palaentology: Darren Naish

REGIONAL REPRESENTATIVES

Scotland: Tom Anderson
Surrey: Nick Smith
Somerset: Dave McNally
West Midlands: Dr Karl Shuker
Kent: Neil Arnold
Gtr Manchester & Cheshire: Allen E Munro
Hampshire: Darren Naish
Leicestershire: Alistair Curzon
Cumbria: Brian Goodwin
Yorkshire: Steve Jones
Tyneside: Simon Elsdon

USA: Loren Coleman
Denmark: Dr Lars Thomas, Erik Sorensen
Republic of Ireland: Daev Walsh
Spain: Alberto Lopez Acha, Angel Morant Fores
Germany: Hermann Reichenbach, Wolfgang Schmidt
France: Francois de Sarre
Mexico: Dr R A Lara Palmeros
Canada: Ben Roesch

"In her abnormalities, nature reveals her secrets"
(Goethe)

WHO'S WHO & WHAT'S WHAT

CONTENTS:

3 Editorial
4 Newsfile
14 Wolverines: a Reply - Chris Moiser
16 George Lekaukau - Roy Kerridge
20 Bestiary: The Chimaera - Ade Dimmick.
22 Crypto-Curiosities of Kent's Past - Neil Arnold

27 How many Kiwi species are there? - Darren Naish
31 Big in Japan - Richard Freeman
35 ESP in Animals: the Goverment Connection - Nick Redfern
39 Eternal Cat - Marcus Matthews

40 Letters
42 What's Afoot - Richard Freeman
43 Book Reviews - Richard Freeman
45 Subscriptions & Payments
46 CFZ Publications
47 Back Issues

ANIMALS & MEN

CFZ, 15 Holne Court, Exwick, Exeter, Devon, EX4 2NA, England

email adddress: cfz@eclipse.co.uk

SUBSCRIPTION DETAILS:
PLEASE SEE PAGE 45

---

http://www.eclipse.co.uk/cfz

BOOK ORDERS & PAYMENTS:
PLEASE SEE PAGE 45

ANIMALS & MEN # 20

EDITORIAL

THE GREAT DAYS OF ZOOLOGY......
.....ARE NOT DONE

Dear Friends,

It is well over six months since the last issue of this magazine arrived on your doormat. Unfortunately, since issue 19, various members of the Editorial team have been otherwise occupied – mainly due to financial considerations and the necessity of having to earn a living, but now the short term problems which have beset us over much of this year appear to be over and we are able to get on with the business at hand.

It is all change at the Centre for Fortean Zoology. Thanks to generous donations by Wolfgang Schmidt and Joyce Howarth we have now acquired new video and printing equipment. We are now working on several projects that we have been planning for several years.

* The chronicles of our Puerto Rico and Mexico expedition of 1998 will soon be available both as a book and a video.

* The results of our investigation into the south Devon dolphin mutilations will also be available on video withinon the next few months.

* The Owlman film will be finished very soon and available from April. It is being premiered at the 2000 UnConvention at the Commonwealth Institute in London, and will be available on video shortly after.

* We are planning a major expedition for next year and will announce details in the next issue.

Because of a dispute with the management we are no longer associated with Domra Publications of Corby. My books which were published by them are temporarily out of print. However the following titles will be reissued by the CFZ next year:

- The Owlman and Others (A revision of the first edition rather than the substandard Domra edition)
- Smaller Mystery Carnivores of the Westcountry (Revised second Edition)
- The Rising of the Moon (Revised second edition)

and we will also be issuing two new books:

- Only Fools and Goatsuckers – the hunt for the Chupacabra
- The Blackdown Mystery

Because of financial strictures, but mostly because of lack of time there will not be a yearbook for the year 2000 but we hope to recommence production for the following year. Unfortunately we are no longer able to print the monthly newsletters because of our other commitments and so outstanding subscriptions for newsletters will be added on to your subscription to this magazine.

At the moment we are not sure what is happening to our sister magazine *The Goblin Universe*, but we hope to be able to resume publication next year. There is also a possibility that it will be transferred to a different publisher. For the moment we would just ask for your patience!

Also next year, we are proud to announce the return of the Crypto Shop – bigger and better than ever! Together with Danish cryptozoologist Erik Sorenson we intend to be able to offer the biggest and best selection of second-hand cryptozoology books in the world!

Finally, we would like to both apologise and thank our good friend John Tait who designed both this and the last cover. He has given the magazine a facelift which will take us proudly into the new Millenium and we were crass enough to omit his name from the last issue. Many apologies.

Slainte

Jon Downes

NEWSFILE
compiled and edited by the boys from the old brigade

CONSERVATION

RELEASE THE BATS
According to the *Sunday Times*, on the 23 May 1999 there is a disturbing and illegal trade in the meat of protected bat species in British shops and restaurants. *"Despite international laws outlawing the trade in bats or their consumption for food in Europe, The Sunday Times found fruit bats openly on sale in British shops and restaurants last week.*

One reporter was offered a lump of smoked bat at a shop in south London. A worker at a cash-and-carry in Brixton pulled the meat from a box and wrapped it in brown paper. He boasted the meat was imported from Ghana and charged £1.86 for the hand-sized portion. Analysis of the meat by independent scientists found that the bones within it matched those of fruit bat samples. The meat was virtually rancid and partly decomposed. It was infested with foreign beetle larvae."

The newspaper continued with revelations that: *"In Birmingham, a reporter who posed as a meat trader was promised bats 'within a few days' by a vendor at the city's daily meat market. Another reporter was offered bat meals in a cafe off the Old Kent Road in southeast London. The reporter asked a waiter in the African restaurant if bat was being served and was offered a curry, served with vegetables and rice."*
Tony Hutson, from the Bat Conservation Trust, said: *"This is the first time we have heard of bat meat being openly sold in Britain. It is obviously a serious concern for us."*

MYSTERY CATS

USA

New Hampshire
Bradford, - Two construction workers are the latest to spot what they say was a mountain lion, although wildlife biologists maintain that the animals disappeared from New England at the turn of the century. Still, about a half dozen people every year in New Hampshire call Fish and Game to say they have seen a mountain lion. None of the sightings have been confirmed, said Mark Ellingwood, a wildlife biologist. *USA TODAY* - Monday, July 19, 1999

Michigan
A Green Oak Township family's introduction to their new home included sighting what police said may have been a panther.

Darlene Wiljanen noticed the black cat-like creature about 9:15 a.m. at the back of the family's 5-acre property, near a wooded area across from Island Lake Recreation Area. After watching it prowl for several minutes, she got the family's video camera and taped the animal for three or four minutes, said her husband, Matt Wiljanen.

ANIMALS & MEN # 20

"I don't know what a panther looks like, but this animal looked too darn big to be a cat," he said.

Matt Wiljanen described the animal as about 4-feet [sic] long, not including its tail, and about 1 1/2- to 2-feet [sic] tall. It looked like a shorthaired black cat, but about the size of a bobcat. It seemed to be stalking something, he said. After videotaping the animal, Darlene Wiljanen called Green Oak Township Police. Police called the Michigan Department of Natural Resources and the Fish and Wildlife Service, who sent officers to investigate the incident. They found tracks and said they were too large to be those of a housecat. The Wiljanens moved to their home on Bishop Road a week before. *"On the first day, our furnace went out,"* he said. *"Yesterday it was the panther. What next?"* The Ann Arbor News Saturday, April 3, 1999

CANADA

EDITOR'S NOTE: although there is no doubt that *f.concolor* does exist in Canada, this story from the Toronto Globe and Mail 19 June 1999 caught our eye........

Claiming to have seen a cougar in Ontario was once akin to confessing to drinking bouts with an invisible rabbit. Now, with a simple stoop-and-scoop manoeuvre, Lil Anderson has changed all that. Ms. Anderson, a resource management technician with Ontario's Ministry of Natural Resources, has the poop on the big cat. Found on a trapline near Kenora last year, the fecal matter "is the first solid or semi-solid piece of proof we've had for the cougar's existence," says wildlife biologist Neil Dawson. Listed as an endangered species and protected against hunting, the eastern cougar was supposed to have been driven out of the province during the past century. "There are still a lot of cougar skeptics out there," Mr. Dawson concedes. "But with Lil's finding, I think the tide is turning."

Cougars, also called pumas, mountain lions and panthers, once roamed throughout much of North America. Nearly two metres long and weighing as much as 60 kilograms, the big tan-coloured cats became increasingly scarce as forests gave way to farms and they were persecuted as livestock killers. Ontario's last known cougar was shot near Creemore, north of Toronto, in 1884. Since then,

NEWSFILE

at least 1,000 cougar sightings have been reported in the province, all without definite proof of the animal's existence--until last year, when Ms. Anderson found herself hot on the trail of the mysterious cat. Responding to a call about possible cougar tracks northeast of Kenora, Ms. Anderson and Natural Resources technician Rob Moorley found another set of tracks. "They were so fresh, we were expecting a close encounter of the furred kind," Ms. Anderson says.

They soon found the crucial evidence, still unfrozen despite the $-15^{\circ}C$ temperature. Ms. Anderson scooped up the deposit--technically known as scat--and shipped it to the Edmonton forensic laboratory of Alberta's Natural Resources Service. There, forensic biologist Tom Packer subjected the stool to thin-layer chromatography, a process that separates the chemicals found in an animal's bile salts into a pattern specific to individual species. He compared the results with scat obtained from an Alberta cougar. The patterns matched.

On the surface, the finding is good news. Top predators are a sign of a healthy environment, and should indicate the existence of both good habitat and abundant prey. On the other hand, as loggers, hunters and campers push into previously untracked wilderness, there may simply be more pressure on the cougar's habitat, and greater opportunities to catch sight of the beast.

Reliable cougar sightings have ranged from Manitoba to Quebec borders, and from Hearst in the north to Bracebridge and Pembroke in the south. For Ms. Anderson's part, she is still on the case. The next time cougar scat falls in the forest, she hopes someone will notice and call the ministry. *"My big goal is to see and photograph a cougar,"* she says.

UK

EDITOR'S NOTE: we are still trying to get hold of these pictures although we are reliably informed by Chris Moiser who *has* seen them that they are unfortunately inconclusive.....

ANIMALS & MEN # 20

According to *The Electronic Telegraph* - 3 September 1999 a puma has been recorded prowling around a factory by its surveillance cameras. The 3ft-long cat was spotted by a security guard at Blockleys, a brickmakers in Telford, Shropshire. An RSPCA spokesman is reported to have said: "We have used specialist equipment to analyse the film and measure the cat and are of the opinion that this specimen was a puma. It has now been spotted there three times this year." She said the animal was not dangerous but urged people not to try to track it down or trap it.

OUT OF PLACE

Cue a string of Rod Hull Jokes....

Susan Roos was tooling along in her Land Rover when she crossed a rise and slammed on the brakes, startled by a bird the size of a teenager. *"I actually thought my eyes were bad,"* Roos said. *"I see this giant bird. It must have been 5 feet tall. It's running back and forth across the road. The long neck is going up and down like crazy. I slow down and stop, and then I realize what I'm seeing is actually real."* What she was seeing was an emu, and in Pound Ridge such encounters are common enough - and frightening enough - that the Town Council in this well-to-do New York suburb has just doubled the loose-emu fine. Not that Roos had any idea she was seeing an emu. She sped to the Town Hall and rushed in, shouting, *"There's an ostrich loose!"* *"Everybody looks up calmly and sort of nods and says, 'Oh, I guess there's an emu out again,'"* Ms. Roos said. *"What did I know?"*

NEWSFILE

The escaped emus in Pound Ridge apparently are pets. A Buddhist retreat keeps some on its property. Some other residents with large parcels of land keep emus among their exotics. None would return calls. The new ordinance, which went into effect last month, means an escaped emu - or other "livestock" - can cost its owner as much as $200. "Usually our problems are with crowing roosters or horses or cows that get loose and wander around on the roads," said Councilwoman Nancy Jane Woolley. "We didn't even know we had emus until they started getting out, because they don't have to be registered or licensed or anything."

"They can give you a real kick, and they can kick behind or in front. That's their defense, plus the pecking. They can hurt you. But normally they're not going to bother you if you're not bothering them," said Paul Kupchok, director of the Farm and Wildlife center at Green Chimneys in Brewster, where animals are used as therapy for troubled children. Green Chimneys has two emus and turns away others every month or so. *"Emus were all the rage there for a while,"* Kupchok said. *"It seems there's something new every year. Vietnamese pot-bellied pigs, miniature horses, emus, llamas. After a while, people call us, hoping we'll take the animal off their hands."* Kupchok fears some owners may simply have released their birds. *"Once they escape, they're not coming back,"* he said. *"Emus have no homing instinct."*

However, as so often seems to be the case within the annals of fortean zoology (and indeed forteana as a whole) this was not an isolated incident. Emus were figuratively popping up all opver the place. An amusing story in the *Milwaukee Journal Sentinel* on July 24, 1999 told how an emu *"ran through the local Burger King drive-through"*, in Palmyra, Wisconsin *"fueling all sorts of new Whopper jokes, no doubt, before hightailing it down Highway 59 with the local constabulary in pursuit. To the constabulary's credit, the authorities did their jobs well, corralling the bird without injuries to anyone and then giving it a temporary home. Under those lazy, hazy, crazy days of summer, chalk this up under crazy - and to a local tradition of strange sightings. Apparently the Emu was reclaimed by its owner and is now safely back where it belongs.*

ANIMALS & MEN # 20

An Emu in Foristell, Missouri was less lucky. According to the *St. Louis Post-Dispatch* on August 21, 1999: *"A man shot and killed an emu after a St.Charles County animal control officer tried unsuccessfully to tranquilize it. The emu was reported running loose around 9:30 a.m. along Highway W in Foristell. A sheriff's deputy responded to the area and found the 6-foot, 125-pound bird running along Schultz Road. He followed it north along Ditrich Road, where the bird nearly caused two accidents as drivers tried to avoid it, authorities said. When it ran back onto Highway W and nearly caused accidents again, an animal control officer shot it with a tranquilizer gun. The tranquilizer didn't work, however, which can happen if the animal's adrenaline is high or if the chemicals are past their shelf life, a county health department official said.*

The emu then ran into a yard in the 800 block of Highway W, where a farmer became frightened and shot it. Authorities could not immediately locate the owner. Authorities suspect that the emu was released by someone who had invested in selling the birds as meat."

Moose On The Loose

According to Reuters on July 20, 1999, the Danish authorities were engaged in a hunt for a moose which swam over the narrow sound separating Sweden from Denmark and disappeared into forest north of Copenhagen. An elderly couple walking along the beach at the resort of Hornbaek were shocked when the young moose emerged from the sea after swimming five km (three miles) over the sound from Sweden.

Moose are unknown on the Danish side of the strait but media in Sweden, where the animal is a national symbol, are closely following the saga of the moose on the loose, with appeals to Danes not to shoot it. For what it is worth Denmark's ambassador in Stockholm gave assurances that the moose will be returned home safely if caught. From a cryptozoological point of view this incident is interesting because of Dr Lars Thomas` theory that many of the sightings of the lake Seljord `Monster` are actually swimming moose. If this most recent incident has any great historical precedents then it is quite possible that many of the sea serpent sightings from northern waters can now be easily explained.

NEWSFILE

NEW AND REDISCOVERED

JAWS 25?

Claims that *"25 New Shark Species"* have been found In Philipino waters may have been exageratted. On July, 7 1999, Alex V. Pal, of the Philippine Daily Inquirer Visayas Bureau announced: *"Local fishermen had been catching them for years, even for generations. But little did they know that some of the little sharks in their harvest could have earned for them a moment of fame in scientific books. After studying shark specimens collected for five months, scientists have learned that about 25 species have yet to be given names. The first such study on elasmobranchs sponsored by the World Wildlife Fund could put Dumaguete on the scientific map after Australian scientists confirmed the discovery."* However, shark expert John Stephens commented: *"Don't believe everything you see in the papers! There are new chondrichthyan taxa in the Philippines but we have more work to do yet before we know how many. There are some 25 species in the collection which we cannot currently put definate names on. Many of these specimens will have to be compared to material from other areas. The newspaper somehow got hold of this and twisted it around."*

ANIMALS & MEN # 20
FISHY STORIES

Less contentious are the following discoveries of new fish species reported by Yahoo! News:
http://dailynews.yahoo.com/h/ap/19990907/sc/science_meets_movie_1.html

Here is the news item in full:..

WASHINGTON (AP) - When the Smithsonian Institution and the IMAX Corp. decided to make a movie about the Galapagos Islands the result went beyond the giant screen - scientists squeezed in enough research to discover more than a dozen marine species. ``Galapagos,'' the new 3D film focusing on the unusual wildlife on and around the Pacific island group west of Ecuador, will premiere Oct. 27 at the Smithsonian's National Museum of Natural History. It follows explorations of marine biologist Carole Baldwin in the sea surrounding the 19 islands and also visits the rare and unusual land animals.

*``I think I was chosen because I had never been there, and they wanted a scientist with fresh eyes, someone the audience could follow. It was fantastic,''* she said in a telephone interview. She pronounced the resulting three-dimensional film, displayed on a giant screen, as great.`` *The only thing missing in the theater is the cold and wet,''* she said. *``Otherwise, you're there.''* But Baldwin didn't settle for just making a movie. *``My goal was science.''*

The filmmaker's goal was certainly to make a film. The film was being funded by the Smithsonian Institution and IMAX, so the idea was to make the film about research,'' she said.

So, research she did.

``We still don't know exactly how many new species we have,'' she said.

The scientists, now back at the museum, must take each of the new finds and compare it with thousands of others in the Smithsonian collection to verify it was not previously known.`` *`I would say its like dozens'' of new finds,* she added. The researchers used a submersible vessel to study the largely unexplored waters between 200 feet and 1,000 feet deep. The area is to deep for scuba diving, and previous studies using submersibles concentrated on deeper waters.

NEWSFILE

"Finding a dozen new vertebrate species in that length of time is almost unheard of," she said. "But the deep sea is so unexplored its not uncommon to find new things every time you go down." Researchers and film crews stayed 14 weeks inthe Galapagos with the only two IMAX 3-D cameras in the world. They visited more than 80 locations, including dives in the four-person submersible. Among Baldwin's discoveries: anthiine bass, a new type of sea bass; an unusual wrasse, a small striped fish that cleans larger fish, from about 400 feet down; a new cat shark; and several new scorpion fish. Baldwin concentrates on fish, but other researchers turned up new types of sponges, urchins and gastropod mollusks, she said.

The new species will be added to the Natural History Museum's 8 million-specimen collection of preserved fish as well as to the collections of the Charles Darwin Research Station in the Galapagos, and the California Academy of Sciences.

Located on the equator 600 miles west of South America, the Galapagos have been called the laboratory of evolution, its strange plants and animals the inspiration for Charles Darwin's theories that became known as Darwinism.

The film is to run four times daily on the giant IMAX screen at the National Museum of Natural History. It will be the first regular giant-screen 3-D film shown at the museum. Later it will tour other IMAX theaters around the world.

However these were not the only discoveries of new fish species in recent months.

Dr. Dominique Didier Dagit, Assistant Curator and Acting Chair of Ichthyology at The Academy of Natural Sciences and a world authority on chimaeroid fishes, discovered a new species of Chimaera - an ancient deep-sea relative of sharks from the coastal waters off New Zealand. Interestingly the new species,, named *Chimaera panthera* or the leopard chimaera was discovered whilst she was while visiting a museum.

ANIMALS & MEN # 20

The fish had been given to the National Museum of New Zealand, Te Papa Tongarewa, by a local fisherman. Dagit, because of her expertise with these fishes was immediately called to examine the specimen. She determined Chimaera panthera was a new species because of its distinguishing leopard-like brown spots that cover the body and fins. This is the first species of Chimaera to be discovered in New Zealand and the sixth species to be recognized in the genus.

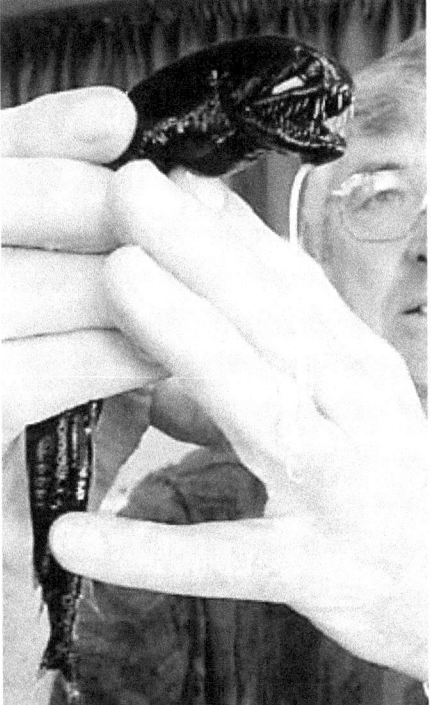

Several new species of deep water fish with 'big eyes and teeth' were reportedly discovered in Hawaiian waters in recent months as well. Although details are scant the Copyright Liberation Front was able to get hold of this picture of Dr Peter Herring, an Ichthyologist with a gloriously lexilinked name, displaying a specimen believed to be a new species of dragonfish. For more details go to

http://starbulletin.com/1999/06/29/news/story7.html

NEWSFILE

IT WOULD BE BETTER IF IT HAD BEEN THE OWLMAN BUT...

Fieldwork by a University of Kansas ornithol-ogist continues to reveal the extent of biological diversity of the New World tropics - even as deforestation poses a mounting threat to the survival of many species - with the discovery of a new species of pygmy-owl.

In a cover story published in the April 21 issue of the "Auk," a leading ornithological journal, Mark Robbins, the KU Natural History Museum's collection manager for birds, and his co-author, Gary Stiles of the National University of Colombia in Bogota, name the new species Glaucidium nubicola, or Cloud-forest Pygmy-Owl.

The bird inhabits the Pacific slope of the Andes in Ecuador and Colombia, and with its discovery and the elevation of a previously identified subspecies to full species rank, Robbins and Stiles revise the taxonomy

ANIMALS & MEN # 20

of the often overlooked and elusive group of pygmy-owls.

The Cloud-forest Pygmy-Owl is the latest new discovery to result from Robbins' work in Ecuador. During the past decade, Robbins has described four new bird species to science. Because birds are perhaps the best known group of organisms, the discovery of a new species is a relatively rare event, with an average of only one new species described every year.

NEW CLASS FOR GALAPAGOS

EDITOR`S NOTE: We have been lucky enough to have been able to report on the discovery of quite a few new species over the past twenty issues of A&M but seldom has there been news as potentially momentous as this. We therefore print the entire news story in full and refrain from comment:

20 June, 1999

Charles Darwin Research Station

The natural fauna of the Galapagos Islands contains four of the five classes of vertebrates. Various species of fish, reptiles, birds and mammals have been present in the Islands for the last several million years. One class, amphibians, has been unable to colonize the remote oceanic archipelago during all of that time primarily due its intolerance of salt water. Recent human activity and climatic fluctuations may have combined to alter the situation and frogs are now another introduced species within the Galapagos.

It appears that reproducing populations of frogs have become established on at least two of the five populated Galapagos Islands. A small (2 - 3 cm) arboreal frog of the Tree frog family Hylidae has been found increasingly frequently in Puerto Ayora, Isla Santa Cruz since 1998. The species, Scinax quinquefasciata, is a common frog of coastal lowlands in Ecuador. Seven individuals have been captured from three general areas within Puerto Ayora, the busiest port in the Galapagos.

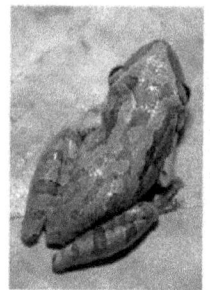

Scinax quinquefasciata

The frog introduced to Galápagos in 1998/1999

Additional observations and captures have occurred in Villamil on Isla Isabela, and observations of an apparently similar frog have been made in Puerto Baquerizo Moreno on Isla San Cristobal. One individual has been captured aboard a local boat, and another observed aboard a second vessel. Over the last 20 years individual frogs of at least two other species have been occasionally sighted within the ports of Galapagos, but breeding populations were apparently never established.

These populations represent the first known colonization by amphibians of the Galapagos Islands. Amphibians are generally conspicuously absent from the native faunas of oceanic archipelagos because their permeable skins place them in a negative water-balance with salt water.

When in contact with the sea, amphibians dry out as they lose fluids via osmosis to the more concentrated saltwater.

Because of their inability to withstand even brief periods in salt water amphibians rarely survive long enough to reach oceanic islands by natural means such as rafting with floating mats of vegetation or floating across expanses of ocean. However, increasing human activity within the Galapagos archipelago requires large amounts of materials from continental Ecuador. Materials reach the islands as freight aboard one of five cargo ships making monthly calls to Galapagos ports or airfreight aboard one of the

ANIMALS & MEN # 20

three jets arriving daily. Some of the frogs mentioned above where found within packages of vegetables from the continent and in standing water in stored automobile tires, others were found active upon the ground or in trees calling at night.

There is little published about the ecology of Scinax quinquefasciata, although a captive individual reportedly lived for nearly 4 years. Other species of the genus Scinax are resistant to desiccation and inhabit terrestrial environments where water is not always available. Breeding occurs in small temporary pools where females their eggs, which hatch quickly into tadpoles. The larval stage is relatively short and metamorphosis into froglets occurs quickly. Small pools of water and moist soil are common in gardens and around cisterns and leaking pipes within Puerto Ayora. Moist soil is more common in the highlands of Santa Cruz, but there have been no frogs captured there yet. While no tadpoles have been discovered yet, the numbers, distribution, and sizes of adults suggests that breeding is occurring.

The first observations of this species within Galapagos occurred during 1998 at the height of the 1997-1998 El Nino event. Conditions were wetter during parts of those years than at any time since 1983. Severe flooding occurred throughout the coastal regions of Ecuador and reports of unusually dense populations of frogs were common. The current hypothesis of the dispersal of this frog to the Galapagos proposes that abundant populations in the continental port of Guayaquil allowed individuals to take refuge in materials bound for Galapagos by ship or plane. Once they arrived in the islands the unusually wet conditions allowed establishment, which has persisted due to the increased availability of suitable microhabitats associated with human habitation.

It is impossible to predict the potential impacts of these frogs on the indigenous fauna of Galapagos. Frogs are mostly insectivorous so this species is presumably eating a variety of Galapagos insects and other invertebrates but we have no idea of the numbers nor species being consumed. Many frogs have poison glands within their skin, and introduced frogs have caused striking declines in the populations of naive native predators in other parts of the world. At this time we don't know if *Scinax quinquefasciata* possess such glands, nor if any Galapagos organisms are eating them. However,

NEWSFILE

the general policy of the Galapagos National Park Service is to treat all alien species as potential threats to the natural biological diversity of Galapagos and to promote their eradication or control.

The current priorities concerning this newly introduced species aim to determine its distribution and rate of dispersal, compile information about potential means of eradication, search for breeding sites, and perform some simple experiments to explore the potential toxicity to indigenous predators. All frogs found during these activities will be preserved; none will be left in the field.

MORE MONKEY BUSINESS

A monkey weighing less than an ounce was born in captivity in the Brazilian Amazon and could be a new species, Dutch zoologist Marc van Roosmalen said in a statement recently DNA tests will determine its genus and species, but Roosmalen said the monkey could be *"an anomaly developed by the dwarf marmoset to survive in the rain forest"* threatened by deforestation. "The monkey has hands with claws like the dwarf marmoset, but its size and weight are distinctive," said Roosmalen, who works at the National Institute of Investigations in the Amazon in Manaus, the capital of Amazon state. The monkeys were found in the same region along the Aripuanan River in the western Amazon where Roosmalen discovered the dwarf marmoset last year. He is convinced this monkey, which has not been named, *"is a different species, because the mothers have only one baby at a time and care for only one baby, while the textbook dwarf marmoset has twins 80 percent of the time."* The monkey weighs less than 2 ounces now. As an adult, it probably will only weigh between 5 and 6 ounces, Roosmalen said.

MUNTJAC NEWS

In a flurry of news items, Muntjacs have again been capturing the imaginations of the fortean zoological community.

ANIMALS & MEN # 20

NEWSFILE

Roosevelt's Bark-ing Deer *(Muntiacus rooseveltorum)*'. in *the Journal of Mammalogy* (80: 639-43.)

Data in this study confirms the validity of a species of muntjac that has been controversial for 60 years. Diagnostic DNA characters are presented for each species examined including the *M. rooseveltorum* holo-type. Three specimens of a recently collected small Laos barking deer have identical sequences to the type specimen of *M. rooseveltorum*

Regular readers of these hallowed pages will be aware that we have been monitoring the spate of new zoological discoveries in Hong Kong with someinterest and have repeatedly claimed that the discoveries in this tiny and overcrowded corner of the world are of far more significance than other more widely publicised zoological discoveries worldwide.

It therefore comes as no great surprise to us to find that yet another new species has been added to the mammal list of this former British colony. According to the most recent issue of *Porcupine* - the journalof the department of Ecology and Biodiversity at Hong Kong University, it seems that whereas it has been known for many years (atleast since the days of Robert Swinhoe) that one species of muntjac *(M.reevesi)* lived in the more remote parts of the territory, it now seems as if a second species *M muntiacus* is also present there.

As we have said on so many occasions over the past four or five years, if such discoveries can be made in such a tiny and well explored area of the globe, Gawd alone knows what lurks in the Amazon.......

n recent years there have been several new species of muntjac found in southeast Asia. Most recently George Amato, Mary G. Egan, George B. Schaller, Richard H. Baker, Howard C. Rosenbaum, William G. Robichaud, & Rob DeSalle, published a paper entitled 'Rediscov-ery of

Possibly most exciting is the discovery of an entirely new species of muntjac measuring just 20 inches at the shoulder and weighing no more than 25 pounds. This is the world's smallest deer, according to a recent study led by the Bronx Zoo-based Wildlife Conservation Society (WCS).

The "leaf deer" or "leaf muntjac," which lives in remote mountain regions of Southeast Asia, was first seen by WCS biologist Alan Rabinowitz in 1997 during field surveys in northern Myanmar (Burma).

After obtaining specimens from local hunters, Rabinowitz brought samples to New York for DNA analysis. The results of the genetic work, published in the recent issue of the journal Animal Conservation, confirmed the leaf deer as unique. *"Through DNA sequencing, we were able to determine that this particular species of mutjac was clearly distinct,"* said the study's lead author, Dr. George Amato, director for conservation genetics for WCS. *"It's a very exciting discovery."*

ANIMALS & MEN # 20

Monsters of the next millennium

Richard Freeman

The last century has brought us many spectacular new creatures, the mountain gorilla, the komodo dragon, the okapi and others on the list of new animals we are so fond of reciting. At the turning of a new century who among the zoological outcasts will lumber, slither, hop, or flap out of the twilight zone of science and into our textbooks? Here, gentle reader, I present my top ten of likely cryptozoological discov-eries for the next 100 years and offer a pint of beer to each reader for any not found by the year 2100.

I omit out-of-placers like big cats, as most aren't true cryptids and it's bloody obvious that most exist.

1: The thylacine. We know it existed up till 1936, it has been seen at close quarters by a zoologist and a wildlife ranger, and has been predicted by computer program. This is the pony to back and few doubt that its rediscovery is only a matter of time.

2: Delcourt's giant gecko. Not many cryptids are stuffed and mounted in museums, but this little blighter is. As with the thylacine we know the world's largest gecko really did exist and sightings of a big arboreal lizard in northern New Zealand suggest it still scampers through the tree tops in parts of this island.

3: The giant anaconda. O.K., anacondas *exist*, but how big do the buggers get? Being live-bearers, they don't have to come ashore to lay eggs. By being buoyed up in the water they can hypothetically reach huge sizes. Finally they lurk in some of the most ill-explored areas on Earth. I think 15 to 18 metre uncommon specimens may exist.

4: The yeti. Our first "major league media monster" to make it into the top ten. One of the pillars of science is repeatable experiments that get the same results. In several separate laboratories in England, China, and US, yeti hair has been analysed by proton-induced x-ray emission. Guess what conclusion all the scientists came to? - unknown primate. Don't be too supprised if one day you see a King Kong lookalike gazing at you from the front page of your newspaper.

FEATURE

5: Orang Pendek. The yeti's "little brother" is possibly a large, robust, ground dwelling gibbon. It has been seen by W.A.S.P. scientists, what more could you want? With all the unrest (what a soft name for massacres) perhaps a larger Western presence in Sumatra will finally find this creature.

6: Megalania prisca. The great Australian dragon has recently received a big boost in the credibility stakes with the discovery of a Megalania hip bone unfossilized and possibly only 100 years old. Add this to Aboriginal folk lore, modern sightings (including a herpetologist), livestock kills, and tracks, then you have a big surprise for zoologists and a big worry for sheep, cattle, and hikers.

7: Giant eels. Anyone with any sense knows there are no pre-historic reptiles in Loch Ness but a 9-meter eel is well within the bounds of possibility. Many sea serpent and lake monster reports seem to refer to gargantuan eels whose flexible bodies could present all the outlines shown by aquatic monsters. An old trawlerman once told my grandfather of his encounter with such a being off the Devon coast in the early 70s.

8: Mokele-mbembe. The consistency and history of the Congo monster sightings suggest that *something* big, amphibious and long necked lives in these rain forests. My guess: a long necked semi-aquatic monitor lizard; similar length to Megalania but more slender.

9: The lusca. Controversy still rages over the samples of flesh taken from a massive carcass washed up in Florida in 1896. Some say it was an octopus of Toho Studios dimensions, others that it was a decomposing sperm whale. The Lusca lurks in holes on the sea bed (blue deeps), occasionally surfacing - an octopus of whose dimensions H. P. Lovecraft would have approved.

10: The giant ground sloth. South American Indian sightings of a monster that resembles a mylodont sloth stretch coincidence to breaking point. The natives endow this beast with body armour beneath the skin, except for the stomach. In reality this matches the dermal scutes of the mylodont. Dr David Oren is on the monster's trail and has found its tracks and heard its eerie cry. How much longer until he catches up with his quarry?

ANIMALS & MEN # 20

Wolverines: a reply

by Chris Moiser

When I researched and wrote my article *"Wolverines or Muddy Badgers?"* for *Animals and Men* 17, I had no idea how much interest and controversy I would be stirring up.

It is very pleasing to know that several people felt the need to put pen to paper in response to my article, and I also feel that the debate has opened up some useful discussion. It was particularly gratifying to see the reference that Tom Anderson made to a 'glutton' being mistaken for a badger in nineteenth century Canada, or British North America, as it would be then. This is a reference that I was not aware of, and I am grateful for it.

A possible initial point that I should mention is the photograph of the muddy badger on the cover of Animals and Men 17. This photograph was not taken by me, but by a friend at Porfell Animal Land, not using expensive photographic equipment, but a reasonably cheap, compact camera with a built in flash gun. This photograph was not intended to suggest that a muddy badger, viewed that closely, or from that angle, could be mistaken for a wolverine. It was only intended to show that white badgers can get muddy! It does not, perhaps, take a great deal of imagination to think of seeing this animal in the distance, sideways on, in poor light, when it *could* be mistaken for a wolverine.

The badger concerned has been living in this area for several years, and although I have not seen it in as muddy a condition as it appears in the picture, I have seen the animal on at least three occasions. I am also aware of other white badgers in the Devon and Cornwall area, and in other parts of the country. As I think that I suggested previously, white badgers, unlike other white mammals, seem to survive to live something like a normal lifetime because they do not, in this country have a top predator that eats them regularly, and could therefore more easily find a white individual. Terry Hooper's article, "The return of *Gulo gulo*" (Hooper, T. 1998 22 - 24), whilst interesting and capable of promoting a lot of sensible debate, does present an idea of there being a number of separate wolverine populations within the United Kingdom. I find this idea preposterous. Whilst it is possible that there may be one or two groups, the idea of 7 separate populations is frankly ridiculous for the reasons that were stated in my original article.

To summarise them, we are considering an animal that was not imported in any great numbers at all because it was not a popular zoo exhibit; was rarely, if ever, farmed for fur; and had no merits as a pet. The only zoo to exhibit wolverines in England in recent times, that I can find, is Norfolk Wildlife Park. Clinton Keeling has also told me of a pair at Regent's Park in the *1950s/1960s*.

As far as I know neither collection have had any escapes and these areas do not overlap with any of those that Terry mentions. Whilst I respect the need for some confidentiality in running an organisation such as the Exotic Animals Register I think that we are starting to have problems in this area with the credibility of Terry's reports when he claims confidentiality so often. The need for confi-dentiality is particularly questionable with the alleged group of Wolverines referred to as group A , in the English - Welsh border area. If

ANIMALS & MEN # 20

these animals were originally here as early as 1969, there surely can be no need for any confidentiality? I base this statement on the following facts.

1. The longest recorded longevity of the wolverine in captivity is 17 years 4 months, so any there now as a result of the happenings of 1969, must be, at least, from the second generation after release.

2. There would be no offence committed in releasing them back in 1969, (the offence of releasing exotic animals into the U.K. was created in 1981). Even if it had been an offence back in 1969 then the statutory limitations would probably have now run out.

3. Revealing the site where the animals were liberated in 1969 would hardly pose much danger to the current population, who will, presumably have moved some distance away in the interim period.

4. Whilst Terry refers to a "loony fringe" of hunters travelling round with illegal high power weapons, and other "hunters for hire", we do, in this country, have some of the toughest fire-arms laws in the world, and some of the strongest anti-hunting feeling in the world. Anybody caught committing any fire-arms offences is in grave danger, *inter-alia,* of losing their fire-arms licence: a major discouragement from hunting on other peoples property without consent.

If these animals have really survived to the third (or more) generation(s), they have done so despite any local knowledge of them, or by remaining so secretive that they have escaped notice in the area in which they live. I would also suggest that if wolverines were really to be present in the numbers that Terry has indicated he is being most irresponsible in not drawing the attention of the Ministry of Agriculture to them. I say this on the following grounds. The wolverine has been absent from this island for several thousand years, and there are now no biological controls on its numbers if it were to establish here. Whilst I am more tolerant than many biologists to the idea of introduced species in the United Kingdom, the wolverine is clearly a species that would not fit well into our current ecology. It could have a disastrous effect on much of our indigenous wildlife and cause many problems with our domestic livestock. Terry's own descriptions of attacks on sheep may perhaps confirm this.

If I may draw an analogy with mink; mink have become established here following releases and escapes from fur farms. It seems unlikely now that we will ever eradicate them from this island. MacDonald (1989), quotes the mink as weighing 1.1 - 3.3 lbs. (0.3 - 1.1 kg). This animal is known for its vicious attacks on ground dwelling waterbirds in particular. Imagine the presence of the wolverine, on average ten times the size, (or larger!) and with similar carnivorous habits, but a reputation for attacking prey larger than itself! The ecological effects if this species were to become established throughout the country would be catastrophic. At the very least a proper scientific study should take place to establish when an eradication policy should be implemented.

References:

Hooper, T. 1998 The return of *Gulo gulo. Animals and Men* 18

Macdonald, D. (ed.) 1989 *The Encyclopaedia of Mammals* Unwin Hyman, London.

ANIMALS & MEN # 20

George Lekaukau

by Roy Kerridge.

"I must pray for England! Right or wrong, England is the mother country!"

The occasion was the outbreak of the Gulf War, the place was the middle of the Kalahari Desert and the speaker was George Lekaukau, an elderly cattle herder of fiercely majestic appearance. His voice did not match his looks, for over the years it had shrunk into a sinister sand-blasted whisper. A firm believer in witchcraft, George himself possessed an occult aura, and his pale eyes sometimes blazed alarmingly from his gaunt features, as he whispered an ominous Delphic utterance.

My mother, my two brothers and an anthropologist I shall call Eric were crossing the Kalahari by Landrover, an expedition that was half-work, half-play and all Adventure. George was the "native guide", in time-honoured fashion. However, my family risked starting a new fashion by bringing George home to England afterwards as a house guest.

Eric had first met George's son, now a member of the Botswana government. To Eric's surprise, he learned that George Senior, despite being able to read, write and of course speak English, had returned to a traditional way of life. As such, he was the answer to an anthropologist's dream. So, without delay, George was contacted. His cattle seemed able to look after themselves with only a nephew left to draw water and fill their troughs. George seemed happier as a hunter and tracker, one who blithely disregarded game laws imposed by namby pamby conservationists. And so the expedition set out. Some of George's stories and observations were noted down by my mother beneath an African sky, others by myself beneath a Kensal Green lampshade.

Each evening, camp beds would be arranged around a fire; the sky above, a glittering Planetarium. George took the main watch, ever ready to chase a lion with a burning brand. Once, so he said, he had done this in vain, as a huge maned lion seized a Bushman friend of George's by the head and bore the unfortunate man away. George kept the white antelope skin on which his friend had been sleeping. By day, so George said, lions were in awe of Bushmen. "The lion is the Bushman's gun", was one of George's whispered utterances.

By this he meant that the lion would kill animals for the Bushmen to eat - not through altruism, however. Bushmen hunters follow a lion until it makes a kill. When the animal has sated its hunger, the Bushmen drive it away and seize the remains of the meal for themselves. My mother later met English people who had seen this. If the lion is the Bushman's gun, could the wolf once have been the caveman's spear? Could the domestication of wolf-into-dog have been brought about by prey-robbing cavemen? Perhaps the cheated wolf thought, "If you can't beat them, join them", and so

- 16 -

joined the human race for the sake of a share in its own kill.

Eric and George, both men of some self-importance, hit it off very well and would sit drinking canned lager and discussing women together in a man-to-man fashion. Some-times Eric would slip away, for he had anthropologised this part of the Kalahari many times before, and had an African girlfriend waiting for him in a thatched hut in almost every settlement. These girls and their children appear to have been somewhat ostracised by the other villagers, and were dependent on Eric's occasional expeditions for their support. Often, Eric spoke about the book he was writing. He now had a new idea to bring prosperity to Botswana: big game hunting.

"You must tell everyone you know not to kill lions", he instructed George. "Then the lions will increase and rich Germans and Texans will come to shoot them."

George nodded respectfully. Instinctively he had gauged the white man's "class system", for Eric was the expedition's only public school man. Sometimes George would tell stories, translating tribal tales into English and singing the songs that embroidered the fables in his Tswana language. My mother recognised the Brer Rabbit story where the fox plays dead, but the rabbit tricks him into revealing his mortality by saying "If he was really dead, he'd kick up his leg and shout 'Wahoo' like all dead folks."

In George's story, the rabbit was a hare and the fox a jackal. George accounted for several jackals on the trip, and made their soft silvery hair into a robe. Here is another of his stories:

"The Lion grew old and could no longer hunt, so his servant the Jackal told pretend to be dead. Then the Jackal ran far and wide crying 'King Lion is dead: everyone must come and pay their respects to his body.' Most of the animals were pleased to hear that Lion was dead, but thought it only right that they should pay their respects. One by one they entered the cave, where they were quickly killed and eaten by Lion, who was in reality very much alive. At last it came the turn of Hare, who noticed that footprints went into the cave, but none came out.

'Aren't you going to pay your respects?' barked Jackal, noticing that Hare stood still. 'Yes, I will, but just now I'm cold', said Hare. 'I'll light a fire, get warm and then pay my respects.'

So Hare made a fire, and the wind blew the smoke to the entrance of Lion's cave. Hare put more and more green leaves on the fire, so a thick cloud of smoke poured into the cave. A moment later, out came Lion, coughing and wiping at his eyes with his paws. His cave was full of smoke.

'Run! See, Lion is alive!' called Hare.

ANIMALS & MEN # 20

So most of the animals escaped, thanks to the cleverness of Hare."

As the expedition rattled deeper into the Kalahari, George kept a look out for Bushmen, traceable by their wispy grass shelters and secret signs to show the underground presence of water or edible tubers. At villages, humble chiefs, very much at one with their people, would greet the party with happy politeness.

Village Africans are very formal. The villages themselves consist of huts within compounds of sticks and clay, these small compounds being scattered over an area of twenty miles or more. In a few villages made prosperous by a new road, round clay huts with thatched roofs have been replaced by garage-like square buildings made of breeze blocks, with corrugated iron roofs. Unlike huts, these had been built with furniture and a Western interior in mind. Today, Beauty and Poverty may go hand in hand. I say "may", because George didn't seem to appreciate the beauty of the wild animals of the Kalahari.

"When I see an animal, I must kill, eat!" he once declared fiercely. "No time to look at beauty, it might get away! I only kill what I need, and I only kill lions if they raid my cattle.

In our front room at Kensal Green, George watched the black and white version of "King Solomon's Mines" on television, with great relish, believing the story to be true and the actors 'real.' At the Natural History Museum, he believed the roaring automated dinosaurs to be real, but stood his ground stoically, St. George to the robot dragon.

People in England don't need Bushmen, as they don't witchcraft each other. When we get witchcraft, we swell inside. We go to Bushmen, they cut us and take out the poison. "Once I was very ill. I could feel a thing scratching inside me, so I went to the Bushmen. One cut me and took out a small snake. They are wise, they cut people and take out snakes and scorpions.

Again and again, George's conversation turned to lions. In this, he was the complete opposite of West Africans I have met in London, who often say "I suppose you think Africa is a place full of lions - well, I've never seen a lion."

George *had* seen lions.

"One night, I was riding home on a horse, with a Bushman friend behind me on a donkey. A lioness appeared suddenly from behind a tree. We froze, the Bushman with one foot on the stirrup and one on the ground. The lion looked so surprised! It was really surprised to see us there. I could see that it wished to speak to us, to ask us what we were doing. But it could not speak our language

We could not speak its language. At last, the Bushman shouted 'Kwai! Kwai!' The lion ran away quickly. Only then it realised we were human beings.

"Another time, a friend and myself tracked and killed a gemsbok that had a dead shrivelled-up lion on its horns. It had impaled the lion on its long curved horns and then

ANIMALS & MEN # 20 — FEATURE

could not get them free. So it had to drag the dead lion about - such a heavy load." The gemsbok is a large beautiful desert antelope, first cousin of the Arabian oryx, the animal said to have once been mistaken for a unicorn. It is an Official Protected Species.

I had already discovered that, to many Africans, National Parks are "game preserves". George and his friends shoot only for food. No part of the gemsbok is wasted, for bags and garments are made from the hide. Moffat, Livingstone's mentor (1795-1883) brought the plough and the muzzle-loading gun to the Kalahari in the nineteenth century. Horses and donkeys followed.

"Would you believe it, these people never even had the plough?" marvelled the well-meaning white men of Moffat's day. After a brief bonanza of crops and a mountain of bullet-shot meat, the Kalahari became the barren, sandy place it is today. In George's grandfather's time, giraffes and elephants roamed the plains. The plough soon destroyed the soil and the gun accounted for much of the big game. Until horses and donkeys were introduced, the ox was a riding-horse. Now cattle are kept mainly for meat and prestige. Talking to George about cattle was rather tricky, as it involved a breach of Kalahari etiquette. Cattle to George represented wealth, and asking about them was rather like saying "How much do you earn?" or "What are you worth?"

At first, so I learned, George wondered to himself where the Londoners and other English kept their cattle. Later, he realised that they had none, and his scorn knew no bounds. What a nation of paupers!

Innocently, my mother once asked George if he milked his own cows. His eyes blazed in fury, there was a dark silence, then he snapped out, "Am I not a man?"

It transpired that, among George's people, milking the cattle was very much a man's job.

At night, on the edge of the Kalahari, lone cows sometimes passed by in the darkness. "That's so-and-so's cow," George would say, as if each animal made a recognisable sound. Long years of breeding had brought into being a large, healthy glossy breed of "homing cattle". Soil sandy enough to bear grass can now only be found a day's journey from each village. Cattle set off, not in herds, but in ones and twos, in search of food. Two days later, perhaps, the animals return for a deep drink and a sleep in the shade. Then off they go again, com-ing and going all the time, with no herder - true "homing cattle." Western cattle farmers might well envy George's people.

"My people were pressed into the Kalahari by the Zulus!" George said. "We lost all our cattle and had to start afresh by raiding cattle from the Ngama tribe. What! What do you mean, 'stealing'? It was *not* stealing, we won those cattle in fair war!

- 19 -

ANIMALS & MEN # 20 FEATURE

"Now, when a man is hungry, he can go to his well and kill a cow or a goat. When there is a wedding, there is a great feast, presented by the father of the bride. Guests arrive with presents, we sit and eat around the fire outside, with music from speakers and people dancing. Then we eat meat."

George would get angry if I referred to him as "a Tswana", as he felt that he belonged not to a tribe, but to a clan. "Tswana" is the name of a language, but the speakers of that language are divided into clans, each clan headed by a totem animal (as with the Clan Chattan, or Cat Clan of Scotland. We learned of an Ostrich Clan, a Porcupine Clan and of George's own clan, the Clan of the Multi-Coloured Cow. Unfortunately for George, his association with magic-practising Bushmen led his Chief to brand him as a witch. He had no hut, but lived and slept under a tree.

"I can live like a Bushman, and dig up tubers to eat", he said. "I just drink my gin. Once I couldn't find my way, so I took off my coat, went to sleep, and when I woke up I knew where I was."

English country people, when "pixie-led" or unaccountably lost in their own fields, used to take off their coats and put them on again inside-out. Having done this, they could find their way. Unlucky, George had lost not only his clan, but his country. Through most of his life, Botswana was Bechuanaland, a British Protectorate. George appeared to think that he once had belonged personally to Queen Victoria, a happy state of affairs now vanished. "Independence" for George (one of the most independent men I have met) spelled Doom.

"It was good when I belonged to the Queen", he reminisced in rueful anger. "Suddenly a man from my enemy clan appeared and said 'Now you belong to me!'

'Why is this?' we asked.

'You just do!' was the reply. So now we are ruled from the city of Gabarone - ha! Those who rule us, do you know what they call us? Ha! They are our enemy. This is what we would like to know - has the Queen forgotten us?"

It was hard to explain to George that the present Queen herself is ruled by a set of politicians probably as bad as those in Gabarone. In fact, the Gabarone politicians my mother and brother met seemed remarkably mild. However, according to Eric the Overpaid Anthropologist, George's own son now worked for the government in the capital, and pretended that he was a member of the ruling clan. Apparently, if it were known that George's once-adoring son was a member of the Multi-Coloured Cow Clan, he would lose his job.

Whether in the Kalahari or Britain, George never lost his stiff almost contemptuous sense of pride. His opinion of London may be judged by the speed with which he rushed towards his aeroplane at Heathrow, glancing back only for a moment before galloping off to the sanity of Africa, a land where men are men and own the cows to prove it.

ANIMALS & MEN # 20

BESTIARY

by Ade Dimmick

THE CHIMAERA

The Chimaera or Chimera was a fire-breathing creature from classical mythology.

It was described by Homer as having the foreparts of a lion, the middle of a goat, and the hindparts of a serpent. A 5th century Etruscan bronze depicts the creature as having a lion's head, a goat's head protruding from its body and a serpent's head at the end of its tail. Other descriptions have referred to the 'Divine Nymph', and having the face of a beautiful maiden.

The Chimaera was the female offspring of the snake goddess Echidne and the storm god Typhon. Although there was only one Chimaera she is usually depicted as having swollen teats beneath her body, which may suggest suckling young. This however, could be largely symbolic, and the Chimaera's young need not be of the same species given the diverse nature of mythological reproductive cycles.

It is said that the Chimaera originated from Lydia in Asia Minor and is generally associated with the Near East and the Mediterranean region - although a statue of a Chimaera-type creature was discovered in China, dating from the Han Dynasty.

The Chimaera was renowned for such qualities as strength and swiftness, as well as symbolising storms, wind and danger. She was also seen as representative of the Divine Feminine, latterly becoming synonymous with evil.

It is written that the Chimaera would regularly wreak havoc upon the land, killing anything that got in the way of its fiery breath. At some point the Chimaera also became the household pet in the court of the king of Caria!

The unfortunate creature was eventually destroyed by Bellerophon who, riding upon the recently tamed Pegasus, cast lead into her mouth. Her fiery breath melted the lead which ran down her throat, searing all her vital organs. (There is no record of which mouth; one would assume it was the lion's.)

Robert Graves, believed that the Chimaera was a calendar beast symbolic of the tripartite year of the Great Goddess, with the lion, goat and serpent representing Spring, Summer and Winter respectively. Another related theme is that the Chimaera's death was symbolic of the destruction of the shrine of the Great Goddess who had previously reigned supreme.

Another theory is that the Chimaera was a figurative description of a volcanic mountain in Lycia (Hence the fiery breath.) At the summit was a lair of lions and in the middle was a pasture of goats and serpents infesting the foothills. In his Natural History, Pliny referred to a volcano called Chimaera near Phaselis, Lycia.

The legacy of the Chimaera is still with us, having crept into modern language.

Today a Chimaera is an illusion or fabrication of the mind. And to "chase the Chimaera" is to indulge in useless flights of fancy. Scientifically, a Chimaera refers to an organism containing genetically different tissues formed by the fusion of early embryos.

ANIMALS & MEN # 20　　　　　　　　　FEATURE

CRYPTO-CURIOSITIES OF KENT'S PAST

by Neil Arnold

The foliage of Robin Hood Wood spills like a green liquid, linking the thickets of Blue Bell Hill, Maidstone, Boxley, Goudhurst, Malling and Aylesford. These heavy and historic pastures throughout the Weald of Kent are steeped in mystery, especially the phenomena of ghostly activity. Yet through the spooky occurrences and spectral incidents it is fair to say that the eerier situations have overshadowed other form of strange phenomena.

Now, Kent can stand alongside the West country as bearing a great variety of phenomena and it makes me proud to say that the hitch-hiker of Blue Bell Hill and Pluckley's twenty-something apparitions are now joined by a number of unusual beasts that have in fact inhabited this rural abode for many hidden years. Whilst some dazzling UFO cases have emerged over the years, the sightings - and even reports of landings - have been overshadowed by Kent's more ghostly occurrences. However, at the moment the 'big cat flap' cannot be ignored and so gives me reason to retell a few tales of out of place animals and weird creatures, as well as recount some other incidents not heard before.

Hounds From The Outer Edge

Joan Forman is a respected author on the supernatural and had a weird encounter with a peculiar creature during the 1950s. At the time Joan worked at a village school in Goodhurst and for the first few nights she slept in the oldest part of the building. At 3:30am she awoke to see a strange beast crouching in the corner of the room and staring at her with wide eyes. The 'thing' just sat there looking at her for some hours, yet gave off a menacing aura. Joan described the creature as being two feet in length, much bigger than a domestic cat and unlike anything she'd seen before. The strangest thing occurred as dawn gradually rolled in: the thing just seemed to fade with night's exit.

Immediately then, we have to consider some kind of supernatural entity, as it didn't just get up and walk out of the room. However sleepy a person may be we have to trust their eye for detail and so it seems this creature may have been more akin to the phantom black dogs rather than a real creature. Even an out of place big cat seems out of the question for although Joan would not have expected to see a large feline, she would surely of recognised its form? So, was this beast some kind of omen or a warning? However, if this beast was actually there only for her it does not explain the other sightings made by other women in the building who also saw similar forms.

I have mentioned in a previous article that my mother has seen a ghostly black dog in her bedroom. This was a traumatic time of illness and yet the odd apparition proved to be a symbol of good will.

A similar case concerns an aunt of mine who was extremely poorly, at unrest and very troubled due to an infection in her blood. She has never had any interest in or knowledge of the paranormal but she also saw a small, black and quite ghostly dog during a stressful night. The dog seemed to be a symbol of better things to come, as she soon recovered from her illness.

ANIMALS & MEN # 20

Four miles west of Maidstone lies Trottiscliffe (pronounced Trosley) and it is here that a weird creature resides. The famous Pilgrims Way path that runs from London to Canterbury splices the Trosley area and in its wooded area a gigantic frothing hound roams. Nothing is really known about the huge animal. It has only been sighted in this area and on just a few occasions.

Although the known path cuts through the heavy foliage of the North Downs it does not seem as though the beast has been mistaken for one of the many big cats in the vicinity. There are no tales pertaining to the hounds legend which is why the story is hardly featured anywhere. Maybe it just boils down to a straight forward haunting or maybe something more sinister.

Five miles east of Maidstone sits the beautiful structure, Leeds Castle, a picturesque masterpiece shrouded in history and blanketed by an eeriness that does not just hold phantom people in its stony walls. The Black Dog Of Leeds is considered to be the bringer of misfortune, the conjurer of ill-will, as it prowls the cold halls.

However, on one occasion the mysterious creature actually saved a woman's life. The hound attracted the attention of a lady who was sitting on a bay at a window overlooking the wonderful moat. The woman was intrigued by the weird animal and stood up to follow it. As she neared the creature it simply vanished and at that moment the bay cracked and collapsed, plummeting to the murky depths below. And so this spectral hound, hitherto known as a symbol of grief, was on this occasion a saviour.

The black dog lore is famous throughout Britain and some kind of pattern does emerge from the sightings reported. Some of the hounds never really give much indication that they are actually etherial creatures although fiery eyes and a 'Baskerville' glow are reported. It seems that the larger hounds, like the evil Black Shuck, are indeed a signification of misfortune. The smaller dogs, even if they do appear malevolent, certainly appear to be of good cause. It seems unusual that some greater, unseen force should use a dog to represent grief but there is certainly something odd about the creatures, otherwise people would surely pass the animal off as your average four-legged friend. A majority of the time, the beast is there to cause fear, emitting some kind of menace.

If You Go Down To The Woods Today..

I always thought over-sized rabbits and spectral bunnies were the spectacle of magical movies like "Alice In Wonderland" and "Watership Down". However, a recent issue of "Encounters" magazine featured a letter regarding the sighting of a twelve-foot tall rabbit.

This brings to mind a strange incident that took place in the '70s. It happened in Robin Hood Woods, an area that must conceal a haunted history. Rumours of a voodoo woman that runs across the country fields could well be connected to the fiend that was spotted. It's a case I have not read anywhere; it comes from a friend who I trust and as it concerns a six-foot tall bunny I don't think the witness would have rushed to tell the authorities due to the possibility of becoming a laughing stock. However, this person is sure that what they saw in the woodland was a white rabbit, not standing on its back legs, and measuring a 'whopp-

ANIMALS & MEN # 20

-ing size'. This furry fright caused a lot of stress to the witness who probably thought he would be perceived as a mad hatter. Since then, no other sightings have occurred. Maybe the bestial bunny was some kind of weird spectre, but explaining its size is something beyond me. The animal was described as 'giant' and adds a whole new meaning to the name Thumper. The closest thing I can compare to this creature would be an out of place kangaroo which would surely have shocked the witness enough to cause confusion. Not everyone expects to see a kangaroo in the woods of Kent so misidentification was possible. However, on both accounts it is still weird.

About eight years ago myself and some old friends decided to let some fireworks off in nearby woodland, an area overlooked by the haunted Blue Bell Hill. It was November time, a smoke-filled night and being the lads we were, we ventured to the dark woods firing rockets and generally messing about. The woodland had a path that at the time was not illuminated so we walked in blackness. We reached a central area of the woods huddled together and trusting our senses. We decided to light a fire. After about half an hour we decided to make our way home as the fire was becoming a little uncontrollable. We began to walk along the path, still shuffling nervously, until the embers were out of sight. One of my friends was worried about the flames so wanted to go back and put the fire out properly. We walked half way, then let him go on alone - but, as he came to the flames, he got the fright of his life. He screamed and ran back to us, waffling in an hysterical manner. We made our way out the woods in a scramble and made it to a nearby estate before my friend told us of his encounter. He said he saw a head pop up out of the darkness and then saw a creature, like a large ferret with white fur, stand up. Apparently, like in the good old films, they both terrified each other. I know for a fact he wasn't 'winding us up', as he was in such a state especially as the creature was almost as tall as him. He stands at about five foot eight. (about 1.6 metres.) To this day, I can remember that night. I can never explain the over-sized animal but imagine something with a ferret's head and snow-white in colour. Whatever it was it wasn't seen again. This is not thick woodland but due to the creature's reactions it seems as though it was real; for, let's face it, you never hear of a frightened ghost!

FEATURE

PHANTOM OR FLESH ?

It is November 1963. The fireworks are just dying out over Sandling Park in Hythe. Four friends are strolling home after a dance and they are attracted by a weird light floating over the trees nearby. They become worried by the orb which moves towards them before dropping behind some more trees. One of the boys, seventeen year old John Flaxton is becoming extremely cold as the group become disturbed by the light which has reappeared. It is following them and every time they stop in their motion the light seems to halt too. It then disappears behind more trees. The boys then spot a strange humanoid figure waddling towards them. It is tall, dark and appears headless. The leathery creature bears two wings and continues to shuffle towards them. The boys run for their lives before the thing gets any closer for them to notice any other details.

The following days throw up evidence in the form of three footprints of unusual character and the surrounding woodland is bathed in a peculiar light for a short time. Mothman had come. This sighting of extreme strangeness spawned many other odd experiences around the globe. Many people were seeing birdrnen, the bat-squatch and leather-winged humanoids. But why? Surely not some form of undiscovered creature ?

ANIMALS & MEN # 20 — FEATURE

Not a lot of evidence points to this theory and it seems the thing was more of a spectral manifestation rather than real creature. Who knows why only three prints were found or why the creature appeared in this area at all because Hythe is no hot-spot for any sort of strange phenomena. John Keel said that maybe the area was some kind of 'window' to another dimension but since that sighting there have been no other events to suggest a UFO flap or any kind of enigma pertaining to the fortean world. Maybe the boys are similar to the witnesses (women mainly) who have spotted Owlman of the West country. Maybe only a certain type of adolescent or teenager can see this being. It could be part of some mental vortex but whatever the case, Hythe was certainly an unusual place for this thing to show itself.

And why the light? Well, there is the old theory that the creature was some sort of alien and emerged from its flying saucer but maybe the light was simply given off as the creature actually flew through the air, because what is the point in having a UFO if you've got wings...? Maybe Mr. Mothman can't fly through our sphere on mere wing power. Other UFO sightings were reported in the Hythe area but this does not mean we must connect the creature with the saucer phenomenon for UFOs are basically seen everywhere nowadays. And so the mystery remains. I also feel that the creature may not have been headless and that its features were concealed by the enshrouding wings. But whatever those boys saw it was very disturbing.

There may be no connection here but a few years back my father (who isn't very open on the paranormal) was angling on Hythe sea-front. It was a winter night and around midnight when my father was approached by two peculiar characters that my father could only describe as 'ninjas'. These two 'men' came out of nowhere and stood watching my father. They were 'dressed' from head to toe in black, even their heads were masked. My dad acknowledged them but they just turned and walked off. Of course, I am not saying that these two beings were from another planet or indeed anyway related to the winged creature but I think their presence *was* mysterious.

More Beasts...

In January 1973 a Folkestone man was driving from Capel to Alkham and saw a strange creature cross the road directly in front of his car. The man was not sure what he'd seen but a few days later a gamekeeper and RSPCA inspector found a few paw-prints and said they were made by a big cat, possibly a puma.

In the early '70s Kent was not exactly the big cat hot-spot it is today but after the Alkham sighting other witnesses stepped forward. One man said he saw a large feline at 3:30am whilst driving between Canterbury and Lympne. During this time this may have been the same creature spotted for there was no estimated report as to how many big cats were loose in the wilds of Kent. There can be no questioning their realism as many private collections have been released but zoo escapes have not been in abundance enough in the past to suggest the cats have broken free. In the early part of the 1900s Blue Bell Hill bore Drakes Zoo, a small business that ran a small train through the village and into the zoo grounds. Although the zoo was more of a 'farm' it still housed a number of larger creatures which may have escaped unnoticed as the park gradually became dilapidated.

Certainly one of the most peculiar, and oldest sightings comes from the year 1205. Although little is written on the incident I am eager to find out more about it as it is such a weird occurrence. It happened in Maidstone and the tale was told by an Abbot Ralph of Coggeshall. In his writings he mentioned a huge, raging storm of lightning bolts and thunder claps. On this torrid night a strange beast was struck by lightning and left as a charred, smoking mass. Apparently the odd corpse that gave off such a vile stench was unlike any other creature. It was described as having the head of an ass, the belly of a human and limbs all differing from each other. The strange thing is, there doesn't seem to be any record of sightings in regards to this sort of beast so scepticism does arise. One thing I am not is a sceptic but the evidence for this time is extinct.

The thing is, how do we know that it was not a normal animal like a dog that had been burnt to an unrecognisable mess ? If the corpse was not badly scorched then the beast would have maintained its form but as it was it was surely too much of a state to identify it. Whatever the case, this is still an unusual moment in Kent's history and if we are looking at an unknown creature then this is a very bizarre case indeed. I'm sure that many documents of the past would be very fascinating in regards to strange creature sightings but getting hold of them is a task in itself.

In 1975 on the banks of the River Stour, at Sandwich, witnesses reported seeing a large, out of place reptile. Although the reports were ignored at first they were soon taken notice of when many people saw a crocodile, over five-feet in length bathing on the banks. This is obviously a case of zoo escape or more likely someone's own creature being unleashed due to the authorities being 'onto' them. It is fortunate that no swimmer or angler disturbed the creature; yet it proves that Kent's tranquil countryside is a more than sufficient habitat for large out of place animals.

APPARITIONS OR ANIMALS?

Some people do seem to be the target of paranormal incidents. They are susceptible to the world of the supernatural. They are plagued by ghosts, by UFOs, by poltergeist phenomena and on a more sinister note they seem open to ghastly manifestations that either appear as over-sized known creatures or completely hideous and unrecognisable things.

Deciphering the apparition from animal is no easy task, for there are indeed strange creatures lurking in the shadows, and for a person to see a real crocodile is almost as shocking as seeing a ghostly dog. There is no doubt that some reputedly haunted areas are conjuring up creatures that are 'targeting' sensitive people on a mental level. On the other hand, however unusual some out of place sightings are we must accept that there's literally hundreds of roaming creatures in the wrong place at the wrong time.

And not all of them seem to be God's great creatures.

So how many kiwi species are there?

by
Darren Naish

The exact number of kiwi species was until recently a fairly stable situation - there were three species, one of which, the Brown kiwi, could be subdivided into three subspecies. However, new studies on kiwi DNA indicate that things might be more complex than this. The history of the different kiwi species is also interesting - over time, various workers have regarded different populations as worthy of their own specific or subspecific status. The discovery of the three universally accepted kiwi species was in fact a rather slow and drawn-out affair that spanned much of the 19th century.

The first kiwi to be described and named, the **Brown kiwi (*Apteryx australis*)** Shaw 1813, was not joined by a second species until 1847 when John Gould named *A. owenii*, the **Little spotted kiwi**.

While there have been a few (unsuccessful) attempts to give *A. owenii* its own genus, it has retained its original name and, aside from Rothschild's unsuccessful attempt in 1893 to create a new subspecies (*A. owenii occidentalis*), it has remained undivided. A kiwi named *A. mollis* by Thomas Potts in 1873 has since proved to be a junior synonym of *A. owenii*. The smallest and one of the rarest kiwis, *A. owenii* was formerly widespread on both North and South Island but is now restricted to five special island reserves. With a population of around 1,110 (as of mid 1999), it is reportedly increasing in numbers.

In 1850, Bartlett decided that the Brown kiwis from North Island were worthy of specific status - they were smaller, darker and with coarser plumage than South Island birds - and he named them *Apteryx mantelli*.

Zoologists disagreed about Bartlett's suggestion over the following years and McLennon (1991) notes that 14 papers were published on this one issue alone. In 1888, Sharpe took things a step further and argued that some *A. mantelli* specimens deserved to be regarded as yet another new species, *A. bulleri*. The latter species proved to be unwarranted, but Bartlett has been partly vindicated in that it has become generally accepted that the North Island birds do warrant separate recognition, but as a subspecies (the **North Island brown kiwi *A. australis mantelli***), not as a species. The south

Animals & Men Collected Editions Volume 4 — New Horizons

ANIMALS & MEN # 20 — FEATURE

Illustrations by the author

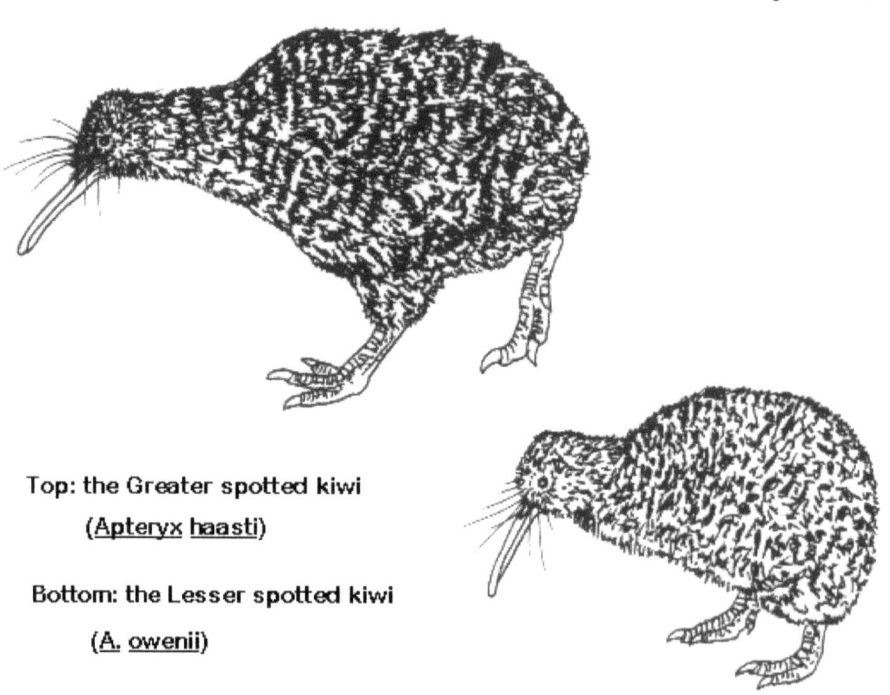

Top: the Greater spotted kiwi

(Apteryx haasti)

Bottom: the Lesser spotted kiwi

(A. owenii)

Island brown kiwi thus became the nominate version of *A. australis* and is now *A. a. australis*. A new species named by Potts in 1873, *A. fusca*, has proved to be a synonym of *A. a. australis*.

The last great discovery in kiwi taxonomic research (perhaps) was the naming in 1871 of **Apteryx haastii**, the **Great spotted kiwi**, by Potts following his examination of two skins collected from Westland. Potts named this species in honour of Julius von Haast, then the director of the Canterbury Museum and a scientist who had spent much time searching for kiwis and other birds in the countryside of New Zealand. *A. haastii* is believed to be the same as *A. maxima*, the name created by Jules Verreaux based on anecdotal tales of an especially large and aggressive kiwi (and not based on any specimen or backed up by a description). As noted below, other workers regarded *A. maxima* as the same as the brown kiwis from Stewart Island, while some

ANIMALS & MEN # 20 — FEATURE

cryptozoologists have even suggested that *A. maxima* may have been based on observations of emeid moa. What was regarded as another new species of kiwi, the **Stewart Island kiwi**, was described by Walter Buller in 1890. Noting the large size of his specimen, Buller regarded this kiwi (confusingly) as the same as *A. maxima*. Pointing out the problematic lack of a type specimen and description for this alleged species in 1893, Walter Rothschild argued that Buller's kiwi must be given a new name, and he called it *A. lawryi* (the *lawryi* honours Buller's middle name). Subsequent work showed that the Sewart Island kiwi was distinct from other types, but it was

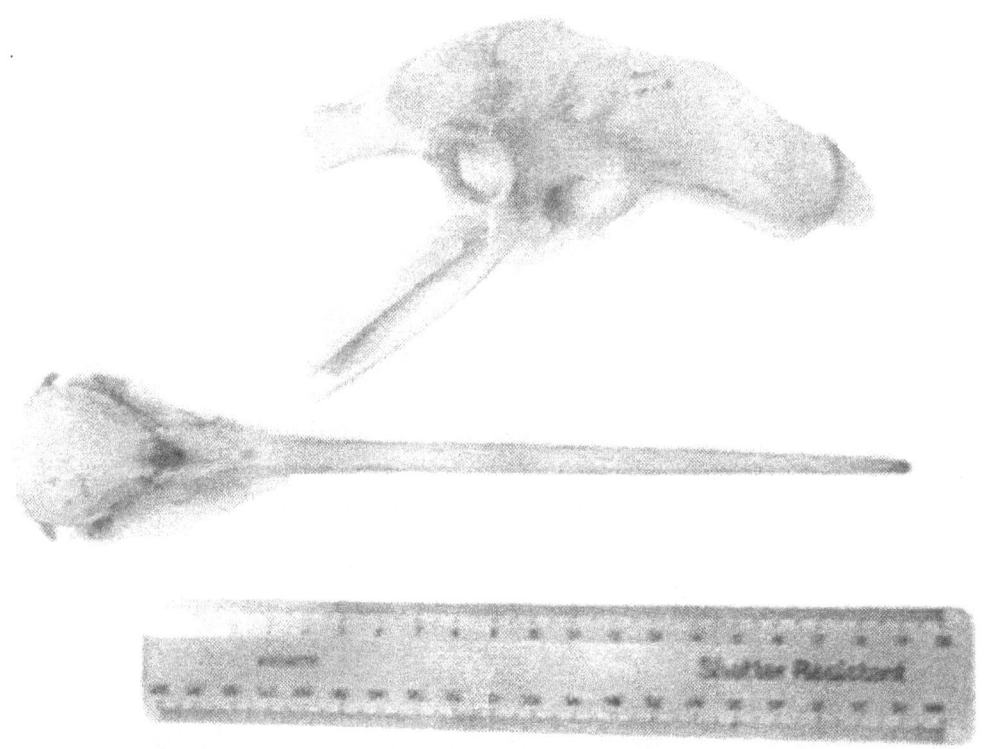

Skull and pelvis of Stuart Island brown kiwi (Apteryx australis lawryi). Note the extraordinary length of the bill.

ANIMALS & MEN # 20

downgraded to a subspecies of *A. australis*, thus becoming ***A. a. lawryi***.

Amongst brown kiwis, the Stewart Island form is quite distinctive with a particularly large beak and legs. Unlike other brown kiwis (where they are light brown), in the Stewart Island form these features are bluish grey.

Thus by the end of the 19th century, kiwi taxonomy had stabilised and there appeared to be three good species (the Little spotted (*A. owenii*), Great spotted (*A. haastii*) and Brown (*A. australis*)), the last of which could be subdivided into a South Island (*A. a. australis*), North Island (*A. a. mantelli*) and Stewart Island (*A. a. lawryi*) subspecies.

However, this three-fold classification was complicated in 1993 when Charles Daugherty and Alan Baker analysed the DNA of kiwis previously regarded as belonging only to *Apteryx australis*.

Finding that birds from three southern populations (Haast, Fiordland and Stewart Island) were genetically similar to one another but different from other brown kiwis, they proposed that this newly recognised form be named **Tokoeka** ('Tokoeka' is actually the Maori word for the Weka (*Gallirallus australis*)).

Further research has shown that the Haast population - informally dubbed the **Haast tokoeka** - is distinct from the two other populations (now referred to as **Southern tokoeka**) and may warrant separate recognition.

Curiously, the tokoekas bear a superficial resemblance to the Great spotted kiwi. This may indicate that our understanding of kiwi interrelations is set for some major changes.

A further surprise is that some South Island brown kiwis - a group currently known as the **Okarito brown kiwis** - are also genetically distinct, and far more closely related to North Island brown kiwis than to tokoekas. Okarito browns have proved to be critically endangered - the popula-tion is estimated at 200 individuals and is restricted to just 40 km^2 of forest.

Research continues on the affinities of these forms and a formalised nomenclature has yet to appear.

- - - - - - -

ANIMALS & MEN # 20 — FEATURE

Big in Japan
Richard Freeman

Japan conjures up images of an ultra high-tech society, towering sky-scrapers, flashing neon signs, overpopulation, a world akin to "Bladerunner". As with most foreign images of other countries it is wrong. Almost 90 per-cent of Japan is covered with mountains. Most of the population is urban and crowded into the cities in the few flatter areas. It may seem odd that such an advanced country still harbours unknown animals but the monsters that still walk beneath the rising sun are some of the strangest in the world.

Hibagon: A Japanese ape?

It is fitting that one of the world's most mountainous countries should have its own version of the *Yeti*. Though somewhat smaller than its Himalayan cousin the Japanese *Hibagon* is nonetheless a terrifying beast.

Inhabiting the mount Hiba area and its surrounding wilderness in the Hbayama national park, it is said to stand 5 feet tall, is covered with bristly brown hair turning white on the chest, and resembles a gorilla. It possesses a snub nose, long muscular arms and smells like a rotting cadaver. The monster first appeared in 1970 and terrorized the district for several years.

A typical sighting was that of Reiko Harada, a 46 year old seamstress, and her young son in 1972. Whilst walking home she saw a *Hibagon* standing by the roadside.

The creature raised its hands as if signalling her to stop. Reiko went numb with terror and shook violently. Eventually she managed to pick up her child and run home. A search later revealed crushed shrubs and a stench akin to a decomposing body.

There is a type of large monkey in Japan, the Japanese macaque (*Macaca fuscata*). These are the famed "snow monkeys" renowned for bathing in hot springs then drying out in the steam. They also live at a higher altitude than any other primate.

However this animal is less than half the size of *Hibagon*. As stated before, most of Japan is sparsely settled mountain wilderness. It is far from impossible that a moderately sized unknown ape or giant short tailed monkey still inhabits the mountain forests. Most fascinating of all, could this creature's frightening appear-ance be the genesis of the demonic *Oni*? These are Japanese devils with animalistic red faces. They walk the earth in search of souls to drag back to hell.

One particularly vile demon was Kappa. This creature had the head of a monkey, the shell of a terrapin, and the body of a frog.

Despite its small size this aquatic demon was extraordinarily strong and could drown a horse.

Like all the best demons Kappa was fond of human flesh. His power came from a magick liquid in a concave depression in his skull.

The best way to defeat Kappa was to bow upon meeting him. Despite his evil nature Kappa had Japanese politeness and would bow back spilling his liquid and losing his strength.

Kappa was also addicted to the

ANIMALS & MEN # 20   FEATURE

taste of cucumber and could be influenced by anyone who fed him this vegetable.

Issie and its kin: the modern day dragons of Japan.

Perhaps the most celebrated of movie monsters is Godzilla. Created in the 50s by Toho studios the 350 foot tall, radioactive fire breathing, mutant *Tyrannosaurus rex* has rampaged his way through dozens of films, destroying Tokyo countless times in battles with foes ranging from giant blobs created by pollution to robot replicas of himself.

Godzilla has his roots in the legends of Japanese dragons. These magnificent monsters resemble Chinese dragons but have some important differences. They have only three claws on each foot, unlike the imperial dragon of China, who had five talons. They also lacked the Chinese dragon's complex, staged life cycle. Japanese dragon's eggs resembled precious stones and once hatched the dragons attained huge size very quickly. One tale tells of a peasant boy who brought home dragon eggs believing them to be jewels. Small holes opened in their tops and tiny dragons flew out. The little reptiles swelled at an astounding rate and smashed through the roof of his house.

Some early travellers descriptions of dragons kept and worshipped in Japanese temples resemble crocodiles. Indeed the Indo-pacific crocodile that can reach 30 feet in length sometimes strays into the waters around Japan's southernmost islands. Such a monster would make a fine blue print for a dragon. If Japanese mariners travelled as far afield as their Chinese counterparts they may have encountered *Megalania prisca*, the 30-ft Australian monitor lizard. Even on the cusp of the millennium dragon-like creatures are still reported.

Lake Ikeda near the city of Kagoshima on the island of Kyushu has an interesting legend attached to it. The story goes that in ancient times a white horse and her foal grazed close to the waters of this extinct volcano. One day a samurai took the foal away, doubtless to raise it as his steed. The mare leapt into the lake searching for her offspring, occasionally surfacing, to the amazement of locals. There may be some grain of truth in this story, as strange creatures are reported today in lake Ikeda. The reports describe a massive animal over 30 feet in length with a snake-like head and neck, and a long humped back.

Several photographs of the animal have been taken. Mr Tosiaki Matsuhara took the first in 1978. He was a folklorist who had been investigating the legends of the lake. His pictures seem to show to individuals together. They are hump-backed and creating waves. The creatures have been christened *Issie,* much like Loch Ness's *Nessie* and have been seen by many respectable people including the president of a construction firm. This man, Yutaka Kawaji and 20 members of his family observed a black skinned animal showing some 6 to 9 meters of its body above the water. Mr Kawaji persuaded the animal in a motor boat, it dived and re-surfaced several times. *Issie's* description is a familiar snake necked, humpbacked beast much like the Loch Ness monster.

Issie has counterparts in other areas of Japan; also on Kyushu, Lake Toya has reports of a similar beast. On Hokkaido island, Lake Kutcharo is the home of *Kussie* another monster for whom local citizens have formed a protection society.

The Shamanu: Japan's dwarf wolf.

The shamanu of Japanese wolf (*Canis lupis hodophila*) was the smallest of all the wolves reaching only 41 inches in length. It was also the most distinctive of the wolves unequally marked with grey, white and russet fur. The Ainu people of northern Japan worshipped it and called it the howling god. Elsewhere it was known as *Okami* (great god), *Magami* (true god), and *Kami* (mountain god). Its skull was believed to ward off demons. There is a legend of a blind lute player who was lost in the mountains in a wild snow storm. He feared he was doomed but eventually met someone in the wilderness and was led down by what he thought was a hunter. Upon reaching his home he found it was a kindly shamanu.

This changed with the coming of "civilisation". With deforestation, the introduction of firearms, and the spread of farming the shamanu's range began to shrink. Throughout the 19th century they were extensively hunted and the last one was supposedly killed near Washikaguchi on Honshu in 1905.

The whole sorry tale is strikingly reminiscent of that of the Tasmanian marsupial wolf or Thylacine (*Thylacinus cynocephalus*) and like this animal the shamanu is rumoured to survive in remote areas and has been glimpsed many times since its supposed extinction. It would be a great triumph for both conservation and the Japanese nation if the howling gods could be proven to still haunt the mountains at the dawn of the 21st century.

A flat snake and a hairy fish : real life "pokemon!"

The Japanese video game Pocket Monsters (pokemon) for short has become a runaway success both in its homeland and in the West. Players create their own small monsters each with unique powers and pit them against other player's creations. The game has spawned an addictive Manga cartoon that follows a young pokemon trainer as he collects all 150 species. The made up monsters are fascinating, each with its own ecological niche (if some are a bit surreal!).

There are two small Japanese monsters that one could easily believe were the products of obsessive pokemon players, but apparently are based in reality.

The *tzuchinoko* is a snake that looks as if it has lost an altercation with a steamroller. Dorso-ventrally flattened (like a stingray) it bears horn like ridges, facial pits, and a well-defined neck that is narrower than the body. A dorsal ridge runs along it's spine and a triangular head. It would seem to be an aberrant pit viper, perhaps one adapted for lurking in rock crevasses. There are several tortoise and lizard species adapted in this way. Known for centuries in Japan it only became known in the West as recently as 1987. A type specimen has yet to be procured by science.

Some antique manuscripts in Japan refer to a "hairy fish" (putting one in mind of the famous fur-bearing trout hoax). These peculiar piscines were 4 to 5 feet long and covered with hair. Oddly for fish they would come out on land and gambol around making load noises. They were aggressive to humans, sometimes killing them but never eating the corpses. All in all these sound more like pinnipeds than fish. Seals and sealions can deliver a powerful bite and one only has to look at an animal like the leopard seal to know it could easily kill a man. Perhaps a forgotten and possibly now extinct species of freshwater seal is being spoken of here. The small Baikal seal of Russia is land-locked and exists entirely in fresh water. Alternatively these writings could refer to a known species that swam up river in land.

We all know seals make it into Loch Ness and a leopard seal once was killed 48 kilometres up the Sholhaven River in Australia. If the measurements were correct, however, our Japanese seals would be a new species, the smallest ever known.

ANIMALS & MEN # 20

ESP in Animals: the Goverment Connection
by Nick Redfern.

The idea that elements of the United States Intelligence community have an active interest in determining the validity or otherwise of extra-sensory perception (ESP) in animals, sounds like something straight out of an episode of The X-Files. Just occasionally, however, truth is far stranger than fiction...

At various times since the early 1970s, the US Defence Intelligence Agency (DIA) has been acutely aware of (and at times, highly alarmed by) purported advances in parapsychology on the part of the former Soviet Union. In addition, the DIA has produced a number of quite astonishing reports detailing its findings on (amongst other topics) telepathy; out-of-body experiences; remote viewing; psychokinesis; claims of teleportation; hypnotism; and much more.

Moreover, far from being an obscure agency of no particular merit, the DIA was created in 1961 by US Defence Secretary Robert McNamara and brought together the military intelligence branches of the US Army, Navy and Air Force.

Currently, the DIA satisfies the foreign intelligence and counter-intelligence requirements of the Secretary of Defence, the Joint Chiefs of Staff, various components of the Department of Defence and provides the military intelligence contribution to national intelligence.

In other words, the DIA is a highly-respected and vital component of the US Government; and with this is mind, let us turn our attention to the DIA's findings with respect to ESP research and the animal kingdom.

In a September 1975 paper titled 'Soviet and Czechoslovakian Parapsychology Research' made available to me via the US Government's Freedom of Information Act, the DIA reveals its findings on this fascinating area of research. Given its contents, I make no apologies for quoting the paper without deletion:

TELEPATHY IN ANIMALS.

Soviet and Czechoslovakian parapsychologists have not reported in animals in recent years; instead, they have emphasised research on biological energy transfer. Soviet parapsychology research is multi-disciplinary and indistinguishable from conventional Soviet physiological research. Both disciplines are presently involved in attempts to identify the sources of internally generated and externally imposed stimuli underlying physiological processes.

Soviet research on telepathy in animals in the 1920s and 1930s was devoted largely to proving that telepathy between man and animals did indeed exist.

A good example of the early Soviet approach was research conducted by VIM. Bekhterev of Leningrad University, in collaboration with a circus performer, V.L. Durov. Bekhterev reported that Durov's trained dogs successfully solved arithmetic problems and identified or retrieved objects solely on the basis of their trainer's mental suggestion.

The results of these tests were controversial, since the dog's performances were good when Durov was present and supplied the "suggestions", but deteriorated markedly when he was absent and another individual attempted to mentally control them.

Bekhterev's original objective was to demonstrate that telepathy between man and animals was mediated by some form of electromagnetic radiation (FMR), but by 1937, he and other Soviet parapsychologists had concluded that no known form of EMR was the carrier of thought transmission.

The EMR theory of information transfer is still unresolved by the Soviets, but is still the major basis underlying much of their research.

ANIMALS & MEN # 20 — FEATURE

In 1962 B.S. Kazhinskiy advanced the theory that animals are capable of visual and aural perception and reflex understanding of the behaviour of other animals or humans. He postulated that this ability resulted from the capacity of one animal to detect (via its nervous system), analyse, and synthesise signal-stimuli given off by another animal. According to Kazhinskiy, the signals were transmitted in the form of a "bioradiational sight ray" and analysed by the percipient animal as a result of its Pavlovian conditioning. The term "bioradiational rays" is still used by some Soviet and Czech parapsychologists to refer to focusing and concentration of biological energy by the brain and the optical neural channels.

Present day Soviet and Czech parapsychology research with animals is devoted almost exclusively to investigation of sources of biological energy involved in physiological processes, the interactions of such energy with external fields, and the effects of externally generated fields on animal physiology. Reference to telepathy in the sense of communications by transmission of total, conceptual, mental formulations is seldom made.

A significant advance toward identification of the EMR source of biological energy transfer was gained from recent research conducted at the University of Novosibirsk. Scientists there investigated the release of energy during cell division and during cellular damage and repair resulting from viral infection or toxic chemicals. In over 5000 experiments with cell cultures and animal organs it was shown that damaged cells radiated some form of energy and that the energy released was capable of causing damage in adjacent control preparations of organs or cells. Further investigation revealed that a uniform pattern, code, or rhythm of radiation was emitted by normal cells. This pattern was disturbed when cellular damage occurred, becoming quite irregular.

It was also found that the patterns were transmitted from experimental to control preparations only when the cells or organs were cultured in quartz containers. Since quartz transmits ultraviolet (UV) radiation and standard laboratory glassware does not, the Soviets concluded that UV radiation mediated cellular information transfer. The researchers subsequently correlated given irregularities of emission with specific diseases and are now attempting to develop techniques for diagnosis and therapy by monitoring and altering cellular radiation codes.

Czechoslovakian research on energy transfer between animal muscle preparations from animals to man, and from man to man, has also demonstrated EMR as the vehicle of biological energy transfer. In experiments conducted between 1948 and 1968 at the Okres Institute of Public Health, Kutna Hora, Czechoslovakia, Dr. Jiri Bradna demonstrated contactless transfer (myotransfer) of stimuli between frog neuromuscular preparations. Bradna placed identical preparations side by side; stimulation of one preparation with electric pulses at frequencies between 10 and 30 pulses per second caused contraction and a recorded electromyographic response in the other. In other experiments, stimulation of muscle preparations influenced the oscillations of a pendulum and increased the muscle tension of a human subject. Bradna obtained objective proof that energy in the very high frequency (vhf) range mediated the stimulus transmission. He also demonstrated that myotransfer could be blocked with ferrous metal filters and aluminium, could be deformed with magnets, ferrites and other conductors, could be reflected and transmitted over waveguides, and shielded with grids. Bradna concluded that primary perceptual and informational pathways between animals are based on metabolic processes at the macromolecular level and that the magnitude of energy transfer depends on muscular adenosine triphosphate (ATP) energy release.

Bradna has reported successful application of myotransfer in physiotherapy.

It has been found to be effective for both individuals and groups. In the latter case, the summation of stimuli has been shown to enhance the neuromuscular responses of individuals within the group. Bradna feels that such stimuli influence the herd of animals and may also be a factor in altering human behaviour under conditions of isolation or overcrowding.

In the Soviet Union, Doctor Y.A. Kholodov has investigated the effects of a constant magnetic field (CMF) on rabbits. Whole-body exposures to fields between 30 and 2000 oersteds* resulted in nonspecific exchanges in the electroencephalogram but no other directly measurable physiological responses. Kholodov showed that weak magnetic as well as other externally generated radiation fields have a direct effect on nerve tissue, and for this reason he feels that natural and artificial fields in man's environment may have an influence on health and behaviour via the nervous system and the hypothalamus. Kholodov's research is representative of current Soviet efforts to explain paranormal phenomena on the basis of known physical and biological parameters.

Another Soviet scientist, A.S. Presman, feels that biological energy and information exchange between living organisms is the result of electromagnetic field (ENF) interactions between individuals or between the individual and the environment. He and other Soviet scientists have recorded EMF's from man, frogs, and insects of various species at ranges from several centimetres to several metres from the body surface. The frequencies of the ENF's were found to correspond to various biorhythms of organs, rhythms of movement and acoustic signals and bioelectric rhythms. Presman thinks that in groups of animals, electromagnetic oscillations are synchronised by frequency matching and that the cumulative intensity may grow in proportion to the square of the number of individuals. Such cumulative emission is also thought to be possible as the result of synchronisation of the emissions of many cells in animals in a highly excited state.

Presman, like Kholodov, feels that the effects of sub-threshold stimuli are mediated through the hypothalmic region of the midbrain. The hypothalamus regulates diverse physiological processes in the organism (pulse, body temperature, oxygen consumption, carbon dioxide liberation, urine volume, urine nitrogen concentration, etc.) and these are the functions most commonly disturbed by changes in EMF' s.

Presman believes that electromagnetic signalling is universal between animals, but not between humans who may have lost the capability for such communication as a result of evolution and the development of verbal and artificial communication channels. He does not rule out the possibility that "spontaneous telepathy" may occasionally occur, but regards such occurrences as rare cases of atavism. Consequently, he regards man as the least suitable animal for studying electromagnetic communication. It is important that the increased degree of sophistication which has occurred in Soviet ESP or telepathy research since 1960 be understood. At present the terms "ESP" and "telepathy" are seldom used. It is possible that the newer terms "biocommunication" and "psychotronics" will vanish in the near future only to be replaced by conventional high-energy physics terminology, or term such as "interpersonal subconscious reactions" or "mention" forces. In any event, the classical ESP experiments with animals are no longer of interest in the USSR. The typical Vasilev experimentation from 1920 to 1955 has been replaced with sophisticated research protocols which study complex interactions between man, animals and plants.

Dr. Pavel Naumov, who bears no relation to the now imprisoned Edward Naumov, conducted animal biocommunication studies between a submerged Soviet Navy submarine and a shore research station: these tests involved a mother rabbit and her newborn litter and occurred around 1956, three years prior to the USS Nautilus disclosure [Authors note: this is a reference to an ESP study allegedly undertaken by the US Navy in 1960].

According to Naumov, Soviet scientists placed the baby rabbits aboard the submarine. They kept the mother rabbit in a laboratory on shore where they implanted electrodes (EEG?) in her brain. When the submarine was submerged, assistants killed the rabbits one by one. At each precise moment of death, the mother rabbit's brain produced detectable and recordable reactions.

As late as 1970 the precise protocol and results of this test described by Naumov were believed to be classified. Many examples can be found in Soviet literature with dogs, bears, birds, insects and fish in conjunction with basic psychotronic research. The Pavlov Institute in Moscow may have been involved in animal telepathy until 1970.

In essence, that is the document. Of course, the fact that it is now a quarter of a century old surely begs the question: at what level

ANIMALS & MEN # 20 FEATURE

is government knowledge of ESP in animals at in 1999...?

Nick Redfern is the author of a number of best-selling books, including 'A Covert Agenda', 'The FBI Files' and 'Cosmic Crashes'. He also likes his booze and punk rock.

- Oersteds are a measure of the intensity of a magnetic field.

The Eternal Cat
Marcus Matthews

A 6½ inch (16cm) statuette, found in a grotto at Austerlitz in the Pyrenees has been dated to the Aurignacian culture, portrayed a creature with a large head, short body, long, powerful limbs, a short tail and heavy, powerful lower jaw. On another fragment from Isturitz are the shoulders and head of another feline with an even deeper jaw.

We associate lions with warm climates, though, in fact, they are perfectly at home even in the snow of our zoos and safari parks. We also know they were found throughout Pleistocene Europe even during periods of intense cold.

At this period there were actually several large cats, such as Owen's panther, the cave lion and the sabre-toothed lesser scimitar cat in Europe. The last allegedly became extinct 500,000 years ago, although it is depicted in later artefacts. The cave lion became extinct as recently as 40,000 ago. While lions are not commonly portrayed in cave-paintings, some are known, such as in the Cave de Trois Freres in France and the frieze of lions from the Cave de la Vache in the Ariege. One of the lions in this image possesses a well-defined disabled tuft, proving it is indeed a lion and not a cave-tiger as, at one time, palaeontologists believed.

It has been suggested that the lions depicted on the Assyrian monuments may actually have been cave lions, hot lions were certainly in Europe much later. In 480 BC, according to Xenophon and Herodotus, lions in Greece attacked the baggage train of Xerxes, the Persian king.

Although the sabre-toothed tiger was believed to have died out at least 500,000 years ago, a 12,000-year-old piece of Sythan goldwork portrays a struggle between hunters and a beast that resembles one. One reason why such creatures were hunted was for their skins that had been traded worldwide from earliest times. The oldest record of their use in clothing goes back to 6500BC. At the site of Catal llayuk in Turkey images of dancers wearing leopard skins have come to light. They were probably being worn for ritual purposes, the wearers believing that the skin of the animal imparted to them something of its power, ferocity and agility. We certainly know that Aztec warriors dressed in jaguar pelts, while the Masai tribesmen of east Africa adopted the lion's mane as part of their costume and the fierce Dayak warriors of Sarawak donned the skins of clouded leopards when going into battle. There was widespread use of skins in China and elsewhere in the Far East. In Africa, chieftains used lion skins as a means of establishing authority over their subjects. But the skins were also thought to impart magical powers, for they were worn by witch doctors in

Africa as well as by shamans in many countries. However, the hunting of 'big game' became a pursuit of the ruling classes quite early on. Assyrian kings are portrayed pursuing lions from chariots, though it has been suggested their prey was actually bred in captivity to provide them with sport. The pharaoh, Amenophis Ill (1405-I 367BC) was said to have killed over 100 lions during his 10-year reign.

The Roman also organised hunts, though here their aim was to provide live animals for the circus. A picture in a 300AD Roman villa at Bône in Algeria shows lions, leopards and cheetahs being driven into a stockade of netting reinforced with thorns. Meat or tethered live creatures such as goats, calves or dogs could be used as bait. Nets could also be dropped from trees or animals captured by the use of running nooses attached to heavy logs. Once it set its foot in the noose, it was pulled tight and movement impeded by the log which it had to drag with it. This made it easy prey for trappers.

The third century poet Oppian describes a methods of capturing leopards in which waterholes were drugged with strong wine. The stupefied animals were said lie down to sleep off a hangover, though it has to be said that there are many who believe that Oppian was making rather free with his poetic licence.

Once they had arrived in Rome or any of the other major cities of the empire, they would be prepared for arena. Here they could participate in spectacles which involved appalling cruelty, not only to the humans pitted against them, but also to other animals who would be goaded into fighting one another.

When not thus employed, these creatures formed part of menagerie, but the origins of these well pre-dated the Romans. The earliest recorded zoos were at Saqqara in Egypt and go back to 2500BC.

Ptolemy II (283-2465BC) established a great menagerie at Alexandria, while a century earlier Alexander himself, after his conquests in India, had sent tigers back to home to be exhibited.

Despite - or perhaps because of - their fierceness, both lions and tigers became virtually royal fashion accessories. Ramses the Great had a lion he used in battle against the Hittites. Nero had a pet tiger he called Phoebe; Caligula lion called Acinares or 'Scimitar', and both Mark Antony and the Carthagian general Hanno had pet lions.

If the big, wild cats have repeatedly proved that they can be tamed, it was their smaller relative who developed into the domestic cat. And they had a very different history. By the third millennium BC the Egyptians were already using them to protect their grain stores from rodents. From I600BC, on the evidence of tomb paintings and other records, the cat was forming part of home and family life. According to Peter Neville in *Do Cats Need Shrinks*, it is possible the formerly wild creature had underdone a genetic change, making it tolerant of humans.

Cats became so much an accepted part of the Egyptian family life that their passing was lamented in the same way as the passing of any other family member, their owners shaving off their eyebrows in the traditional sign of mourning. Cats were even embalmed like their human owners. Several hundred thousand of them cats were found in central Egypt in the late nineteenth century and a cargo of 19.5 tons was brought to Liverpool. A few specimens went to the Natural History Museum and other collections, but the bulk were auctioned at between £3.50 and £4.25 per ton were sold to farmers for use as fertiliser.

ANIMALS & MEN # 20 — FEATURE

Egypt may well have been the original cradle of the domestic cat, possibly resulting from the crossing of the Euro-African wild cat and the jungle cat.

Further hybridisation would have led to the emergence of the strains we now know, such as a long-haired so-called Persian, which may have resulted from a cross with the central Asian Pallas cat. Siamese cats share characteristics, such as voices, coats and characters, with the golden cat of south east Asia. Supremely graceful and elegant, they may well have enjoyed sacred status and would have been owned only by the priests and perhaps members of the aristocracy. Certainly the cat figures in Egyptian mythology where the villain Seth attempts to eat a divine cat in the presence of its mother Bastet.

Nearer home, in the British Isles, the lynx, a member of the cat family, and the Scottish wild cat were part of the native fauna. Remains found at an Iron Age site near Glastonbury in Somerset suggests cats may have been eaten, though in this connection we have evidence of a form of divination practised by the Iron Age Celts which involved chewing the flesh of, among other creatures, cats.

The domestic cat may possibly have been brought to Britain by Phoenician or Greek traders, but they were definitely present by Roman times. In the Roman town of Silchester, their footprints have left been on the soft clay of tiles which had been left out to dry, and the skull of a domestic cat was found in the remains of a villa which burnt down about 4BC.

There is little doubt that cats were to be found in many households. While the main reason for keeping them would have been to keep down vermin, it is also possible, as Miranda Green suggests, that they were also kept as pets. In any case, they were plainly highly regarded by the Celts, as is shown by such artefacts as a mid-fourth century BC a bronze, coral-inlaid brooch from Czechoslovakia with a terminal in the form of a cat's head. Of laws to protect them we have the first written evidence in the British Isles about 936AD in the laws of Hywel the Good, ruler of South Wales. These include the fine to be imposed for killing the cat which guards a royal barn. 'The animal's body is to be held downward by the tail with its head touching a clean, level floor. Wheat is then to be poured until the pile becomes so large that the tip of the upright tail disappears'. The same document also provides a list of the points by which a cat is to be judged. It should be perfect in ear, eye, tail, teeth and claw. It should kill mice, not devour its young and 'should not be caterwauling every new moon'.

LETTERS

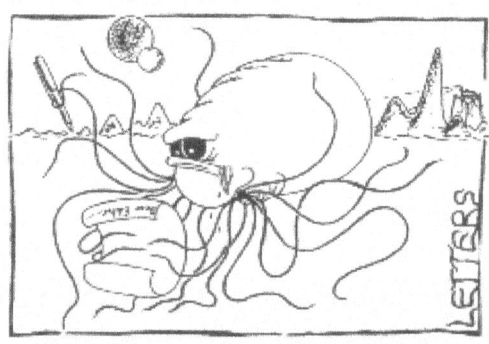

Dear Jon,

Hope all is well at CFZ. Issue 19 was excellent, especially Neil Arnold's piece on Cobtree Manor which particularly interested me as someone who grew up in Kent.

Another Kentish story surfaced

ANIMALS & MEN # 20 — LETTERS

See out website for updates! - Graham.

Crocodiles

in the Guardian on 13/9/99, which you probably saw, but just in case:

Wild boar chases man up tree

A man took refuge up a tree when chased by a wild boar yesterday near Port Lympne wild animal park in Kent.
He called for help on his mobile. When police arrived the boar had gone but the man was still up the tree - shocked but uninjured.

Made me smile, anyway.

OK, no more mister nice guy - where are my copies of A&M no's 1 and 2? Graham managed to finally sort out all the other back issues, but I am still awaiting these two (and have been for quite a while). I think you were having problems getting them reprinted, but it would be nice to see them one of these days....

All the best,
David Sutton

Graham Inglis, deputy director of the CFZ and 'admin supremo' replies:

While things are generally fine at the CFZ, I admit that the books and magazines mail-out service has been pretty lousy all through 1999.

In part, Jon and I can blame pressure of work (*Quest* magazine work, etc) but administrative bungling has undoubtedly played a big part too. We're determined to get things sorted soon - perhaps not yet to the extent of drawing up a charter of prompt service - but everyone still waiting for back issues, etc, should, we hope, see the orders filled before years' end. Apologies for all the delays.

Richard Freeman states in Issue 19 of this publication [letters page] that the *Crocodylus niloticus* dislikes salt water and would not have been able to reach the island of Rhodes unaided by boats. This species is recorded from coastal West Africa and one individual has been sighted 7 miles (11 km) from the Zululand coast. *C. niloticus* has in fact crossed to Zanzibar and Madagascar by crossing the sea and there is no reason that *C. niloticus* could not have reached Rhodes from the coast of the mainland. I suspect that *C. niloticus* has travelled further in the Mediterranean. Certain lake monster sightings from Italy have been likened to crocodiles and there is no reason *why C. niloticus* should not be a possible candidate for similar Mediteranean sightings.

Allan Edward Munro
Leigh, Lancashire

Richard Freeman, author of the letters page comment in question, replies:

The Madagascan crocodiles are a distinct sub-species who reached the island before its breakaway from Africa. The crocodiles that untill recently inhabited other Indian ocean islands such as Mauritius have been found to be Indo-pacific crocodiles. The West African specimens were probably washed out to sea by floods or storms. The only species of crocodilians who habitualy enter salt water are the Indo-pacific and American crocodiles.

ANIMALS & MEN # 20

What's a-foot?

by
Richard Freeman

Well, we almost made it. The editorial team of Animals and Men nearly had its own T.V. show...

For the best part of two years the south west regional independent television company had been telling us that it was "99 percent" sure that our proposed show "Weird about the West" would be going into production. A few weeks ago Carlton television brought out Westcountry and all our hard work was tossed uncere-moniously onto the scrap heap (doubtless in favor of some mindless swill for the brain-dead, that T.V.'s bottomless slop bucket of dross churns out unendingly these days).

There is a spark of light on the horizon however. In August we made a short film for H.T.V. They were so impressed that there is now talk of our own series! What was this film that caused such excitement? It was entitled:

The Brassknocker Hill Project

Regular readers will remember the beast of Brassknocker Hill, a simian creature that haunted the Bath area some 20 years ago. The sightings probably had their genesis in several baboons that had escaped from Longleat Safari park. We were perplexed when a production company approached us wanting to make a film on this subject. It had a fairly prosaic explanation, had occurred two decades ago, and most witnesses had moved away or died. However, the film turned out to be nothing like we had envisioned.

WHAT'S AFOOT

We have done so many T.V shows that we have become quite blasé about them. Another documentary about some out of place beast? Run of the mill stuff - or so we thought.

The director, Damien Wild, recently returned from the U.S, decided to cash in on the success of the Blair Witch Project and made the film a "video diary" of our attempts to find the beast. So Jon, Graham, and myself, together with Phil Williams, a new addition to the team, trundled off to Bath to make our first fictional film.

Phil was used like a cross between a packhorse and a deep south cotton plantation slave, forced to carry all our equipment and luggage whilst being whipped and swore at by Jon. As a workshy, dole scrounging, soap dodger this was his lot. Graham looked like a particularly sleazy drug dealer with a blue suit, shades, and a suitcase. I more or less played myself, a roguish, dashing, gothic cryptozoologist. (Yeah, Right - Ed.)

We had been "sent" a photograph of the beast, purporting that it had finally returned after 20 years. In fact this was me in a bigfoot mask hiding behind a bush. As we investigate we get picked off by the creature one by one, except Phil who becomes possessed by some forest elemental and changes into a fire wielding maniac jester. The film features me trying to bait the beast out with peanuts whilst making various simian vocalisations through a megaphone, Jon acting (!?) like a pompous, insufferable bastard, and Phil descending into a yawning canyon of supernatural madness.

Is it really the beast that kills us, of the mad jester? Are the two in cahoots? Are they one of the same, a manifestation of the forest spirit?

ANIMALS & MEN # 20

God alone knows what the viewing public, expecting an investigative documentary, thought of these monkeyshines, but enough of them watched it to make the H.T.V. "big cheeses" interested.

Currently we are awaiting a meeting with the producer of the show to discuss a series. Watch this space... (to probably be informed that we were rejected in favor of "topless pensioner indoor bobsleighing").

Phil Jester Williams

The Brassknocker Hill film was transmitted on HTV West on 21 Sep 1999 as part of the "Heads and Tails" series.

BOOK REVIEWS

Book Reviews
by Richard Freeman

Fossil Remains of Mythical Creatures by Bob Slaughter
(Smilodoness books IBSN 0-9651349-0-3)

Bob Slaughter is a professional palaeontologist who came up with a novel idea, a book of bogus fossils belonging to creatures from folklore. His idea is that legendary beasts are the inversion of extinct ones. With the latter we have the bones but not the information on there colour, behaviour etc. With the former we have a wealth of information on there lifestyle and appearance but no fossils to back them up. Ergo this book was born. Sounds great doesn`t it? The trouble is he chose some very mundane subjects. I was expecting spectacular dragon skeletons, fossil gryphons, giants and unicorns, but no, Slaughter`s book is full of obscure and dull specimens. There are some nice fairies but the rest of the collection is frankly as dull as ditch water. This is an A-1 example of a splendid idea appallingly executed. I only hope someone else tries this out and makes a better job of it.

Truly Weird: Real life cases of the Paranormal by Jenny Randles
(Collins & Brown IBSN 1-85585-442-2)

Jenny Randles is a prolific writer, mainly known in the field of U.F.O logy. Here she has widened her scope to write about many Fortean subjects. This book is really a coffee table book for

ANIMALS & MEN # 20

those new to paranormal studies and as such is a fine introduction. Subjects tackled are as diverse as simulacra to poltergeists. She makes one minor error in describing the yeti as having white fur, in fact its fur ranges from reddish brown to black (one report on the Russian / Chinese border in the 50s spoke of white fur but this was seen by moonlight). This however is a minor gripe and the books is intelligently written with a fine level of scepticism. In the author's verdict section at the rear of the book she always approaches each subject from a rational view. A fine gift for a budding Fortean.

Mysteries of Planet Earth by Dr Karl P.N.Shuker (Carlton IBSN 1 85868 679 2)

Without a doubt, this must be the book of the year. Even before one opens the cover up the sheer quality of the publication grabs you. It is plush and impressive and the contents match the sleeve.

This is Karl's finest work since "The Lost Ark" and is crammed so damn full of new information you just don't know were to begin. I pride

BOOK REVIEWS

myself in cryptozoological knowledge but there's stuff in here I've never heard of. Earth hound, weird subterranean carnivores that burrow into graves to devour cadavers, the sandewan, a Zimbabwean entity who's calling-card is a constant trail of blood, giant blue eels in the Ganges, and legions more.

Reading this book I felt like a kid at Christmas unwrapping exciting new gifts of cryptozoological information. In short, if this book were a woman it would be Winona Ryder and if you don't buy it you are a southern shandy drinker.

The History of British Mammals
by Derek Yalden
(Poyser natural history IBSN 0-85661-110-7)

This remarkable book, the first of its kind in 117 years, charts the mammalian fauna of the British Isles from the primitive insectivores that scurried in the shadow of the dinosaurs to our modern day species.

The book comes into its own in the ice age with records of where the differing species of megafauna have been found. From glacial times it follows the effects of changing climate and mankind on our native mammals.

Perhaps the most fascinating part of the book is its look at the possibility of returning formerly extinct species to Britain. Could the wolf, the bear, the wolverine, the lynx, the beaver, the bison, and the moose ever return to our land? The danger would surely be from us to them not vice-versa. The wild boar has already returned after two groups escaped in south east England 10 years ago and now a population of at least 200 live wild. It will be interesting to monitor the progress of this magnificent species. – RF

ANIMALS & MEN # 20

Psycho-Electrics: A theory offering rational explanations for paranormal phenomena by John Ivimy
(Pen Press IBSN 1-9007-9606-06)

Although not all unexplained phenomena are covered by this book a surprising amount are looked on in a new light of a new theory. Ivimy's idea revolves around electro-magnetic currents that cause airplane crashes, U.F.O sightings and spontaneous human combustion. A group of air crashes in New York in 1951 are looked at in detail.

This book holds interest for the UFOlogist, the Earth mystery buff and the physicist.

Pen Press are a publishing company to watch, with many more Fortean titles. - RF

The Encyclopaedia of the Loch Ness Monster by Paul Harrison
(Hale IBSN 0 7090 6461 6)

There have been enough books written on the Loch Ness Monster to fill Godzilla's rucksack but this one stands out as totally unique. I'm amazed someone has not come up with such an excellent idea before. Just about everything you could want to know about the monster is included in this humdinger of a book. Witnesses, experts, theories, investigators, locations; the whole shebang painstakingly cross referenced. Just thinking about the amount of work that went into this book gives you admiration for its author.

It does have a lack of illustrations and a couple of printing errors (240 foot basking shark? Surely he means 24 foot) but these do not detract from a truly wonderful book.
One thing puzzles him, why is Nessie referred to as female. Well, I know the answer to that one

BOOK REVIEWS

Paul, so get in touch and I'll let you know...
- RF

SUBSCRIPTION to
ANIMALS & MEN

For a 4-issue (one year) subscription:
£8 UK   £9 EC
£14 US / Canada / Oz / NZ (airmail)
£15 Rest of World.

METHODS OF PAYMENT

Subscription rates INCLUDE postage. On other orders, postage and packing is extra: please add 25p (£0.30 outside UK) per magazine and 75p (£0.90 outside UK) per book.

Payment can be made in UK cash, by IMO (an international money order), Eurocheque, or by a cheque drawn on a UK bank.

Please make all cheques payable to Jonathan Downes.

Britain is one of the few countries in the world where US dollars do **not** circulate. If making payment in US$ then please add $14 to cover the currency exchange fee.

Please send all orders to

CFZ, 15 Holne Court,
Exwick, Exeter, Devon, EX4 2NA,
England.

- 45 -

ANIMALS & MEN # 20

ANIMALS & MEN
BACK ISSUES: £2 each

Back issues are available from the editorial address. Please see "methods of payment" on p.45.

CONTENTS (all issues also contain news pages, reviews and letters):

1 Relict Pine Martens, Giant Sloths, Sumatran and Javan Rhinos, Golden Frogs, Frog Falls.
2 Mystery bears in Oxford and The Atlas Mountains, Loch Ness reports, Green Lizards, Woodwose, The Tatzelwurm.
3 Giant Worm in Eastbourne, Lake Monsters of New Guinea, Giant Lizards in Papua, Mystery Cats, Black Dogs on Dartmoor, Scorpion Mystery.
4 Manatees of St Helena, Migo: The Lake Monster of New Britain, The search for the Tasmanian Thylacine.
5 Mystery cats, Loch Ness, More on the "Migo Video", Boars and Pumas, The Hairy Hands of Dartmoor.
6 The Owlman Special; also the Humped Elephants of Nepal, Mystery Cats, Sabre-toothed cats, Mysterious hominids of Africa, The British Nandi Bear?, Bibliography of Cryptozoology books part 1 (by Dr Karl Shuker).
7 Mystery Whales, Strangeness in Scotland, On collecting a cryptid, Bodmin Leopard Skull, Shuker's Cryptozoological Bibliography pt 2.
8 Green Cats and Dogs, Mystery Whales, Quagga Project, Bibliography of Cryptozoological books (3rd & concluding part), Malayan Man Beast.
9 Hong Kong Tiger, Horseman of Lincolnshire, Scottish BHM, Congo Peacock, Mystery Whales.
10 Mystery Moth of Madagascar, Bengal Leopard Cats, The Derry, Wild Boars in Kent, a new Irish lake monster, mystery whales and the truth about the Essex Beach Corpses.
11 The "Walruses Special", also: Feathered Dinosaurs, Ground Sloth Survival in North America, Mystery Whales, Initial Bipedalism.
12 Lions: The Barbary Lion, etc. More Feathered Dinosaurs, Chinese Crabs in the Thames, Mystery Animals of Germany, News from New Zealand.
13 Pangolins; also Moby the Sperm Whale, Barking Beast of Bath, Yorkshire ABCs, Molly the Singing Oyster, Leatherback Turtles, Walruses.
14 The Dragons of Yorkshire, Irish mystery animals, In Search Of "Gambo", Charlie Fort and the Vampire Sheep Slayer - and Jackals; and the first of Clinton Keeling's Cogitations - comments on the previous issue.
15 Lake Dakataua "Migo" monster update, The Weird Warbling Whatsit of the Westcountry, The Beast of Llangurig, The Waspman, The Bigfoot "Murders", and three articles on Beavers.
16 Expedition Report: The Search for El Chupacabra; Quagga Project update; Bestiary #1; Snakes with Legs; Eastern Cougars; Giant Lizards in the English Countryside?
17 British Wolverine - or muddy badger?, Turtle Tales, Killer Bees, The Ziphiidae - possible new species, Vertebrate palaeontology, Video: the Beast of Bodmin press conference.
18 GUST expedition; Wolverines; crypto sharks; Puerto Rican lamprey; Out-of-place animals in Kent; Quaggas and hybrids.
19 The Case of the British Thylacine; Bestiary - The Rukh; Coypu in a Yorkshire Attic, Sweet Wallaby of Mine; Sipandjee - An Unidentified Ape; Ayrshire Tales; Curiosity Killed the Cat; Ground Sloth Survival.

BACK ISSUES

THE GOBLIN UNIVERSE
BACK ISSUES: £2 each

Back issues are available from the editorial address. Please see "methods of payment" on p.45.

CONTENTS (all issues also contain news pages, letters, and record, magazine and book reviews):

4 Witches, Hellhounds and Capel's tomb. St. Leonards Vampire. Cattle Mutilation. Psychic Detectives.
5 Crop Circles & Animal Mutilations. Glamis Castle ghosts. Communication with UFOs.
6 Rendlesham "UFO crash site" in Suffolk. Mystery Planets. Cannibalism in Scotland. DIY countries.
7 The Terror of Gloucestershire. Telpas. Barnum & Tom Thumb. The Making of "The Owlman" film. KKK operations in Scotland?
8 Kent witchcraft; Nick Redfern interview; King Arthur; Dorset Hellstones; The Poultrygeist; Whales.

ANIMALS & MEN # 20

THE OWLMAN AND OTHERS

NEW UPDATED EDITION
by
Jonathan Downes

£12.95
"Anomalist" award winner 1997

Pleaase see page 45 for more information on ordering books from the CFZ, or visit our website on

www.eclipse.co.uk/cfz

OUR OWN PUBLICATIONS

CFZ YEARBOOK 1999

Containing longer articles than published in *Animals & Men* magazine.

Includes

Surviving Neanderthals - a search for man's closest relatives
- by Jonathan Downes and Richard Freeman.

The Beast of Bluebell Hill - by Neil Arnold:
Sightings of a mystery animal in Kent.

Wolverines in Wales? - by Roy Kerridge

Waitoreke: The Enigma from New Zealand
- by Craig Heinselman

The evidence thus far; varying descriptions from otter-like, beaver-like, or seal-like. The theories (through behaviour, anatomy and habitat).

Folk tales involving were-beasts from Ghana - by Louis Baba

Pelorus Jack -
The text of the 1911 booklet by James Cowan on on the solitary white dolphin off N.Z.

Chance would be a Fine Thing - by Graham Inglis.
Life on other planets? It's certainly a possibility...

£10.75 (UK)
£11.50 (overseas)

Prices inclusive of postage & packing

- 47 -

Animals & Men Collected Editions Volume 4 — New Horizons

ISSN 1354-0637
Typeset by a funk soul brother
"check it out now..."

THE CENTRE FOR FORTEAN ZOOLOGY

So, what is the Centre for Fortean Zoology?

We are a non profit-making organisation founded in 1992 with the aim of being a clearing house for information, and coordinating research into mystery animals around the world. We also study out of place animals, rare and aberrant animal behaviour, and Zooform Phenomena; little-understood "things" that appear to be animals, but which are in fact nothing of the sort, and not even alive (at least in the way we understand the term).

Why should I join the Centre for Fortean Zoology?

Not only are we the biggest organisation of our type in the world, but - or so we like to think - we are the best. We are certainly the only truly global Cryptozoological research organisation, and we carry out our investigations using a strictly scientific set of guidelines. We are expanding all the time and looking to recruit new members to help us in our research into mysterious animals and strange creatures across the globe. Why should you join us? Because, if you are genuinely interested in trying to solve the last great mysteries of Mother Nature, there is nobody better than us with whom to do it.

What do I get if I join the Centre for Fortean Zoology?

For £12 a year, you get a four-issue subscription to our journal *Animals & Men*. Each issue contains 60 pages packed with news, articles, letters, research papers, field reports, and even a gossip column! The magazine is A5 in format with a full colour cover. You also have access to one of the world's largest collections of resource material dealing with cryptozoology and allied disciplines, and people from the CFZ membership regularly take part in fieldwork and expeditions around the world.

How is the Centre for Fortean Zoology organised?

The CFZ is managed by a three-man board of trustees, with a non-profit making trust registered with HM Government Stamp Office. The board of trustees is supported by a Permanent Directorate of full and part-time staff, and advised by a Consultancy Board of specialists - many of whom are world-renowned experts in their particular field. We have regional representatives across the UK, the USA, and many other parts of the world, and are affiliated with other organisations whose aims and protocols mirror our own.

I am new to the subject, and although I am interested I have little practical knowledge. I don't want to feel out of my depth. What should I do?

Don't worry. We were *all* beginners once. You'll find that the people at the CFZ are friendly and approachable. We have a thriving forum on the website which is the hub of an ever-growing electronic community. You will soon find your feet. Many members of the CFZ Permanent Directorate started off as ordinary members, and now work full-time chasing monsters around the world.

I have an idea for a project which isn't on your website. What do I do?

Write to us, e-mail us, or telephone us. The list of future projects on the website is not exhaustive. If you have a good idea for an investigation, please tell us. We may well be able to help.

How do I go on an expedition?

We are always looking for volunteers to join us. If you see a project that interests you, do not hesitate to get in touch with us. Under certain circumstances we can help provide funding for your trip. If you look on the future projects section of the website, you can see some of the projects that we have pencilled in for the next few years.

In 2003 and 2004 we sent three-man expeditions to Sumatra looking for Orang-Pendek - a semi-legendary bipedal ape. The same three went to Mongolia in 2005. All three members started off merely subscribers to the CFZ magazine.

Next time it could be you!

Project Kerinci, Sumatra - 2003
In search of the bipedal ape Orang Pendek

How is the Centre for Fortean Zoology funded?

We have no magic sources of income. All our funds come from donations, membership fees, works that we do for TV, radio or magazines, and sales of our publications and merchandise. We are always looking for corporate sponsorship, and other sources of revenue. If you have any ideas for fund-raising please let us know. However, unlike other cryptozoological organisations in the past, we do not live in an intellectual ivory tower. We are not afraid to get our hands dirty, and furthermore we are not one of those organisations where the membership have to raise money so that a privileged few can go on expensive foreign trips. Our research teams, both in the UK and abroad, consist of a mixture of experienced and inexperienced personnel. We are truly a community, and work on the premise that the benefits of CFZ membership are open to all.

What do you do with the data you gather from your investigations and expeditions?

Reports of our investigations are published on our website as soon as they are available. Preliminary reports are posted within days of the project finishing.

Each year we publish a 200 page yearbook containing research papers and expedition reports too long to be printed in the journal. We freely circulate our information to anybody who asks for it.

Is the CFZ community purely an electronic one?

No. Each year since 2000 we have held our annual convention - the *Weird Weekend* - in Exeter. It is three days of lectures, workshops, and excursions. But most importantly it is a chance for members of the CFZ to meet each other, and to talk with the members of the permanent directorate in a relaxed and informal setting and preferably with a pint of beer in one hand. Since 2006 - the *Weird Weekend* has been bigger and better and held on the third weekend in August in the idyllic rural location of Woolsery in North Devon.

Since relocating to North Devon in 2005 we have become ever more closely involved with other community organisations, and we hope that this trend will continue. We also work closely with Police Forces across the UK as consultants for animal mutilation cases, and we intend to forge closer links with the coastguard and other community services. We want to work closely with those who regularly travel into the Bristol Channel, so that if the recent trend of exotic animal visitors to our coastal waters continues, we can be out there as soon as possible.

We are building a Visitor's Centre in rural North Devon. This will not be open to the general public, but will provide a museum, a library and an educational resource for our members (currently over 400) across the globe. We are also planning a youth organisation which will involve children and young people in our activities.

Apart from having been the only Fortean Zoological organisation in the world to have consistently published material on all aspects of the subject for over a decade, we have achieved the following concrete results:

- Disproved the myth relating to the headless so-called sea-serpent carcass of Durgan beach in Cornwall 1975
- Disproved the story of the 1988 puma skull of Lustleigh Cleave
- Carried out the only in-depth research ever into the mythos of the Cornish Owlman
- Made the first records of a tropical species of lamprey
- Made the first records of a luminous cave gnat larva in Thailand
- Discovered a possible new species of British mammal - the beech marten
- In 1994-6 carried out the first archival fortean zoological survey of Hong Kong
- In the year 2000, CFZ theories were confirmed when an new species of lizard was added to the British list
- Identified the monster of Martin Mere in Lancashire as a giant wels catfish
- Expanded the known range of Armitage's skink in the Gambia by 80%
- Obtained photographic evidence of the remains of Europe's largest known pike
- Carried out the first ever in-depth study of the *ninki-nanka*
- Carried out the first attempt to breed Puerto Rican cave snails in captivity
- Were the first European explorers to visit the `lost valley` in Sumatra
- Published the first ever evidence for a new tribe of pygmies in Guyana
- Published the first evidence for a new species of caiman in Guyana
- Filmed unknown creatures on a monster-haunted lake in Ireland for the first time
- Had a sighting of orang pendek in Sumatra in 2009
- Published some of the best evidence ever for the almasty in southern Russia

EXPEDITIONS & INVESTIGATIONS TO DATE INCLUDE:

- 1998 Puerto Rico, Florida, Mexico *(Chupacabras)*
- 1999 Nevada *(Bigfoot)*
- 2000 Thailand *(Giant snakes called nagas)*
- 2002 Martin Mere *(Giant catfish)*
- 2002 Cleveland *(Wallaby mutilation)*
- 2003 Bolam Lake *(BHM Reports)*
- 2003 Sumatra *(Orang Pendek)*
- 2003 Texas *(Bigfoot; giant snapping turtles)*
- 2004 Sumatra *(Orang Pendek; cigau, a sabre-toothed cat)*
- 2004 Illinois *(Black panthers; cicada swarm)*
- 2004 Texas *(Mystery blue dog)*
- Loch Morar *(Monster)*
- 2004 Puerto Rico *(Chupacabras; carnivorous cave snails)*
- 2005 Belize *(Affiliate expedition for hairy dwarfs)*
- 2005 Loch Ness *(Monster)*
- 2005 Mongolia *(Allghoi Khorkhoi aka Mongolian death worm)*
- 2006 Gambia *(Gambian sea monster, Ninki Nanka and Armitage's skink*
- 2006 Llangorse Lake *(Giant pike, giant eels)*
- 2006 Windermere *(Giant eels)*
- 2007 Coniston Water *(Giant eels)*
- 2007 Guyana *(Giant anaconda, didi, water tiger)*
- 2008 Russia *(Almasty)*
- 2009 Sumatra *(Orang pendek)*
- 2009 Republic of Ireland *(Lake Monster)*
- 2010 Texas *(Blue dogs)*

Other books available from
CFZ PRESS

THE OWLMAN AND OTHERS - 30th Anniversary Edition
Jonathan Downes - ISBN 978-1-905723-02-7

£14.99

EASTER 1976 - Two young girls playing in the churchyard of Mawnan Old Church in southern Cornwall were frightened by what they described as a "nasty bird-man". A series of sightings that has continued to the present day. These grotesque and frightening episodes have fascinated researchers for three decades now, and one man has spent years collecting all the available evidence into a book. To mark the 30th anniversary of these sightings, Jonathan Downes has published a special edition of his book.

DRAGONS - More than a myth?
Richard Freeman - ISBN 0-9512872-9-X

£14.99

First scientific look at dragons since 1884. It looks at dragon legends worldwide, and examines modern sightings of dragon-like creatures, as well as some of the more esoteric theories surrounding dragonkind.

Dragons are discussed from a folkloric, historical and cryptozoological perspective, and Richard Freeman concludes that: "When your parents told you that dragons don't exist - they lied!"

MONSTER HUNTER
Jonathan Downes - ISBN 0-9512872-7-3

£14.99

Jonathan Downes' long-awaited autobiography, *Monster Hunter*...

Written with refreshing candour, it is the extraordinary story of an extraordinary life, in which the author crosses paths with wizards, rock stars, terrorists, and a bewildering array of mythical and not so mythical monsters, and still just about manages to emerge with his sanity intact.......

MONSTER OF THE MERE
Jonathan Downes - ISBN 0-9512872-2-2

£12.50

It all starts on Valentine's Day 2002 when a Lancashire newspaper announces that "Something" has been attacking swans at a nature reserve in Lancashire. Eyewitnesses have reported that a giant unknown creature has been dragging fully grown swans beneath the water at Martin Mere. An intrepid team from the Exeter based Centre for Fortean Zoology, led by the author, make two trips – each of a week – to the lake and its surrounding marshlands. During their investigations they uncover a thrilling and complex web of historical fact and fancy, quasi Fortean occurrences, strange animals and even human sacrifice.

**CFZ PRESS, MYRTLE COTTAGE,
WOOLFARDISWORTHY BIDEFORD,
NORTH DEVON, EX39 5QR
www.cfz.org.uk**

Other books available from
CFZ PRESS

CFZ PRESS

ONLY FOOLS AND GOATSUCKERS
Jonathan Downes - ISBN 0-9512872-3-0

£12.50

In January and February 1998 Jonathan Downes and Graham Inglis of the Centre for Fortean Zoology spent three and a half weeks in Puerto Rico, Mexico and Florida, accompanied by a film crew from UK Channel 4 TV. Their aim was to make a documentary about the terrifying chupacabra - a vampiric creature that exists somewhere in the grey area between folklore and reality. This remarkable book tells the gripping, sometimes scary, and often hilariously funny story of how the boys from the CFZ did their best to subvert the medium of contemporary TV documentary making and actually do their job.

WHILE THE CAT'S AWAY
Chris Moiser - ISBN: 0-9512872-1-4

£7.99

Over the past thirty years or so there have been numerous sightings of large exotic cats, including black leopards, pumas and lynx, in the South West of England. Former Rhodesian soldier Sam McCall moved to North Devon and became a farmer and pub owner when Rhodesia became Zimbabwe in 1980. Over the years despite many of his pub regulars having seen the "Beast of Exmoor" Sam wasn't at all sure that it existed. Then a series of happenings made him change his mind. Chris Moiser—a zoologist—is well known for his research into the mystery cats of the westcountry. This is his first novel.

CFZ EXPEDITION REPORT 2006 - GAMBIA
ISBN 1905723032

£12.50

In July 2006, The J.T.Downes memorial Gambia Expedition - a six-person team - Chris Moiser, Richard Freeman, Chris Clarke, Oll Lewis, Lisa Dowley and Suzi Marsh went to the Gambia, West Africa. They went in search of a dragon-like creature, known to the natives as `Ninki Nanka`, which has terrorized the tiny African state for generations, and has reportedly killed people as recently as the 1990s. They also went to dig up part of a beach where an amateur naturalist claims to have buried the carcass of a mysterious fifteen foot sea monster named 'Gambo', and they sought to find the Armitage's Skink (*Chalcides armitagei*) - a tiny lizard first described in 1922 and only rediscovered in 1989. Here, for the first time, is their story.... With an forward by Dr. Karl Shuker and introduction by Jonathan Downes.

BIG CATS IN BRITAIN YEARBOOK 2006
Edited by Mark Fraser - ISBN 978-1905723-01-0

£10.00

Big cats are said to roam the British Isles and Ireland even now as you are sitting and reading this. People from all walks of life encounter these mysterious felines on a daily basis in every nook and cranny of these two countries. Most are jet-black, some are white, some are brown, in fact big cats of every description and colour are seen by some unsuspecting person while on his or her daily business. 'Big Cats in Britain' are the largest and most active group in the British Isles and Ireland This is their first book. It contains a run-down of every known big cat sighting in the UK during 2005, together with essays by various luminaries of the British big cat research community which place the phenomenon into scientific, cultural, and historical perspective.

**CFZ PRESS, MYRTLE COTTAGE,
WOOLSERY, BIDEFORD,
NORTH DEVON, EX39 5QR
w w w . c f z . o r g . u k**

Other books available from
CFZ PRESS

THE SMALLER MYSTERY CARNIVORES OF THE WESTCOUNTRY
Jonathan Downes - ISBN 978-1-905723-05-8

£7.99

Although much has been written in recent years about the mystery big cats which have been reported stalking Westcountry moorlands, little has been written on the subject of the smaller British mystery carnivores. This unique book redresses the balance and examines the current status in the Westcountry of three species thought to be extinct: the Wildcat, the Pine Marten and the Polecat, finding that the truth is far more exciting than the currently held scientific dogma. This book also uncovers evidence suggesting that even more exotic species of small mammal may lurk hitherto unsuspected in the countryside of Devon, Cornwall, Somerset and Dorset.

THE BLACKDOWN MYSTERY
Jonathan Downes - ISBN 978-1-905723-00-3

£7.99

Intrepid members of the CFZ are up to the challenge, and manage to entangle themselves thoroughly in the bizarre trappings of this case. This is the soft underbelly of ufology, rife with unsavoury characters, plenty of drugs and booze." That sums it up quite well, we think. A new edition of the classic 1999 book by legendary fortean author Jonathan Downes. In this remarkable book, Jon weaves a complex tale of conspiracy, anti-conspiracy, quasi-conspiracy and downright lies surrounding an air-crash and alleged UFO incident in Somerset during 1996. However the story is much stranger than that. This excellent and amusing book lifts the lid off much of contemporary forteana and explains far more than it initially promises.

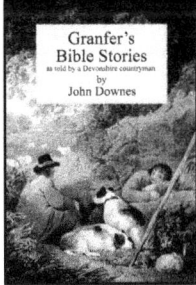

GRANFER'S BIBLE STORIES
John Downes - ISBN 0-9512872-8-1

£7.99

Bible stories in the Devonshire vernacular, each story being told by an old Devon Grandfather - 'Granfer'. These stories are now collected together in a remarkable book presenting selected parts of the Bible as one more-or-less continuous tale in short 'bite sized' stories intended for dipping into or even for bed-time reading. `Granfer` treats the biblical characters as if they were simple country folk living in the next village. Many of the stories are treated with a degree of bucolic humour and kindly irreverence, which not only gives the reader an opportunity to re-evaluate familiar tales in a new light, but do so in both an entertaining and a spiritually uplifting manner.

FRAGRANT HARBOURS DISTANT RIVERS
John Downes - ISBN 0-9512872-5-7

£12.50

Many excellent books have been written about Africa during the second half of the 19th Century, but this one is unique in that it presents the stories of a dozen different people, whose interlinked lives and achievements have as many nuances as any contemporary soap opera. It explains how the events in China and Hong Kong which surrounded the Opium Wars, intimately effected the events in Africa which take up the majority of this book. The author served in the Colonial Service in Nigeria and Hong Kong, during which he found himself following in the footsteps of one of the main characters in this book; Frederick Lugard – the architect of modern Nigeria.

**CFZ PRESS, MYRTLE COTTAGE,
WOOLFARDISWORTHY BIDEFORD,
NORTH DEVON, EX39 5QR
w w w . c f z . o r g . u k**

Other books available from
CFZ PRESS

ANIMALS & MEN - Issues 1 - 5 - In the Beginning
Edited by Jonathan Downes - ISBN 0-9512872-6-5

£12.50

At the beginning of the 21st Century monsters still roam the remote, and sometimes not so remote, corners of our planet. It is our job to search for them. The Centre for Fortean Zoology [CFZ] is the only professional, scientific and full-time organisation in the world dedicated to cryptozoology - the study of unknown animals. Since 1992 the CFZ has carried out an unparalleled programme of research and investigation all over the world. We have carried out expeditions to Sumatra (2003 and 2004), Mongolia (2005), Puerto Rico (1998 and 2004), Mexico (1998), Thailand (2000), Florida (1998), Nevada (1999 and 2003), Texas (2003 and 2004), and Illinois (2004). An introductory essay by Jonathan Downes, notes putting each issue into a historical perspective, and a history of the CFZ.

ANIMALS & MEN - Issues 6 - 10 - The Number of the Beast
Edited by Jonathan Downes - ISBN 978-1-905723-06-5

£12.50

At the beginning of the 21st Century monsters still roam the remote, and sometimes not so remote, corners of our planet. It is our job to search for them. The Centre for Fortean Zoology [CFZ] is the only professional, scientific and full-time organisation in the world dedicated to cryptozoology - the study of unknown animals. Since 1992 the CFZ has carried out an unparalleled programme of research and investigation all over the world. We have carried out expeditions to Sumatra (2003 and 2004), Mongolia (2005), Puerto Rico (1998 and 2004), Mexico (1998), Thailand (2000), Florida (1998), Nevada (1999 and 2003), Texas (2003 and 2004), and Illinois (2004). Preface by Mark North and an introductory essay by Jonathan Downes, notes putting each issue into a historical perspective, and a history of the CFZ.

BIG BIRD! Modern Sightings of Flying Monsters

Ken Gerhard - ISBN 978-1-905723-08-9

£7.99

From all over the dusty U.S./Mexican border come hair-raising stories of modern day encounters with winged monsters of immense size and terrifying appearance. Further field sightings of similar creatures are recorded from all around the globe. What lies behind these weird tales? Ken Gerhard is a native Texan, he lives in the homeland of the monster some call 'Big Bird'. Ken's scholarly work is the first of its kind. On the track of the monster, Ken uncovers cases of animal mutilations, attacks on humans and mounting evidence of a stunning zoological discovery ignored by mainstream science. Keep watching the skies!

STRENGTH THROUGH KOI
They saved Hitler's Koi and other stories

£7.99

Jonathan Downes - ISBN 978-1-905723-04-1

Strength through Koi is a book of short stories - some of them true, some of them less so - by noted cryptozoologist and raconteur Jonathan Downes. The stories are all about koi carp, and their interaction with bigfoot, UFOs, and Nazis. Even the late George Harrison makes an appearance. Very funny in parts, this book is highly recommended for anyone with even a passing interest in aquaculture, but should be taken definitely *cum grano salis*.

CFZ PRESS, MYRTLE COTTAGE, WOOLSERY, BIDEFORD, NORTH DEVON, EX39 5QR

CFZ PRESS

Other books available from
CFZ PRESS

BIG CATS IN BRITAIN YEARBOOK 2007
Edited by Mark Fraser - ISBN 978-1-905723-09-6

£12.50

People from all walks of life encounter mysterious felids on a daily basis, in every nook and cranny of the UK. Most are jet-black, some are white, some are brown; big cats of every description and colour are seen by some unsuspecting person while on his or her daily business. 'Big Cats in Britain' are the largest and most active research group in the British Isles and Ireland. This book contains a run-down of every known big cat sighting in the UK during 2006, together with essays by various luminaries of the British big cat research community.

CAT FLAPS! Northern Mystery Cats
Andy Roberts - ISBN 978-1-905723-11-9

£6.99

Of all Britain's mystery beasts, the alien big cats are the most renowned. In recent years the notoriety of these uncatchable, out-of-place predators have eclipsed even the Loch Ness Monster. They slink from the shadows to terrorise a community, and then, as often as not, vanish like ghosts. But now film, photographs, livestock kills, and paw prints show that we can no longer deny the existence of these once-legendary beasts. Here then is a case-study, a true lost classic of Fortean research by one of the country's most respected researchers.

CENTRE FOR FORTEAN ZOOLOGY 2007 YEARBOOK
Edited by Jonathan Downes and Richard Freeman
ISBN 978-1-905723-14-0

£12.50

The Centre For Fortean Zoology Yearbook is a collection of papers and essays too long and detailed for publication in the CFZ Journal *Animals & Men*. With contributions from both well-known researchers, and relative newcomers to the field, the Yearbook provides a forum where new theories can be expounded, and work on little-known cryptids discussed.

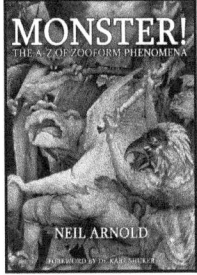

MONSTER! THE A-Z OF ZOOFORM PHENOMENA
Neil Arnold - ISBN 978-1-905723-10-2

£14.99

Zooform Phenomena are the most elusive, and least understood, mystery `animals`. Indeed, they are not animals at all, and are not even animate in the accepted terms of the word. Author and researcher Neil Arnold is to be commended for a groundbreaking piece of work, and has provided the world's first alphabetical listing of zooforms from around the world.

**CFZ PRESS, MYRTLE COTTAGE,
WOOLFARDISWORTHY BIDEFORD,
NORTH DEVON, EX39 5QR
w w w . c f z . o r g . u k**

Other books available from
CFZ PRESS

BIG CATS LOOSE IN BRITAIN
Marcus Matthews - ISBN 978-1-905723-12-6

£14.99

Big Cats: Loose in Britain, looks at the body of anecdotal evidence for such creatures: sightings, livestock kills, paw-prints and photographs, and seeks to determine underlying commonalities and threads of evidence. These two strands are repeatedly woven together into a highly readable, yet scientifically compelling, overview of the big cat phenomenon in Britain.

DARK DORSET
TALES OF MYSTERY, WONDER AND TERROR
Robert. J. Newland and Mark. J. North
ISBN 978-1-905723-15-6

£12.50

This extensively illustrated compendium has over 400 tales and references, making this book by far one of the best in its field. Dark Dorset has been thoroughly researched, and includes many new entries and up to date information never before published. The title of the book speaks for itself, and is indeed not for the faint hearted or those easily shocked.

MAN-MONKEY - IN SEARCH OF THE BRITISH BIGFOOT
Nick Redfern - ISBN 978-1-905723-16-4

£9.99

In her 1883 book, *Shropshire Folklore*, Charlotte S. Burne wrote: *'Just before he reached the canal bridge, a strange black creature with great white eyes sprang out of the plantation by the roadside and alighted on his horse's back'*. The creature duly became known as the `Man-Monkey`.

Between 1986 and early 2001, Nick Redfern delved deeply into the mystery of the strange creature of that dark stretch of canal. Now, published for the very first time, are Nick's original interview notes, his files and discoveries; as well as his theories pertaining to what lies at the heart of this diabolical legend.

EXTRAORDINARY ANIMALS REVISITED
Dr Karl Shuker - ISBN 978-1905723171

£14.99

This delightful book is the long-awaited, greatly-expanded new edition of one of Dr Karl Shuker's much-loved early volumes, *Extraordinary Animals Worldwide*. It is a fascinating celebration of what used to be called romantic natural history, examining a dazzling diversity of animal anomalies, creatures of cryptozoology, and all manner of other thought-provoking zoological revelations and continuing controversies down through the ages of wildlife discovery.

**CFZ PRESS, MYRTLE COTTAGE,
WOOLFARDISWORTHY BIDEFORD,
NORTH DEVON, EX39 5QR
w w w . c f z . o r g . u k**

Other books available from
CFZ PRESS

DARK DORSET CALENDAR CUSTOMS
Robert J Newland - ISBN 978-1-905723-18-8

£12.50

Much of the intrinsic charm of Dorset folklore is owed to the importance of folk customs. Today only a small amount of these curious and occasionally eccentric customs have survived, while those that still continue have, for many of us, lost their original significance. Why do we eat pancakes on Shrove Tuesday? Why do children dance around the maypole on May Day? Why do we carve pumpkin lanterns at Hallowe'en? All the answers are here! Robert has made an in-depth study of the Dorset country calendar identifying the major feast-days, holidays and celebrations when traditionally such folk customs are practiced.

CENTRE FOR FORTEAN ZOOLOGY 2004 YEARBOOK
Edited by Jonathan Downes and Richard Freeman
ISBN 978-1-905723-14-0

£12.50

The Centre For Fortean Zoology Yearbook is a collection of papers and essays too long and detailed for publication in the CFZ Journal *Animals & Men*. With contributions from both well-known researchers, and relative newcomers to the field, the Yearbook provides a forum where new theories can be expounded, and work on little-known cryptids discussed.

CENTRE FOR FORTEAN ZOOLOGY 2008 YEARBOOK
Edited by Jonathan Downes and Corinna Downes
ISBN 978 -1-905723-19-5

£12.50

The Centre For Fortean Zoology Yearbook is a collection of papers and essays too long and detailed for publication in the CFZ Journal *Animals & Men*. With contributions from both well-known researchers, and relative newcomers to the field, the Yearbook provides a forum where new theories can be expounded, and work on little-known cryptids discussed.

ETHNA'S JOURNAL
Corinna Newton Downes
ISBN 978 -1-905723-21-8

£9.99

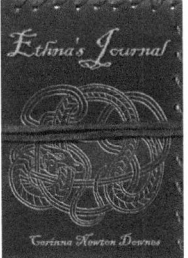

Ethna's Journal tells the story of a few months in an alternate Dark Ages, seen through the eyes of Ethna, daughter of Lord Edric. She is an unsophisticated girl from the fortress town of Cragnuth, somewhere in the north of England, who reluctantly gets embroiled in a web of treachery, sorcery and bloody war...

**CFZ PRESS, MYRTLE COTTAGE,
WOOLFARDISWORTHY BIDEFORD,
NORTH DEVON, EX39 5QR
w w w . c f z . o r g . u k**

Other books available from
CFZ PRESS

ANIMALS & MEN - Issues 11 - 15 - The Call of the Wild
Jonathan Downes (Ed) - ISBN 978-1-905723-07-2

£12.50

Since 1994 we have been publishing the world's only dedicated cryptozoology magazine, *Animals & Men*. This volume contains fascimile reprints of issues 11 to 15 and includes articles covering out of place walruses, feathered dinosaurs, possible North American ground sloth survival, the theory of initial bipedalism, mystery whales, mitten crabs in Britain, Barbary lions, out of place animals in Germany, mystery pangolins, the barking beast of Bath, Yorkshire ABCs, Molly the singing oyster, singing mice, the dragons of Yorkshire, singing mice, the bigfoot murders, waspman, British beavers, the migo, Nessie, the weird warbling whatsit of the westcountry, the quagga project and much more...

IN THE WAKE OF BERNARD HEUVELMANS
Michael A Woodley - ISBN 978-1-905723-20-1

£9.99

Everyone is familiar with the nautical maps from the middle ages that were liberally festooned with images of exotic and monstrous animals, but the truth of the matter is that the *idea* of the sea monster is probably as old as humankind itself.

For two hundred years, scientists have been producing speculative classifications of sea serpents, attempting to place them within a zoological framework. This book looks at these successive classification models, and using a new formula produces a sea serpent classification for the 21st Century.

CENTRE FOR FORTEAN ZOOLOGY 1999 YEARBOOK
Edited by Jonathan Downes
ISBN 978 -1-905723-24-9

£12.50

The Centre For Fortean Zoology Yearbook is a collection of papers and essays too long and detailed for publication in the CFZ Journal *Animals & Men*. With contributions from both well-known researchers, and relative newcomers to the field, the Yearbook provides a forum where new theories can be expounded, and work on little-known cryptids discussed.

CENTRE FOR FORTEAN ZOOLOGY 1996 YEARBOOK
Edited by Jonathan Downes
ISBN 978 -1-905723-22-5

£12.50

The Centre For Fortean Zoology Yearbook is a collection of papers and essays too long and detailed for publication in the CFZ Journal *Animals & Men*. With contributions from both well-known researchers, and relative newcomers to the field, the Yearbook provides a forum where new theories can be expounded, and work on little-known cryptids discussed.

**CFZ PRESS, MYRTLE COTTAGE,
WOOLFARDISWORTHY BIDEFORD,
NORTH DEVON, EX39 5QR
www.cfz.org.uk**

CFZ PRESS

Other books available from
CFZ PRESS

BIG CATS IN BRITAIN YEARBOOK 2008
Edited by Mark Fraser - ISBN 978-1-905723-23-2

£12.50

People from all walks of life encounter mysterious felids on a daily basis, in every nook and cranny of the UK. Most are jet-black, some are white, some are brown; big cats of every description and colour are seen by some unsuspecting person while on his or her daily business. 'Big Cats in Britain' are the largest and most active research group in the British Isles and Ireland. This book contains a run-down of every known big cat sighting in the UK during 2007, together with essays by various luminaries of the British big cat research community.

CFZ EXPEDITION REPORT 2007 - GUYANA
ISBN 978-1-905723-25-6

£12.50

Since 1992, the CFZ has carried out an unparalleled programme of research and investigation all over the world. In November 2007, a five-person team - Richard Freeman, Chris Clarke, Paul Rose, Lisa Dowley and Jon Hare went to Guyana, South America. They went in search of giant anacondas, the bigfoot-like didi, and the terrifying water tiger.

Here, for the first time, is their story...With an introduction by Jonathan Downes and forward by Dr. Karl Shuker.

CENTRE FOR FORTEAN ZOOLOGY 2003 YEARBOOK
Edited by Jonathan Downes and Richard Freeman
ISBN 978 -1-905723-19-5

£12.50

The Centre For Fortean Zoology Yearbook is a collection of papers and essays too long and detailed for publication in the CFZ Journal *Animals & Men*. With contributions from both well-known researchers, and relative newcomers to the field, the Yearbook provides a forum where new theories can be expounded, and work on little-known cryptids discussed.

CENTRE FOR FORTEAN ZOOLOGY 1997 YEARBOOK
Edited by Jonathan Downes and Graham Inglis
ISBN 978 -1-905723-27-0

£12.50

The Centre For Fortean Zoology Yearbook is a collection of papers and essays too long and detailed for publication in the CFZ Journal *Animals & Men*. With contributions from both well-known researchers, and relative newcomers to the field, the Yearbook provides a forum where new theories can be expounded, and work on little-known cryptids discussed.

**CFZ PRESS, MYRTLE COTTAGE,
WOOLFARDISWORTHY BIDEFORD,
NORTH DEVON, EX39 5QR
w w w . c f z . o r g . u k**

Other books available from
CFZ PRESS

CENTRE FOR FORTEAN ZOOLOGY 2000-1 YEARBOOK
Edited by Jonathan Downes and Richard Freeman
ISBN 978-1-905723-19-5

£12.50

The Centre For Fortean Zoology Yearbook is a collection of papers and essays too long and detailed for publication in the CFZ Journal *Animals & Men*. With contributions from both well-known researchers, and relative newcomers to the field, the Yearbook provides a forum where new theories can be expounded, and work on little-known cryptids discussed.

THE MYSTERY ANIMALS OF THE BRITISH ISLES: NORTHUMBERLAND AND TYNESIDE
Michael J Hallowell
ISBN 978-1-905723-29-4

£12.50

Mystery animals? Great Britain? Surely not. But is is true.

This is a major new series from CFZ Press. It will cover Great Britain and the Republic of Ireland, on a county by county basis, describing the mystery animals of the entire island group.

The Island of Paradise: Chupacabra, UFO Crash Retrievals, and Accelerated Evolution on the Island of Puerto Rico
Jonathan Downes - ISBN 978-1-905723-32-4

£14.99

In his first book of original research for four years, Jon Downes visits the Antillean island of Puerto Rico, to which he has led two expeditions - in 1998 and 2004. Together with noted researcher Nick Redfern he goes in search of the grotesque vampiric chupacabra, believing that it can - finally - be categorised within a zoological frame of reference rather than a purely paranormal one. Along the way he uncovers mystery after mystery, has a run in with terrorists, art historians, and even has his garden buzzed by a UFO. By turns both terrifying and funny, this remarkable book is a real tour de force by one of the world's foremost cryptozoological researchers.

DR SHUKER'S CASEBOOK
Dr Karl Shuker - ISBN 978-1905723-33-1

£14.99

Although he is best-known for his extensive cryptozoological researches and publications, Dr Karl Shuker has also investigated a very diverse range of other anomalies and unexplained phenomena, both in the literature and in the field. Now, compiled here for the very first time, are some of the extraordinary cases that he has re-examined or personally explored down through the years.

**CFZ PRESS, MYRTLE COTTAGE,
WOOLFARDISWORTHY BIDEFORD,
NORTH DEVON, EX39 5QR
w w w . c f z . o r g . u k**

Other books available from
CFZ PRESS

Dinosaurs and Other Prehistoric Animals on Stamps: A Worldwide Catalogue
Dr Karl P.N.Shuker - ISBN 978-1-905723-34-8

£9.99

Compiled by zoologist Dr Karl P.N. Shuker, a lifelong, enthusiastic collector of wildlife stamps and with an especial interest in those that portray fossil species, it provides an exhaustive, definitive listing of stamps and miniature sheets depicting dinosaurs and other prehistoric animals issued by countries throughout the world. It also includes sections dealing with cryptozoological stamps, dinosaur stamp superlatives, and unofficial prehistoric animal stamps.

CFZ EXPEDITION REPORT 2008 - RUSSIA
ISBN 978-1-905723-35-5

Since 1992, the CFZ has carried out an unparalleled programme of research and investigation all over the world. In July 2008, a five-person team - Richard Freeman, Chris Clarke, Dave Archer, Adam Davies and Keith Townley went to Kabardino-Balkaria in southern Russia in search of the almasty, maybe mankind's closest relative. Here, for the first time, is their story...With an introduction by Jonathan Downes and forward by Dr. Karl Shuker.

CENTRE FOR FORTEAN ZOOLOGY 2009 YEARBOOK
Edited by Jonathan Downes and Richard Freeman
ISBN 978 -1-905723-37

£12.50

The Centre For Fortean Zoology Yearbook is a collection of papers and essays too long and detailed for publication in the CFZ Journal *Animals & Men*. With contributions from both well-known researchers, and relative newcomers to the field, the Yearbook provides a forum where new theories can be expounded, and work on little-known cryptids discussed.

THE MYSTERY ANIMALS OF THE BRITISH ISLES: KENT
Neil Arnold
ISBN 978-1-905723-36-2

£12.50

Mystery animals? Great Britain? Surely not. But is is true.

This is a major new series from CFZ Press. It will cover Great Britain and the Republic of Ireland, on a county by county basis, describing the mystery animals of the entire island group.

**CFZ PRESS, MYRTLE COTTAGE,
WOOLFARDISWORTHY BIDEFORD,
NORTH DEVON, EX39 5QR
w w w . c f z . o r g . u k**

Other books available from
CFZ PRESS

GIANT SNAKES
By Michael Newton
ISBN: 978-1-905723-39-3

£9.99

In this exciting book, Michael Newton takes an overview of the most terrifying uberpredators in the world - giant snakes. Outsized examples of known species as well as putative new species are looked at in detail.

**THE MYSTERY ANIMALS OF THE BRITISH ISLES:
THE WESTERN ISLES**
Glen Vaudrey
ISBN 978-1-905723-42-3

£12.50

Mystery animals? Great Britain? Surely not. But is is true.

This is a major new series from CFZ Press. It will cover Great Britain and the Republic of Ireland, on a county by county basis, describing the mystery animals of the entire island group.

Strangely Strange but Oddly Normal
Andy Roberts
ISBN 978-1-905723-44-7

£14.99

An anthology of writings from one of Britain's most respected Fortean authors, covering everything from UFOs, to the Rolling Stones, and from psychedelic drugs to ancient fertility symbols, the Incredible String Band, and government cover-ups.

China: The Yellow Peril?
Richard Muirhead
ISBN 978-1-905723-41-6

£7.99

Richard Muirhead takes an in depth look at the history of Western relationships with China. If some Victorian antiquarians are to be believed contact between the Chinese Empire and other Middle Eastern and Western Empires goes back to times long before the birth of Christ, such as the ancient Egyptians and the Roman Empire.

**CFZ PRESS, MYRTLE COTTAGE,
WOOLFARDISWORTHY BIDEFORD,
NORTH DEVON, EX39 5QR
w w w . c f z . o r g . u k**

Other books available from
CFZ PRESS

STAR STEEDS AND OTHER DREAMS
By Dr Karl Shuker
ISBN-13: 978-1905723409

£8.99

Today, Dr Karl Shuker is a world-renowned author on cryptozoology and animal mythology, with over a dozen books and countless articles to his name, but long before his first book on such subjects had been published he was already a prolific poet. Yet in stark contrast to his continuing output of scientific writings, his poetry has remained largely unseen by the outside world - only his family, friends, and selected colleagues have ever read any of his very sizeable collection of poems...until now.

PREDATOR DEATHMATCH
By Nick Molloy
ISBN: 978-1-905723-45-4

£8.99

Predator Deathmatch is the first ever book to study apex predators and actually pose the question of who is/was the ultimate predator by pitting them against each other. The author has carefully profiled each contender with a mixture of historical data, information from the fossil record and current observations of wild animal behaviour. .

CENTRE FOR FORTEAN ZOOLOGY 2009 YEARBOOK
Edited by Jonathan and Corinna Downes
ISBN 978-1-905723-52-2

£12.50

The Centre For Fortean Zoology Yearbook is a collection of papers and essays too long and detailed for publication in the CFZ Journal *Animals & Men.* With contributions from both well-known researchers, and relative newcomers to the field, the Yearbook provides a forum where new theories can be expounded, and work on little-known cryptids discussed.

A DAINTREE DIARY
By Carl Portman
ISBN: 978-1-905723-53-9

£9.99

Carl Portman, tarantula expert from the West Midlands travels to Queensland with two Sheilas in search of spiders and adventure. He finds both in this engaging and oddly heartwarming book. A must for anyone interested in the natural world. A glorious mix of arachnology and adventure, with a smattering of silly humour. Not to be missed

**CFZ PRESS, MYRTLE COTTAGE,
WOOLFARDISWORTHY BIDEFORD,
NORTH DEVON, EX39 5QR
w w w . c f z . o r g . u k**

Other books available from
CFZ PRESS

MONSTRUM! A Wizard's Tale
By Tony `Doc` Shiels
ISBN-13: 978-1905723553

£9.99

A timely reprint of the classic account of monster raising by Tony 'Doc' Shiels, once the Wizard of the Western World, and still the Shamrock Shaman. Owlman, Nessie, Morgawr and much more. This new editikon includes a new `postface` by Doc himself and hitherto unseen illustrations. A fantastic book which has rightly become somewhat of a legend.

Animals & Men collected Editions Vol 4 *New Horizons*
Edited by Jonathan Downes
ISBN: 978-1-905723-56-0

£12.50

At the beginning of the 21st Century monsters still roam the remote, and sometimes not so remote, corners of our planet. It is our job to search for them. The Centre for Fortean Zoology [CFZ] is the only professional, scientific and full-time organisation in the world dedicated to cryptozoology - the study of unknown animals. Preface by Richard Freeman and an introductory essay by Jonathan Downes, notes putting each issue into a historical perspective, and a history of the CFZ.

**CFZ PRESS, MYRTLE COTTAGE,
WOOLFARDISWORTHY BIDEFORD,
NORTH DEVON, EX39 5QR
w w w . c f z . o r g . u k**

Lightning Source UK Ltd.
Milton Keynes UK
UKHW021902220319
339700UK00009B/203/P